THE CONDOR YEARS

Also by John Dinges

Assassination on Embassy Row (with Saul Landau)
Our Man in Panama: The Shrewd Rise and Brutal Fall of Manuel Noriega

THE CONDOR YEARS

How Pinochet and His Allies Brought Terrorism to Three Continents

John Dinges

THE NEW PRESS

NEW YORK
LONDON

Requests for permission to reproduce selections from this book should be made
through our website: https://thenewpress.com/contact.

Originally published in the United States by The New Press, New York, 2003
This paperback edition published by The New Press, 2005
Distributed by Two Rivers Distribution
Extract from Pablo Neruda's "Vienen los pájaros" from *Canto General* is reprinted
by permission of Fundación Pablo Neruda, © 1950 by Pablo Neruda and
Fundación Pablo Neruda

ISBN 978-1-56584-764-4 (hc)
ISBN 978-1-56584-977-8 (pb)
ISBN 978-1-59558-902-6 (ebook)

LIBRARY OF CONGRESS CATALOGING-IN-PUBLICATION DATA

Dinges, John, 1941–
The Condor years : how Pinochet and his allies brought terrorism to three continents /
John Dinges.
p. cm.
Includes bibliographical references and index.
ISBN 978-1-56584-764-4 (hc.) / ISBN 978-1-56584-977-8 (pbk.)
1. Chile—Politics and government—1973–1988. 2. Southern Cone of South America—
Politics and government. 3. Pinochet Ugarte, Augusto. 4. Operaciân Cândor (South
American countersubversion association) 5. Chile. Direcciân de Inteligencia Nacional.
6. State-sponsored terrorism—History—20th century. 7. Victims of state-sponsored
terrorism—History—20th century. 8. Chile—Relations —Foreign countries.
9. United States—Military policy. I. Title

F3100.D565 2004
327.1283'009'047—dc22   2003060265

The New Press publishes books that promote and enrich public discussion
and understanding of the issues vital to our democracy and to a more equitable
world. These books are made possible by the enthusiasm of our readers; the support of
a committed group of donors, large and small; the collaboration of our many partners in
the independent media and the not-for-profit sector; booksellers, who often hand-sell
New Press books; librarians; and above all by our authors.

www.thenewpress.com

Composition by dix!

Printed in the United States of America

For Carolina, my companion in those years and these

Y sobre las plumas carnivoras
volaba encima del mundo
el condor, rey asesino

—Pablo Neruda, from "Vienen los Pajaros" in *Canto General*

CONTENTS

A NOTE ON SOURCES AND ACKNOWLEDGMENTS

This book is in large part underground history. It covers roughly the period 1973–1980, when military dictatorships ruled in most of South America. I have sought out the principal actors—the security forces, the armed leftist groups, and U.S. officials—who went to great lengths to keep their activities secret from the public at the time. Many of those directly involved, especially among the opponents of the military governments, are dead. Many others among the military and even among former U.S. officials continue to conceal what they did. But it was not an impervious group, and I was able to interview or obtain testimony from more than 200 people among those who participated in the events of the period. The second major source of new authoritative information is the plethora of contemporary secret documents that have been discovered, confiscated, officially declassified or otherwise made available in recent years.

I have tried to bring together the documents and the interviews to achieve a laminate of maximum strength in reconstructing the once secret events. Often those interviewed were able to refresh their memories with the documents, but most crucially the contemporary documents provided a factual spine that could not be changed by faulty or self-interested memories. When there was conflict between the documents and memories a quarter century later, I usually gave greater authority to the documents.

Four collections of documents are used most extensively: The U.S. government, by executive order during the Clinton administration, declassified approximately 24,000 documents about Chile and 4,000 about Argentina for the period of the military governments, the latter containing a significant number of documents concerning events in Bolivia, Brazil, Paraguay, and Uruguay. An immense cache of files from Paraguay's intelligence police were discovered in Paraguay in 1992 and are stored in an archive in Asunción. Finally, I obtained copies of the secret correspondence between Chile's intelligence agency, DINA, and the agency's undercover operative in Buenos Aires, numbering approximately 2,400 pages. In addition I received about 2,000 pages of declassified files from U.S. agencies in response to my requests under the Freedom of Information Act.

A word must be said about the secrecy of intelligence documents. Secret documents often have a special aura because they may provide an insider's view of events or reveal actions that have never been made public. But secrecy does not inoculate them against inaccuracy and they are only as factual as the reporting and sourcing that went into them. Whenever possible, therefore, I have attempted to independently confirm events described in the intelligence documents. The fact that these documents have been kept secret for all these years, however, does tell us one important thing: it is highly unlikely the drafters of the intelligence reports were manipulating facts or crafting lies to deceive the public. They were exchanging with each other and with allied intelligence agencies their best information on unfolding events. The documents are therefore a reliable roadmap of what the intelligence officials and their superiors believed at the time to be an accurate version of the facts.

The secret documents demonstrate, for example, that the intelligence agencies were preoccupied with an alliance of leftist armed groups called the JCR and this perceived threat was a major factor in the creation of the military's own alliance, Operation Condor. In reality, the military capability of the leftist groups never presented a serious threat to the dictatorships, and in hindsight the military's portrayal of the threat seems exaggerated. But it is undeniable that the military services gave high credence to the information they were exchanging in secret among themselves.

Detailed notes, particularly regarding documentary sources, are arranged by page and chapter at the end. A keyword is provided to identify the passage to which a note refers. Direct quotation from a conversation is based on the recollection of at least one of the parties to the conversation.

With regard to names of Latin Americans, who use the last names of both their fathers and mothers, I will include both last names in first reference. Thereafter only the patronymic will be used. For example I use Andrés Pascal Allende on first reference, and Andrés Pascal or Pascal thereafter. In some exceptional cases I will continue to refer to the person using both last names, usually because the person is known publicly in that way.

In pursuing this investigation, I rejoined a broad community of journalists, lawyers, judges, and human rights activists who have been working, now into the third decade, to bring truth and justice to bear on the terrible events of these years in the southernmost countries of South America. I learned from them all and in many cases they helped me directly. My thanks and admiration go out to Joan Garcés, who devised the international legal strategy that led to General Pinochet's arrest in London, thus setting a precedent for major advances in international human rights law. That success built on the groundwork of Judge Giovanni Salvi, of the Italian federal court of Rome, former assistant U.S. attorneys E. Lawrence Barcella and Eugene Propper and their FBI colleagues, special agents Carter Cornick and Robert Scherrer, who were the vanguard in investigating and prosecuting the international assassinations documented in this book.

I am also grateful for the insights and generosity of investigating officials Giancarlo Capaldo of the federal court of Rome, Roger Le Loire of the criminal court of France, and Oscar Aguirre, judicial secretary to Judge Rodolfo Canicoba Corral, of the Argentine Federal Court, all of whom are pursuing groundbreaking human rights prosecutions centered on the crimes of Operation Condor. In Chile, Judge Juan Guzmán has done singular work to overcome the hostile judicial climate of post-dictatorship Chile to make once rare human rights prosecutions a matter of everyday news.

Many of the lawyers and investigators who did the behind the scenes work in these milestone cases were extraordinarily generous in helping me. My thanks to Anabel Alcaide, Carlos Zamorano, Sophie Thonon, William Bourdon, Hernán Quezada, Alejandro González, Cristina Mihura, and Giulia Barrera.

In the task of keeping track and making sense of the thousands of documents used in my investigation, and for a host of other indispensable jobs during the three years devoted to this book, I want to thank my able researchers Stacie Jonas, Pascale Bonnefoy, Kate Lasso, Nicholas Udugama, Francisco Rivera, and Karla Polito. In the final stages of the book I relied on Tomás Dinges for crucial fact-checking and a candid editorial eye. The National Security Archive, where I am a senior fellow, supported my document research and FOIA requests. My thanks to director Tom Blanton and to NSA analyst Carlos Osorio, who discovered and shared with me several critical pieces of documentary evidence for the book.

Dean Tom Goldstein of Columbia University Graduate School of Journalism supported my project with encouragement and generous academic leaves. I am grateful to the institutions who provided grants of financial support: The Ford Foundation, and the support of Alexander Wilde, Augusto Varas, and Martin Abregú; The Fund for Constitutional Government, and the support of Conrad Martin; The Freedom Forum Pacific Coast Center; The Sam Rubin Foundation, and the Institute for Latin American Studies of Columbia University.

André Schiffrin and Jonathan Shainin of The New Press gave me unflinching editorial guidance that has made this a better book. Many other friends and colleagues in the United States and in the four countries where I did the bulk of my reporting, Chile, Argentina, Paraguay and Uruguay, helped in a hundred ways but most of all provided a community of friendship and interest during my many trips to their countries. Thanks to Stella Calloni, Miriam Lewin, Alejandro Inchaúrregui, Horacio Verbitski, Luis D'Andrea Mohr, Maria Seoane, Arnol Kremer, Victor Gariboldi, Carlos Libenson, Claudio Jacquelin, and Patricia Nazario in Argentina; to Alfredo Boccia, Martín Almada, Rosa Palau, Julia Fernández Albertini, Carlos Mojoli, and Aldo Zocolillo in Paraguay; to Manuel Flores, Roger Rodríquez, Raul Roncinni, Daniel Gianelli, Danilo Arbilla, Raúl Olivera, Rafael Michelini, Ana Laura Lissardi, Alfonso Lessa, and Luis Nieto in Uruguay; to Monica González, Patricia Verdugo, Ignacio González Camus, Pedro Matta, Manuel Cabieses, Pedro Schwartz, Catherine Kenrick, and John O'Leary in Chile; and in the United States Elizabeth Farnsworth, Martin Edwin Anderson, Franklin "Tex" Harris, Dale Van Atta, Peter Kornbluh, Paz Cohen, Don Bohning, Jeff Stein, and Sarah Anderson.

I want to thank the many other people who consented to interviews and who did their best to help me reconstruct the truth about long past events in their lives and careers. Many are named as sources in the book. Some still cannot be named or preferred not to be named. I hope they will consider the final telling of the story a worthy justification for the time spent with me. For those who disagree with my account in minor or major details, or find that it diverges from some longheld political interpretations of the events of those years, I can only ask that they evaluate the new evidence I have brought to the historical record and judge it with an open mind. I have tried mightily to avoid errors, but lament those that may remain. I am grateful to those who read portions of the book in draft form, especially Ariel Armony, Alfredo Boccia, Martín Almada, Martin Edwin Andersen, Robert Cox, Mónica González, Luis Nieto, Rafael and Zelmar Michelini *(hijo)* and Martín Sivak. Any mistakes will be fewer because of their help.

My family was my anchor in this long and sometimes arduous endeavor. Carolina, my wife, lived through the Condor years with me in Chile, and our son Tomás was born there. Sebastián and Camila have entered young adulthood as this book was conceived and written. They all are my greatest blessing, and their love has given me perspective and joy. They have tried to understand my obsession with establishing the truth of those years so that the pursuit of justice, any measure of justice, will continue to advance no matter how long it takes.

John Dinges, August 2003

Additional investigative findings on the Condor Years, including original documents and document indexes, can be found at http://www.JohnDinges.com/Condor

THE CONDOR YEARS

—

1

THE FIRST WAR ON TERRORISM

On a clear September morning in 1976, Orlando Letelier, an influential former Chilean ambassador to Washington, lay dead and mutilated at Sheridan Circle on Washington's Embassy Row, his car blown apart by a remote-control bomb. Only a few months earlier, death squads in Argentina kidnapped and executed a former president of Bolivia and two of Uruguay's most prominent political leaders. Top-ranking guerrilla leaders from Chile and Uruguay, living underground in Argentina, were also tracked down and killed. Assassination squads landed in European capitals with lists of Latin American exiles. A U.S. congressman was the intended target of one of the plots.

Over a short period of several years an extraordinary list of military and political leaders from the countries of southern South America lost their lives or were targeted for assassination. The victims and targets had this in common: they opposed the anti-Communist military dictatorships that controlled much of Latin America, and they were living in what they thought was safe exile outside their own countries. Some had resorted to violence themselves; most were of the caliber and prominence that qualified them as democratic alternatives to the military strongmen they were striving to remove. In all cases the military governments had come to power with the firm support of the United States, and in all cases it was the military leaders, often working in close collaboration with one another, who organized the assassination teams and sent them on their terrorist missions.

Yet these international crimes were only a small part of the thousands upon thousands of other murders committed by the military governments in South America against their own citizens in these few years—from 1973 to 1980—which I have called the Condor Years. The governments claimed their enemies were "terrorists." While some of them did fit the description, the most prominent victims were respected military and civilian leaders trying to preserve or restore democracy. The vast majority were educated young men and women involved in movements to challenge economic and social injustice. Their deaths are the still-uncounted collateral damage in our hemisphere of the world Cold War to vanquish the Soviet Union and the prospect of Socialist revolution.

The political tragedy of this story is that the military leaders who carried out the assassinations and mass murders looked to the United States for technical assistance and strategic leadership. The U.S. government was the ally of the military regimes. The tragedy is the United States acted not to promote and nurture democracy, but to encourage and justify its overthrow. Even more tragic, and arguably criminal, were the cases in which U.S. officials were directly involved in plots and liaison relationships with those engaged in political assassination and mass murder.

These are not charges that can be made lightly. The story is not simple or one-dimensional. Many U.S. officials were discovering human rights as a policy goal during these years, and there are examples that will be documented in this book of the CIA and other agencies trying to prevent international political assassinations. Yet U.S. diplomats, intelligence personnel, and military officers were also so intimately associated with the military institutions carrying out the repression that that they did little or nothing to discourage the massive human rights crimes about which they were reporting to Washington.

The evidence shows that the messages in favor of human rights and democracy were muted in comparison with the clarion calls to stop Communism at any cost. The signals were mixed at best. They were cynical and intentionally ambiguous at worst. The military rulers appear to have looked at U.S. actions and understood, not unreasonably, that their methods would not be opposed. (Even after the Carter administration made human rights a forceful priority in 1977, the mass killing continued in Argentina.) This book attempts to tell some of the stories of these terror-filled years from the point of view of the covert actors—inside the military governments and their international allies, including the United States, and inside the radical revolutionary groups who were their adversaries.

September 11, 1973, Santiago, Chile, is a good place to begin. It was the day General Augusto Pinochet Ugarte bombed the presidential palace, the symbol of the continent's longest lasting democracy. Pinochet's military coup was warmly embraced by the United States government. The official story, backed by the available evidence, is that the United States was not directly involved. Nevertheless, the same kind of official evidence shows the United States taking the lead in organizing a military uprising only three years earlier. That effort failed, but resulted in the assassination of General René Schneider, the leader of the Chilean armed forces. Both the 1970 U.S.–backed attempt and the 1973 Pinochet coup had the same target: Salvador Allende, a Socialist who had been elected president in impeccable democratic elections.

Where the CIA-organized coup plot failed, Pinochet succeeded. Massive military force quickly smashed Allende's popular but faltering revolution. Allende himself committed suicide rather than surrender to Pinochet after his palace was bombed.

It is a coincidence that September 11 would gain even greater infamy with the World Trade Center bombings in 2001. But the coincidence is not insignificant. The first September 11 was a day after which everything changed in Latin America. Pinochet's coup was not just another military takeover, of which there had been dozens in previous decades. It was the beginning of a total war justified as a "war on terrorism," whose principal targets were the political forces perceived by Pinochet and his allies as infecting their countries with the alien cancer of Communist revolution.

Victory inside Chile was only the first step. Resistance there was short-lived. Many thousands of Allende supporters were crowded into improvised concentration camps, such as Santiago's National Stadium. More than a thousand people were summarily executed, among them two young Americans. Pinochet's military began a tactic new to Latin America: they hid the bodies of executed prisoners in secret mass graves, while denying to families that the prisoners had ever been in custody.

The larger goal quickly became the eradication of all traces of political movements akin to Allende's—in all of Latin America. In some meetings Pinochet's representatives even talked about worldwide eradication of their ideological enemies. It was a war that required new tactics, new organizations, and unprecedented secret agreements among countries in the Southern Cone of South America with long histories of rivalry and animosity.

Latin America, under Pinochet's geopolitical leadership, began a kind of reverse domino effect. Country after country whose democratic system had given leftist ideology a foothold fell under military rule and was subject to merciless political cleansing.

Because the enemy was international in scope, Pinochet devised an underground, international scheme to defeat them. To this end, Pinochet created a secret alliance with other military governments—Uruguay, Paraguay, Bolivia, Brazil, and Argentina. It was called "Operation Condor"—named for the majestic carrion eater that is Chile's national bird. The idea was for the security services to join forces to track down "terrorists" of all nationalities, wherever they resided.

It was certainly understandable that the alliance would go after the militarized guerrilla groups that proliferated in the region in the sixties and early seventies. The groups were themselves organizing an international underground alliance and were gearing up to wage guerrilla war against the military regimes. The Condor strategy was broadened, however, to include the eradication of all rivals, including the military leaders and civilian political leaders determined to restore constitutional government.

Among Condor's tactics was international assassination, and that was what brought the tragedy to Washington, D.C.

Police agencies had long been organized in Interpol, which often provided for effective exchange of information and action in the pursuit of international criminals. Condor was a giant step beyond previous police coordination and intelligence exchange. Where Interpol had international warrants and extradition proceedings, Condor had political data banks and cross-border kidnappings. Condor was operational, and in Latin America (and elsewhere), operations included assassination.

At first, Condor operations were limited to Latin American countries. Each member country allowed the intelligence agencies of other countries to operate inside its borders—capturing exiles, interrogating and torturing them, and returning with them to the country of origin. Condor operations against international targets were intermingled with and often indistinguishable from the massive repression inside each country to defeat domestic opponents of each military government. Almost invariably, Condor victims disappeared. Then, in mid-1976—coinciding with the establishment of military dictatorship in Argentina—Pinochet and two of his Condor allies decided to expand operations beyond the borders of Latin America. Chile, Argentina, and Uruguay created multinational teams, selected targets, and began specialized operational training at military facilities in Argentina.

What did the United States know—and do—about Condor? For decades after these events, the full extent of U.S. knowledge of and contacts with Condor operations has been a carefully guarded secret. What little was initially revealed is contained in my previous book, *Assassination on Embassy Row*, published in 1980 with Saul Landau.

Now, many, but not all, of the secret documents on Chile have been declassified. The previous accounts of U.S. relations with Condor must be drastically revised. The new documents, together with interviews with many of the officials directly involved, demonstrate that the U.S. State Department and intelligence agencies had amazingly complete and intimate details about the functioning and planning of Condor. The documents and interviews also show that officials put out erroneous information minimizing their foreknowledge about Condor's assassination plans. The evidence suggests they did so in order to direct attention away from the possibility that they could have prevented the most notorious act of Condor terrorism, the Letelier assassination in Washington, D.C.

I write this as the nation continues to debate FBI and CIA advance intelligence about the Al Qaeda attacks on the World Trade Center. Had the agencies connected the dots using the abundant information they had received, could they have detected and perhaps averted the worst act of international terrorism on U.S. soil?

The same pattern of abundance of information and the failure to connect the dots is present in both cases, with similarly tragic results, although the magnitude of the tragedies is immensely disproportionate. There was one other enormous difference: in the case of Condor's terrorism, the perpetrator was a close U.S. ally, not an enemy. And the information about upcoming attacks was obtained from sources in the friendly intelligence agencies who were actually planning the attacks.

Evidence now available shows that the CIA knew of Condor's existence within a month or two of its creation. The CIA had long promoted the idea of greater coordination among the region's military, especially with regard to intelligence and communications. When the new organization was first discussed in U.S. cable traffic, it was viewed not with alarm but as a logical reaction to international coordination of armed groups on the left. Condor was seen as an understandable, even laudable, upgrade in the countries' intelligence capabilities.

Did this approval extend to all of Condor's methods, including disappearances, cross-border kidnappings, and assassinations? To be sure, knowledge of those methods is not the same thing as approval. Indeed, there is no evidence at all suggesting any U.S. agency or official knew about or countenanced an assassination in the United States. But neither is there evidence the U.S. agencies, in liaison contacts with their Latin American military counterparts, manifested any clear opposition to such tactics in the fight against Communism. To the contrary, the military leaders knew the CIA itself had used such methods. It is certain that Pinochet and his officers knew that the CIA provided weapons to right-wing plotters who had assassinated the chief of the Chilean armed forces in 1970, then paid the same group $35,000 in hush money after the plot collapsed in failure.

This much is clear from my investigation: U.S. intelligence agencies had excellent sources inside Operation Condor and were monitoring developments closely. Early reporting included Condor's possible link to the assassinations in Argentina of a former Bolivian president and two prominent Uruguayan political leaders. The first evidence of concern came from the State Department's Latin America bureau, which queried the U.S. ambassadors in the region about evidence of security force coordination.

In late July 1976, new reports transformed that concern into a plan of action. The CIA learned that Condor was taking its operations abroad. The CIA briefed the State Department's top Latin American officials that Condor was planning "executive action"—assassinations—outside Latin America. The reports mentioned Paris, then both Portugal and France, as locations for the operations. Teams were already training in Argentina.

Rounding up subversives in their own countries was one thing. Planning assassinations in European capitals was another. Officials at the State Department reacted with the kind of common sense directness that most people would have brought to bear on such a situation: something had to be done to stop this craziness. The officials drafted an urgent and top-secret cable. Signed by Secretary of State Henry Kissinger, the cable instructed the U.S. ambassadors to Chile, Argentina, and Uruguay to contact those governments at the highest level possible to make clear that the United States knew about the plans and opposed them. The language was diplomatic, larded with reassurances that the United States shared the governments' goal in defeating terrorism and subversion, but the message the ambassadors were to deliver was unmistakable: We know what you are planning; don't do it. Kissinger's cable stressed that the ambassadors should act with speed and urgency, containing this sentence in the first paragraph: "Government planned and directed assassinations within and outside the territory of Condor members has most serious implications which we must face squarely and rapidly."

What happened next? Inexplicably, amazingly, nothing happened. Kissinger's orders were not carried out. Chile, Argentina, and Uruguay went ahead with the Condor planning. Weeks went by, and none of the ambassadors delivered the warning.

Twenty-eight days later, on September 21, a remote-control bomb exploded under the driver's seat of a car rounding Washington's Sheridan Circle, on Massachusetts Avenue, only a few hundred feet from the Chilean embassy. Orlando Letelier was General Pinochet's most prominent and effective opponent in the United States. He had been foreign minister and defense minister in the Popular Unity government of President Allende. He had served as Allende's ambassador to Washington. His contacts and access in Washington as well as in the capitals of Europe where he traveled frequently were unmatched. Letelier had had a hand in two recent blows against Pinochet—legislation in the U.S. Congress making respect for human rights a condition for aid, and the cancellation of major Dutch investments in Chile.

His legs severed by the blast, Letelier died almost instantly. A twenty-five-year-old American woman, Ronni Moffitt, staggered from the car, helped by her husband, Michael Moffitt, who had been sitting in the back seat. Shrapnel had sliced her carotid artery, and she drowned in her own blood before an ambulance could arrive. Her husband survived, dazed and shouting that DINA—the Directorate of National Intelligence—Pinochet's secret police, had done this.

The FBI investigation subsequently confirmed that he was right. The investigation also uncovered documentary evidence that the Chilean agents who carried out the assassination used the Condor apparatus to obtain passports and visas intended for use in the plot.

Would Pinochet have called off the assassination planned for Washington if the U.S. ambassador had put him on notice that the United States had discovered Condor and its plans for international assassinations? One U.S. State Department official, Hewson Ryan, was troubled by this question, and expressed his concern about U.S. awareness of Condor in an interview shortly before his death in 1991:

> Whether there was a direct relationship or not, I don't know. Whether if we had gone in, we might have prevented this, I don't know. *But we didn't.* We were extremely reticent about taking a strong forward public posture, and even a private posture in certain cases, as was this case in the Chilean assassination. [Emphasis added.]

There is additional, even more compelling, evidence that U.S. intelligence had in its possession information that could have been used to avert the act of terror in the United States. We now know that there were not one but two Condor-related assassination missions underway in the summer and fall of 1976. Amazingly, both were detected in progress by U.S. intelligence. The plan to send assassins to Paris was one, and it led directly to the Kissinger cable, containing the orders to send the (undelivered) warning message. The second mission was discovered by the U.S. ambassador to Paraguay, George Landau. Paraguayan officials had asked him to provide U.S. visas for false Paraguayan passports for two Chilean security agents on their way to the United States. Landau became suspicious and alerted the CIA in Washington. Landau did not know he had discovered an assassination plot in progress, but his action alerted the U.S. government that Chile security agents were planning something in the United States. Landau's action (he also made copies of the passport photos, one of which was the actual assassin) eventually implicated Chile, Paraguay, and the Condor apparatus in Letelier's death and led to the case being solved by the FBI.

Our concern here—in the weeks prior to the Letelier assassination—is with the advance knowledge. New information was coming in about Chile, Uruguay, and Argentina planning an assassination in Paris; then separate information arrived about Chile planning a suspicious mission to Washington, D.C. The information from both streams was developed during the same period of time (late July, August, and early September) and was handled by the same CIA and State Department officials.

It is reasonable to ask, even after all these years, who aborted the clear instructions intended to stop Condor's assassination plans and why. It is also reasonable to think that a strong and clear warning to Chile about Condor would have caused Pinochet and his security chief to cancel the mission to kill Letelier.

What we know for certain is that the warning to the Condor countries, including Chile, was set in motion, then inexplicably pulled back. The most benign explanation is that the dots were not connected until it was too late, that it was simply an innocuous mistake by busy officials. This explanation, given by several State Department officials, is undermined by the subsequent effort to conceal how much U.S. officials knew about both streams of Condor information. It is further undermined by the State Department's and the CIA's continuing refusal to declassify relevant documents that would answer these still unanswered questions.

This is one of the Condor stories that is the object of this investigation. The missed opportunity to prevent an act of terror and murder on the streets of Washington pales beside the deeper tragedy in Latin America and of the deeper failure of the United States in that period. The historical question is this: How many of the thousands of murders committed by Chile, Argentina, Uruguay, Bolivia, Paraguay, and Brazil could have been prevented if the United States had taken "a strong forward public posture, [or] even a private posture" against the killing, torture, and disappearances its allies in friendly intelligence agencies were carrying out?

2

MEETING IN SANTIAGO

*Chile proposed operations to eliminate enemies all over the world, . . . to elimi-
nate people who were causing harm to our countries, people like Letelier.*

—INTELLIGENCE OFFICER WHO ATTENDED THE MEETING TO CREATE
OPERATION CONDOR

*That these nations face a regional, coordinated terrorist threat is fact, not fiction.
. . . The most rational approach to deal with a coordinated regional enemy is to
organize along similar lines. The U.S. has long urged these countries to increase
their cooperation for security. Now that they are doing so our reaction should not
be one of opprobrium.*

—U.S. AMBASSADOR TO URUGUAY ERNEST SIRACUSA, CABLE TO
WASHINGTON, JULY 20, 1976

November 1975

The meeting to create the Condor system was held in one of the mansions of
fading elegance along Santiago's broadest avenue, the Alameda. The building
housed the Army War Academy, where officers already in service took advanced training in leadership and—more recently—intelligence. It was late
November 1975, a pleasant season, when the days are hot and bright in the
Southern Hemisphere's spring. For most of a week, colonels, majors, and cap-
tains from six countries gathered each morning beneath the arched ceiling of
what once might have been a formal banquet room. They were all intelligence
officials, most with traditional military training, some with police back-

grounds, men whose job it had become to defeat what they variously referred to as subversion, terrorism, or international Communism.

Together, the military forces they represented dominated the lives of more than two-thirds of the population of South America. The geographic area under their sway was only a little smaller than that of the continental United States—spanning the entire Southern Cone of South America, from Chile's 2,500-mile Pacific Coast, south to the Straits of Magellan and Cape Horn, east to the Atlantic shores of Argentina and Uruguay, and then north almost 4,000 miles to encompass the Andes highlands of Bolivia, the plains of Paraguay, and the vast cities and Amazonian expanses of Brazil.

They looked to the United States as their leader in the worldwide Cold War, but they had been shocked, only seven months before, when the United States allowed its ally, the South Vietnamese military government, to fall in defeat in a *guerra de guerrillas*—a war of underground rebels outmaneuvering traditional armies. To these gathered military officers, it was all too ominous, too similar to their own situation. Their own enemies were the bands of young leftists in each of their countries who had taken up arms for the cause of revolution, inspired by Marx and Che Guevara and dedicated to the slogan of repeating "1, 2, 3 Vietnams" in Latin America.

Now, military intelligence had learned that the most dangerous underground groups had joined together in an international campaign combining armed attacks and international diplomacy, with bases all over Latin America and support networks in Europe. Secret intelligence reports from those months show a focus bordering on obsession on the nonviolent threat that the military considered even more dangerous: the nonviolent politicians lobbying in Europe and the United States against the military governments under the banner of democracy and human rights.

Chile had gathered this group of intelligence chiefs to present a plan to strike against these enemies anywhere in the world. General Augusto Pinochet was the host, and he was paying the expenses of all those attending. Pinochet stood stern and tall among the region's military leaders. He had taken power two years before in a ferocious military assault that reversed the growing momentum of radical change in Latin America.

Chile's experiment in democratic revolution, and its leader, President Salvador Allende, died on that day, September 11, 1973. With the coup, Pinochet gained a reputation as a kind of anti-Communist avenging angel.

With aggression and brutality never before seen in South America, he decimated the region's largest and best organized leftist establishment. He did it first with mass arrests, concentration camps, and the summary executions in the days and weeks following the coup. He then moved to the more arduous task of rooting out the clandestine opposition groups. For this he created a new intelligence force, answerable only to him: the Directorate of National Intelligence (DINA). By late 1975, the new tactics had achieved almost total victory inside Chile, and Pinochet and his intelligence chief turned their attention abroad.

Pinochet's success was making him a hero of the world anti-Communists, earning him the gratitude, access, and even friendship, of leaders like Francisco Franco, Henry Kissinger, and Margaret Thatcher.

If Pinochet addressed the assembled intelligence chiefs that balmy Tuesday morning, November 26, 1975, he did it during a ninety-minute opening session scheduled for "ceremonial greetings." Then, the "First Inter-American Meeting of National Intelligence" was brought to order by the chief of DINA, Colonel Manuel Contreras.

This account of the secret proceedings of that meeting is based on the eyewitness account of one of the participants and two documents given to participants. One document is the meeting's program and schedule; the other is the final resolution over the signatures of the heads of delegations of the countries joining Chile's new organization. Additional details are provided by CIA and FBI documents and sources.

Contreras explained the rationale for his plan:

> Subversion, [he wrote], . . . does not recognize borders nor countries, and its infiltration is penetrating every level of national life.
>
> Subversion has developed a leadership structure that is intercontinental, continental, regional and subregional. As examples we can list the Tricontinental Conference of Havana, the Revolutionary Coordinating Junta [JCR] for South America, etc., all of which are given a pleasing face by all kinds of solidarity committees, congresses, Tribunals, Meetings, Festivals and conferences, etc.
>
> In contrast, the countries that are being attacked on the military, economic and political front (from both inside and outside their borders) are fighting back at most only with bilateral understandings or simple "gentlemen's agreements."

The informal cooperation of the past was not enough to combat this "psychopolitical war," he argued. Contreras outlined his proposal for three phases of what he called "effective coordination." The first, relatively innocuous phase was described in detail in the documents. It called for the creation of a Coordinating Center (Centro Coordinator) in Chile to gather, exchange, and communicate information on people and organizations linked to "subversion." The center was to be "similar to that which Interpol has in Paris, but dedicated to subversion."

The system would have what was then the latest technology: "Telex, microfilm, computers, cryptography." In the final document, for approval by each country's president, there is a thinly veiled reference to the expected interaction with the American CIA and FBI: "We recommend the utilization of liaison resources outside the countries of the System, *especially those that are outside the continent*, to obtain information on Subversion" (emphasis added). Contreras would later say publicly that both the CIA and the FBI knew about this intelligence data bank, contributed information to it, and sought information from it.

Phases Two and Three of the new organization were "operations," activities so secret that the word itself does not appear in the documents. In the intelligence world, the distinction between information and operations separates the men from the boys. Operations means planning and executing actions that directly advance the military or political objective the agency is trying to achieve. Sometimes the actions are designed to gather intelligence and serve the information gathering and analysis arm of the agency. Most often operations are designed to attack, incapacitate, or otherwise impede the enemy's ability to act. They include disseminating propaganda ("black" propaganda, meaning the use of lies, also known as "disinformation," to discredit or confound the enemy), surveillance, and location of enemy targets, and covert missions to capture and hold enemy activists.

The pinnacle of intelligence operations is assassination, sometimes called "wet work" in the intelligence world. In the mid-1970s Latin America security parlance, operations was the word used for kidnapping, interrogation under torture, and killing.

Phase Two operations were limited to actions against targets inside the six-member countries. Colonel Contreras's proposal met an obvious need. Activists of all political stripes had moved from country to country as military crackdowns were imposed. Many were refugees under official protection of the United Nations High Commission for Refugees. Tens of thousands of refugees had gathered in Argentina, the only country that did not yet have a military government. As long as the exiles did not break the laws of the country in which they had sought refuge, they were protected—at least in theory—under international law. Contreras's proposal made refugee protection meaningless by creating a mechanism for the intelligence services to conduct operations in each other's countries.

The model for Phase Two was the successful joint operation that had just been completed by Chile, Argentina, and Paraguay in the months prior to the November meeting. Paraguay captured two leftists, a Chilean and an Argentine, arriving from Argentina. They were on the first stop of a mission to several Latin American countries to recruit leftist groups to the new Revolutionary Coordinating Junta (JCR). Chilean and Argentine intelligence officers converged on Asunción to interrogate the two men. After three months of shared interrogation, Paraguay permitted Chile to transport the Chilean prisoner to a clandestine interrogation center in Chile. He was held for another four months, and then disappeared. The operation was one of several documented examples of direct U.S. collaboration with the joint security force actions. The FBI shared and distributed the intelligence product of the Paraguay arrests, even while knowing that the information had been obtained under torture.

The new system would formalize and improve such collaboration, expanding it to include Bolivia, Uruguay, and Brazil. The intelligence services would exchange information, allowing each to keep track of the whereabouts and movements of its enemy targets present in another country. One or both countries would carry out surveillance and capture; all interested countries would participate in interrogation. The reports based on interrogation would be shared, and upon request a captured leftist would be transported to his or her home country for further interrogation and eventual execution.

Torture was an inevitable and integral part of the process of interrogation in all of the countries. Under the system, prisoners in neighboring countries could be interrogated simultaneously, based on quick exchanges of questions and data among the interrogators. Documents captured in raids were to be copied and exchanged for analysis in each country.

What Contreras had in mind for Phase Three stunned even some of this group of hardened intelligence veterans. Phase Three operations would include surveillance and assassination *outside* Latin America. Colonel José A. Fons, Chief of Uruguay's delegation recalled the meeting twenty-six years later in an interview:

> Chile proposed operations to eliminate enemies all over the world, to eliminate people who were causing harm to our countries, people like Letelier. That was an operation that required a lot of preparation, a very well done operation. Chile had the resources and the will to operate. I repeat, Chile had the resources and will to operate.

The five top intelligence officials* endorsed Chile's proposal and signed the final document, dated November 28. A delegation from Brazil attended as observers, but did not formally join until 1976. After consultation with their respective governments, they were to ratify the agreement within sixty days.

The new entity needed a name. A Uruguayan air force colonel, the second ranking member of the delegation, had a suggestion that was incorporated in the final document.

> The present organization will be called CONDOR, by unanimous agreement, in accord with the motion presented by the Uruguayan delegation in homage to the country that is its headquarters.

The Letelier assassination would not take place for another ten months, but it was uppermost in Colonel Fons's mind when he thought back on the Condor meeting. Letelier was the most typical victim—targeted as a dangerous democrat rather than a violent terrorist, a man who worked against Pinochet not in secret but in public corridors of power in the United States and Europe.

---

* The names of heads of delegations to the Condor meeting are known only through this document. They are, as listed: "Jorge Casas, Navy Captain, chief of delegation, Argentina; Carlos Mena, Army Major, chief of delegation, Bolivia; Manuel Contreras Sepúlveda, Army Colonel, Director of National Intelligence, Chile; José A. Fons, Army Colonel, chief of delegation, Uruguay; Benito Guanes Serrano, Army Colonel, chief of 2nd Department, Armed Forces Staff, Paraguay."

The Letelier assassination was to become the single most notorious act involving the Condor alliance being forged at the November 1975 meeting. The Uruguayan officer who described the meeting could have chosen from a stunning list of similar examples, before and after the meeting, of attacks against enemies from all the countries represented, including his own. All fit the international parameters set forth in Chile's proposal for Phase Two and Three operations: the targets were violent or nonviolent enemies residing outside their own country at the time they are attacked.

The high-profile Condor victims include a former president, a dissident military chief, and moderate political leaders with impeccable democratic credentials. Some of the victims, had they lived, would have been at the top of lists for potential presidents when their countries returned to democracy. There were many other lower-profile cases—Argentines, Uruguayans, Chileans, Paraguayans, and Bolivians kidnapped outside their own countries in the period 1974–80. Some were unabashed Marxist revolutionaries planning guerrilla war; some were trying to live in peace. Only a few survived.

All fit the pattern of Phase Two and Phase Three "operations" discussed at the Santiago meeting on inter-American intelligence those days in November 1975. Some of the killing took place before the meeting. Condor operations of both Phase Two and Phase Three reached a peak in the period after the military coup in Argentina in March 1976.

A final case must be noted. In late July 1976, a CIA official in Montevideo, Uruguay, learned that a Uruguayan officer was talking at a cocktail party about killing U.S. Congressman Edward Koch. The congressman had angered the military government by passing an amendment to cut off U.S. military aid to Uruguay. CIA Director George Bush personally called Representative Koch to warn him that there was a "contract" out on his life because of his amendment on Uruguay. The hit was to be carried out not by Uruguay but by Chile's DINA—a detail that betrayed the threat's modus operandi as a Phase Three Condor plan.

The implications are inescapable: U.S. intelligence officials had knowledge about the new organization's assassination plans but treated that information with insouciant disregard bordering on indifference to the possible fatal consequences of its allies' terrorist actions. As will become evident in the course of this book, even more information was in the hands of officials about the planned mission that resulted in Chile's assassination of Letelier around the same time. We will examine in detail the actions taken and omitted that led to the failure to avert that act of international terrorism in the heart of the U.S. capital.

The written documents from the Santiago meeting referred to the Condor System, or the Condor Organization. They maintained Condor's cover, even in the secret documents, that Condor was simply a data bank, an exchange of information, and a communication system. But U.S. intelligence reports referred almost universally to "Operation Condor," capturing more accurately the organization's aggressive, activist nature.

The Santiago meeting and the creation of Operation Condor is a central event in one of the darkest periods in Latin American history, from 1973 through 1980, when countries previously renowned for democracy and civilized virtues submerged themselves in terrorism, clandestine warfare, and systems of repression not experienced before or since. The Condor Years stand for the destruction of more than one hundred years of virtually uninterrupted democracy and rule of law in Chile and Uruguay. Argentina and Brazil had spottier records, going in and out of authoritarian rule, but both were modern societies with enormous economies. Argentina was considered the most "Europeanized" country in Latin America, whose elegant capital, Buenos Aires, was compared in its architecture and broad avenues with Paris. The same sophisticated Argentina that tended to look down on its neighbors as less cultured, less European, was transformed during the Condor Years into the country with a mass-murder body count in the tens of thousands.

Until the late 1960s and 1970s "revolution" usually connoted military imposition of one ruler to replace another. Opponents were arrested and mistreated, even tortured and sometimes killed. It is not to diminish the gravity of the crimes of earlier eras to point out that they differed by many orders of magnitude from the practices of the Condor Years—when the mass arrests, secret prisons, concentration camps, even the use of extermination methods and crematoriums are comparable only with the worst practices of the Nazi era.

Operation Condor itself was responsible for a relatively small proportion of the total deaths and violence, but it represents the final, worst departure from the rules of law and civilized society. States at their highest level of authority entered into an agreement to cooperate in the enterprise of state terrorism. They discarded not only the human rights protections of their own citizens, but conspired to violate the norms of international protections: the right to sanctuary, asylum, protection of refugees, habeas corpus, and the carefully crafted procedures for extradition of those charged with crimes in one country and arrested in another.

As a secret treaty, Condor elevated human rights crimes to the highest level of state policy, under the direct control and manipulation of the heads of state and ministers of government. Its existence as an official policy instrument of six nations made it impossible for those regimes to write off their human rights crimes as isolated acts of aberrant officials or rogue agents.

The story of the Condor Years would be miscast, however, if it were told only as a litany of human rights violations. The story requires an objective and realistic recounting of the Marxist revolutionary side as well. In retrospect, the movements that brandished incendiary rhetoric and real weapons against states they denounced as bourgeois and corrupt may seem in hindsight predestined to defeat. But at the time, the outcome was by no means clear in Latin America. Both the right (ranging from the radical anti-Communism of the traditional land- and business-based rightist parties to the moderately liberal movements whose priorities were democracy and social reform) and the left (populist movements such as Peronism, Soviet-line, and other types of Communist parties, Social Democratic, and Marxist Socialist parties) took seriously the challenge represented by the "extreme" left. The revolutionaries inspired by the example of Cuba and Ernesto "Che" Guevara were convinced they were winning (for a time) and that their pockets of underground guerrilla warfare would become a catalyst for a countrywide, perhaps even continent-wide, uprising in the name of Socialism.

As many as 5,000 members of the Movement of National Liberation-Tupamaros were organized in urban cells in tiny Uruguay and had gained a worldwide reputation as Robin Hood–like romantic revolutionaries. Che Guevara himself seemed to live on even after being captured and executed by Bolivian soldiers and their CIA advisers. Argentina had a variety of radical groups arising from the traditional left and the Peronist movement. By 1974, the Peronist Montoneros had assassinated a former president, General Pedro Eugenio Aramburu, and kidnappings of businessmen for multimillion-dollar ransoms were common.

Chile's extreme left radicalism was mostly at the level of overheated rhetoric. Violence was mostly limited to rock-throwing against rightist youth groups. But in the first year of Allende's government an extremist group assassinated a former cabinet minister, Edmundo Pérez Zucovic.

Paraguay was a perennial caldron of conspiracy. Marxist ideology played little role in the plotting against the dictatorship of Alfredo Stroessner, whose Colorado Party had been in power for twenty years. Young Paraguayans studying in neighboring Argentina, however, were joining Marxist revolutionary groups, and a well-organized but unsuccessful effort was made to kill Stroessner with a car bomb in that year.

It was an era of great violence and great idealism; the most radical groups on both left and right rejected democracy as a solution to society's most pressing problems. It was an era in which the United States itself played a role profoundly at odds with its historical legacy and deepest values. Absorbed by the larger geopolitical competition with the Soviet Union, the United States could no longer be counted as an ally by the political forces in Latin America most committed to democracy.

By 1970, and lasting until the inauguration in 1977 of President Jimmy Carter, the United States in effect had switched sides. In Allende's election democracy had brought to power a Marxist proclaiming he would create a unique and peaceful "Chilean road to socialism," an unacceptable outcome to the United States. Under the leadership of Henry Kissinger, first as Richard Nixon's national security adviser and later as secretary of state, the United States sent an unequivocal signal to the most extreme rightist forces that democracy could be sacrificed in the cause of ideological warfare. Criminal operational tactics, including assassination, were not only acceptable but supported with weapons and money.

A CIA internal memo laid it out in unsparing terms:

> On September 16, 1970 [CIA] Director [Richard] Helms informed a group of senior agency officers that on September 15, President Nixon had decided that an Allende regime was not acceptable to the United States. The President asked the Agency to prevent Allende from coming to power or to unseat him and authorized up to $10 million for this purpose. . . . A special task force was established to carry out this mandate, and preliminary plans were discussed with Dr. Kissinger on 18 September 1970.

To extremists in the military, people like Manuel Contreras and others later placed in charge of security forces, Kissinger and the CIA sent an even more dangerous message that would echo later in Condor operations. The CIA "agreed with" and supported plans by military plotters to kidnap the top commander of the Chilean Armed Forces, an action considered "an essential step in any coup plan." The officer, General René Schneider, was shot to death in the operation. Schneider's offense, according to the CIA, was excessive devotion to democracy: "Schneider was a strong supporter of the Chilean constitution and a major stumbling block for military officers seeking to carry out a coup to prevent Allende from being inaugurated."

According to declassified documents, the CIA provided three submachine guns to one group of plotters at 2 A.M. on the day of the kidnapping. The CIA has always insisted that the weapons were never used and that a different group killed Schneider. Weapons and money were also promised to that second group but were never delivered, according to the CIA. The distinction between the two groups seems insubstantial, however, since the CIA never abandoned the tactic of kidnapping the army chief and was providing support to plotters on the same day it actually happened.

The United States thus gave its operational endorsement to acts of terrorism in furtherance of the cause of anti-Communism. It was okay to remove a moderate leader who became a "stumbling block" to the removal of a perceived Communist threat. The message could only have been reinforced when the agency a few weeks later sent $35,000 to one of the kidnappers who had escaped. The reason given: "to keep the prior contact secret, maintain the good will of the group, and for humanitarian reasons."

The U.S. message about acceptable operational tactics was received directly by some of those who later used those tactics in the Condor Years. Among the members of the group plotting to kidnap Schneider was a former Chilean Naval Academy student, Enrique Arancibia Clavel. In 1974, Arancibia became DINA's operational liaison with Argentine intelligence and organized the murder of another military commander who had become a stumbling block, Pinochet's predecessor General Carlos Prats González.

In my interviews with military officers from Condor countries there was a consistent refrain, "The United States was our leader."

Now, a quarter century later, the countries of the Southern Cone continue to struggle with the events of these years. Chile, Argentina, Brazil, Uruguay, Paraguay, and Bolivia have all enjoyed at least a decade free of military rule. But constitutional government and rule of law are without exception under a shadow cast by the military crimes of the past. That has been the shadow of impunity.

With few exceptions, those responsible for the thousands upon thousands of executions and disappearances, for the systematic use of torture that affected tens of thousands more, and for the international assassinations that are at the core of the Condor system have been able to evade justice. Amnesty laws, accepted by incoming civilian government as the price of military withdrawal from power, were used to shortcircuit even the most cursory judicial investigation of the crimes. The laws protected the military from being charged and even questioned. No officer of state in any country, neither military commander, judge, nor head of government, had the authority to demand that officials tell what they know about the human rights crimes of the past.

As a result, the first and most enduring human rights casualty was the truth. In the absence of official, credible investigations by competent authorities endorsed by democratic legitimacy, the historical record of those years was a matter of political preference. Victims' families and their allies among political and human rights organizations did their best to investigate based on the testimonies of those who suffered, but their conclusions were subject to easy denial by the accused and those on the other side of the political divide. So-called "truth commissions" conducted laudable investigations to clarify the legal status of the thousands of disappeared, but were prohibited in many cases from officially naming the names of those who caused the disappearances.

Officers who once were masters of torture and extermination camps were promoted or retired as their age and career required, with honor and the full benefits of rank. Pinochet was lionized abroad as a strong, no-nonsense leader responsible for the "Pinochet Model," which brought order and economic prosperity. Blatantly illegal international arrangements like Condor were shrouded in secrecy and official denial.

The legal and historical limbo in which the Condor Years were immersed also affected the United States. Having won the Cold War and elicited the peaceful capitulation of its Soviet rival, the United States conferred on itself a kind of de facto amnesty even more encompassing than that enjoyed by its

Latin American allies: no truth commission or any other kind of official investigation was established to look into the human collateral damage of the many
proxy wars we supported in Latin America and elsewhere.

Despite the edifice of legal obstacles, however the pursuit of justice never
ceased. For more than two decades the investigators, journalists, political activists, human rights workers, and a few indomitable judges worked relentlessly
to piece together the facts as they became available and to seize opportunities
for judicial advances as they arose.

The successes in the pursuit of justice were few. Then, in October 1998,
everything changed. Circumstances, hard work, and luck conspired to put a
dictator under arrest in London.

3

TILTING AT WINDMILLS

The charter of this tribunal gives warning for the future, I say, and repeat again, gives warning for the future, to dictators and tyrants masquerading as a state, that if . . . they debase the sanctity of man in their own countries, they act at their peril, for they affront the international law of mankind.

—Sir Hartley Shawcross, Britain's chief prosecutor at Nuremberg, 1945

Pinochet's impunity has never been far from Joan* Garcés's mind. It has been that quiet man's burning passion since September 11, 1973, when as a young aide with Socialist ideals he had been forced to evacuate Chile's presidential palace, La Moneda, before the air attacks that enveloped it in flames. That day, for Garcés, saw the death of the dream of building a just, Socialist society using democracy rather than violent revolution.

Garcés, a Spaniard, had come to Chile a few years earlier to write a thesis on Chilean politics, for his doctorate at the Sorbonne in Paris, and he stayed to become—still only twenty-six years old—one of Salvador Allende's closest political confidants. That last day Allende ordered him to abandon the besieged presidential palace because "Someone has to recount what happened here and only you can do it."

"I was a witness to the great national and collective hope [of the Allende experiment], expressed in a democratically impeccable way. And I was also a witness to the human and social tragedy into which Chile was submerged three years later. My best friends left their lives there, defending their commitment

---

* Joan is a variation of the Spanish name Juan.

to the freedom and dignity of their people. This is something you don't ever forget," he said, looking back.

After the coup, Garcés returned to Spain to a career in law, writing and teaching. He wrote a book on the failed but noble experiment of the "Chilean road to Socialism," one of the first insider accounts of the chaotic political maneuvering of Allende's three years in office. He made the case that Allende was committed to inviolate respect for the law and Chile's constitution.

Impeccable democracy. The rule of law. Applied to the service of the poor, as in no other country of the world before or since. Those were the values that Garcés took away from Chile. Instead, the region began a long journey through a swamp of dictatorship, arbitrary military rule, and violations of individual rights. And the military leaders like Pinochet seemed to be getting off scot-free. Even as the years unfolded and the military governments gave way finally to constitutional rule, the new political leaders—despite their democratic impulses—chose not to prosecute the crimes of the past. Protection of those who had committed unspeakable crimes was the price of peace with a still powerful military. Impunity, sanctioned by the democratic governments, was the rule in Chile and the other Condor countries.

As a sideline to his successful commercial law practice in Madrid, Garcés became one of the respected pioneers in the emerging field of human rights law. One day in the spring of 1996, on the one-hour flight from Barcelona to Madrid after a business trip, Garcés read a short newspaper article that would again return Chile—and the pursuit of Pinochet—to the center of his life. A criminal court in Madrid had begun the prosecution of former members of Argentina's military junta for alleged human rights crimes committed in Argentina two decades before.

"As you can imagine, in a matter of seconds I made the extrapolation," Garcés said. When he landed in Madrid, Garcés made inquiries about the case. It had begun with a hypothetical question discussed by a group of public prosecutors: If Argentina was not able to prosecute its generals for human rights crimes, would Spain have jurisdiction? The prosecutors concluded that Spanish law, combined with international law precedents going back to the Nazi trials at Nuremberg, allowed such charges to be brought in Spain as long as the crimes involved could be considered crimes against humanity.

The prosecutors resolved to test the theory by bringing a case to court, acting not in their official capacity as prosecutors but in a private capacity allowed under Spanish law. On March 28—within days of the twentieth anniversary of the coup that brought the Argentine military to power in 1976—the association's secretary general, Carlos Castresana, drafted and filed a formal accusation (*denuncia*) charging the members of the Argentine junta with genocide and terrorism against ten victims of Spanish nationality. The case had been assigned to a special court in Madrid, called the *Audiencia Nacional*, and to investigating Judge Baltasar Garzón. Garzón had earned a reputation as a press-savvy, crusading judge for his relentless prosecutions of drug traffickers and of police abuses against the Basque separatists, ETA, a group that frequently used terrorist tactics.

Garcés went to talk to Castresana. "Look, I told him, you have the same juridical foundation to bring a case for the same kind of crimes in the country next door," he said. Castresana was interested. He considered Pinochet to be in the same category as the Argentine generals. Garcés offered to provide the factual material for a parallel case against Pinochet. He had the recently published report of Chile's National Commission of Truth and Reconciliation, known as the Rettig Report, which contained the country's most complete human rights investigation, conducted in the first year after Chile's return to democracy in 1990.

Using the information from the report, the prosecutors' association—this time represented by association President Miguel Miravet—presented a second formal accusation, on July 4, naming Pinochet and the other members of the Chilean military junta as the presumed authors of crimes against humanity in Chile, including torture, kidnapping, and disappearances. Seven victims were named, all Spanish citizens.

In a separate, meticulously detailed filing on his own behalf, Garcés linked the Argentina and Chile cases in a way that was later to prove crucial. He charged that the leaders of Chile and Argentina had committed human rights crimes together, as participants in a criminal conspiracy. Little was known in 1996 about that alleged conspiracy, except its name, Operation Condor.

He wrote:

> The persons cited in the current case [against Pinochet et al.] conspired with those of equal rank in the Military Junta of Argentina to coordinate and multiply the scope of the identical crimes of terrorism, assassinations, illegal arrests, torture, kidnapping of minors and disappearances. . . . The criminal conspiracy fol-

lowed a common pattern, with those charged herein using public functionaries under their command to commit their crimes . . . and financing their terrorist activities with the National Budget, and whose victims include Spaniards and also tens of thousands of citizens of other countries, who were assassinated, kidnapped or "detained and disappeared" in actions committed in many states of America and Europe. The conspiracy . . . received the name Operation Condor.

As evidence, Garcés cited the only authoritative document known at the time, an FBI cable published in the author's 1980 book on the Letelier assassination.

The cable was an intelligence report written a week after that assassination by the FBI man in Argentina, Robert Scherrer:

"OPERATION CONDOR" IS THE CODE NAME FOR THE COLLECTION, EX-CHANGE AND STORAGE OF INTELLIGENCE DATA CONCERNING SO CALLED "LEFTISTS," COMMUNISTS AND MARXISTS, WHICH WAS RE-CENTLY ESTABLISHED BETWEEN COOPERATING INTELLIGENCE SER-VICES IN SOUTH AMERICA IN ORDER TO ELIMINATE MARXIST TERRORIST ACTIVITIES IN THE AREA. IN ADDITION, OPERATION CON-DOR PROVIDES FOR JOINT OPERATIONS AGAINST TERRORIST TARGETS IN MEMBER COUNTRIES OF "OPERATION CONDOR." CHILE IS THE CEN-TER FOR "OPERATION CONDOR" AND IN ADDITION TO CHILE ITS MEM-BERS INCLUDE ARGENTINA, BOLIVIA, PARAGUAY AND URUGUAY. BRAZIL ALSO HAS TENTATIVELY AGREED TO SUPPLY INTELLIGENCE INPUT FOR "OPERATION CONDOR." MEMBERS OF "OPERATION CON-DOR" SHOWING THE MOST ENTHUSIASM TO DATE HAVE BEEN AR-GENTINA, URUGUAY AND CHILE. A THIRD AND MOST SECRET PHASE OF "OPERATION CONDOR" INVOLVES THE FORMATION OF SPECIAL TEAMS FROM MEMBER COUNTRIES WHO ARE TO TRAVEL ANYWHERE IN THE WORLD TO NON-MEMBER COUNTRIES TO CARRY OUT SANCTIONS UP TO ASSASSINATION AGAINST TERRORISTS OR SUPPORTERS OF TERROR-IST ORGANIZATIONS FROM "OPERATION CONDOR" MEMBER COUN-TRIES.

Both court filings made the impunity argument: In Chile there had been "not even a single judicial investigation" against the military leaders despite many futile attempts by victims families to bring such charges in Chile's courts. To the contrary, the military leaders had decreed a "self-amnesty" in 1978 to prevent such court actions. By the end of July 1996, Court numbers 5 and 6 of the Spanish National Court *(Audiencia Nacional)* had ratified the legitimacy of the criminal cases, allowing the investigating judges to examine evidence for formal indictments of the accused Chilean and Argentine officers.

The aggressive judicial actions were unprecedented. Neither the crimes, nor the alleged criminals, nor the victims were in the territory of Spain at the time of the events. Yet, once the specific legalities were cleared away, the courts' decisions in accepting the cases were based on a fairly simple principle of international law: that truly egregious crimes, those that rise to the level of crimes against humanity such as those forever engraved in human consciousness by the Nazi atrocities of World War II, are matters of universal jurisdiction. In other words, if the state in which they are committed is unable or unwilling to bring such crimes and criminals to justice, any other state is empowered to do so.

It was a principle buried in disuse during the tense decades in which the anti-Communism of the Cold War superceded the struggle against German Nazism. But in Spain that summer of 1996, a few determined lawyers and risk-taking judges revived and fortified the principle.

The actions taken by Castresana, Garcés, and the Spanish judges went virtually unnoticed in the international press in the summer of 1996. Yet the filings set in motion legal proceedings that were destined to change the course of international human rights law. In addition, the resulting judicial investigations led directly and indirectly to the release of voluminous new documentation on the inner workings of the secret security agencies and their allies in the six Condor countries.

A few months after filing the case, Garcés flew to Washington, D.C., and called his old friend Saul Landau. Landau was a fellow in the moderate left-leaning think tank the Institute for Policy Studies, an organization with a unique history in the battle against Pinochet. Founded by two former White House officials from the most idealistic wing of the John F. Kennedy presidency, the Institute's fellows were in the front lines of the 1960s intellectual and political battle against the war in Vietnam. In the 1970s it naturally evolved into a cen-

ter of opposition to U.S. government alliances with South American dictatorships such as Pinochet's.

At Landau's invitation, Orlando Letelier came to the Institute soon after his
release from a Chilean prison camp in 1974 and used it as a base of operations
in lobbying U.S. and European political leaders to throw up obstacles to the
dictatorship. Letelier was on his way to work at the Institute's Dupont Circle
offices the day he was assassinated. After Letelier's assassination, his widow, Isabel Margarita Morel de Letelier, continued as a fellow at the Institute, and
with Landau mounted an unrelenting campaign to push forward the U.S. investigation of Letelier's murder.

Arriving in Washington, Garcés asked Landau to arrange a meeting. He
wanted to enlist the support of the prosecutors and FBI agents, now retired,
who had conducted the investigation of the Letelier assassination. That investigation had produced an enormous body of information about the workings of
the Pinochet military and had led to the public discovery of Operation Condor.
Most importantly, the still secret files held by major U.S. agencies—the Justice
Department and FBI, the CIA and the State Department—contained what was
undoubtedly the most complete investigative record of the inner workings of
the Pinochet government and its relations with the United States.

The U.S. Justice Department's investigation had been the only successful
international prosecution of crimes committed by the Chilean dictatorship.
But its success was limited—the conviction of several Cuban exiles who assisted
Chilean agents in the assassination. One of the assassins, American-born
Michael Townley, pleaded guilty and cooperated with the U.S. prosecution.
Colonel Manuel Contreras and other DINA officers were indicted, but Chile
refused to extradite them to the United States. In 1990, Pinochet ended his
seventeen-year dictatorship (while remaining as chief of the armed forces). For
the first time, Chilean courts began an untainted investigation of the Letelier
assassination, and in 1995, DINA Chief Contreras and his deputy, Colonel
Pedro Espinoza, were convicted. Both were serving sentences in special military prisons at the time of Garcés's arrival in Washington.

Former Assistant U.S. Attorney E. Lawrence Barcella, one of two lead prosecutors in the case, hosted the meeting at his law offices on Pennsylvania Avenue, just three blocks from the White House. Lead FBI investigator Carter
Cornick also attended. Garcés laid out his plan and progress so far since the
charges had been filed in Spain. The goal, he said, was to achieve a formal in-

dictment by the Spanish court and an order of arrest, which would have the effect of preventing Pinochet from traveling freely abroad. Finding the truth and documenting it in a credible international court, sending a message for history about the end of impunity—these were measures of justice as important as any possible punishment of the guilty.

The Spanish judge, García-Castellón, calling on the provisions of the Mutual Legal Assistance Treaty (MLAT), a 1990 agreement signed by Spain and the United States, had made a broad, bold request—called "letters rogatory"—for U.S. secrets about Chile and Pinochet, both subjects of nettling historic sensitivity. Garcés knew the request for cooperation would languish in benign neglect unless he could neutralize the expected knee-jerk opposition from those in the U.S. government who thought it best to bury embarrassing secrets about U.S. support for Pinochet in the obscurity of the past. The letters rogatory asked for all documents in U.S. archives about Pinochet, his secret police, and Operation Condor. CIA operational files, which had never been released, were specifically requested. The CIA was sure to hold a trove of information on its relationship with Chile's DINA, but no one was optimistic about prying loose such potentially embarrassing information.

The clear conclusion was that Garcés needed the United States government to send a signal, if possible from the very office of the president, that the United States looked on the investigation with at least friendly neutrality. Though skeptical, Barcella and Cornick promised their help.

U.S. response to the request for cooperation moved at a snail's pace. No documents that had not already been made public were provided to Spain. No new documents were declassified, and the idea of CIA help barely reached the level of hypothetical possibility. Nevertheless, in the hypersensitive world of international law and diplomacy, signals were sent and received. Nothing was done or said to throw cold water on the Quixotic Spanish case. That abstention from discouragement was a positive signal in itself.

But as long as the MLAT request was lodged at the Department of Justice, the position on declassification was a simple "no"—don't declassify anything in response to a court request. It could set a dangerous precedent and any number of investigations in foreign countries about which there might be information in U.S. files.

After a bit of prodding from U.S. Congressman John Conyers, a Justice Department official promised publicly the United States would cooperate "to the extent permitted by law." Barcella was given approval to go to Spain to testify. And in January 1998, Judge García-Castellón brought a "rogatory commission" to Washington, and received full Justice Department cooperation. García-Castellón was able to obtain the testimony of the other principle investigators in the Letelier investigation. (Michael Vernon Townley, the principal assassin and chief witness in the case, and the Cuban exiles still serving their sentences, refused to testify because García-Castellón declined to grant them immunity from future prosecution.)

For most of two years, Garcés built a case against Pinochet that was overwhelming in sheer volume. He organized a gigantic pro bono legal operation on several continents that allowed victims of the Pinochet regime to join the suit wherever they were. Volunteer lawyers in Spain, Washington, and Santiago expanded the list of plaintiffs from seven dual Spanish-Chilean nationals to more than 3,000 documented cases of torture, execution and disappearance. Victims' families joined by organization: the entire membership of the Families of Disappeared Detainees registered with the court with legal representation by Garcés's team of volunteers. The families of two Americans who had been killed in Chile, Charles Horman and Frank Teruggi, added their names to the list of plaintiffs.

Court filings ran to hundreds of pages, often reading like narrative history, describing incidents such as the so-called "Caravan of Death" in which Pinochet's officers traveled from city to city ordering summary executions to clean out the jails of political prisoners. A long section details the systematic use of torture based on the testimonies of dozens of prisoners who survived.

The Spanish and Latin American press covered the developments in some detail. But in the United States, newspapers were fashioning a softer view of the aging dictator. Pinochet was going to step down in March 1998, after almost twenty-five years as commander in chief of the Chilean armed forces. As he prepared to join the pantheon of the twentieth century's great dictators, writers reflected on Chile's own emotional ambivalence about their most powerful leader ever: "Chilean Strongman to Exit a Hero; Darker Side of Pinochet Regime Played Down," headlined the *Toronto Star*. The *Washington Post*, looking back, saw in Pinochet a " 'National Father' or Bloody Killer? As Ex-Dictator Retires From Military, Chile Is Divided Over His Legacy."

The grandfatherly Pinochet of 1998 had replaced the forbidding 1973 image of dictator in gray cape and dark glasses. He was poised to become Chile's respected ex-president and elder statesman.

A little noticed story in London's *Financial Times*, however, was to prove prophetic. The story said Pinochet, angered at Spain for permitting the criminal case against him from going forward, had ordered the closing of Chile's military office in Madrid. Established during the Franco regime, it was used to procure military supplies and armaments from European dealers, and had been a major avenue to circumvent the U.S. arms embargoes placed on Chile for human rights reasons.

London was to be the site of the new European procurement office, chosen, the article said, because General Pinochet has been a "frequent, if discreet," visitor there.

In September 1998, Pinochet arrived in London for what was to be his final, fateful visit.

He and his wife, Lucía, stayed at the Park Lane Intercontinental Hotel. They spent a few gracious hours at formal tea with Pinochet's longtime friend Margaret Thatcher at her home. Their friendship was based not only on shared dedication to reversing the political gains of the left. Thatcher was also grateful for Pinochet's military support in the Falklands/Malvinas War in 1982, in which Chile was the only Latin American country to oppose Argentina's attempt to occupy the islands that are Britain's last colony in South America. Never had a word of criticism for Chilean human rights violations escaped Thatcher's lips.

For the first time Pinochet was traveling as a civilian. His retirement from the army on March 11 had been less than smooth. Celebrated by his military colleagues with parades and speeches as the man who had saved Chile, Pinochet also faced the repudiation of thousands of protesters, who had to be held back by riot police. Chile's government, despite its democratic spirit, was placed immediately in the politically awkward position of protecting the retired dictator.

Pinochet had not left to chance the legal impunity he had enjoyed since 1973. In 1978, the toughest years of repression behind it, the military government issued decree law 2191, which granted amnesty to anyone ("authors, accomplices or concealers") responsible for political crimes since the coup. The law was intended to wipe from the courts all investigations of military actions during the period when most deaths and disappearances occurred, and that was its immediate effect. To that was added parliamentary immunity. Pinochet had rewritten the constitution in 1980 to grant himself the rank of senator for life (*senador vitalicio*), as a former head of state. Within hours of his farewell speech to his high-stepping troops, Pinochet was sworn in as senator. His protection from prosecution was continuous and seemingly air-tight, passing from his position as head of state until 1990, to commander in chief of the armed forces until 1998, to lifetime immunity as a senator.

For Pinochet's trip to London, the ever solicitous Chilean Foreign Ministry provided the fledgling senator with a diplomatic passport, even though he was not engaged in any official business for the government. Within days, Amnesty International, with headquarters in London, was alerting its chapters around Europe of his presence and organizing protests in London.

But Joan Garcés, learning from the Chilean press of Pinochet's presence, had another idea. There had been encouraging developments in both Spanish cases. Judge García-Castellón had issued a decree on September 15 reaffirming his court's jurisdiction to investigate the crimes, a preliminary step to issuing an indictment. Garcés also joined Pinochet to the parallel Argentine case in the court of investigating Judge Baltasar Garzón, based on Pinochet's participation in Operation Condor. In March, Garcés filed a criminal complaint in Garzón's case with details about Condor, accusing Pinochet of crimes against Chileans who had disappeared in Argentina. The petition not only introduced Condor and Pinochet into Garzón's case, it also contained a specific demand for Pinochet's arrest. Mirroring the arguments Garcés had made in his 1996 filing, Garzón now was able to identify Pinochet as a participant in the Condor criminal conspiracy and thus a potential defendant in the Argentine investigation. As both courts neared the indictment stage, both now had a common target: Pinochet.

Garcés reasoned that the British government would not move against Pinochet on its own, but might be amenable to cooperating in the Spanish cases. Britain and Spain were signatories of a European extradition treaty that made extradition among European countries almost as easy as among states in the United States. About the time Pinochet was having tea at Margaret Thatcher's home in London, Garcés in Madrid was drafting the legal justification for Spain to ask British authorities to question Pinochet. The request, citing the pledge of international cooperation in the European Convention Against Terrorism, was issued by judges in both the Argentine and Chilean cases. Urgent telegrams transmitted the request—called "letters rogatory"—via Interpol to London's Scotland Yard on Thursday October 15. The requests from the two judges to Scotland Yard were identical; that of Judge Garzón arrived first and was given precedence.

Meanwhile, reports surfaced that Pinochet had checked into an unnamed London hospital for routine surgery to repair a herniated disk in his back. The rogatory petition asked that Pinochet be questioned "when he recovers from surgery and that in the meantime British police should take whatever measures necessary to ensure that he does not leave the United Kingdom until the requested action has been completed." When the pending request was made public, Garzón commented there was no question of trying to extradite Pinochet, only to submit written questions to him.

October 16, 1998, began as a normal Friday at the National Court in Madrid, a low-key prelude to a relaxing weekend. Joan Garcés arrived in late morning and spent more than an hour with Judge Garzón, discussing the case. Less than twenty-four hours had passed since the interrogation request had been transmitted to London and no developments were expected until the coming week. Garzón was glancing at his watch. He said he had plans to drive with his wife to Andalucía, to attend a bullfight. Garcés said his good-byes, wished the judge a pleasant weekend, and left around 2 P.M.

A few minutes later, a fax from Scotland Yard was delivered to Garzón's desk. The message acknowledged receipt of his petition to interrogate Pinochet, but also contained a warning and some unsolicited advice. Scotland Yard had located the hospital where Pinochet was being treated, and had been informed he was well enough to be discharged. An airplane was being readied to fly him back to Chile early the next morning. "We cannot guarantee that the senator will remain here during these proceedings. He is free to leave whenever he wishes," the fax said, adding: "We will be able to hold him only if you decree an order for his arrest."

Garzón's dilemma was acute. An arrest order would include a request for Pinochet's extradition to Spain for trial. Time had suddenly become a critical factor. If he was to dictate an arrest order, it had to arrive in London in time to be executed before Pinochet got away. Garzón had to decide within a very few minutes what he was going to do, and without the benefit of consultations with anyone else involved in the case—Judge García-Castellón had already left the office.

Neither court case had as yet reached a formal indictment, although sufficient evidence had been gathered and it was within the judge's discretion to act. But this was no ordinary criminal case. Judge Garzón was asserting jurisdiction over Pinochet on the grounds that Pinochet's alleged crimes were against humanity as a whole, not just against the societies where the crimes were committed. Pinochet had been a head of state—a status that confers certain protections under international law. He was not a citizen of Spain. His alleged crimes had taken place neither in Britain nor in Spain.

A decision to order Pinochet's arrest was clearly consistent with Garzón's own prior decisions in the case. It would be a decision, however, that would be subjected to worldwide scrutiny of the kind few judges experience in their lifetime. To justify his actions, Garzón had to rely on legal foundations that floated in the nebula of unused and barely defined areas on international law. It would set new precedents of vast impact. If successful. A wrong decision would expose him to ridicule, even put his career at risk. Caution would dictate ignoring the late-arriving fax and letting fate take its course over the weekend.

Instead, Garzón looked at his watch again, opened the safe where the case files were kept, and sat down to write 720 words that were about to change history. In a world of legal documents often running hundreds of pages, Garzón's arrest warrant was stark and showed the roughness of a hurried draft:

> Writ by which the unconditional provisional arrest of Augusto Pinochet is decreed and an international order for his capture is issued.
>
> Facts: Proceedings so far have shown that in Chile from September of 1973, and similarly in the Republic of Argentina after 1976, a series of events and criminal activities occurred under the mantel of the most furious repression against the citizens and residents of those countries. These actions are carried out using plans and goals pre-established by the structures of power and which have as their object the physical elimination, disappearance, kidnapping of thousands of persons, having previously been subject to generalized torture, according to the "Rettig Report."

In the international arena, there is evidence of coordination which would receive the name "Operation Condor," in which several different countries participate, among them Chile and Argentina, and which has the purpose of coordinating repression among the countries.

In this sense, Augusto Pinochet Ugarte, at the time Chief of the Armed Forces and of the Chilean state, carried out criminal activities in coordination with the military authorities of Argentina . . . , giving orders for the physical elimination of persons, torture and kidnapping and disappearance of others from Chile and of different nationalities and in various countries through the actions of the Secret Service (DINA) and within the aforementioned "Plan Condor."

General charges weren't enough. Garzón knew he had to include concrete cases. He quickly extracted details from Garcés's March 1998 complaint on Condor. There were at least seventy-nine cases of Condor crimes, he stated in the warrant, and named one prominent victim, Edgardo Enríquez Espinosa, who disappeared April 10, 1976. It was a name Pinochet was sure to recognize. Enríquez had been the top leader of Chile's most radical revolutionary group, MIR. His capture in Argentina in April 1976 was the culmination of Condor operations in Paraguay, France, Argentina, and Chile. In his haste, Garzón mistakenly wrote that Enríquez had been kidnapped in Chile and transported to Argentina, when in fact the reverse was true.

As important as the facts were the legal justifications. Promising to expand on the presentation later, Garzón stated that the facts presented constituted crimes of genocide and terrorism under the Spanish law designated as article 23.4, which established "Spanish jurisdiction as competent . . ." He therefore proceeded to charge Pinochet for the crimes of genocide and terrorism and to issue a warrant for his arrest and extradition.

Garzón printed out the order and gave a copy to the only staff member still in the office with instructions to fax it immediately to Interpol Madrid, which would transmit it to Interpol London.

Just before 11 P.M., Sergeant David Jones of Scotland Yard arrived at the London Clinic with a detective, a uniformed policeman, and an interpreter. In accordance with British custom, none of the policemen was armed. On the eighth floor, where Pinochet's private room was located, they confronted a Chilean army captain who was in charge of Pinochet's guards.

"You have to leave at once," Jones said.

"I cannot leave my general," the captain responded in Spanish. "I'm a Chilean military officer, and I only take orders from my superiors."

"You can either leave nicely, or you can leave by force," Jones said through the interpreter. One of the Chilean guards reached in his pocket. There was a moment of wide-eyed tension, which was diffused when it became clear the guard was pulling out nothing more threatening than a cell phone. The guards then mildly allowed themselves to be led outside the building.

A nurse entered Pinochet's room to wake him and help him sit up in bed. The Scotland Yard officers waited a respectful quarter hour, then entered the room. Pinochet was alert and visibly angry. "Listen to what the sergeant is going to say," the interpreter said. She translated the order of arrest "for the murder of Spanish citizens in Chile, within the jurisdiction of the government of Spain."

Sergeant Jones read Pinochet his rights to counsel and to remain silent, but Pinochet was sputtering with rage. "I'm a head of state, I'm a diplomat, I'm not a criminal or a terrorist," he said, in apparently genuine protest and surprise. Then came a flash of comprehension:

"I know who is behind this," he growled to the interpreter, "that communist Garcés."

The arrest was the opening act of a legal drama that would last for sixteen months, with advances and retreats on both sides. The British Court granted extradition in principle, then in March 2000 declared Pinochet to be of diminished mental and physical capacity. He was released to return to Chile. It was a technicality that many considered a thinly veiled deal worked out with the Chilean government. Nevertheless, through it all the legal principal of universal jurisdiction for crimes against humanity survived intact. Pinochet's arrest was a revolutionary advance in international law not because it created new law; it didn't. It was revolutionary because it was the first time the principles developed by the victors in World War II were used to prosecute an ally rather than an enemy of the countries bringing the charges. It was the case, arguably, that brought down the curtain on the Cold War, ending its role as spoiler in international human rights law.

On a world stage, the proceedings on Pinochet's extradition were a total vindication of the Nuremberg principles. As military commander, Pinochet was being held accountable for crimes against humanity committed by those under his command. He was denied the traditional shelter that heads of state and former heads of state had enjoyed from prosecution by other states. And Spain's right to put Pinochet on trial was reaffirmed under the Nuremberg principle that his crimes—torture and terrorism—offended all humanity and therefore were subject to prosecution by any state anywhere.

The case broke the tacit agreement among nations that the Nuremberg principles were to be applied solely as "victors' justice"—against the crimes committed by the losing side in a military struggle. Bringing such cases against sitting governments and their former officials was not only a diplomatic nightmare, it raised the specter of tit-for-tat retaliation against a country's own officials—a danger that has colored the United States' opposition to almost all such international prosecutions. For Latin America, where sitting military governments had negotiated transitions to democracy on the condition that they would not be held accountable for past crimes, the prosecution of Pinochet was perceived as an earthquake destabilizing the delicate balance of power with the military establishment.

Chile at the moment of Pinochet's arrest was governed by the same coalition of leftist and centrist parties (including Allende's Socialist Party) that had fought so hard against Pinochet. Yet the arrest of their old enemy brought consternation, not smiles. Chile's ambassador in London rushed to Pinochet's side, and within hours President Eduardo Frei Ruiz-Tagle protested the arrest, saying initially that Pinochet's "diplomatic immunity" had been violated. That claim was swiftly swept aside by Britain (which pointed out that such immunity was a privilege reserved for accredited diplomats and members of government on official visits—not to anyone who happened to hold a diplomatic passport). Chile then centered its opposition on the very nationalist argument Nuremberg was designed to defeat: claiming that since the alleged crimes were committed in Chile, only Chile as a sovereign country had the right to try Pinochet.

Chile's credibility was onion-skin thin on its pledge to bring Pinochet to justice in Chile, considering that Pinochet in recent years had twice used the threat of a new coup to force the government to back off its mild efforts to bring even his subordinates to trial. Chile's position, its leaders said, was that Spain had no right to try Pinochet, and that he should be returned to Chile to allow the Chilean legal system to take its course.

The United States exhibited deep ambivalence, but not outright opposition, to the events in London. The Democratic Clinton administration carried with it the political legacy of the human rights policies of President Jimmy Carter, which had done much to sever the Cold War alliance behind which the Latin American dictatorships had masked their atrocities during the Condor Years.

Secretary of State Madeleine Albright mapped a position that avoided criticism of the actions in London and Spain while basically coming down on the side of Chile.

> The United States is committed to principles of accountability and justice, as shown by our strong support for the International War Crimes Tribunal in former Yugoslavia and Rwanda; and the record of the United States in working to see those responsible for those kind of crimes brought to justice is second to none. . . . At the same time, the United States is also obviously firmly committed to democracy and the rule of law in Chile. I think we believe that in Chile, the citizens of a democratic state are wrestling with a very difficult problem of how to balance the need for justice with the requirements of reconciliation. I think significant respect should be given to their conclusions.

The U.S. position was hashed out in late November in a marathon meeting in Albright's ballroom-size office on the seventh floor of the State Department. Present were twenty-five high officials representing all parts of the State Department. The first legal hurdles in London had made clear that there would be no quick resolution and that Pinochet could stay in custody indefinitely. There was no sympathy for Pinochet expressed in the room, but the proposition that the United States should say something in support of the Spanish extradition request was quickly raised and dismissed. Almost as quickly it was agreed that "deference" to Chile's democracy would be the cornerstone of U.S. policy on the Pinochet issue.

The discussion turned to an action that would please both the Chilean government and those who favored vigorous prosecution of Pinochet. Spain had asked for the release of U.S. classified documents. Chile also favored the full disclosure of U.S. actions in Chile during the Allende and Pinochet periods. It was an elegant middle position. A document release would avoid the pitfalls of taking a position for or against Pinochet's extradition, yet it was an unequivocal step in the direction of historical disclosure and would provide evidence that could be used against Pinochet and others accused in any legal proceedings, whether in Spain, London, or elsewhere.

In a low-key announcement on December 1 in answer to a reporter's question, a State Department spokesman said, "Due to the interest in this case the Administration is conducting a review of documents in its possession that may shed light on human rights abuses during the Pinochet era. We will declassify and make public as much information as possible consistent with U.S. laws and the national security and law enforcement interests of the United States." The action neatly bypassed the hitherto stubborn opposition by all U.S. government agencies to declassifying new documents in response to Spain's request under the mutual legal assistance treaty.

It was a momentous decision, whose importance was belied by the nonchalance of the announcement. President Clinton, on the recommendation of Secretary of State Albright and National Security Adviser Samuel "Sandy" Berger, issued an executive order requiring an unprecedented release of the most secret documents on Chile, including files about CIA operations to prevent Allende from taking power in 1970 and to support the successful rightist campaign to orchestrate his military overthrow in 1973.

The first 5,800 documents were released in June 1999. In all, some 60,000 pages of secret U.S. files on Chile were made public. In September 2002, a smaller collection of State Department documents on Argentina was released. There were still to be arguments about documents withheld or partially blacked out. But the majority of the documents were released without excisions.

When Joan Garcés began his legal pursuit of Pinochet, he didn't dare dream of arrest and trial, but he thought he had a good chance of getting at the truth. The veil of impunity would be removed and replaced by the clear pane of public disclosure. It would be a measure of justice, he reasoned, to find out what had happened to so many victims of the Condor Years. His expectations were far too modest. Garcés's pursuit and that of dozens of other lawyers, judges, and human rights investigators succeeded far beyond the realism of legal action.

Even as Pinochet arrived back in Chile to the euphoria of his die-hard supporters, he had ceased to wield any real power. Politically, he was damaged goods, his impunity in tatters. Indeed, within months, the international legal dragnet widened against Pinochet and other former dictators. New prosecutions based on the Pinochet precedent were opened naming Pinochet and other dictators in Rome, France, Switzerland, and Belgium. Judges in Chile and Argentina, bypassing the amnesty laws, opened new cases, forcing a parade of hundreds of military officers to appear as witnesses or as accused. Pinochet was stripped of his parliamentary immunity and resigned as senator. The trickle of truth, once released, produced a flood of new information. Documents became available from the bowels of the secret police organizations and were open to the arduous but rewarding detective work of those willing to put together the pieces of the puzzle. It is that new information that has finally allowed the full story of those years to be told.

These momentous events in international law had as their common and primary target the crimes of the Operation Condor conspiracy, which in turn stood at the apex of anti-Communist state terror in Latin America. In its conception, Condor was the logical next step for the governments that had come to power for the purpose of fighting the reality and perceived threat of Communist revolution. It is to those days of revolution that we must return to comprehend the story of Condor.

4

REVOLUTION IN THE COUNTERREVOLUTION

It is the fear that individual guerrilla groups throughout South America will unite that has motivated the recent intensification in cooperation among security officials in the Southern Cone.

—CIA MEMORANDUM

To the international strategy of imperialism there is the corresponding continental strategy of the revolutionaries.

—FOUNDING DECLARATION OF THE REVOLUTIONARY COORDINATING JUNTA (JCR)

One improbable fact must be grasped about South America at the time of our story: radical social revolution was a real possibility for millions of people, coloring everyday life with hope or dread depending on the circumstances and political views of each individual. Masses of people were in the streets—supporting change or opposing it, often united not by ideology but by support for a populist strongman. Then, in many of the countries in the continent, the upheaval in the streets was driven underground by the even more violent reality of military counterrevolution.

These were times when, in Chile, for example, half a million people (out of a population of 10 million) would pack Santiago's main avenue, La Alameda, for more than a mile to hear President Allende's speeches. When throngs exceeding 1 million people pressed for the return of perennial populist dictator Juan Domingo Perón in Argentina. When, at one such rally, to welcome their exiled leader home from Spain, Peronists from leftist and rightist factions fought a pitched gun battle with dozens of casualties. In these times in Bolivia, a "people's assembly" made up of miners and peasants threatened to displace Bolivia's parliament during the brief rule of left-leaning general Juan José Torres. Peru's military government also defied stereotypes by proclaiming progressive income distribution and land redistribution policies, then turning to the Soviet Union for military aid and equipment. Those experiences demonstrated that not even the region's military were immune from the contagion of radical ideas.

Revolution was seen as possible. And for those who believed in a Marxist theory of history, it was inevitable. Back then, revolution was concrete reality. It was Fidel Castro's victory in Cuba, in which a small guerrilla army outfought a corrupt dictatorship and brought land reform, expropriations, and unbridled idealism. Revolution was an idea for the immediate future. It was Ernesto "Che" Guevara's idea that a *"foco,"* a concentration of a few dedicated fighters in the mountains, could set the fuse of countrywide, even continent-wide, uprisings of the poor and middle classes. It was a revolution that would spread and spread, by example, by ideology, by house-to-house and factory-to-factory organizing, and—most of all—by what they called *la lucha armada*, armed struggle.

Tens of thousands of young people in South America became the militants in this armed struggle. They adopted for themselves the lofty title of "revolutionaries," and strove to live up to the challenge of Che—their dead, Christ look-alike hero, who told them, "The first duty of a revolutionary is to make the revolution." Uruguay's Tupamaros were the most successful. They brought clandestine warfare to the cities, carrying out bold strikes that included arms raids and the kidnap-killing of a U.S. security adviser, Dan Mitrione, who had been accused of teaching torture techniques. Groups all over the continent—the largest in Chile, Uruguay, and Argentina—translated Che's call to arms into new tactics adapted to city streets as well as mountain paths.

General Pinochet's military takeover in Chile was a crushing blow for those on the side of revolution, but the ultimate outcome was not yet decided. In fact, for the most radical revolutionary groups, Pinochet's coup had an ironic silver lining. By destroying Allende's *"via pacifica,"* the peaceful road to Socialism, Pinochet had legitimized its opposite. Pinochet had proved the revolutionaries right. The violence of the overthrow served to confirm what they had been say-ing all along: that true revolution would triumph not by the gradualism of elec-tions and social reforms but by the force of arms.

There was a further irony in Pinochet's victory. His soldiers swept up tens of thousands of factory workers, peasants, and party members whose radicalism consisted in their vote and public activism in support of Allende's democratic revolution. But the repression barely touched—at first—the revolutionary leaders advocating armed struggle. They had already gone safely underground before the coup.

Those groups prepared to fight on in Chile. With long-standing organiza-tional bases in Argentina, Uruguay, and Bolivia, like-minded groups took the Pinochet coup as their mandate to internationalize the South American armed revolution for the first time.

Chile's group was the Movement of the Revolutionary Left *(Movimiento de Izquierda Revolucionaria)*, known as MIR. Its leaders had come out of the stu-dent movements of the 1960s and had established an important base of support in a few unions and in the shantytown communities surrounding Santiago. They considered themselves a vanguard and advocated a Leninist model of party-led Socialist revolution—meaning that after the revolution, a country would be run by a "dictatorship of the proletariat." President Allende's nephew, Andrés Pascal Allende, was a top MIR leader, and one of the most vociferous in criticizing his uncle's government as timid and reformist.

MIR never carried out armed actions while Allende was president. Never-theless, in the months preceding the September 1973 coup, they embarked on an aggressive military strategy: its main element was an attempt to organize re-sistance to coup plotting inside the Chilean armed forces. MIR had also stock-piled arsenals of light weapons and conducted military training in the hills outside Santiago. MIR central committee chief Miguel Enríquez had publicly called on soldiers to defy orders: "Non-commissioned officers, rank and file and policemen should disobey the orders given by officers involved in a coup, and in that case [of a coup in progress] all forms of struggle will be legitimate," he said in July.

It was not a traditional guerrilla strategy to defeat the armed forces but rather to burrow from within. Commented Andrés Pascal: "We called the military part of the organization the 'central force,' but it was almost like a school. We had some weapons, sure, but it was more like propaganda. The principal military work was inside the armed forces; that is, it was political work directed at the armed forces, to try to recruit, to win people over inside the armed forces to oppose a coup."

MIR's contacts inside the military provided good intelligence about the coming coup. MIR leaders prepared a contingency plan: friendly troops would allow them to break into military arsenals and distribute weapons to loyalist troops as a preemptive strike against the officers' plotting.

From the point of view of Chile's military establishment, no more hostile and dangerous action could be imagined than MIR's attempt to split the military from within. No political group had ever attempted to infiltrate the military. For the officers corps, on both sides of the coup plotting, such a split meant civil war and the specter of military killing military.

It was to avoid such a scenario that General Carlos Prats, Chile's commander in chief and an Allende loyalist, resigned under pressure from his fellow officers. He stepped down in the certain knowledge that, in the name of military unity, he had removed the last obstacle to a military takeover.

So it happened. Pinochet took command when Prats resigned; the military remained united and brutally eliminated the troops and officers who had been prepared to take up arms against their brother soldiers to defend the Allende government. Pinochet had come late to the coup plotting, according to most accounts, but once in charge had transformed it from a so-called "soft coup"—to throw out one civilian government and install another—into a unique historic project to physically eliminate all possibility of another Allende in the future.

There is no way to exaggerate the atmosphere of terror that the military imposed on Chile after September 11, 1973. Pinochet made no attempt to hide the brutality of his counterrevolution. Although he faced virtually no armed resistance, MIR having decided to forego activating its military force in favor of hunkering down for a longer fight, Pinochet's troops occupied the cities with guns blazing. For days, it was common to see bodies along roadsides or floating in the Mapocho River, which traverses Santiago. City morgue workers filled all available refrigeration units and began to stack bodies in corridors, allowing families to walk through to identify relatives.

Automatic rifle fire could be heard every night for months during the dusk-to-dawn curfew. Fortified police and army barricades, manned by troops armed with machine guns, were set up in streets throughout the capital. Commandeered city buses filled with soldiers careened through neighborhoods, stopping to raid individual houses, often after neighbors called in accusations that suspicious foreigners or "bearded subversives" were living there. (Police, alerted by neighbors' denunciations, twice raided the author's house in the middle-class neighborhood of Ñuñoa, near central Santiago, where he was living in a rented house with three Chileans, an American, a Canadian, and a Colombian. One of the Chileans, a graduate student in economics from a working-class family, was arrested when he returned to his school to pick up books. Soldiers released him after midnight, putting him on the street five miles from home during curfew when street patrols had permission to shoot to kill. He crept house to house for hours, finally scaling the fence at our house and banging on the door just before dawn.)

Tens of thousands were rounded up in the first weeks and packed into stadiums and then into hastily constructed concentration camps. In a tactic repeated many times, troops surrounded and raided entire settlements *(poblaciones)* of poor and working-class people considered strongholds of pro-Allende sentiment. By December, the concentration camp population reached 18,000 prisoners.

As terrible as it was, the executions, dumped bodies, concentration camps, and mass arrests were just the visible part of the repression. A good part of the atmosphere of terror came from uncertainty about military actions that were hidden. There was a general awareness that people were dying, but nobody knew how many. Many of those arrested never showed up in the concentration camps; neither did their bodies appear in the morgues or rivers.

Over the years, bodies were found in unmarked plots in cemeteries, at the bottom of abandoned mines and wells. Several hundred bodies were located, but they did not add up to the thousands of names on the lists of the disappeared.

Pinochet's toughest enemies, however, had escaped the country to build resistance abroad. Those who stayed in Chile were creating underground networks to strike back at the military. Stopping those in hiding would require new intelligence capability and systematic operations throughout the country. Defeating subversion abroad was even more difficult. It would be a sustained, international struggle. Pinochet began to develop the long-term international apparatus almost immediately after September 11. According to a CIA report dated October 3, one of his first steps was to reach out to like-minded friends: "The armed forces apparently believe the left is regrouping for sabotage and guerrilla activity. Several friendly governments have been asked to provide counterinsurgency materiel and training."

Brazil and the United States were first in line to help Chile reconfigure its military for the new tasks.

There is a continuing dispute about specific actions by U.S. agents to promote and support the 1973 coup. The record of newly declassified documents is expansive but still incomplete. The most recent official report about the CIA role, the so-called Hinchey Report, released in 2000, reaches a carefully hedged but still disconcerting conclusion:

> Although the CIA did not instigate the coup that ended Allende's government on 11 September 1973, it was aware of coup plotting by the military, had ongoing intelligence collection relationships with some plotters, and—because CIA did not discourage the takeover and had sought to instigate a coup in 1970—probably appeared to condone it.

The official CIA position draws a fine line between instigation (which it denies) and support (which it does not rule out before the coup, and which it acknowledges after the coup). The documentary record on the latter remains fragmentary and inconclusive.

Short of a credible investigation, the documents released so far will be subject to the not unreasonable assumption that they have been carefully redacted to hide the truth of U.S. involvement. That said, the contemporary documents should be analyzed first in terms of their explicit content, and not simply dismissed as lies where they contradict suspicions about U.S. actions.

In that light, there is a fascinating exchange of cables between the Santiago station chief and his boss at CIA headquarters, the chief of the Western Hemisphere Division. The subject is the prospect of a coup against Allende's government. Allende has finished his first year in office, and the CIA officials are discussing how they should influence the Chilean military. The context is the failed CIA attempt to instigate a coup a year earlier.

November 12, 1971, Santiago chief of station to CIA Headquarters:

> We recognize that the [redacted] program's end objective, a military solution to the Chilean problem, must be sought within very carefully drawn guidelines. . . .
>
> There should be a high probability for success before we weigh in in favor of a coup. . . .
>
> We therefore restrict our discussions of the mechanics of a coup to recruited sources and are discreet in our discussion with the other military officers. . . .
>
> Taking into consideration all the caveats and limitations noted above, we conceive our [redacted] mission as one in which we work consciously and deliberately in the direction of a coup.

To this point in the exchange, it is clear that the CIA station chief, who has been identified as Ray Warren, believes that his goal is to cause a coup, and that the discussion is about "how." The next cable in the sequence is even more explicit, and it contradicts the station chief's understanding of his job.

December 1, 1971, CIA headquarters to Santiago station chief:

> We hope that the following comments will explain and define the limitations on [redacted] operations as well as provide practical and acceptable guidelines for the future. . . .
>
> Since we do not have [redacted] approval to become involved in any coup planning, we cannot accept your conclusion in [your cable] that the [redacted] mission is to "work consciously and deliberately in the direction of a coup." Nor can we authorize you to "talk frankly about the mechanics of a coup" with key commanders, because the implications of that amount to the same.
>
> On the other hand, the monitoring and reporting of activities, events and attitudes of the Chilean armed forces and their leaders has become increasingly important. . . . There is of course a rather fine dividing line here between merely "listening" and "talking frankly about the mechanics of a coup" which in the long run must be left to the discretion and good judgment of the individual case officer.
>
> The essential fact . . . is that we do not have any authority to state, or even to imply, that [redacted] favors a coup as a solution to the Chilean dilemma.
>
> In sum, stay with history as it unfolds, don't make it.

The coup occurred twenty-two months later, ample time for the on-again, off-again U.S. coup policy to switch back in the other direction. But it must be said that the available documents do not suggest that such a switch in fact happened. In the absence of further evidence, the Hinchey Report's conclusion stands, namely, that the United States worked to undermine the Allende's democratically elected government and ardently desired its overthrow, but had no direct role in the military coup itself.

Our concern here is to examine the alliances that grew up around Pinochet's blow to the Latin American left and how the United States influenced the Pinochet regime after it took power, particularly in supporting, training, and gathering intelligence from the security agencies most responsible for Operation Condor assassinations and other systematic human rights violations.

The Hinchey Report, despite its generally hedging tone, points to intense activity by U.S. agencies to help Pinochet's regime prepare for the coming security challenge.

> CIA actively supported the military Junta after the overthrow of Allende. . . . Many of Pinochet's officers were involved in systematic and widespread human rights abuses following Allende's ouster. Some of these were contacts or agents of the CIA or US military. The IC [Intelligence Community] followed then-current guidance for reporting such abuses and admonished its Chilean agents against such behavior.
>
> Liaison with Chilean Security Services. The CIA had liaison relationships in Chile with the primary purpose of security assistance in gathering intelligence *on external targets*. The CIA offered these services assistance in internal organization and *training to combat subversion and terrorism from abroad*, not in combating internal opponents of the government. [Emphasis added.]

"Subversion and terrorism from abroad" was precisely what Pinochet's advisers envisioned as their most serious long-term threat. The operational brain center for planning the new intelligence apparatus was the *Academia de Guerra*, the War Academy, a French colonial–style building along Santiago's Alameda, at the corner of García Reyes Street. It had housed the school for advanced officers training since 1886. In 1973, it had been a meeting place for the coup plotters, and continued after the coup as a kind of think tank for the officers advocating the most hard-line methods in the struggle they considered to be a world war against Communism. The officer Pinochet put in charge was Lieutenant Colonel Manuel Contreras Sepúlveda, a tough leader who was popular with his troops and had a reputation for being a devout Catholic and something of an intellectual. He had already come to the attention of U.S. intelligence officials in Chile as one of the best and the brightest. Contreras gave the new apparatus the name Directorate of National Intelligence (Dirección de Inteligencia Nacional), to distinguish it from the existing military intelligence organizations within each branch of the armed forces. It became universally known as DINA.

The September 11 coup also spurred the toughest revolutionary groups into action.

Thousands of Allende supporters who escaped arrest fled the country, many by walking over the Andes separating Chile and Argentina, others making their way through the northern Atacama Desert to Peru. Argentina was in what was to be a relatively brief period of civilian rule. The military, which had ruled since overthrowing Juan Domingo Perón in 1956, had allowed elections earlier in 1973, which were won by a Perón surrogate, Héctor Cámpora. Perón returned from his long exile in Spain and unceremoniously pushed Cámpora aside. Perón, seventy-eight years old and in failing health, won new elections in a landslide and took power just a month after the coup in Chile.

Hated by the most conservative sectors of the military, Perón balanced extreme right-wing and left-wing factions within his own Justicialista Movement. Peron's crafty power maneuvers had included overt encouragement of armed action by leftist allies he referred to with affection as *los muchachos*— "the boys." He had made clear his sympathy for Allende, and he had reopened diplomatic relations with Cuba, breaking the U.S.-sponsored embargo. With Perón's populist restoration, Argentina became a haven for political refugees and revolutionary organizations. As military dictators closed down politics in one country after another, Bolivians, Uruguayans, Paraguayans, Brazilians, and now Chileans all flocked to take advantage of the heady freedom in Argentina.

The radical revolutionaries now making Argentina their home base had spent the early 1970s under the protection of Allende's Chile. Most of the top leaders made their escape from Chile in the weeks prior to the coup. The most committed veterans were Uruguay's Tupamaros and Bolivia's National Liberation Army (*Ejército de Liberación Nacional*—ELN). The Bolivian group had inherited the mantle of revolution from Che Guevara himself, who had fought in a *guerra de guerrillas* in the mountains of Bolivia, until he was captured and executed in 1967 (by counterinsurgency troops accompanied by CIA trainers). Thousands of Tupamaros were imprisoned in Uruguay, but hundreds more had escaped and were preparing a counteroffensive from outside the country.

In Argentina, they were welcomed by the most formidable group of all, the Argentine People's Revolutionary Army (*Ejército Revolucionario del Pueblo*— ERP) and its above-ground political organization, the Revolutionary Workers Party (*Partido Revolucionario de los Trabajadores*—PRT). Mario Roberto Santucho, an accountant, had led the group from its origins in Argentina's bickering Trotskyist factions to a disciplined, ideologically united party. Having grown up as a clandestine organization under military rule, ERP was not reluctant to translate its violent rhetoric into military actions. Its members had carried out a series of kidnappings and assaults that had led to its banning in 1972. With some 5,000 militants deployed in cells throughout Argentina's cities, the PRT/ERP was rich and well organized, and itching for the revolution to start.

The ERP leaders saw the coup in Chile as confirming their conviction that Latin America was embarked on an irreversible road to revolution. "We were in one of our best moments in the political bureau," said Luis Mattini, one of the few top ERP leaders still alive to describe the events of the 1970s. "The mass movement was at its peak. We decided to deploy all necessary effort to help Chile—such as mass demonstrations of solidarity in Argentina, but above all military preparation and material support for MIR. . . . We firmly concluded that the coup was not a setback but rather the removal of an obstacle. We thought the Chileans would rise up in arms, and given the degree of politicization and socialist conviction they had we thought they would be unstoppable."

The revolutionary groups were ready to move forward with a common strategy to defeat the military dictatorships. In early November, Santucho gathered representatives from all four groups for a secret meeting at one of the ERP safe houses in Buenos Aires. It was a revolutionary summit of ERP, MIR, Tupamaros–MLN, and the Bolivian ELN.

The leaders all knew one another well. They had already met several times to discuss the idea of a unified revolutionary organization—the brainchild of MIR leader Miguel Enríquez. MIR, ERP, and Tupamaros leaders held the first meetings in October 1972 in Chile. The Bolivians joined the group at a subsequent meeting in June 1973 in Argentina. Each organization had been sending cadres to Chile for military and ideological training in camps deep in the Andes Mountains, at Cajón del Maipo. In August, just a month before the coup, the four organizations had approved a formal alliance, called the Revolutionary Coordinating Junta (*Junta Coordinadora Revolutionaria*—JCR).

Now, with the obstacle of Allende's peaceful road to Socialism out of the way, it was time for the JCR to transform its strategy into action.

The men who took part in those meetings were the general staff of a grandly conceived continental revolution. For ERP, Mario Roberto Santucho was seconded by Luis Mattini, Domingo Menna, and Enrique Gorriarán Merlo. MIR leader Miguel Enríquez led the meetings in Chile, but was represented in Argentina by his brother, Edgardo Enríquez; Andrés Pascal; Nelson Gutiérrez; and military chief Alberto Villabela. Tupamaros leaders present were Efraín Luis Martínez Platero and William Whitelaw.

The Bolivians were represented by two men with stellar revolutionary reputations: Osvaldo "Chato" Peredo was the surviving brother of several who had fought with Che in Bolivia; Major Rubén Sánchez had fought on the other side, as an officer of the Bolivian army. He had switched sides ideologically during the short-lived revolutionary government of General Juan José Torres, and now served as Torres's aide in exile in Argentina.

The JCR was no mere alliance, nor was it a merger of the separate organizations. Enriquez's proposal was that no country's revolutionary movement would be subordinate to another's. Each group would fight according to its own timetable and with its own methods. As long as Allende remained in power, for example, MIR did not challenge the government with armed force—a principle the coup had made moot. Each member organization would choose when and how to take up arms. But together they would create an infrastructure—an international apparatus to provide mutual logistical, financial, and military support.

In the concept developed by Enríquez and his ideological partner Santucho, the JCR was for Latin America what the Third and Fourth Internationals had been for the world Socialist movement growing out of the Russian Revolution. Just as the Third International was the Communist Party's instrument to defend the Soviet Revolution, and the Fourth International embodied Leon Trotsky's idea of permanent revolution in many countries, the JCR was the Fifth International representing Latin America's continent-wide revolution. Its heart was closer to Trotsky than to Stalin. The JCR was an implicit rebuke of a basic tenet of the international Communist Party, under the leadership of the Soviet Union—the idea that revolution should be consolidated in "one country," namely Russia, before spreading worldwide.

This new organization was to be the fulfillment of the strategic vision of Che Guevara. In 1966, just before he left Cuba to take the revolutionary cause to Africa and the rest of Latin America, Che declared in a speech to an audience of revolutionaries from all over the world, gathered in Havana, that armed groups in Latin America should join together to "form something like *Juntas de Coordinación* (Revolutionary Coordinating Councils or boards) to make the repressive work of Yankee imperialism more difficult and to facilite their own cause."

Che's statement was quoted in a long manifesto, "To the Peoples of Latin America," stating the JCR's goals and strategy. The JCR, it said, would take up Che's call to arms: to "develop a bloody and prolonged revolutionary war that will make the Latin American continent the second or third Vietnam of the world."

The heated Marxist rhetoric is from another era, but is essential reading to understand the events that followed in the Condor Years. In this logic of revolution, the defeats in Chile and elsewhere showed the futility of "reformist" strategies such as Allende's recently failed Popular Unity in Chile and the current danger of Perón's populism in Argentina. The left was at a crossroads. Only one strategy could lead ultimately to victory—the continent-wide guerrilla war set in motion by the Junta Coordinadora. Some excerpts:

> We are united in the realization that the strategy of revolutionary war is the only viable strategy in Latin America. And we realize that this revolutionary war is a complex process of mass struggle, armed and unarmed, peaceful and violent, in which all forms of struggle converge harmoniously around the axis of armed struggle.
>
> ... The continental character of the struggle is determined fundamentally by the presence of a common enemy. North American imperialism is carrying out an international strategy to stop socialist revolution in Latin America. It is

no accident that fascist regimes have been imposed in countries where a mass movement in ascendancy has threatened the stability of oligarchic power. The international strategy of imperialism requires a continental strategy by the revolutionaries.

. . . The road to travel in this struggle is not short. . . . Therefore our revolutionary war is one of attrition in the first stages, until we form as a popular army that is superior to the forces of the enemy. This process is gradual, but it is paradoxically the shortest and least costly path to achieve the strategic objectives of the neglected classes.

PEOPLE OF LATIN AMERICA: TO ARMS

We are living decisive moments in our history. In this awareness, the MLN Tupamaros, the Movement of the Revolutionary Left MIR, the National Liberation Army ELN and the People's Revolutionary Army ERP call on the exploited workers of Latin American, the working class, the poor farmers, the poor of the cities, the students and intellectuals, revolutionary Christians and all elements originating from the exploited classes willing to collaborate with this just popular cause, to take up arms with decision, to actively incorporate themselves to the anti-imperialist and socialist revolutionary struggle that is already breaking out in our continent under the banner and example of Comandante Guevara.

The audacity of such an undertaking is breathtaking: to proclaim a revolutionary war at the very moment the military counterrevolution sponsored by the United States was at its most intense. In the event, none of the goals of the JCR were achieved, but it would be a mistake to dismiss the call to arms as merely overblown rhetoric. To the contrary, the JCR was taken so seriously by the military governments that it became the principle target of Operation Condor. Secret military documents devoted to analysis of the JCR "threat" show the military interest in the JCR was not merely for propaganda purposes. The secret reports make it indisputable that the military believed in the accuracy of the information about the JCR and acted on it. It is also true that the military propagandists used the specter of the JCR to taint the nonviolent opposition to the military governments with the violent tactics of the guerrilla groups. The ensuing "war on terrorism" against the JCR members was accompanied, not coincidentally, by a string of assassinations of democratic leaders with little or no connection to the radicals operating inside the JCR.

Two decades later, survivors among those who created the JCR would emphasize its relative ineffectiveness. "When we announced the JCR it was like a *campanazo*—like ringing a big bell. They [the military governments] thought it was much bigger than it actually was, and they reacted very rapidly, with devasting force. We were in diapers, with lots of problems, and never really had the opportunity to do what we set out to do," said René Valenzuela, a Chilean who was one of the JCR's chief operatives in Europe.

Those dismal reflections are hindsight. From the point of view of late 1973, the JCR was a burst of earnest energy and revolutionary optimism. "We imagined a sort of an embryonic Vietnam in all of Latin America," said Luis Mattini. "We were going to take the idea of the JCR to Brazil, Peru, Mexico, Caracas. We thought the revolution was about to start in all of Latin America."

Although the JCR agreement already existed before the Chilean coup, the meeting in Buenos Aires was the beginning of concrete action. There was much to be done. As described by participants, the meeting produced a strategy and an ambitious agenda to be accomplished in the coming months.

The immediate priority was support of MIR in Chile. The groups urged MIR to launch a military counterattack as soon as possible. The JCR would provide material support—money and arms—to generate solidarity for Chile and propaganda against the Pinochet dictatorship.

The overall military strategy of the JCR reflected the strong militaristic views of ERP leader Roberto Santucho. Members would coordinate the timing and location of military offensives to create maximum mutual support. The ERP would go first. A band of guerrillas was trained, armed, and ready to launch guerrilla warfare in the mountains of Tucumán Province in northwestern Argentina. Bolivia's ELN and MIR would open supporting offensives across nearby borders—Chile in the south around Neuquén and Temuco, and Bolivia in Tarija Province to the north. Tupamaros, following the directives of their leaders imprisoned in Uruguay, were to strike with a counteroffensive planned for May Day 1974. With wars breaking out almost simultaneously in four countries, it was thought, the military would face internal rebellion, be thrown on the defensive, and eventually collapse.

For the Tupamaros and the ELN, the first task was to reorganize inside their respective countries to prepare their militants for armed struggle. Both groups had been decimated by the military crackdowns of the past two years, and their networks of militants were in fearful disarray. To reconnect the cells and mobilize them for action, the groups needed to build the basic infrastructure of clandestine urban warfare: a secure communications system of couriers, codes, and *"berretines"* (camouflaged hiding places for people, arms, and messages). They needed top quality forged documents, credible front businesses to handle financial transactions and provide cover jobs, and they needed to rent or buy hundreds of secure houses and apartments for operations and living quarters.

Such grandiose goals demanded enormous amounts of money and weapons. The JCR would provide both. The ERP, already the richest of the organizations, was carrying out a series of kidnappings and proposed to dedicate most of the ransom money to JCR projects. The JCR budget was to exceed $20 million.

Acquiring and stockpiling weapons was the most difficult task. In the years before narcotics trafficking, there was no large-scale international arms market in South America, and shipping to the southern parts of South America involved enormous distances and vulnerability to military surveillance. MIR had a practical contribution it was proud to offer to the JCR: a weapons factory. A team of Chilean engineers and metal workers had meticulously copied the design of the Swedish submachine gun, the Karl Gustav, which was a standard-issue weapon to Chile's Carabinero police. Capable of automatic fire, it used relatively easy to obtain nine-millimeter bullets in a thirty-shot magazine. The MIR technicians also had worked up the manufacturing specifications for hand grenades, a grenade launcher, and light mortar. The clandestine factory had started production in Chile. As the coup approached the MIR technicians had moved the operation to Argentina and expected to have the first finished weapons in early 1974.

It was a colossal undertaking, Efraín Martínez Platero said. "We intended to develop a grand, an enormous infrastructure network for all of the countries— Bolivia, Argentina, Chile, Uruguay. That's how we spent all those millions of dollars of JCR money—in buying airplanes and trucks, in creating a structure capable of giving us the possibility of penetrating each of those countries, so that if we wanted to we could transport weapons, fighters, money, people, moving it all in and out at will."

Public relations was an indispensable part of any popular movement, even a clandestine one like the JCR. The JCR members decided they would make a public announcement of the JCR call to arms in the coming months. A thick magazine, called *Che Guevara: Junta de Coordinación Revolucionaria* (of which three issues ranging from forty-eight to seventy-six pages were published in Spanish, English, and other languages), was the international voice of the JCR.

Before going public, however, the new organization needed to advise its friends and potential allies. Above all, almost as monks going to Rome to submit to the authority of the Pope, the JCR leaders wanted to lay the idea at the feet of Fidel Castro. Immediately following the meeting in Buenos Aires, Martínez Platero was designated the JCR's official ambassador, its "international representative," to travel first to Cuba and then to Europe.

Martínez Platero was a logical choice to be the JCR international representative. The Tupamaros had become a household word in Europe, and were universally respected in leftist circles as nonsectarian, Robin Hood revolutionaries. When he arrived in Cuba he went through channels. He first explained the JCR to Manuel Piñeiro, the famous *Barbaroja* (Red Beard), chief of the Cuban Communist Party's Department of America, whose name was synonymous with Cuba's support of revolutionary groups in Latin America. Piñiero had set up military training courses for the hundreds of Tupamaros who had come to Cuba from Chile just before the coup. For some, there was an elite officers course. Martínez Platero inspected the troops in the courses and took part in the "voluntary work" in sugar fields that was expected of visitors of all classes. Still, it was weeks before he was given an audience with Fidel. It came only a few days before he was scheduled to leave for Europe, in late October.

Martínez Platero invoked Che's memory as the inspiration for the Coordinating Junta, but Fidel was dismissive. He was far from opposed to the use of armed struggle to win the revolution, but he considered the JCR's grand strategy impractical and even trivial. And he was disparaging of the Trotskyist ERP.

"I would like to honor you, but it is because you are a leader of the Tupamaros. I never would receive you as the representative of the JCR," Martínez Platero quoted Fidel as saying. "Chico, don't run around with those Trotskyists. It's a waste of time."

He cautioned that a military offensive in Uruguay now would be disastrous and could very well provoke the executions of the imprisoned leadership. He counseled a strategy of building strength while pursuing the establishment of broad coalitions with political parties. Training and support would be given to the Tupamaro militants, but he refused to consider the proposal that Cuba become the operational and training center for the JCR.

Soon after Martínez Platero left Cuba, another JCR representative arrived, the ERP's Luis Mattini. His main agenda was to inform Fidel about ERP's plan to launch a guerrilla campaign in the mountains of Tucumán Province. In an all-night meeting on January 5, 1974, Fidel reminisced about his own experience using rural guerrilla tactics in his war against Cuban dictator Fulgencio Batista in the 1950s. But he refused to consider giving military aid and training to the Argentine guerrillas. Perón's government had opened lucrative trade relations with Cuba, with a long-term line of credit exceeding a billion dollars.

Fidel gave an even more politically cautious criticism of the launching of the JCR. "I quoted Che on the need to coordinate revolutionary forces," Mattini recalled. "Fidel said, 'you're right, you have to coordinate. Unity is good. But it should be secret. You should not make it public.' " Already a veteran in world Communist infighting, Fidel saw the JCR as a challenge to the traditional Soviet-line Communist parties in the four countries where it was operating.

"Our reasoning was just the opposite to Fidel's," said Mattini. "We wanted the JCR to be public in order to attract other organizations to join us in a united armed revolution." The old-line Communists were mired in "reformism"; the revolution, led by the JCR, was rightfully leaving them behind.

The other pillars of the JCR plan were soon in place. On December 6, 1973, Victor Samuelson, the dapper young general manager of the Argentine branch of Exxon Corporation, was taking a leisurely walk around the swimming pool at the company's private club outside Buenos Aires. A voice behind him growled, "Don't go any farther. The place is surrounded." A dozen ERP troops had taken control of the club. They grabbed Samuelson and shoved him into a car. For the next few days he was stashed in an underground pit that had been used to change the oil on cars. When negotiations for a ransom began, he was moved to a more comfortable safe house, where he played games of chess in which he routinely beat his captors.

Kidnapping had become alarmingly common in Argentina. So common that Exxon officials negotiated directly with the ERP without involving the Argentine Federal Security Police (*Seguridad Federal*), itself a force with a shady reputation whose officers were known to have pulled off a few lucrative kidnappings of their own. The bidding started at $4 million, which was about what the ERP leaders expected to get. The initial negotiations were handled by Tupamaros. When Exxon stalled at a low $2 million offer, Roberto Santucho gave the job to one of his toughest officers, Enrique Gorriarán. Months passed. In March, Exxon made a "final offer" of $10 million, and Santucho said, "OK, Take it, we can't keep this gringo here forever." Gorriarán, recalling the episode from his prison cell in Argentina, said he thought he could push for more. "I told them, "$14 million or we send you his ears,' " he said. According to Exxon officials, the threat was more deadly. Gorriarán met with the Exxon negotiator at a café in late February and delivered an ultimatum—which was later put in writing—that Samuelson would be executed in seventy-two hours if the ransom demand was not met. Exxon agreed and reached the ERP negotiator only an hour before the midnight execution deadline.

The ransom—$14.2 million—was flown from New York and delivered in packets of $100 bills packed in six suitcases. Exxon agreed to pay for food and clothing to be distributed to poor people in a Buenos Aires suburb—which accounted for the somewhat lopsided ransom amount. The ransom was by far the largest ERP had ever obtained in the half-dozen kidnappings the organization had pulled off in previous years.

Besides Samuelson, ERP kidnapped two other foreign businessmen to raise money for the JCR, according to Gorriarán. Firestone paid $3 million, and Swissair paid $3.8 million to free their executives. In the early months of 1974, the revolutionary war chest had fattened to more than $20 million.

In late January, the guerrillas' military offensive opened in Argentina. A force of eighty troops led by ERP military commander Enrique Gorriarán made a late-night frontal assault on the Azul army base, a tank garrison in Buenos Aires Province. Armed with antitank grenade launchers and automatic rifles, they broke through the main gate with trucks intended to transport weapons and ammunition stolen from the base's arsenal. The guerrillas killed the commander of the base and captured the second in command, then retreated under heavy fire after a seven-hour battle. They lost four men and failed to capture any weapons. The attack failed in its military objective, and ERP leaders criticized Gorriarán's conduct of the battle. But the Azul battle succeeded grandly as propaganda. It was the closest a guerrilla force in Argentina had ever come to waging conventional warfare.

The ERP used the Azul battle as the occasion to announce the creation of the Coordinating Junta. On the morning of February 14, a small bus usually used for businessmen's tours of Buenos Aires picked up six journalists at pre-designated locations and drove them to a restaurant and dance hall a few miles outside the city, in the town of Villa Bosch. Gorriarán, tautly muscled and balding, in his early thirties, was flanked by masked gunmen as he spoke to the journalists against a backdrop of posters of Che Guevara and Argentine military hero General José Francisco de San Martín.

Gorriarán said the Azul attack was just the beginning of an offensive against the army and denounced President Perón as a "bourgeois reformist." In response to the ERP attack, Perón had pushed through new Draconian antiterrorist laws greatly increasing the army's power. Other leftist groups in Argentina had denounced the ERP's attack as a provocation whose main effect would be a crackdown on their legitimate activity. They favored giving the newly elected Perón—who had finally displaced the military—an opportunity to prove his independence. But for ERP, there could be no truce. "We consider that to halt or diminish the fight against the oppressor army would allow it to reorganize and to pass over to the offensive," Gorriarán said.

Gorriarán distributed a six-page pamphlet containing the JCR's manifesto, "To the Peoples of Latin America." But stories on the clandestine press conference, including a twenty-five-inch story on an inside page of the *New York Times*, gave only brief mention to the formation of the four-country guerrilla front. A simultaneous announcement of the JCR formation was issued in Lisbon, Portugal.

The JCR organizations embarked on a period of intense preparations for the coming offensive. The ransom money from the three kidnappings ensured that whatever the guerrillas needed they could buy at top price. The sums of cash were so enormous, they created a financial and logistical problem. The money had to be converted into local currencies. At one point after the delivery of the Samuelson ransom, ERP operatives were delivering a daily suitcase of dollars to their black market money changer at the Liberty Hotel and bringing it back filled with Argentine, Chilean, and other currencies.

Sources differ somewhat about the distribution of the cash. MIR, ELN, and Tupamaros received $2 million apiece, according to Tupamaro leader Martínez Platero, and MIR's Pascal Allende concurs that $2 million was earmarked for MIR. Luis Mattini recalls that it was $1 million each. A U.S. cable based on intelligence reports cites an "ERP communiqué stating that it had given $5 million to its sister organizations in the JCR. The money was part of the ransom from the ERP kidnapping of a U.S. Exxon executive. According to a usually reliable source, the MIR's portion was $3 million."

The guerrillas took the military initiative in Argentina. A group of thirty well-equipped ERP combatants infiltrated into the mountains of Tucumán Province in northwest Argentina and established a base camp. On May 29, they descended from the camp and took over the small town of Acheral. They gave speeches to the populace, hung banners, stayed all day, and departed in the evening without encountering the slightest resistance. On the same day, another ERP commando attacked an army communications battalion in Rosario Province, hundreds of miles from Tucumán. Santucho's guerrillas also planted a bomb at a Rosario police headquarters.

ERP units found recruiting to the revolution was fruitful among the tens of thousands of young men who had lost jobs in Tucumán's collapsing sugar economy. Other high profile military operations kept ERP in the headlines. For a time, their challenge seemed more than the corruption-riddled Argentine military could handle. In a daring strike in August that demonstrated their ability to move about the country at will, seventy guerrillas from Tucumán drove in a rented bus and participated in a successful attack on the Villa María army munitions factory in Córdoba Province. Another group of guerrillas were caught, however, as they marched on foot back to their hideouts after the attack. Sixteen were killed, in what those who escaped charged was a massacre following surrender.

Despite the casualties, the ERP's so-called Mountain Company seemed to be following the pattern of Castro's victorious offensive in Cuba's Sierra Maestra that led to the fall of the Batista dictatorship. Tucumán had dense jungles and high mountains, ideal for impregnable "liberated zones," which Santucho predicted would be the next step. Progress was also evident among the other JCR member organizations. In Chile, a secure infrastructure for the clandestine MIR was in place and plans were being laid for a military campaign to open within a year. The JCR was also supporting the reorganization of the ELN inside Bolivia, and ERP was helping a fledgling group of Paraguayan revolutionaries. The revolution in the counterrevolution seemed to be on course.

———

The United States had little time to bask in Pinochet's victory in Chile. The administration was immediately faced with decisions about what to do next. Like an alcoholic agonizing over one more drink before going on the wagon, officials debated whether they should end the covert action programs that the CIA had been running since at least 1958, when Allende first ran for president.

CIA covert action had been used to undermine democracy; now the issue was whether to use it *against* Pinochet in favor of democracy. In one document, two deputy assistant secretaries in the State Department's Latin America bureau disagreed about continuing CIA financial support for Chile's Christian Democratic Party now that Pinochet was in power. Covert money and CIA propaganda operations had been propping up the party for more than a decade and had been instrumental in electing President Eduardo Frei Montalva in 1964. The Christian Democrats, Chile's largest party, had opposed Allende, but now were likely to oppose Pinochet as it became clear he had no intention of returning Chile to democracy.

Harry Shlaudeman favored helping the party even in opposition to Pinochet:

> If we held off now we could be causing ourselves trouble, for it would look as if we had been interested simply in knocking off Allende.

Jack Kubisch was con:

> . . . The secretary [Henry Kissinger] had made it clear that the change in regime in Chile was very much in our interest and that we should do all we could to help the Junta succeed. In view of the Secretary's remarks, he [Kubisch] would not be comfortable recommending assistance to any element in Chile that was not completely identified with the Junta. It was not essential to the success of the Junta that the PDC [Christian Democrats] survive as an entity.

Shlaudeman:

> What was important was that we not give the impression that we had no problems with a right-wing dictatorship and that we had no interest in the survival of democracy after all that we had said over the years. . . . It would be best to tell the PDC that we would finance it for three to five months but that we were getting

out of this kind of activity for good in very short order. . . . He was worried about the effects of a drastic, immediate cut off right now, especially since we had been saying every since 1962 that our primary interest in Chile was the survival of democracy.

Mr. Kubisch responded that Chilean democracy had taken the country close to disaster.

It was a debate over the dispensability of democracy as a goal of U.S. policy. The premise was that "knocking off Allende" in favor of a "right-wing dictatorship" was the successful outcome of the most recent U.S. covert action programs. As the choice of dictatorship versus democracy would present itself again and again in the post-coup period, democracy had few defenders among those making policy decisions. In this remarkably candid document, Secretary of State Kissinger is portrayed as setting an early and unequivocal policy for U.S. activities in Chile: Help the Pinochet junta and only the junta.

5

AGENTS IN ARGENTINA

*In the year 1974, in the month of March, the president [Pinochet] sent me to the
United States. . . . I met with [CIA deputy director] Vernon Walters about how
to do national intelligence. So the CIA promised to help us. I spoke with Vernon
Walters, and he sent us eight high-level CIA agents to organize courses or seminars here in Chile, which lasted until the middle of August of 1974. . . .*

*We eliminated the terrorists from Chile, throwing them out of the country,
detaining them in Chile, putting them on trial, with the result that we produced
very few dead compared with other countries. . . . [I]n Chile there were 3,000
dead.*

— MANUEL CONTRERAS, JUNE 2002 INTERVIEW

*It was—I'll get jumped on for this—but it was a patriotic request, if you will, and
I did it.*

— MICHAEL VERNON TOWNLEY, EXPLAINING WHY HE HAD AGREED TO ASSASSINATE
GENERAL CARLOS PRATS

For people trying to get back to their normal lives in Chile, there was reason to
breathe easier in the early weeks of 1974. It was summer—for many, a time to
go to the beach and try to forget the traumas of the past months, to try to believe the worst was behind them. Nightly gunfire had stopped; the press was no
longer filled with reports of "extremists" killed while "trying to escape"—a
common explanation for summary executions. From all appearances, far fewer
people were being killed.

The National Stadium no longer held prisoners and was being cleaned up
for the coming soccer season. Eighteen thousand prisoners still being held

were distributed to less high-profile concentration camps in sparsely populated desert towns, with quaint names like Chacabuco, Pisagua, Melinka, and Isla Rieseco in the north.* The Catholic Church had joined with other religious organizations to create the first human rights organization, the Peace Committee *(Comité Pro Paz)*, and its internal reports carefully documented arrests, disappearances, executions, and prison populations. The month-by-month reports noted a remarkable decline in deaths—to a low point of one disappearance in February. Many found reason to hope that the orgy of violence had spent itself.

The optimists were misled by the calm. In the underground world of the military, the first steps to even greater violence were already being taken. Manuel Contreras and his team at the War Academy finished their planning for the new intelligence organization, and the junta ordered it into action in the first days of the new year. The creation of the Directorate of National Intelligence *(Dirección de Inteligencia Nacional*—DINA) was a carefully guarded secret—an official decree was eventually published, but hid DINA's real powers in secret provisions. U.S. military personnel in Chile, however, were well informed. The defense attaché sent to Washington a full biographical workup on Contreras, documenting Contreras's promotion to full colonel and appointment on February 24, 1974, as head of DINA.

The U.S. military intelligence reports described DINA from the beginning as an extraordinarily powerful, sui generis security force unlike anything the Chilean military had ever seen. Even though its director was only a colonel, DINA was independent of the military chain of command, a power unto itself. A U.S. naval officer reported on his conversation with a concerned and nervous Chilean officer. "The DINA, contrary to original plans . . . , is directly subordinate to Junta President General Pinochet. When R[eporting] O[fficer] asked why this was so, source replied, 'That's too sensitive to discuss, even with you.' " DINA was pushing the regular military intelligence units aside, the officer reported, and—worse—DINA operatives were identifying themselves as working for army or navy intelligence when they conducted raids and deten-

---

* Concentration camps: According to Peace Committee tracking, the number of prisoners in the publicly recognized concentration camps declined to 10,000 by March, and to 7,000 by September 1974. In addition, approximately 5,000 mostly Latin American political refugees who had sought asylum in embassies and international organizations were allowed to leave the country under protection of the U.N. High Commission for Refugees.

tions. "The service intelligence departments and the CECIFA (Armed Forces Counterintelligence Center) personnel refer to DINA as 'the monster'. . . ."

Another concern was DINA's torture methods: "Another major problem of the DINA is its system of interrogation. Source said that their techniques are straight out of the Spanish Inquisition and often leave the person interrogated with visible bodily damage. The CECIFA and service intelligence departments are upset about this, essentially feeling that in this day and age there is no excuse for the use of such primitive techniques. Source said the CECIFA and service intelligence department interrogations usually take place in the presence of a qualified medical doctor to insure no permanent physical or mental damage is done to the person being interrogated."

Contreras was given power to commandeer officers and troops from any of the branches of the armed forces and to hire civilians to fill the growing ranks of DINA. The best and the brightest young officers, some of whom had studied under Contreras when he was a professor of intelligence at the War Academy, competed to be chosen to serve in DINA. They were exempt from wearing uniforms, and wore their hair long. DINA service meant long, irregular hours, but also excitement, access to women, cars, and money. And for some, it would mean international travel.

The U.S. military intelligence officers put DINA in the same category as Nazi and Soviet repressive apparatus, describing it as a "modern day Gestapo" and "a KGB-type organization".

Already in February 1974, DINA was being ascribed nearby absolute power. "No judge in any court or any minister in the government is going to question the matter any further if DINA says that they are now handling the matter," the U.S. air attaché reported to the Pentagon. His source said "there are three sources of power in Chile, Pinochet, God and DINA."

Pinochet and Contreras made themselves the domineering father and all-knowing mother dispensing all things good and evil in Chile's newly totalitarian family. Pinochet was an aloof, public, and inflexible figure who cast himself as the embodiment of the *patria*, the fatherland. Contreras worked behind the scenes, controlling life and death in the country through the intimacy of his bond with Pinochet. In dealings with his equals, there was an exterior pleasantness, an almost feminine softness about Contreras. An American intelligence officer described him based on frequent meetings in the 1970s: "Contreras is mild-mannered and polite. When you talk to him he seems gentle and disarming. He doesn't whistle or bark orders to his subordinates. He's not your typical Chilean officer—who usually puts on a Prussian military manner. He comes across as reasonable and likes intelligent conversation." Friends and subordinates referred to him as "Mamo," a derivative of Manuel. Physically he was equally unimposing. Even as a young officer, he was pudgy, carrying 185 pounds on a 5'8" frame. His face was smooth and round, drooping into jowls as he grew older.

As a young officer, Contreras was known to be a fervent Catholic, a *beato*, fervent bordering sanctimoniousness. During a posting in the south of Chile, he organized special masses on base that attracted lay people from the surrounding community as well. Another American military friend went on maneuvers with Contreras in the late 1960s and was deeply impressed by his competence in command and by the bond he achieved with his men. His strength was the ability to think strategically, to view the larger picture in a given tactical situation. The solutions he devised tended to be systems and plans rather than short-term fixes. He had the mind of an engineer, which was his military specialty and the subject of the only formal course he is known to have attended in the United States.

This well-regarded officer was the architect of a unique intelligence system that was about to embark on an orgy of mass murder. Where Contreras received his intelligence training—other than in routine courses at the War Academy—could not be learned. Robert Scherrer, the FBI official who knew Contreras well, concluded that Contreras must have received training in Brazil. There is no doubt that Contreras and DINA had a close operational relationship with Brazil's intelligence service, SNI. U.S. documents confirm that Brazilian intelligence officers came to Chile to interrogate prisoners after that coup and that Chilean officers were sent for intelligence training in Brazil.

Years later, Contreras is proud to discuss the inspiration and concept of DINA, and its effectiveness. As Contreras describes it, Chile was armed with an inadequate intelligence-gathering capacity at the time of the coup. Each branch of the armed services had its own "institutional" intelligence branch, trained primarily to gather information about possible military actions involving other countries, such as Peru or Argentina, with whom Chile had been in intermittent conflict going back at least a century. Political intelligence—keeping track of the political enemies of whatever government was in power—had been the job of the detective branch of the civilian police known as *Investiga-*

ciones. During the Allende government, the chief of the political police was a Socialist and was executed by the military immediately after the coup.

The new military government had completed the relatively easy task of rounding up known suspects cowering in their homes, but was unprepared for the arduous work of rooting out a tough enemy in exile or hidden inside Chile.

"I had two missions," Contreras said in an exclusive interview.*

> The first was to provide national intelligence—something that was not done in Chile until 1973—to provide national intelligence to the government. I was to gather information from four fields of action, that is, internal, external, military and economic. That was the first mission. The second mission that DINA had was based on the state of siege. Thus we were ordered to repress subversion and terrorism that existed in Chile in that epoch. . . . We were ordered to do that, and we accomplished that, and Chile was the first country in the world that succeeded in eliminating terrorism from its territory. . . . We eliminated the terrorists from Chile, throwing them out of the country, detaining them in Chile, putting them on trial, with the result that we produced very few dead compared with other countries, which still have terrorism. Even in Latin America itself we have Peru with more than 200,000 dead, El Salvador with more than 200,000 dead, Argentina with 30,000, and in Chile there were 3,000 dead. Nevertheless, that hasn't been taken into account by foreign countries, who unfortunately still don't accept our argument.

Contreras's acknowledgment of the death toll is striking, and accurate. In the strange moral calculus of mass murder, 3,000 deaths in the war on terrorism is for Contreras not only justifiable but an argument for the relative moderation of his approach. Contreras exaggerates the death tolls in Peru and El Salvador, but his figure for Chile is close to the 3,197 deaths documented by Chile's official human rights inquiry. His count for Argentina is also in the range widely accepted among human rights groups.

Contreras's concept of national intelligence was aimed not only at repression of the left but at establishing total control of every aspect of government and social life in Chile. Repressing "terrorism" inside and outside of Chile was

---

*The interview was conducted by journalist Amaro Gómez-Pablo in June 2002, using questions on Operation Condor and the CIA provided by the author.

only one of several major tasks. National intelligence meant his agents had to penetrate and control the government bureaucracy itself, with particular focus on the economy. He also had to monitor the military for potentially disloyal officers—classic counterintelligence. What Contreras appeared to have in mind was to combine in one colossal agency the domestic detective work of the FBI, the counterintelligence capability of the Pentagon, and the international espionage skills of the CIA.

Contreras knew he needed help. In March 1974, he traveled to the United States to get it. It is a trip that is still kept secret by the U.S. agencies who worked with Contreras and DINA, including the CIA. It involves CIA training on site in Chile and material support never acknowledged by U.S. officials, although general references in key documents confirm that CIA training of DINA took place. The context of the period of training is important: as the trainers arrived in Chile, DINA launched its first massive assault on the underground opposition inside Chile and opened its principal operations center for torture and interrogation, a walled complex in a Santiago suburb known as Villa Grimaldi. In June, July, and August, DINA agents, often in pickup trucks with camper-type coverings in the back, swept up hundreds of people. About 10 percent of those captured simply "disappeared," a grim realization that for families and colleagues did not sink in for months. In those inaugural months of CIA training, the number of disappeared multiplied: seventeen in June, forty-six in July, forty-nine in August, forty in September. Almost all of the disappeared were suspected MIR militants.

The CIA trainers departed from Chile sometime in August. Within weeks, DINA conducted its first international assassination, of Pinochet's rival and predecessor, General Carlos Prats, in Argentina.

The story of the CIA training must be unraveled with care. It starts with Contreras's words:

> In the year 1974, in the month of March, the president [Pinochet] sent me to the United States. . . . I met with [CIA deputy director] Vernon Walters about how to do national intelligence. We were just starting to organize the mission of national intelligence, about which there was no background in Chile—we only knew about [military] institutional intelligence. So the CIA promised to help us. So the president sent me to the United States to see those who will help us. I spoke with Vernon Walters, and he sent us eight high-level CIA agents to orga-

nize courses or seminars here in Chile, which lasted until the middle of August of 1974. In those courses or seminars they trained the officers and noncommissioned officers in all the measures that should taken and instructions that should be carried out in order to set up what is called national intelligence.

They only acted on the theoretical part. We didn't get to the practical part. In other words, they only taught us, they didn't participate in anything.

Well, August of '74 came, and the chief of the delegation, together with the chief of station* of the CIA, who was permanently in contact with us, they asked to stay here in Chile, to take jobs inside DINA. I opposed that, and the president said, "absolutely not." So I opposed it and I said to him [the CIA chief], "No, you have to return to your country."

The chief of the delegation, who had been sent by Vernon Walters, became quite upset, and he told me that we were going to have consequences because we wouldn't accept this [arrangement].

Such a scenario cannot be considered factual solely on Contreras's word. He has shrewdly used his relationship with the CIA to embarrass the United States and has charged that the CIA was responsible for some of the crimes of which DINA has been accused, including the Letelier assassination. In this case, however, there is a significant body of corroborating evidence for Contreras's statement about CIA training of DINA.

DINA already had 700 employees (not counting the web of paid and unpaid informants) in January 1974. The U.S. defense attaché in Chile reported on its training needs: "The major problem of DINA is that its personnel, a mix of military and civilians, are not properly trained for their jobs. They especially lack elementary training in intelligence and interrogation techniques and tend to be extremely secretive."

That the CIA provided such training is established by several official sources. The Hinchey Report, in a passage first cited in Chapter 4, refers to CIA training of DINA "to combat subversion and terrorism from abroad, not in combating internal opponents of the government." A still secret 1979 report of the Senate Foreign Relations Committee corroborates elements of Contreras's

---

* Stewart D. Burton was chief of station at the time. In another interview, *La Tercera*, September 21, 2000, Contreras identifies Burton as the CIA official with whom he was dealing in 1974.

story directly. "Shortly after DINA was established, Director Contreras came to the United States to seek American assistance. According to the CIA, the United States made clear to Contreras that no training or support which could aid internal repression could be given. Agency officials did, however, brief Contreras on the fundamentals of intelligence organization and management."

Declassified CIA documents are mum about the details of the training and about Contreras's assertion that eight CIA trainers spent several months in Chile. On the crucial fact of the CIA trainers' presence, Contreras is corroborated by his chief of operations, Colonel Pedro Espinoza. In subpoenaed testimony in 2000 Espinoza said he set up an intelligence school partly based on "courses given by the CIA instructors in Santiago." My interviews with two lower ranking former DINA agents provide other evidence. One said he attended lectures given by Americans he presumed to be CIA. The sessions took place at Contreras's Tejas Verde regiment, the site of DINA training. The other agent said he saw CIA manuals of procedure and intelligence instruction. Before he learned of the U.S. role, he said, "I thought Contreras was some kind of genius to have built up such a large, complicated apparatus in such a short time."

Finally, there is corroboration for Contreras's claim that the CIA attempted to post its own agents in operational jobs inside DINA. I learned that a similar arrangement was in place in Venezuela. The country's intelligence service, manned by CIA-trained officers, many born in Cuba, had become a virtual subsidiary of the CIA—what Contreras says the CIA had in mind for Chile. I interviewed Orlando Garcia, of the Venezuelan intelligence service, DISIP, and Carlos Andrés Pérez, who was president at the time. Both confirmed that at least one CIA officer was posted full time and had operational duties in the offices of the Armed Forces Intelligence Service in Caracas, which was the Venezuelan equivalent of the CIA.

There are three additional pieces of evidence of the CIA's intimate relationship with Contreras around this time. The CIA ordered a "covert name trace" on Contreras on May 20, 1974—during the time Contreras alleges the CIA trainers were present in Chile. A name trace is an elaborate security procedure involving queries to all CIA stations and records searches about the person. It is a CIA prerequisite to establishing a close, often paid, relationship with a source. Contreras received at least one payment from the CIA, in mid-1975, of an undisclosed amount, according to the Hinchey Report. (The same document that revealed the name trace also says that the CIA security files on Contreras were destroyed in 1991, an act of extraordinary arrogance by the agency to prevent further embarrassing disclosures about its working relationship with Contreras.)

The third piece of information is a CIA memo written about the time Contreras was in Washington in early 1974. It contains a detailed insider account of Pinochet's rivalries with his fellow generals. An annotation indicates it was written with input from General Vernon Walters, then deputy director of the CIA. Its primary focus is on Pinochet's efforts to neutralize the other members of the ruling junta and concentrate power in his own hands:

> Pinochet has had disagreements with a number of generals. One important general recently was eased into retirement following a series of personal and policy disputes with the junta president. Some senior officers who were most active in the plotting against Allende look upon Pinochet as a late-comer to that effort and probably feel that others are more deserving of the presidency. Pinochet appears determined to prevent the emergence from within the military of potential rivals for power. His position now is firmly enough established for him to deal forcefully with disgruntled officers, and further changes in the high command and cabinet shifts probably will take place.

The CIA was also well informed about DINA's first expansion of operations beyond its borders. "In early 1974, security forces from Argentina, Chile, Uruguay, Paraguay, [and] Bolivia met in Buenos Aires to prepare coordinated actions against subversive targets," a CIA report said, noting, however, that the coordination was not yet "very effective." U.S. embassy officials began to hear of regular meetings of the security and intelligence forces for the five countries in the region, sometimes including Brazil as well. They knew it as the "coordinating group," whose most important meetings were held at Campo de Mayo army base in Buenos Aires.

As predicted, Pinochet began to deal with "disgruntled officers." No military rival was as threatening to Pinochet as his predecessor, General Carlos Prats, who was living in voluntary exile in Argentina. Prats's resignation as commander in chief in August 1973 had preserved unity in the armed forces and removed the last obstacle to the coup plotters' move against Allende. Shortly after the coup, he accepted an offer of support and protection from Argentine President Juan Domingo Perón. Prats and his wife, Sofia, took up residence in a comfortable apartment—subsidized by his hosts—in the affluent Palermo district. Argentine as well as Chilean military officers were frequent visitors. The discreet former general made no public comments, but to his visitors, Prats made no secret of his disgust with the brutality and antidemocratic character of Pinochet's regime. He had regular, friendly conversations with the Chilean military attaché in Argentina, who reported on his activities to SIM, the military intelligence service. Prats's correspondence with officers in Chile was also voluminous and open. He conducted himself as a proud military man who had served his country while in office and had nothing to fear or hide in retirement.

Prats began writing a memoir of his military service, intended as an *apologia* for military subordination to the constitution, the guiding principle developed by his assassinated predecessor General René Schneider and ultimately repudiated by Pinochet. He had taken his private papers with him into exile and used them to reconstruct a day-by-day account of the events inside the military leading to the coup. Prats wrote daily until late at night, even while holding a regular job at an export-import firm to support his family. By September 20, 1974, he had finished the manuscript, more than 100,000 words. That day, he composed a fifteen-page handwritten prologue, titled "Letter to my fellow citizens"—a letter that, along with his memoir, would not become public for more than a decade.

> I feel it is my duty to make public "My Testimony."
>
> Because destiny placed me inexorably in a critical moment of history. . . .
>
> Because I had the opportunity to know secrets of state that have not been made public and which should become part of the History of Chile.
>
> Because I was a witness to the noble attitudes of high level personalities . . . who have prematurely disappeared from this earthly existence; just as [I have been a witness] to contemptible attitudes of others, also in high positions, who in anxiety would like to keep their actions hidden forever.

The plot to assassinate Prats began to unfold in the months of June and July 1974, about the time Prats lost the protection of President Perón, who died on July 1 and was replaced by his ineffectual widow, Isabelita (María E. Martínez), and a cabal of mostly right-wing Peronists.

This account of the crime is based on new information developed by Argentine investigating judge María Servini de Cubría and her staff and on the never before published confession of DINA's American-born assassin, Michael Vernon Townley.

Townley, captured by the FBI in April 1978 for his role in the Letelier assassination, has provided hundreds of hours of testimony for other investigations in Europe and Latin America. He has long been linked to the Prats murder—stamps in his passport place him in Buenos Aires at the time—but he had always refused to talk about his role. A plea bargain agreement, in exchange for his full testimony in the Letelier case, seemed to shield him from being questioned about murders outside the United States. Then, in 1999, in secret testimony in an Alexandria, Virginia, federal court, in the presence of Judge Servini, Townley finally described in detail what happened on those days in late September 1974.

Born in Waterloo, Iowa, Townley moved to Chile as a boy when his father was made general manager of Ford Motor Company's operations there. In his twenties, he was caught up in fighting against the Allende government. He first came to the attention of the CIA in 1970—a covert name trace was done just as it would later be done for his future boss, Colonel Contreras. Townley wanted to fight world Communism as a CIA agent, but the CIA maintains he was never more than a wanna-be, and spurned his overtures. Failing to find CIA employment, Townley made contact with DINA in June 1974 to pursue his ambition to be an undercover agent.

At about the same time, another agent began to operate in Buenos Aires. Enrique Arancibia Clavel was the black sheep of one of Chile's most prominent military families. He had attended Chile's Naval Academy but was forced to leave because of his homosexuality.

Arancibia and Townley both were veterans of the violent gangs carrying out petty terrorism and some serious crimes against the Allende government. Townley had broken into a television station in 1972 and killed a guard. Arancibia, nicknamed "*el Dinamitero*," led a group of upper-class youths that set off a series of bombs. He was on the fringes of the group that kidnapped and murdered armed forces chief René Schneider in 1970. He joined those who escaped into exile in Argentina. Now, in 1974, both Arancibia and Townley were seeking membership in a new gang, DINA. The Prats murder was their test of fire.

Sometime in the middle of 1974, according to Townley, Pinochet took up the matter of Prats in a meeting with the chiefs of DINA. Pinochet knew that Prats was writing his memoirs and had refused warnings to desist. He described Prats as "a dangerous man for Chile." Pinochet's words were all the mandate Contreras needed. He gave the job of eliminating Prats to his chief of operations, Colonel Pedro Espinoza, and to the head of DINA's newly created Exterior Department, Colonel Raúl Iturriaga Neumann.

The first plot was expensive and badly botched. According to evidence gathered by the Servini investigation, Iturriaga traveled to Buenos Aires in late July with a bag of cash to hire assassins and to coordinate the operation with the Argentine service, SIDE (*Secretaría de Informaciones de Estado*). Enrique Arancibia was DINA's point man. He distributed $20,000 to the would-be assassins, including Juan Martín Ciga Corréa, a leader of a fascist group called Milicia and a member of the Triple A, a death squad that had begun to operate after the death of Perón. The plotters were an unwieldy conglomeration of military, government, and civilian participants who kept DINA's money but failed to carry out the assassination. Townley commented, in later testimony, "the Argentines didn't have the guts to kill them."

The assassins, acting with impunity in a country that, in mid-1974, was approaching lawlessness, apparently talked openly about their plans in military and extreme rightist circles. Accurate information about the plot was picked up in mid-August by intelligence agencies in France and East Germany.

In East Berlin, exile leader Carlos Altamirano, head of Chile's Socialist Party, received a visit from Markus Wolf, chief of international intelligence for East Germany's Stasi intelligence service. Altamirano knew Wolf well and owed him his life. At the time of the coup in Chile, Altamirano went into hiding and sought Stasi's help to evade Pinochet's roundups of opposition leaders. He was one of the most wanted and hated figures by the military, not least because his party was organizing opposition to the coup inside the armed forces. Wolf, a fluent Spanish speaker who ran Stasi operations in Chile during the Allende government, set up a system using false compartments in cars to smuggle fugitives like Altamirano across the border into Argentina.

In August 1974, Wolf was on an errand to save another Chilean. He told Altamirano he had impeccable information of a DINA contract on Prats in Buenos Aires. The assassination was imminent. "They are going to kill Prats, it could only be a matter of hours," he said, according to Altamirano. "You have got to get him out of Argentina." Altamirano immediately called a friend in Buenos Aires, who personally carried the message about the threat to Prats. Prats said he, too, was aware that his life was in danger, but refused to leave the country until he had a Chilean passport. It was a matter of military honor. His application for the passport had been languishing in the Chilean bureaucracy for months.

Altamirano also received information from French intelligence with a similar warning about Prats, adding that another Chilean exile, Orlando Letelier, was also in danger. Letelier had recently been released after a year in Pinochet's Dawson Island concentration camp for high-ranking prisoners from the Allende government. He was in Caracas.

As days passed, Altamirano and Wolf put a plan in motion to try to rescue Prats. Wolf provided a false but perfectly crafted Chilean passport in Prats's name. He also turned over enough money for Prats and his wife to travel comfortably and to establish themselves in another country. "He has got to stop being silly," Wolf said.

Altamirano summoned a young Socialist Party member, Waldo Fortín, who had the documents and clean record to allow him to travel freely in Latin America. Altamirano instructed Fortín to get on a plane immediately to Caracas and Buenos Aires. "I was going to offer Prats every possible kind of support to get him to Europe, to fly him to Paris or wherever he wanted to go. I would offer him money if he needed it," Fortin said in an interview.

At DINA headquarters in Chile, realizing that the assassins hired by Arancibia were not going to deliver, Contreras moved to plan B—Michael Townley. When Townley finally confessed to his role twenty-five years later, he said DINA operations chief Pedro Espinoza gave him the assignment, but he didn't want to call it an "order."

"I would use a term more like inveigled . . . hoodwinked, tricked. . . . I eventually said, well, I'll try."

Townley was working as a car mechanic in Santiago in June 1974 when Pedro Espinoza began the process of recruitment. Townley knew Espinoza slightly from past years in the struggle against Allende. They talked, they had drinks, Espinoza hired him to do small electronics jobs for DINA. Espinoza brought up the subject of Prats. He dangled the possibility of working full time for DINA. Townley was drawn in:

I can't tell you over what period of time there was this conversation about the danger Prats represented . . . without asking, without suggesting, without anything going from that to "Do you think you could?" to "Will you?" to "When?" And I can't give you the transition points or anything else. But obviously in getting to know me, inviting me to his home, and coming to my home for dinner, in bringing me a few pieces of equipment, cheap radio equipment, "Could you fix this, could you look at this for me?"—like these were favors for him on a personal basis—to "You know that there is an organization that may be getting formed here, you might be able to do this on an ongoing basis for them." It was a situation that devolved into "Yes."

Espinoza turned Townley over to Exterior Department chief Iturriaga, who provided him with two chunks of C4 explosive, the clay-like "plastique" that was a favorite of assassins and terrorists in the 1970s. He built a remote-control bomb from a CB radio transmitter, primacord blasting caps, and what he called "a tone device buzzer thing."

Townley flew to Buenos Aires in early September, taking his wife Mariana Inés Callejas. The bomb mechanism was hidden in a portable radio. Claiming he couldn't locate Prats, he returned to Santiago. Iturriaga sent them back to try again, and this time he joined them. He met Townley and his wife and led them to Prats's apartment on Malabia Street, just a block from Libertador Avenue, a major thoroughfare in the Palermo neighborhood.

Townley and his wife kept an eye on the apartment, and the following Friday evening spotted Prats driving into the parking garage under the building. Townley waited until about 9:30 P.M., when the building's janitor opened the garage door and left it open for a few minutes. Townley slipped into the garage with the bomb in a satchel. He quickly realized he had made a serious mistake—he had his passport and identification papers on him. He hid them inside a pipe that served as a railing. He found Prats's car and slid underneath. He tied the bomb to a bar supporting the transmission, almost exactly in the middle of the car. Carefully he set the switch connecting the batteries to the blasting cap. Now armed, the bomb was ready to be detonated by a radio signal from Townley's modified CB transmitter.

By the time he finished, the door was closed and Townley had to spend most of the night hiding in the garage.

On Sunday night, September 29, Prats and his wife spent the afternoon and evening with former Chilean ambassador to Argentina, Ramón Huidobro. Just before midnight, the couple drove home, turning off Libertador a block from the apartment building. As Prats turned left to drive the last one hundred feet to the driveway of his building, he passed a Renault parked at the corner, lights off, with a man and a woman inside.

Townley and Mariana had been waiting for hours. He saw that Prats was not alone, but he thought it was now or never. "The car turned, it came around, it slowed at the intersection and then sped on to enter the garage. All I could see was the back of the car. We're talking near midnight. The illumination down the street I think was bad," he testified.

Mariana had the detonator. "I'm sitting at the steering wheel, she's sitting on the other side. It's sitting in her lap. She picks it up and says what do I do. . . . She's fumbling with it, she's pushing it, whatever. It wasn't even turned on."

Prats's car had turned in and stopped. The man who dared to challenge Pinochet by writing the true story of the coup got out to open the garage door just as Townley grabbed the device from his wife, quickly switched it on, and pressed the button.

Nearly two pounds of explosive incinerated the car with such force that the roof of the car was found on the roof of a nearby building. Carlos Prats González and Sofia Cuthbert de Prats were dead within seconds.

Michael and Mariana Townley returned to the Hotel Victoria, on Calle Florida, in the main business district. In the morning they caught a plane to Montevideo, and from there returned to Chile the same day. Enrique Arancibia also arrived in Santiago that day, staying at his mother's house. A friend of the family testified she was talking to Arancibia's mother by phone, commenting on the assassination. She heard Arancibia shout in the background, "*Así mueren los traidores*"—"This is how traitors die."

In Caracas, Socialist Party member Waldo Fortín got up early and caught the first plane to Buenos Aires. He was carrying the false passport, the money, and the offer to help the Prats family relocate to Europe. Fortín got off the plane in Buenos Aires and heard the news. Prats had been assassinated only a few hours before. He was too late. (Fortín had stopped first in Caracas to give a similar offer of help to Orlando Letelier, who would move a few months later to work in Washington, D.C.)

News of the assassination also brought a sickening realization to a Chilean embassy official, Guillermo Osorio, who had been trying to help Prats get his passport. The requests had been tied up for months, and now Osorio and other consular officials knew the delay was no mere bureaucratic tangle. A message from a military officer at the Chilean Foreign Ministry, received the day of the murders, settled the matter in a single cold sentence: "*Inconveniente otorgar pasaportes a personas indicadas. . . .*"—"It is inconvenient to grant passports to these persons." In a conversation with his brother, Renato, a few days after the murder, Osorio said he knew the order had been intended to prevent Prats and his wife from leaving Argentina. When his brother asked who he thought was responsible for the murder, Osorio said, "The hand of Pinochet is very long."

Guillermo Osório was well on his way to becoming the man who knew too much. Posted in Chile in 1976, he was the man in the Foreign Ministry in charge of acquiring false official documents for DINA, including the passports used in the plot to assassinate Orlando Letelier in Washington. In October 1977, as FBI investigators were closing in on Chile, Osorio was found dead of a gunshot wound at his home. Osorio's brother, Renato, pleaded with the U.S. embassy to investigate the case, which he said was a murder disguised as a suicide.

The Argentine investigators gathered voluminous evidence for the conspiracy to kill Prats, linking military and police officials in Argentina and Chile and civilian terrorists from both countries. Townley claimed in his long-delayed confession that he had no contact with Argentine co-conspirators as he was carrying out his assignment, but investigators think he is concealing what he knows about those contacts. Evidence of Argentine involvement cited by investigators includes: multiple phoned death threats to Prats; withdrawal of police from the street outside Prats's home; darkening of street lights near the Prats's apartment in the hours prior to the assassination; the fact that Townley and his wife could park for hours waiting for Prats's car to return without fear of detection; and the presence of other DINA agents in Buenos Aires, including Iturriaga, his deputy José Zara, and Arancibia.

Moreover, Townley talked specifically about the involvement of SIDE and Milicia in conversations with U.S. investigators, including FBI agent Robert Scherrer. A former Italian terrorist and friend of Townley said Townley told him the operation against Prats could not have been carried out without prior approval by Argentina.

Townley and Arancibia were rewarded for their work in the Prats assassination. Both were promoted from sporadic collaborators to full-time employees of DINA. Contreras bought a sprawling house in the hills above Santiago and turned it over to Townley and his family. Townley would continue to work on electronic and radio operations, and he would be asked to carry out more assassinations.

Arancibia returned to Buenos Aires within a week and began a new career as DINA's clandestine liaison to the increasingly active military and civilian operational groups—death squads such as the infamous Triple A—waging undercover war against leftists. On October 10, he sent his first report, consisting largely of newspaper clippings on the crisis in Argentina. He used the false name Luis Felipe Alemparte Díaz. Arancibia kept meticulous files of his correspondence with his DINA superiors in Santiago. The letters and reports were kept in boxes at his office at the Buenos Aires branch of Chile's Banco de Estado, his cover job. His sloppy tradecraft was to preserve a bonanza for investigators.

In the correspondence, Arancibia said little openly about Prats but clearly was well plugged in. In a December 6 dispatch he notes that he has been in contact with Martín Ciga, a Triple A operative working as head of security at Buenos Aires University—one of those later indicted for involvement in the Prats murder. Then he adds: "The group that eliminated Prats is said to have a list of eight more Chileans, one of whom is [former ambassador Ramón] Huidobro." Huidobro, a close friend who was with Prats the evening of his death, had fled Argentina after receiving death threats.

Arancibia's boss in DINA sent instructions, always signed "Luis Gutiérrez"—a pseudonym for Iturriaga, but also used for whoever was in charge of the Exterior Department. He urged him to be careful in making contacts. "They are of maximal interest, but take appropriate caution not to awaken even the most minimum suspicion and not to compromise yourself." Two weeks later, he instructed Arancibia to investigate a MIR pamphlet, presumably published in Argentina. And he informed his agent that DINA was expanding its operations in Argentina and sending a new officer:

> Col. Juan Barria Barria has been appointed as delegate for National Intelligence in Baires, occupying the post of counselor in our embassy. This officer will be in charge of official contacts with the embassy and with the Intelligence Services.
> . . . A member of SIDE is here [in Santiago] in the Argentine embassy in contact with us.

Col. Barria is an official representative, and you are a chief of Clandestine Information.

Arancibia's reports showed DINA's early preoccupation with coordination with other intelligence agencies. "There is an idea to create an anti-Communist information community at the continental level with Uruguayan and Argentine military and they are interested in making contact with Chileans," he wrote in his memorandum number 2.

The CIA and U.S. military intelligence in Argentina also were monitoring developments in the Prats murder and the move toward greater coordination. Defense Attaché Colonel Samuel Stapleton reported within hours that Prats's murder was surprising because he appeared to be living in Buenos Aires "with the blessing of Pinochet," and that he "had faithfully carried out his restrictive instructions" to refrain from public statements. The CIA report was better informed. It cited "official Argentine government circles" as attributing the assassination to "the work of Chileans." Another CIA source had visited General Prats a few days before the assassination and gave an account of one of the phone calls warning Prats. "The caller warned Prats that a team was preparing to assassinate him, the caller adding that he opposed the assassination. According to Prats, the caller suggested that Prats hold a press conference to announce this threat. . . . The caller also suggested that Prats should carry out his planned trip to Brazil. Prats told [redacted] that he had not contemplated such a trip but that he had used alleged travel to Brazil as a pretext with Chilean consul General Alvaro Droguett to obtain a passport."

The document suggested a motive: "Prats had nearly completed his memoirs which strongly condemned many non-Popular Unity politicians and military officers."

The CIA also put the Prats assassination in the context of the soon to be created Operation Condor, according to the Hinchey Report:

"Knowledge of Operation Condor." Within a year after the coup, the CIA and other US Government agencies were aware of bilateral cooperation among regional intelligence services to track the activities of and, in at least a few cases, kill political opponents. This was the precursor to Operation Condor . . . established in 1975.

The Prats operation was Chile's first foray into international assassination. It succeeded despite what we now know were massive intelligence leaks, most likely the result of the clumsy coordination with the Argentine participants. It bears noting how different were the actions of the intelligence agencies receiving the leaks. The French and East German agencies immediately set in motion actions to prevent the assassination. The CIA, learning of the planned assassination in Buenos Aires, could easily have arranged a discreet but visible show of U.S. interest and support of Prats—a luncheon or a visit from the U.S. defense attaché. Nothing was done.

Future operations would improvise and improve on the model. The next targets were located not only in Latin America, but in Europe as well.

6

MISSION IN PARAGUAY

According to information provided by the subject during various interrogation sessions by the Police of the Capital in Asunción, he admitted he is a member of the Junta Coordinadora and he was acting as a courier for that group. . . . The FBI has initiated an investigation in the United States. . . .

—FBI LIAISON ROBERT SCHERRER, INFORMING CHILEAN POLICE
ABOUT THE CAPTURE OF A JCR OPERATIVE

For the left and their democratic allies, 1975 was to be a year of regrouping and counteroffensive. Prominent Chilean moderates were establishing bases of operation in the United States and Europe. Socialist leader Orlando Letelier worked in Washington, D.C., Carlos Altamirano was in Paris and East Berlin, Christian Democrat Bernardo Leighton was in Rome, and Gabriel Valdés, a former foreign minister, was in New York. Their strategy: build an international coalition of democratic countries to ostracize the dictatorships. Political leaders of Uruguay, Bolivia, and Paraguay continued even after the Prats assassination to base themselves in Argentina, taking advantage of its proximity to their countries and the openness of the Peronist government.

The extreme left, now organized in the JCR, began to see on the horizon the realization of their dream of military victory, of "many Vietnams," as Roberto Santucho liked to say. There was apparent success in Argentina. The ERP's "Compañia del Monte Ramón Rosa Jiménez"—the mountain guerrilla offensive in Tucumán Province—was launching hit-and-run operations that were confounding the government's clumsy counterguerrilla operations. The guerrilla force never exceeded ninety fighters, including ten women, but by January, the ERP units were operating in almost one-third of the province.

The other members of the JCR sent soldiers to Tucumán to gain combat experience. Of ten soldiers from Chile's MIR, four were killed in action. MIR's imported arms factory went into production in Argentina using plans, tools, and technicians brought over from Chile. By April, the first nine-millimeter submachine guns, christened the *"JCR Uno,"* were delivered to the Tucumán fighters, and finished parts for 4,000 other units had been machined and were ready for final assembly. Two radio transmitters were smuggled into Tucumán to complete Roberto Santucho's vision of a Vietnam-like liberated zone from which the revolution would spread.

The PRT/ERP newspaper, *El Combatiente*, was published from a fully appointed printshop in the vaulted chambers of a tunnel—another page from the Vietcong playbook. Tucumán was the beginning, Santucho wrote in a tone of triumph. "We are living a situation of a mass uprising toward Socialism in all the Latin American countries. . . . If it is to find an adequate channel, it must depend on the role of the revolutionary vanguard in building up parties and mass military and political forces. It is in this perspective that we understand the true importance of the JCR and its strategic importance, and [we comprehend] the role of the liberated zones, whose concrete possibility is beginning to be seen."

Yet, the revolutionary war that Santucho and the other leaders of the Revolutionary Junta hoped to ignite in Latin America remained a series of brush fires, despite their efforts to will it into a continental conflagration. "Voluntarism" is the special term in the revolutionaries' lexicon for the error of a leader who allows optimism for victory to blind him to the realities on the ground. The desire, the sheer will to bring the revolution becomes the basis for actions and decisions. In proclaiming the success of his fledgling guerrilla war, he was following Che Guevara's maxim that the mere presence of a small *foco* or pocket of fighting will ignite revolutionary action in a much wider area as soon as people learn of its existence. In other words, propagating the news of success is as important as military success itself.

The reality facing the revolutionaries in mid-1975, however, was stark. More than a year following the creation of the JCR, international guerrilla activity remained sporadic. Hundreds of thousands, even millions, of dollars were being spent to build and maintain revolutionary infrastructure in the four JCR member countries. Once the fighting in Tucumán got underway, JCR strategy called for the opening of simultaneous fronts elsewhere. "The idea was that Argentina would not be the only battle front, that there would also be armed action in Chile and in Uruguay, even in Bolivia," said Luis Alemany, the Tupamaro military chief at the time. But it wasn't happening according to plan.

Alemany, from his base in Argentina, was preparing Tupamaro units for an ambitious counteroffensive scheduled for May Day, 1974. The attack was to include a wave of kidnappings and a prison break, using airplanes and a ship, to free the Tupamaro leadership. Uruguayan police discovered safe houses and plans before the operation got off the ground, however, and the plan was aborted. The leadership, disillusioned by the failure, split into factions and by the end of 1974 the Tupamaros ceased to exist as an effective military force. They had also been penetrated. The safe house where they held their final, fiery meeting was bugged and Argentine agents received transcripts of the debates that preceded the breakup.

MIR in Chile had the strongest military capacity outside of Argentina. Santucho was particularly galled at what he considered a dangerous excess of caution, even timidity by the Chileans. In meetings and exchanges of letters, Santucho cajoled and criticized, but MIR continued to postpone its planned counteroffensive against the Pinochet regime. Instead, DINA now was on the offensive in Chile. In October 1974, tortured MIR suspects had led a DINA commando to the hideout of MIR leader Miguel Enríquez, and he was killed in a furious gun battle.

In Bolivia, the ELN had reorganized, at the urging of their JCR comrades, as the Revolutionary Workers Party of Bolivia (*Partido Revolucionario de Trabajadores de Bolivia*—PRTB). JCR support helped them successfully reinfiltrate to establish organizational bases in miners unions, peasant organizations, and among other remnants of the followers of former president Juan José Torres. A mass protest supported by armed guerrillas in Cochabamba Province was short-lived, but it put dictator President Hugo Banzer on notice that he faced an international threat. His foreign minister and army chief began to ask the U.S. ambassador to provide U.S. intelligence reports on terrorist activity beyond Bolivia's borders.

There had been incipient military action even in quiet Paraguay, where Stroessner's twenty-year-old dictatorship was thought to have long since stamped out all overt resistance. An eclectic group of disgruntled former Colorado party members, radical students, and Argentine-trained Marxists embarked on a plan to assassinate Stroessner with a car bomb. The group had ties to ERP and Montoneros, but was not formally allied in the JCR. The younger members of the group had been trained by ERP while they were students at the University of La Plata in Argentina. Two surviving members disclosed in interviews that the bomb intended for Stroessner was built by Montoneros in Argentina and smuggled into Paraguay by the group's leader, Augustín Goiburú. Twice, the group positioned the bomb in a van along the route frequented by Stroessner, and twice the bomb failed to detonate. Finally, in November 1974, Stroessner's security police arrested a militant who had tried—in an act of colossal foolhardiness—to purchase fresh explosives for the bomb from a navy officer. After being tortured, he led the police to the group's safe house, and dozens were arrested. A CIA report on the plot noted that, "Despite the stupid blunder that produced the mass arrests, the game plan to blow up Stroessner's automobile was the most sophisticated of many attempts to oust the President since he came to power twenty years ago."

In Tucumán, even as Santucho was proclaiming success, the military campaign was losing momentum. The Argentine army in February pushed aside the cruel but ineffective federal police and began a concerted counterattack called Operation Independence. In April, shortly after the ERP newspaper *El Combatiente* trumpeted that the JCR was manufacturing its own "JCR Uno" submachine guns, the military raided one of the arms factories in a basement in the Caseros neighborhood of Buenos Aires. Then, in late June, the military routed a poorly armed ERP battalion at Manchalá in Tucumán. Soon after the army moved into the capital city of Tucumán to decimate the ERP noncombatant support structures that had been operating undisturbed for more than a year. For the rest of the year the army kept the ERP guerrilla force on the defensive. As one observer commented, the ambushers had become the ambushed, and the guerrilla campaign was "bemired, as had been all of the rural [guerrilla] *focos* in the history of Argentina."

It was clear that the Tucumán campaign—with its evanescent "liberated zone"—could not long survive in isolation. It needed more international solidarity than it had received so far. If the JCR was ever to prove its strategic value as a regional force, it was at this critical juncture. Until this point, the JCR had established its international network almost exclusively in Europe, with offices and support organizations in Paris, Lisbon, Rome, and Bonn. European Social Democratic parties had received the JCR emissary, Tupamaro Efraín Martínez Platero, with respect and solidarity in early 1974, but flatly rejected the JCR request for support for the JCR's guerrilla warfare strategy. European enthusiasm and financial aid was limited to "solidarity" with refugees, political exiles, and other victims of mounting human rights abuses. The guerrilla strategy was embraced by Europe's many ultra-left extremist groups, but the JCR tried to keep them at arm's length to avoid alienating the more important Social Democratic support. Surviving JCR leaders—Pascal, Mattini, Martínez Platero—unanimously insist they had no operational ties with the many violent radical groups in Europe, such as the Baader-Meinhof "Red Army" of Germany, although friendly personal relationships were common. Europe provided a rear guard for financial and propaganda operations, they said, but military action was off limits.

The JCR network in its home base of Latin America was less well developed. A curious phenomenon had occurred growing out of the availability of millions of dollars in the ERP war chest. The JCR became a kind of revolutionary funding organization, a crypto-Rockefeller Foundation of the radical Marxist left, receiving proposals and doling out grant money. "We had lots of money. Movements from all over were coming to ask us for money. We gave out $10,000 here, $40,000 there. If they were involved in armed struggle, it was all the more likely they would get the money," said ERP leader Luis Mattini. For a time the visiting revolutionaries were invited to attend military training courses at the ERP's clandestine schools. The largest grant was $150,000 to a leftist group getting organized in Portugal to take advantage of that country's brief military-sponsored revolution. Jaime Bateman, leader of Colombia's M-19 guerrillas, the most active leftist military force outside of the Southern Cone, sent a representative to Buenos Aires in 1974 to plan regional strategy and to discuss the possibility of joining as a formal member of the JCR.

It was time for the JCR to get serious about creating the "Latin American International" contemplated in the JCR charter. In May 1975, the JCR Executive Commission decided to send two JCR emissaries on a mission to spread the JCR's message of regional revolution to other countries in Latin America. The first stop was Paraguay. It was a trip that was to intended to spark the expansion of the JCR and its revolutionary strategy. Instead, however, the JCR mission almost immediately became the target of concerted action by the security forces of Chile, Argentina, and Paraguay. The FBI also was brought into the intelligence loop and initiated a follow-up investigation of JCR activity in the United

States. One can draw a direct line from the capture and shared interrogation of the two JCR emissaries to the creation of Operation Condor six months later.

The mission to Paraguay was planned in early May. Edgardo Enríquez had taken over leadership of MIR after his brother was killed in the DINA attack the previous September. Edgardo, a dark, gangly man, had been dividing his time among Cuba, Europe, and Argentina, since leaving Chile clandestinely in February 1974. Enríquez had only recently arrived in Buenos Aires from Paris in early May. He came with fresh ideas and a determination to make his way back to Chile, where MIR would finally launch the long-delayed military offensive. In a meeting of the JCR Executive Commission he proposed an immediate mission to recruit new JCR member organizations outside of the Southern Cone.

For the trip to Paraguay and beyond, the commission chose two second-ranking figures, Amílcar Santucho, Roberto's older brother, and Jorge Fuentes, who had been MIR's factotum in Buenos Aires since early 1974. Santucho and Fuentes were the organization and money men of the JCR. Fuentes's main job for MIR was to keep a steady flow of cash going across the border to meet MIR's needs in Chile.

Amílcar Santucho, already in his fifties, with five grown children, did not fit the profile of an underground revolutionary. He was a well-known and successful criminal trial lawyer with longtime membership in the Argentine Communist Party. The oldest of eight Santucho brothers and two sisters—four of whom were leftist activists—Amílcar joined his brother Roberto in 1973 to work full time in the PRT/ERP after deciding—according to younger brother Julio—that "Robi had matured a lot politically" and his organization held promise for revolutionary success.

"I remember exactly the objectives of the trip by Amílcar and Fuentes," said Luis Mattini. "It was an incursion as well as an informational trip to carry out a survey of the level of determination (*voluntad*) of the Latin American revolutionaries. It was like a preliminary probe. Afterwards they were supposed to deliver a report and then go out again to cement alliances or memberships [in the JCR] . . ."

One of their duties, according to two sources, was to explore the feasibility of moving JCR headquarters to another Latin American country. Lima, Peru, and Caracas, Venezuela, were on their itinerary. They were to bring $5,000 in cash to the Peruvian group, the Popular Army of Peru, which years later was renamed for the Indian hero Tupac Amaru and in 1996 carried out the spectacular siege of the Japanese embassy in Lima. In Colombia, in addition to following up the contact with Bateman's M-19, they were going to meet representatives of FARC—the Revolutionary Armed Forces of Colombia.

The night before departing with Santucho, Fuentes met for a farewell drink with his closest MIR colleagues, Edgardo Enríquez and René Valenzuela. To an observer in the bar they would have appeared to be three neatly dressed office workers getting together for a few beers and a few laughs after work.

Fuentes no longer looked like the gregarious student radical he had been in Chile, where he was widely known as "El Trosko"—a nickname he gained because of his vociferous opposition to Trotskyist influence in MIR. He had been elected president of the Federation of Chilean Students, the country's most important student organization. The son of an army sergeant, he was an achiever, one of the many young people from lower-class backgrounds who took advantage of the opportunities for education and advancement offered by Chile's decade of progressive governments.

After the coup, he had escaped via Peru to Cuba, where Castro's tradecraft specialists trained him in underground activity and changed his appearance. False teeth changed his recognizable smile, and his distinctive black horn-rimmed glasses were replaced by contact lenses. Valenzuela tried to talk Fuentes out of going by bus to Paraguay. "I told him, Why don't you take a plane. You are a professional, a sociologist. Someone of your status wouldn't travel by bus. They would fly."

But Fuentes was not a person to make decisions based on status, and his attention to the details of security was lax at best. He preferred to travel in the company of a comrade. So early the next morning, Friday, May 16, he boarded the Buenos Aires–Asunción express bus with Santucho for the nearly ten-hour ride. Both had false passports, but in another violation of tradecraft, the two men sat side by side. When the bus arrived at a point twenty miles south of Asunción, it was transported across the Paraguay River on a small ferry, to the port of Itá Enramada on the other bank, where Paraguayan border police checked passports.

How police were alerted is not known, but they boarded the bus with the clear objective of arresting the older revolutionary, Amílcar Santucho, who was immediately taken into custody and taken off the bus. Fuentes, apparently undetected, was allowed to continue his journey to Asunción. U.S. intelligence showed keen interest in the police action. The most detailed account available is in a cable from the U.S. embassy in Buenos Aires, presumably based on Paraguayan and Argentine intelligence sources: "A Paraguayan national noticed Santucho's unusual behavior at border crossing point where he appeared to be signalling for a contact with a folded copy of ERP newspaper. Paraguayan police were informed when bus entered Paraguayan terrritory . . . He was also carrying a false bottom suitcase which contained ERP documents and contact information regarding other leftists in various other Latin American countries. Santucho and Chilean MIR companion, Jorge Isaac Fuentes, were evidently transiting Paraguay for a meeting in Peru of *Junta Coordinador[a] Revolucionario* (JCR)."

It is hard to believe that Santucho would make such a stupid move as to display a clandestine newspaper while on a secret mission. The embassy's intelligence sources may have invented that detail to hide the fact they had Santucho under surveillance. Several other sources confirm that Santucho was carrying JCR documents in a hidden compartment in his suitcase, and one source who talked to Santucho said he was carrying a large quantity of cash.

Arriving in Asunción, Fuentes remained free only long enough to check into a hotel and send a postcard. The next day Paraguayan security police, the Department of Investigations of the Police of the Capital, arrested him at the Hotel España in downtown Asunción.

By any measure the capture of Santucho and Fuentes was an intelligence bonanza. Documents they were carrying included address books and lists of JCR contacts. Most were protected by only the flimsiest codes. In their heads they carried the names, positions, and pseudonynms of hundreds of underground activists—although compartmentalization procedures ensured that they knew very little about the physical location of the activists. They had attended the most secret meetings of the PRT/ERP, MIR, and JCR, and Santucho had served as official note taker. They knew plans, strategy, infrastructure, financial transmissions, and a wealth of detail about past guerrilla operations. Paraguayan security police quickly realized that these two men could provide a roadmap of JCR military activity in the Southern Cone. They also knew details of the JCR structure in a half-dozen European countries and of the solidarity infrastructure being set up all over Latin America, Europe, and the United States.

It was intelligence of vital interest to all of the security forces and intelligence agencies operating in South America. Traditionally wary of intelligence sharing, the agencies began to collaborate in unprecedented ways. The handling of the Fuentes-Santucho case created the mold into which six months later Operation Condor was poured.

One of the first to share in the bonanza was the FBI. The Bureau's man on the ground in South America was Robert Scherrer, whose official title was legal attaché to the U.S. Embassy in Buenos Aires, In fact, he was a one-man intelligence station whose sources in all of the Southern Cone countries were the envy of the CIA and U.S. military intelligence. A red-haired Brooklyn native of Irish-German descent, Scherrer didn't try to blend into the Latin culture, despite his near perfect Spanish. His official assignment included police liaison with Chile, Uruguay, Paraguay, and Bolivia in addition to Buenos Aires. He had had almost six years to build up his sources and network of contacts in those countries, and he had devoted special attention to Paraguay—a backwater country that could have given birth to the term. He traveled there regularly, sometimes taking his wife, Rosemary.

Scherrer knew General Benito Guanes, head of G2, the intelligence department of the General Staff of the Armed Forces. He was on a first-name basis as well with Pastor Coronel, head of DICP (Department of Investigations of the Police of the Capital)—who was holding Fuentes and Santucho at his headquarters in downtown Asunción. Most likely it was one of them who had tipped Scherrer to the capture of the two revolutionaries. It is also likely that Scherrer flew to Asunción. Top-secret intelligence work of this nature was not conducted by phone. In any case, by the first week of June, Scherrer had been briefed on what Fuentes and Santucho were telling their interrogators under torture. He was filing reports, writing letters, and beginning a follow-up investigation on possible U.S. links to the JCR. His report to FBI headquarters in Washington, released to the author under the Freedom of Information Act, is dated June 6.

The FBI officer went a significant step further and thus became—to the extent that documentary proof has come to light—the first documented case of U.S. official participation in the multicountry operations against the JCR. Scherrer sent a letter informing his main police source in Chile, General Ernesto Baeza, about the JCR arrests. Chilean and Argentine security force interrogators also soon arrived in Asunción, and the interrogations of Fuentes and

Santucho became the preoccupation of three countries in the ensuing weeks and months. But before we continue with that story—which culminates in the formal creation of Operation Condor at year's end—we must follow the action of the FBI investigation of the JCR as it took a detour to the United States.

Scherrer's letter to the Chilean police officer eventually was turned over to the official human rights investigators, the Rettig Commission, who stored it in the commissions "reserved" or secret section. There, the author was allowed to read and copy the letter, reproduced here in translation:

Embassy of the United States of America
Buenos Aires, Argentina

Office of the Legal Attache
June 6, 1975

<u>My letter #3</u>

General Ernesto Baeza Michaelsen
General Director of Investigations
General Direction of Investigations
Santiago, Chile

Attention: Inspector Jaime Vásquez Alcaino

Concerning: Jorge Isaac Fuentes (aka) Auriel Nodarse Ledesma

With consideration:

I have learned that the captioned subject is a Chilean citizen and member of the MIR. He was detained May 17, 1975, in Asunción, Paraguay, after entering the country illegally from Argentina carrying a Costa Rican passport number 142302/74 under the identify of Auriel Nodarse Ledesma. The subject was accompanied by Amílcar Santucho, brother of the maximum leader of ERP, Mario Roberto Santucho.

According to information provided by the subject during various interrogation sessions by the Police of the Capital in Asunción, he admitted he is a member of the Junta Coordinadora and he was acting as a courier for that group.

In his address book, the subject had the following notations about individuals and addresses in the United States.

1. Margaret Sun
C/o Maria Brandao
440 West End Ave.
Apt. 16-E
NY, NY 10024

2. Sonia Bacicalupe
8024 Rothington Road
Dallas, TX 75227

3. Calle Padre Colon 256
Rio Piedras, Puerto Rico

I have learned that Bacicalupe is the sister of the subject. The FBI has initiated an investigation in the United States concerning these persons and addresses mentioned above. I will inform you of the results of the investigation as soon as I have them in my power.

I take this opportunity to send my most attentive greetings.

(Original signature)
Robert W. Scherrer
Legal Attache

Scherrer's report to FBI headquarters has similar language, although it is heavily redacted. It confirmed the U.S. investigation. "The bureau is requested to instruct the Dallas, New York and San Juan offices to conduct appropriate investigation," he wrote.

When the existence of the Scherrer letter first came to light, in a *New York Times* story by reporter Tim Weiner, the FBI was quoted as calling the investigation a "routine and traditional form of cooperation," and the reporter was told the FBI could not find the people cited in the letter.

That wasn't true. Not long after Scherrer's report, Fuentes's sister, Sonia Fuentes Bacicalupo (the correct spelling), was teaching her grade school class at St. Phillips Catholic school in a Dallas suburb. She said a priest came to her classroom and told her an FBI agent was looking for her. The agent wanted to know when she had last seen her brother, Jorge, and whether he had ever lived with her in the States. She said she hadn't seen her brother since she'd left Chile several years before the coup. The agents gave her no information about his arrest in Paraguay; it would be many months before she would find out the fate of her brother.

Scherrer, who died in 1995, discussed the Fuentes and Santucho arrests in interviews with the author in 1979 in the context of Scherrer's key role in the FBI investigation of the Letelier assassination. He raised the Paraguay arrests of the JCR operatives on his own initiative as an example of international intelligence coordination against terrorism that was formalized in Operation Condor. In that interview, he talked about the brutality of the Paraguayan police and their use of torture, but he did not reveal that he had been briefed on the interrogation of the two men nor that he had shared the information with his Chilean counterpart, General Baeza.

Scherrer said he considered it part of his job to exchange information with the South American police in their pursuit of "terrorists"—and he considered Fuentes and Santucho to fit into that category. "They should be rounded up. But they should be tried, not slaughtered," he said. The military governments in the region considered the United States a "haven for terrorists" under the guise of human rights activists, and Scherrer said that in 1975 the governments formally proposed that the FBI have a "more open exchange of information with them" about the activities of people they considered "terrorists" in the United States.

Scherrer volunteered a story linking the arrests in Paraguay to a famous terrorist incident in Paris a few weeks later. He said the wealth of intelligence gleaned from Fuentes and Santucho had provided an important clue that helped track down one of the most famous international terrorists of the era, Ilich Ramírez Sánchez, better known as Carlos the Jackal, the Venezuelan-born operative living in Europe.

According to Scherrer, Paraguayan police found a reference to a "Carlos" in Santucho's address book with an address or telephone number in Paris. They thought it was a clue to the whereabouts of Santucho's brother, Roberto, whose code name in ERP was Carlos. They passed the intelligence on to the French security service, DST. As it happened, on June 27—forty days after the arrests in Paraguay—three DST agents and an informant knocked on the door of a Paris apartment where Ilich Ramírez, the Venezuelan Carlos, was posing as a student and living with his girlfriend. After letting them enter, Carlos pulled a gun and shot all four, then escaped. According to Scherrer, "They were looking for Roberto Santucho, using the alias 'Carlos.' The [French] agents went at the apartment to get Roberto, but instead they found the real Carlos, the Jackal. He had an arsenal and bodyguards. They shot their way out and killed the agents."

French intelligence sources did not confirm Scherrer's story. In a briefing, they said an informant led them to the apartment and that they intended to question Carlos, not arrest him. He panicked and started shooting when he realized the agents knew of his connections to the Popular Front for the Liberation of Palestine (PFLP), they said. Carlos the Jackal remained free for more than twenty years, committing ever more egregious acts of terror, including the kidnapping of OPEC oil ministers later that year and the hijacking of an Air France jet that ended in a spectacular—and bloody—Israeli commando raid at the airport at Entebbe, Uganda. Carlos once bragged he was responsible for the deaths of eighty-three people.

Was the famous raid on Carlos the Jackal the result of the tip from South America? There is independent corroboration for Scherrer's story.

The first is DICP chief Pastor Coronel, who wrote about the Carlos connection in secret documents found in the Paraguay Archives. Coronel was in a position to know, since he was in charge of the interrogations of Fuentes and Santucho. More than once he claimed credit for leading the French police to Carlos. In a paper prepared for presentation at a 1976 meeting of several intelligence services and in two other documents, he reported on the capture of Santucho and Fuentes, describing them as "high level leaders of the Revolutionary Junta [JCR]":

> The documentation found on them shows that their stay in Paraguay was linked to the organization of terrorism and cell groups [*grupos de base*]. Later on they were going to move on to other American countries, and finally arrive in Paris.
>
> In Paris they had established an address for a contact. We informed the French authorities of this address. French police raided and two officers died at the hands of the famous terrorist, Carlos. The internationalization of terrorism, thus, has another element of proof.

Other Paraguay Archive documents show that Pastor Coronel followed up on the Carlos investigation. Soon after the arrests, he requested and received a photo of Carlos from Argentine SIDE chief Otto Paladino. Other supporting information comes from Venezuela, whose police had a vital interest in Carlos, a Venezuelan citizen. Venezuela's intelligence service, DISIP, also claimed credit for the raid on Carlos's apartment. "We knew he [Carlos] was in France and we told French police," said Orlando García, who was DISIP General Commissioner at the time. Whether the Venezuelan information had its origin in the Paraguayan arrests or was entirely separate could not be learned.

In March 2001, I was able to ask Carlos himself—imprisoned in Paris—about the matter. The most obvious explanation for the reference to Carlos in Santucho's address book was that there was a relationship between the Venezuelan extremist Carlos and ERP or the JCR. Such a relationship is asserted in later CIA and DIA reports and was widely believed by other intelligence agencies in South America. In a faxed exchange of letters from La Santé Prison, where he is serving a life sentence for the shootings, Carlos acknowledged a relationship between his organization, the Popular Front for the Liberation of Palestine (PFLP), and ERP. In the handwritten letter, Carlos also said, "My contact with MIR comrades [in the Middle East] was of a social nature."

Such international connections fed the already heightened paranoia of the security forces in the Southern Cone. They saw the JCR as the hub of an impending offensive from outside Latin America. The security forces knew of the existence and goals of the JCR, at least from the time of the clandestine press conference in February 1974, but as far as is known, no JCR official of any importance had ever been captured alive. Fuentes and Santucho were the first. Their capture generated an elaborate paper trail in the intelligence agencies—now available in document collections obtained for this book.

Intelligence reports on the JCR, including those released by the CIA and other U.S. agencies, are suddenly filled with rich detail on the internal workings of the JCR. Some of the reports are within weeks of the Fuentes and Santucho arrests. From Paraguay, we have at least twenty documents found among the roomful of DICP archives confiscated by a Paraguay judge in 1992. From Argentina, the files of DINA operative Enrique Arancibia Clavel, first described in Chapter 5, allow us to track Chilean and Argentine intelligence operations following up on the arrests. Also from Argentina, analytical reports ranging from fifteen to forty pages on the JCR were obtained from among the documents turned over to Argentine courts for trials in the mid-1980s. From Chile, interviews with a former DINA agent and fellow detainees provided additional firsthand descriptions of what happened.

Stroessner's enemies who survived years of imprisonment and interrogation in Paraguay called one of the prisons *El Sepulcro de los Vivos*—"the tomb of the living." The man in charge of day-to-day security operations was DICP Chief Pastor Coronel, who liked to conduct the most important interrogations and torture sessions at DICP headquarters on Presidente Franco Street, a narrow, busy thoroughfare only a few blocks from the Paraguayan Parliament. Pastor Coronel had a large suite of offices facing the street on the second floor, framed by five once elegant, floor-to-ceiling French colonial windows. Other investigators' offices were on the first floor. The fifteen or so prison cells were to the rear, in what once had been a separate building crudely joined to the headquarters building by narrow doors carved out of walls and ramps bridging the differences in floor elevations. The prison space had a bizarre, disorienting effect. Walls stopped short of the ceiling, columns left over from some previous construction supported nothing. Stairways dead-ended in brick walls. There were no windows to the outside. Cell doors were covered with sheets of iron with a small slit as the only opening. There was only one bathroom, on the ground floor, but prisoners were not allowed to use it. Instead, each cell had a large tin can.

The cells had all been full for months when Fuentes and Santucho arrived in May. Six months earlier, in November 1974, DICP rounded up hundreds of suspects thought to be connected to the group that had tried to assassinate President Stroessner with a car bomb. The cells could not hold them all. Many had to spend the days sitting on the stairs, and sleep on the concrete floors of the corridors. Now only a few dozen were left, thought to be the hard-core operatives directly involved in the plot.

Torture in Paraguayan jails was routine, but hardly scientific. Coronel and his men used a short, crude whip, called a *tejuruguai*, made of heavy cable and pieces of metal wrapped in leather. Cast-iron shackles and leg irons immobilized the prisoners, sometimes for days at a time in their cells. To those methods, which had changed little since the dungeons of the Dark Ages in Europe, the policemen added the newer Latin American techniques of electric shock and submersion in water, sometimes in combination.

One routine described by the prisoners may have been unique to Paraguay. When a prisoner was broken and ready to talk, Pastor Coronel would convene an interrogation session in his spacious front offices. High officials from Stroessner's government and foreign military attachés were invited to attend the secret sessions. The prisoner, sometimes blindfolded, was brought in and made to stand or sit next to Pastor Coronel's desk. Dark-suited waiters serving coffee and snacks circulated among the dozen or so officers seated in semicircle rows around the prison. One prisoner forced to undergo this routine described it as a tribunal, with questioning from the foreign visitors as well as from Pastor Coronel and his interrogators. Several prisoners interviewed said they could tell from the questions and accents that the visitors included Chileans, Argentines, Uruguayans, and Brazilians. One prisoner said he was convinced that Stroessner himself was in the room for his interrogation.

Santucho, who eventually was released, described such a session in Pastor Coronel's office soon after he arrived, with questioning from Argentines. "The interrogation took place in the office of the chief of investigations. It was during this interrogation that they applied electric shocks to my ears. There were several Argentines, I don't know if they were police or military. I somehow got the impression they were personnel of the Argentine embassy in Paraguay." In later interrogation sessions, Santucho said he was questioned by men he concluded were military officers from Chile, Argentina, and Uruguay.

Among the documents in the Paraguay Archive are five pages of detailed questions for Santucho. More than half of the sixty questions concerned the Junta Coordinadora or ERP and their alleged relationship with Paraguayan militants. This early questionnaire reflected little inside intelligence about JCR operations, however, and appeared to be more of a fishing expedition than a systematic interrogation.

That changed quickly after the first weeks as information for the interrogations flowed in from Chile and Argentina. Questioning shifted from Paraguay to clandestine activities in Buenos Aires and Santiago. Documents that appear to be notes taken by interrogators show they are trying to get the two prisoners to help them locate important targets in Buenos Aires. Notes and a hand-drawn map refer to the "Meeting House of the Junta"—a reference to the

JCR—and to an "ERP Military School" outside Buenos Aires. In a signed "Interrogation Statement," Pastor Coronel asked questions based on intimate knowledge of clandestine MIR activities in Chile. One series of questions involves the telephone number of a person in Santiago who is supposed to act as an emergency contact with "Benjamín," the code name for MIR leader Andrés Pascal. The exchanges are clear evidence that Pastor Coronel was interrogating Fuentes for the benefit of DINA in Chile, and was sending and receiving information in order to advance the questioning. Fuentes is asked—but gives few details—about methods for sending letters back and forth to Chile, and about plans to infiltrate weapons into Chile.

Another set of documents shows the involvement of the Argentine intelligence officer, Major José Osvaldo Riveiro, who will become an important operative in later Condor activities. A handwritten letter dated June 23 is addressed to "Benito"—military intelligence chief Colonel Benito Guanes—and signed "Osvaldo." The two officers clearly have just gotten off the phone—"No sooner did I talk to you than I dedicated myself to fulfilling your requests." The letter is five pages long, and is accompanied by five additional documents for use in the questioning.

The correspondent refers to Fuentes as *"el Nene"*—the kid. Enclosure four is a handwritten, nearly illegible list of fifteen detailed questions and a typed page with a picture attached. The questions appear to concern Fuentes's contacts and activities in Buenos Aires, especially with regard to transfers of messages and money. A photograph of Bolivian JCR member Rubén Sánchez is enclosed with a request that Fuentes be interrogated about his whereabouts and activities.

In the letter, Osvaldo stresses that the interrogation is "very important, because we almost have him located." Osvaldo's main target, it is clear from other documents, was MIR's top leader, Edgardo "Pollo" Enríquez, whose presence in Argentina most likely was learned in the interrogations—Fuentes and Santucho both knew of Enríquez's recent arrival from Europe. The information obtained by torturing Fuentes and Santucho had launched a massive manhunt for JCR leaders that would occupy Chilean, Argentine, and other intelligence services for more than a year. We will return to that account and to "Osvaldo" shortly. First our story shifts back to Colonel Manuel Contreras at DINA headquarters in Santiago.

7

THE CONDOR SYSTEM

By April 1975, intelligence reporting showed that Contreras was the principal obstacle to a reasonable human rights policy within the Junta, but an interagency committee directed the CIA to continue its relationship with Contreras . . . [E]lements within the CIA recommended establishing a paid relationship with Contreras . . .

—H<small>INCHEY</small> R<small>EPORT</small>

We will go to Australia if necessary to get our enemies.

—C<small>OLONEL</small> M<small>ANUEL</small> C<small>ONTRERAS,</small> <small>AS QUOTED BY THE</small> CIA

The terrible but seldom discussed secret of underground revolutionary organizations of this era was that torture, methodically and universally applied as it was by DINA and the other security forces, converted most human beings into sobbing, broken, and submissive puppets under the control of the interrogator masters. Humiliation was total. Manacled on a metal bed frame, naked and spread-eagled, with electric current delivered to their most intimate and sensitive body parts, victims lost all physical control. Sphincters released, muscles cramped in spasms. The entire body quivered and shook in waves of violent seizures. Hangings, dunkings, asphyxiation, beatings, rapes, and mock executions were variations on the basic routine. Some prisoners were run over with trucks. This was real-life horror with sweat and smells and screams, cracking bones and the gushing of every manner of human effluent.

Successful resistance was measured not in silence but in how many hours a person could delay giving the information that would lead the agents to their comrades' safe houses. Militants were trained—"instructed" is a better word, since real training was impossible—to use layers of cover stories and other subterfuges to resist talking for twenty-four hours. After that it was assumed that every prisoner was providing at least some information.

Talking under torture was not necessarily a betrayal, but for the victims of torture the shame of having provided information was one of the most demoralizing scars. Not only did they suffer the guilt of survivors; they knew the information they provided may have led to the death of their revolutionary colleagues and friends.

Each country's apparatus of death had its peculiar characteristics. DINA's methods were selective. Torture was a tool, not primarily a punishment. Such a cruel system had its rationality, but was not totally rational. Captives who had a leadership position or were connected in any way to MIR's military arm—called *La Fuerza Central* (the Central Force)—were condemned to almost certain death and disappearance. Many others died because of the excesses of torture; others for no discernible reason. Perhaps 90 percent of those detained by DINA survived in Chile. It was a system that killed and spared with caprice. In DINA's first year, 1974, the system of torture and secret execution consumed the lives of 421 people. The number of people kidnapped and held by DINA is not known, but is estimated by researchers to be at least 4,000 for that year.

The DINA apparatus was working at full speed, operating out of the walled compound of a former nightclub known as Villa Grimaldi. The process was systematic: agents first detained lists of people thought to have some connection to the Socialist Party and MIR. The prisoners were forced to give up additional names and locations, and those people were picked up. Eventually, the agents penetrated the most secret layers of the underground cells organizing resistance to Pinochet.

The system led to an early and spectacular success. In September 1974, DINA located the house where the leader of MIR, Miguel Enríquez, was living. When the DINA squadron closed in on the house, Enríquez and several lieutenants grabbed their weapons and fought their way out the back to a prepared escape route. But a grenade exploded near his companion, Carmen Castillo, who was six months pregnant, and she was knocked unconscious. Enríquez took her back inside and laid her down behind some heavy furniture, then he tried to reach the escape path again. As he crossed an open patio, DINA agents on the rooftops brought him down with a fusillade of automatic rifle fire. Enríquez was killed; Castillo was captured inside the house, critically wounded, but she survived.

There was grand publicity given to the attack. Enríquez had been a major figure in Chilean politics for a decade and was one of the most famous and divisive people in the country. The gun battle was used as proof of the continuing "terrorist threat" Chile still faced a year after the coup. But in fact, there had been not a single armed confrontation initiated by MIR or any other opposition group since the coup. DINA had also penetrated and destroyed the leadership structure of the underground Socialist Party. Chile was quiet. CIA and DIA reporting to Washington reported on DINA's victories in dispatches that displayed a sense of awe at the effectiveness of its operations.

Contreras, however, was not ready to declare victory. Lack of extremist violence inside Chile was only a sign that the enemy had gone deeper underground and was organizing outside Chile's borders. Contreras continued to expand DINA to face a permanent, international threat. He first needed to position DINA within the armed forces as an integral and permanent institution apart and superior to the traditional intelligence apparatus. Whereas before each branch of the armed forces had its own intelligence branch and training facilities, Contreras now staked DINA's claim to monopoly control of all aspects of intelligence, both military and civilian. He created the National Intelligence School as an advance course for officers and put his DINA operations chief, Colonel Pedro Espinoza, in charge. With its direct connection to DINA operations, the school did not impart abstract instruction. Patterned on the National Information School that was the powerful adjunct to Brazil's SNI intelligence service, Contreras's new school put officers directly in contact with repressive operations and used them as a research staff for DINA's growing empire.

It was time again to consult with Washington. As was the case when DINA was a start-up, the new Contreras initiative coincided with a new round of meetings with the CIA. In early January 1975, Contreras flew to Washington with two key officers, Operations Chief Espinoza and Captain Cristoph Willeke, both of whom had had roles in the Prats assassination the previous September. They all took their wives, according to a description Espinoza gave of the trip in testimony to a Chilean investigating judge. The trip included participation in a meeting with other Latin American intelligence schools. Espinoza said the group left Washington January 12.

The CIA, in many rounds of declassification and in specific Freedom of Information Act requests from the author, has never acknowledged a meeting with Contreras and his men in January 1975. One document from the CIA, however, provides evidence that such a meeting took place. It appears to be talking points for a meeting with General Vernon Walters, the deputy director of central intelligence (DDCI) and the same official who, according to Contreras, organized the CIA training for DINA the year before. Dated January 5, the document is a memorandum from the CIA's Latin America operations chief about "possible topic of conversation with [Contreras]." Contreras's name is mentioned in unexpurgated text only once, but I have concluded based on context that his name is blanked out in several other mentions, in which he appears to be the source of the information on the current security picture in Chile. I have written in his name in brackets where I think it should appear in the redacted text:

> Colonel Contreras was the only senior official who had voiced strong objections to any relaxation in present tough security practices. . . . Having the above facts in mind, the DDCI may want to exercise some persuasive influence on [Contreras] in favor of liberalizing practices involving human rights that would not have a serious effect on Junta control of subversive elements. It should be noted that [Contreras] recently reported [to the CIA station chief] that the MIR, extreme left elements of the Socialist Party, and smaller left extremist groups have been crushed during the Government's counter terrorist campaign. The Chilean Government will now focus on the Communist Party of Chile. [Contreras said] the security situation in Chile is much less serious than it was.

The Hinchey Report, perhaps based on the same CIA reporting, portrayed the CIA's two-headed relationship with Contreras more bluntly: "By April 1975, intelligence reporting showed that Contreras was the principal obstacle to a reasonable human rights policy within the Junta, but an interagency committee directed the CIA to continue its relationship with Contreras." Now, the CIA went a giant step further: "In May and June 1975, elements within the CIA recommended establishing a paid relationship with Contreras to obtain intelligence based on his unique position and access to Pinochet." The Hinchey Report says the request was at first overruled because of DINA's notoriety for human rights abuses. "However, given miscommunication in the timing of this exchange, a one-time payment was given to Contreras." The CIA did not reveal the amount of the payment. But it is probably no coincidence that a deposit for $6,000 was made into Contreras's account in Riggs Bank in Washington in June 1975, according to subpoenaed Riggs Bank records.

It is a strange world we have entered. The CIA's words are laden with concern for human rights; yet CIA interactions with Contreras go in the opposite direction. One wonders at the still secret story that must be behind that single euphemism "miscommunication."

In July and August, around the time Contreras was put on the CIA payroll, Contreras flew to Washington twice to meet with Walters. We have much more information about these trips and the direct relevance of the second trip, in late August, to the organization of Operation Condor. The CIA and Walters have acknowledged that the trip took place—it is the CIA's sole admission of a meeting with Contreras. It was a visit hard to conceal, since Contreras also had meetings, arranged by the State Department, with several congressmen, including Representative Donald Fraser and Senator Frank Church, both tough critics of Chile, in an attempt to persuade them to change their position on Chile.

The trip, according to Contreras's own account, grew out of an official request by Pinochet to the U.S. ambassador that senior officials receive Contreras in Washington so that he could convey Chile's "position on the human rights issue to Secretary Kissinger." The context was that Chile had barred a delegation of the United Nations Human Rights Commission from entering Chile, and there was going to be an effort to expel Chile at the upcoming U.N. General Assembly in September. That the notorious head of Chile's secret police would serve as Pinochet's spokesman on human rights seemed like an incongruous idea, even to the CIA. A CIA cable warned that the visit would be "counterproductive" if it were to leak that Contreras was in Washington.

But at CIA headquarters, the welcome was effusive. On August 25, Walters hosted a formal luncheon at CIA headquarters for Contreras, then met privately for forty-five minutes with Contreras. A declassified memo on the conversations says only that Walters "took the opportunity to express concern over the human rights situation in Chile . . ."

Contreras later made an extraordinary charge: that Walters in that meeting suggested he pay off U.S. congressmen. "Vernon Walters proposed that we take on a lobby of North American senators, to get them to stop harassing

Chile in the international arena," he told a Chilean newspaper reporter. He said Walters suggested he contact five unnamed senators from both parties, "who would be paid $2 million a year so that they will act in favor of Chile." Contreras said he took the idea back to Chile, but it was never implemented.

Contreras provided additional details about the trip to Washington in answer to questions from the author. He said that he was bringing "information" to Washington to back up his message "that we are in a war against terrorism and subversion, and [to disprove] what they have been saying that in Chile we are doing a little less than killing all the people." Walters was Contreras's go-between with Kissinger, according to Contreras: "I met with Mr. Vernon Walters. He met with Mr. Kissinger about the information I was bringing, [and] about the kind of support we needed to avoid this problem. Kissinger supported us. He supported us in avoiding that Chile would be expelled from the United Nations."*

What was the information Contreras brought that was so important it was taken to the number two man in the CIA and was so persuasive it was passed on to Henry Kissinger? There is nothing in the declassified record. It was *not* in all likelihood a recounting of leftist resistance inside Chile, since the CIA's own intelligence—based on information provided by Contreras—was portraying that threat as "much less serious."

Other evidence suggests that Contreras was in Washington to talk about ways to confront the new and powerful international threat presented by the

---

* Walters conveyed a similar message a few weeks earlier to the White House. In a memo to President Ford's national security aide, General Brent Scowcroft, July 25, 1975 (Chile Project), Walters is the go-between to the White House for another message from Pinochet. He writes:

What Pinochet wanted basically was:

1. Understanding for the Chilean decision not to receive the United Nations Human Rights Commission which they regarded as highly prejudiced.
2. Assurance of U.S. support against any effort in the United Nations to expel Chile and, if necessary, a veto.
3. Chileans know they cannot get direct aid because of Congressional opposition. Wonder if there is any way they could get it indirectly via Spain, Taiwan, Brazil or the Republic of Korea.

(signed) Vernon A. Walters, Lieutenant General, USA, Deputy Director.

JCR. We know about the intelligence bonanza DINA and the other security forces had recently discovered with the capture of JCR couriers Fuentes and Santucho. The intelligence being developed in weeks and months of interrogation of the two men provided a picture of the JCR strategy as a continent-wide guerrilla threat.

It makes sense, if we take CIA documents at their word, that Contreras would find a warm reception for his strategy to defeat this international threat. Several documents cited previously emphasize that it was in the international area that CIA was willing to be most helpful to DINA.

There is other direct evidence that Contreras had a plan in his briefcase to defeat this new international threat. We know this because Contreras went directly from Washington to Caracas, Venezuela. There, in conversations, with Venezuelan intelligence officials, Contreras laid out the detailed plans that would eventually have the name Condor.

Contreras and another DINA officer arrived in Caracas on August 27, just two days after his lunch with Walters. According to Contreras, it was Vernon Walters who suggested he go to Caracas. Three other DINA officials had flown in separately from Santiago—a level of staffing that indicates it was not to be a casual meeting. Rafael Rivas Vásquez, head of the intelligence service DISIP, met Contreras at the airport, then took him to dinner with DISIP's general commissioner, Orlando García.

"Then, on the following day, we had a whole session of talks about the possibility of service-to-service exchange," Rivas Vásquez later testified. He said Contreras bragged that he had great power and resources at his disposal and that "he was building up this grandiose scheme of a very big and powerful service that could have information, worldwide information."

In an interview, DISIP commissioner García said Contreras presented a plan for an organization that would allow the participating countries to track down leftist enemies in each other's countries. "He came to ask for our collaboration, to unite our service in collaboration [with DINA]. . . . Contreras wanted us to capture Chilean exiles [in Venezuela] and turn them over to Chile with no legalities. He wanted us to just put them on a plane and Chile would pay the fare."

"He said, 'we have to eliminate the enemies,' " García remembered. "I knew that to eliminate meant only one thing—we knew the people he captured would be tortured and killed."

Contreras was not talking about abstract cooperation. He had concrete items to offer Venezuela, and specific requests.

Venezuela's role was key, since many of Chile's most prominent exile leaders had settled in Caracas. Contreras made a formal request for DISIP to provide him with "information about the activities of all the Chilean exiles living at that time in Venezuela," including flight information about their travels. Contreras had important intelligence to provide in exchange, information about the JCR he had obtained from the interrogations of Fuentes and Santucho. The most important item was a warning that the JCR was planning to move its headquarters from Buenos Aires to Caracas.

Contreras described some of the ways the new international security organization would operate. "Contreras explained that DINA was being expanded as an intelligence service, that they would have foreign agents in the embassies abroad; that they . . . were already training all the third secretaries in the Chilean embassies—putting them through a basic intelligence course, so they could serve as case officers abroad," Rivas Vásquez testified. If Venezuela signed up, DINA would assign a DINA liaison officer to its embassy in Caracas. Contreras gave DISIP a set of "codes and ciphers" to be used in telex communications for the new system. "He talked about computers, which got our attention since we were still using a card filing system," García said. Contreras said his meetings in Venezuela were just one stop on his itinerary to "sell" the plan to the intelligence services of other countries. They were invited, all expenses paid, to a meeting in Santiago to plan the new system.

President Carlos Andrés Pérez vetoed any participation in the plan. Pérez, one of the few democratically elected heads of state at the time in the continent, was a fervent anti-Communist but an equally adamant opponent of Pinochet's destruction of Chilean democracy.

Back in Chile, Contreras moved ahead with the plan to create an international security organization. He needed money, and he needed Pinochet's approval. A memorandum purportedly from Contreras to Pinochet, which Chilean opposition leaders claimed was leaked to them in 1977, contains a request for $600,000 in special funding for the new operation. Although the document's origin inside DINA has never been established, its signature and format match other DINA documents and the content of the letter coincides with what else is known. The key fact, Contreras's request for money, was corroborated by a firsthand source.

Dated September 16, 1975, about two weeks after Contreras's return from Washington and Caracas, it reads in part:

> Pursuant to what was agreed with Your Excellency, I detail the reasons I consider it indispensable to request an addition of 600,000 dollars for the budget of this Directorate in the current year.
>
> 1. Increase of DINA personnel attached to Chile's diplomatic missions. A total of ten people: 2 in Peru, 2 in Brazil, 2 in Argentina, 1 in Venezuela, 1 in Costa Rica, 1 in Belgium and 1 in Italy.
>
> 2. Additional expenses for the neutralization of the principal adversaries abroad of the Junta Government, in particular in Mexico, Argentina, Costa Rica, USA, France and Italy.

Around the same time as the letter's date, one of Pinochet's top aides came into a meeting with Pinochet in which the subject of money and international operations was being discussed. The aide, who described the meeting on the condition his name not be revealed, said the participants included Air Force Colonel Mario Jahn, the deputy director of DINA, who was briefing Pinochet on DINA's international expansion.

Jahn was the man Contreras had put in charge of the project, the source said. "He was Conteras's internationalization man *(hombre de la internacional-ización),*" the source said. "He was having a meeting in one of the presidential dining rooms. He was saying, 'This is the moment to move, to advance and bring the struggle to the world level.' He was asking for money. He said the Americans were helping through Brazil."

Pinochet said little, but seemed to be giving the floor to Colonel Jahn so that he could convince the source, a high-ranking civilian, of the need for the international project. The source, an avid Pinochet supporter who at one time conducted a daily morning briefing with the president, was wary of the DINA plans and tried to learn more. He said he was told by others that CIA training was provided through Brazil, and that Brazil was the "pipeline" through which DINA operatives learned interrogation and torture techniques. (Asked about the Contreras-Pinochet memo, he said he had never seen it.)

The source said DINA's international expansion—which he later knew as Operation Condor—was an important step in the struggle for power going on around Pinochet at the time. Many of Pinochet's close advisers—both civilians and military—were recommending that Pinochet lift the state of siege and begin the process of reconstructing the political system as an anti-Communist "protected democracy." Contreras opposed this, even though internal resistance had been defeated. Contreras used the argument of the international threat to convince Pinochet to continue the expansion of Contreras's own power.

"Those of us closest to Pinochet considered Contreras a danger to Pinochet. His influence was harmful to the cause we supported, which was the reconstruction of the country," the source said. On the other side were hardline military and powerful groups of extreme rightist civilians who opposed any relaxation of the airtight security in the country. Next to Pinochet, they considered Contreras their leader and expected him to succeed Pinochet when the time came.

The source, who still has great affection for Pinochet but considers him a failed and somewhat tragic figure, said he concluded that Contreras compromised Pinochet in the international assassinations as a way to consolidate his leverage with the president. Indeed, it was around this time that Contreras displaced Pinochet's daily briefer and was able to position himself as the official Pinochet met with first each day, in the half-hour early morning ride from Pinochet's residence to the presidential headquarters.

As Contreras was laying the groundwork with Pinochet for the ambitious new organization, he was benefiting from the success of the first multicountry collaboration.

On September 23, at DINA's main operational center, Villa Grimaldi, three officers arrived in high spirits from Paraguay. They brought with them a very important prisoner, JCR courier Jorge Fuentes.

"No problems," reported Captain Miguel Krasnoff. "We gave him the pills and put him to sleep. *Vino tranquilito*—He came along as tranquil as could be." Krasnoff also had brought a present for a young DINA secretary, Luz Arce. A former Socialist who became a DINA collaborator after being broken by torture, she witnessed Fuentes's delivery. Now living in Mexico, she has become an important source to human rights investigators. She described Fuentes arrival in an interview.

Fuentes was barely alive when he arrived at Villa Grimaldi, according to Arce and a dozen surviving prisoners who saw him there. His body was infested with scabies, a contagious skin parasite associated with poor sanitary conditions. He was starving. "Villa Grimaldi was a five-star hotel compared to Paraguay," Arce said. The prisoner was cleaned up and given medication, but he was housed in a small, windowless wooden structure in the outside patio, probably to avoid contagion. The prisoners referred to it as "Trosko's dog house." For the first few days Fuentes was there, other prisoners heard him crying out from inside the box, saying his name was Jorge Fuentes and he had been detained in Paraguay and brought to Chile.

The interrogations and torture that had begun in Paraguay continued in Chile. Fuentes still had much to contribute to the security forces' knowledge of the JCR and MIR. He remained in Villa Grimaldi until January, then disappeared.

Two days after Fuentes arrived, Colonel Contreras wrote to thank his colleagues in Paraguay. Addressing his Paraguayan counterpart, Police Investigations chief Pastor Coronel, Contreras conveyed "the most sincere thanks for the cooperation given us in the mission my personnel had to carry out in the sister republic of Paraguay, and I am sure that this mutual cooperation will continue and increase in the accomplishment of the common objectives of both services."

Contreras's promise of mutual cooperation was not empty. The Fuentes and Santucho arrests had provided a unique opportunity to coordinate interrogations among Paraguay, Argentina, and Chile. The other key piece was Paraguay's assent to transferring Fuentes physically to Chile. Information exchange and operational cooperation were the two elements of this new level of collaboration among the security forces. What Contreras had in mind was to institutionalize this model in a formal organization.

In the first days of November, Contreras took the next step. DINA deputy director, Colonel Mario Jahn—the man Contreras had put in charge of the project—arrived in Asunción, Paraguay. He carried a formal invitation from Contreras, addressed to the chief of Paraguay police, General Francisco Britez, to attend a "strictly secret meeting," in Santiago from November 25 to December 1. DINA would pay all expenses. Britez's memo on Jahn's visit, Contreras's letter, and an accompanying ten-page agenda for the "First Working

Meeting on National Intelligence" were found in the Paraguay Archive, providing the first direct evidence in documents generated by the security forces themselves of the existence and purposes of Condor. Colonel Jahn continued on what was to be an intense five-day trip, delivering the secret invitations to the other future Condor countries: Argentina, Bolivia, Uruguay, and Brazil.

Joint operations that had begun with the Fuentes and Santucho capture were intensifying. In the previous chapter we met the Argentine intelligence agent "Osvaldo," who participated in the interrogation of Fuentes and Santucho while they were in Paraguay. We have his handwritten letter to the Paraguayan military intelligence chief suggesting questions. He became the Argentine point man in a joint Chilean-Argentine operation in the coming months to find and eliminate the remaining JCR leaders in Argentina.

Osvaldo's real identity was Lieutenant Colonel José Osvaldo Riveiro, assigned to Intelligence Battalion 601, the main operational unit of the Army Intelligence Service (SIE). For his clandestine work he used the pseudonynm Jorge Osvaldo Rawson.

For purposes of our investigation, Osvaldo's operation against the JCR is unique. It is the only case where we possess the actual correspondence of a DINA agent involved, giving us an almost day-by-day account of the intelligence reports and detentions that resulted. The documents that tell this story are those confiscated from one of Chile's principal DINA operatives in Buenos Aires, Enrique Arancibia Clavel, whom we also encountered previously, in his role in the Prats assassination. When we left Arancibia in the previous chapter, he was setting up shop after the assassination as a clandestine DINA operative in Buenos Aires, spying on Chilean exiles and sending regular written reports back to DINA headquarters in Santiago.

Arancibia begins to write glowing reports about his new source. "The best information that has been obtained on [the JCR] guerrilla organization was provided . . . by the number 2 chief of SIE [Army intelligence service—*Servicio de Inteligencia del Ejército*], Lt. Col. Jorge Osvaldo Rawson."

Suddenly Arancibia's reports are filled with details about JCR meetings in Switzerland and France, and the names of JCR intermediaries in Paris, with addresses.

Rawson had already been traveling frequently between Asunción, Santiago, and Buenos Aires in trips involving the interrogation of Fuentes and Santucho. His relationship with DINA intensified, and DINA began to foot the bill for his travel. When Rawson learned that "Trosko" Fuentes has been transported to Chile, he pestered Arancibia to share DINA's interrogation reports, especially any details about JCR activity in Argentina. DINA in Santiago instructed Arancibia that he was to be responsible for all contacts with Rawson, in effect making him Rawson's case officer for intelligence and operational exchanges. Rawson was working in the most clandestine part of Army Intelligence, and all contacts were to be clandestine and compartmentalized. DINA's officers stationed in the Chilean embassy were instructed to have no contact with Rawson.

One of the reasons for this kind of spy versus spy tradecraft was Argentina's bizarre political situation. Military officers like Rawson were, in effect, running clandestine operations inside their own institutions. The shaky but constitutional government of Perón's widow, Isabelita Perón, had turned over the task of repressing the leftist revolutionaries to the brutal but ineffective federal police and paramilitary death squads called the Triple A. The army was fighting the antiguerrilla war in Tucumán, but its intelligence arm was not supposed to have an operational role in the rest of the country. Gangs of thugs paid by the government's Social Security agency roamed the city in government cars—the modest Ford Falcon became their feared trademark. Leftist intellectuals, church activists, and dissident labor leaders were put on death lists, and scores were kidnapped and killed. The government campaign inspired terror, but had little impact on the well-organized underground groups such as the ERP and Montoneros.

The country in late 1975 had the worst of all possible scenarios: a serious guerrilla campaign in the mountains of Tucumán Province, isolated but unchecked armed actions by ERP and Montoneros all over the country, and—on the part of the Peronist government—an ineffective but bloody death squad campaign targeting public figures identified with the left. Some newspapers were openly calling on the military to take over and bring order.

A military coup was still half a year in the future, but in early October—following a Montonero attack on an army installation in Formosa Province—the government capitulated to military demands that the army take over the fight against the subversives in the entire country. Decree 2770 gave the army virtually unlimited power, and its draconian language was seen in retrospect as an invitation to the mass murder that was to ensue. The decree empowered the armed forces "to execute any military and security operations that might be necessary for the purpose of anihilating the action of subversive elements in all national territory."

In case there was any doubt about the new mandate, Armed Forces Chief General Jorge Videla made it even clearer in a statement at a meeting of fellow Latin American military leaders several weeks later in Montevideo: "If needed, in Argentina as many people will have to die as are necessary to achieve peace in the country."

In the realm of intelligence, the new authority was of monumental importance. It meant that all intelligence operations directed against political and guerrilla targets were now centralized in the army and its security forces were able to operate all over the country. The Army Intelligence Service (SIE), given the cover name Intelligence Battalion 601, became the most powerful security and intelligence apparatus, to which all other security units were subordinate. Intelligence Battalion 601—where Rawson served—became the "Center of Reunion" coordinating all other intelligence units. This included the federal police and SIDE, the government's State Information Service, which had had a role in the Prats murder. SIDE had been originally designed to be a kind of central intelligence agency under the control of the civilian government, but it was widely disparaged as subject to political influence and was even thought to be infiltrated by the left.

Now, for the first time, the Argentine military had the operational power, similar to that enjoyed by DINA in Chile, to launch a concerted drive against the underground left. And for the first time, real operational coordination across borders was coming into place.

The next major blow against the JCR was struck in Chile. On October 15, just after midnight, a DINA squadron attacked a small vegetable farm near the village of Malloco, a few miles west of Santiago. A captured suspect had led them to the headquarters of Andrés Pascal, where he was gathered with MIR's most important underground leaders. There was a fierce gun battle. MIR military chief Dagoberto Pérez was killed while holding off the attackers with automatic rifle fire and grenades at the main entrance. Pascal and five other leaders retreated on foot through fields at the back. To cover their escape, they set on fire an outbuilding where weapons were stored, and there was an enormous explosion.

The escaping Miristas, one of whom was seriously wounded, commandeered a car and made their way to Santiago, but their network of safe houses
was so compromised, they dared not use it. Instead, they went to the house of a
Catholic priest, who agreed to hide them and arrange medical treatment. At
one point, Pascal—an AK-47 assault rifle in his backpack—his companion,
Mary Anne Beausire, and an American priest rode a motorcycle to a hiding
place in a Trappist monastery in the Santiago foothills. A few days later Pascal
and Beausire were smuggled into the Costa Rican embassy, where they were
granted asylum.

A personal footnote: When photos of Andrés Pascal and his companion
Beausire appeared in newspapers, I understood more about a terrifying event
that had happened to me several months before. In April 1975, two carloads of
DINA agents came to my house east of Santiago, in the village of Lo
Barnechea. Carolina Kenrick—who became my wife a year later—and I lived
there with another couple. At first the agents pretended to be police investigating a car accident in which a little boy had been hit. Quickly it became clear we
were being detained, and agents with automatic rifles began searching the
house. They showed us pictures of two men and two women—one of whom
bore a strong resemblance to Emma, the other woman in the house. I didn't
recognize the picture, but six months later—after the Malloco raid—I saw the
same picture published in the newspaper. It was Mary Anne Beausire, the fugi-
tive companion of Pascal.

First the agents took Emma away in a car, then they loaded me, the other
man, and Carolina into a pickup truck with a camper cover in the back. They
taped our eyelids shut with Scotch tape, but I could see a little by looking
downward. I tried to keep track of where we were going. I knew we had descended toward Santiago, then climbed again toward the mountains on another road. The truck stopped, and someone banged on a metal door. We
drove inside a large compound—I kept track of every detail I could see beneath
the tape—the cobblestone driveway, a shallow drainage ditch, the steps up to a
building with a veranda and columns. Later, I was able to confirm I was in
DINA's most notorious detention camp, Villa Grimaldi.

It was midafternoon on a Sunday, and we had been in custody almost all day.
Carolina and I were interrogated separately—she was asked whether I was a

"good American" who supported the anti-Communist side in the Vietnam War, which had just ended in victory for the North Vietnamese Communist side. I was asked only perfunctory questions about why I was in Chile. By that time the agents had confirmed that none of us were the people they were seeking. Emma, who looked like Mary Anne Beausire, actually had an identification card as an employee of the government's economic planning commission. "You have to understand why we have to do these things," the officer in charge of my questioning said. "There are Marxist terrorists all over the country, and we are trying to catch them to protect people like you Americans." The agents put us all back in the truck, eyes still taped, and dumped us near our home. In the coming days, they returned several times to drive by the house and ask trivial questions in a feigned joking manner.

We were lucky. Perhaps my U.S. passport helped. It was the fourth time I had been detained since the coup. I reported the incident to the American Consulate. The vice consul who received me, John Hall, listened noncommittally. He told me he could file a protest if I wanted, but that I had to understand that it would anger the government and they would probably expel me. I later learned, doing research for my book on the Letelier assassination, that John Hall was actually an undercover officer for the CIA.

The Malloco raid was a near-mortal wound to MIR's operations inside Chile. For the second time, their top leadership had been neutralized. Now they had lost a large part of their arsenal, and their carefully constructed underground operations network was in disarray. Documents and correspondence captured at the Malloco farm allowed DINA to complete its accumulating store of knowledge about MIR and its international JCR connections. One letter, for example, made reference to a $1 million grant to MIR from the JCR war chest. Another document contained details of the planned MIR-JCR counteroffensive, which DINA labeled—perhaps with some irony—Operation Boomerang. A map of the Southern Cone, said to have been captured in the Malloco raid, showed guerrilla offensives branching out from Argentina into Bolivia, Chile, Paraguay, and Uruguay. DINA propaganda greatly exaggerated the threat, proclaiming that assassination plans were afoot against Pinochet, and that 1,200 guerrilla troops had invaded from the south. Those claims were without basis. But the offensives described in the captured map coincide almost exactly with those actually being planned by the JCR member organizations. The Malloco raid also revealed the increasing cooperation between DINA and Argentine security forces. A DINA communiqué said the plan had been uncovered and dismantled "in a preventive operation coordinated with authorities of Argentine intelligence."

Now the action moved again to Argentina. Two weeks after the Malloco raid, 601 Battalion operative Osvaldo Rawson, working closely with Arancibia, was closing in on MIR's apparatus in Buenos Aires. Arancibia reported back to Chile that roundups of Chileans had started. He asked DINA to send photos of MIR's leader, Edgardo "Pollo" Enríquez, to help Rawson in his search.

Edgardo Enríquez was in fact in Buenos Aires. The Malloco disaster had left him as MIR's highest ranking officer, and as a result he was accelerating his plans to return to Chile to rebuild the guerrilla force. One of his lieutenants was a Chilean with a French passport, Jean Yves Claudet Fernández, a thirty-six-year-old chemical engineer, who acted as an international courier for MIR. A few days after the Malloco raid in Chile, Enríquez dispatched him to Paris with coded messages about MIR's dire security situation in Chile. In Paris, Claudet met with MIR/JCR representative, René "Gato" Valenzuela.

"I sent Claudet back with letters and money. He was in a hurry to get back to Buenos Aires, even though I told him he could wait," Valenzuela said in an interview.

Claudet arrived back in Buenos Aires early on the morning of October 31. He checked into the Liberty Hotel, at Corrientes and Florida, whose owner Benjamin Taub ran a black market money exchange out of the hotel and had previously handled large amounts of cash from kidnappings for the JCR.* Claudet's planned meeting with Enríquez never happened. He had walked into a trap set by Osvaldo Rawson. He signed the register, took his bags with the money and documents to his room, and the next day disappeared without a trace.

Rawson informed Arancibia about his success, which Arancibia immediately reported to his DINA superiors:

---

* The owner of the Hotel Liberty, Benjamin Taub, had exchanged millions of dollars for ERP, including most of the $14.2 million ransom for Exxon executive Victor Samuelson in early 1974, as described in Chapters 4 and 9.

> I had a meeting with Rawson, who told me the following:
>
> In the latest procedure a courier of the JCR was captured, a Frenchman apparently, last name Claudet. Among his belongings they found 97 microfilms, with the latest instructions [of the JCR] from Paris. . . . After the interrogation of the aforementioned Claudet, they could establish only that he was a courier of the JCR. They were only able to get photographs.
>
> Claudet no longer exists.

But Enríquez, who at one point had shared an apartment with Claudet, escaped the dragnet. Claudet apparently was able to resist under torture, or simply did not have the information to lead Rawson to Enríquez. There was other bad news for DINA. There had been a serious security breach. The captured documents, Arancibia reported, revealed that JCR headquarters in Paris "was informed about [Fuentes's] transfer from Paraguay to Santiago, and even mentioned the agency or a member of the same who was the informant." The search for Enríquez continued intensely for weeks, according to Arancibia's reports, but the MIR leader had given them the slip.

It was the third week of November. The date of DINA's major event, the "First Inter American Working Meeting on National Intelligence," was approaching. The invitations had gone out in October. DINA was footing the bill for the region's top intelligence representatives to converge on Santiago to formalize the kind of joint operations that had been carried out since May with Paraguayan and Argentine agencies. Arancibia lobbied for Rawson to attend, but he wasn't invited. Argentina's delegation would be led by the State Information Service, SIDE, who confirmed they would attend what was now being described as "the cocktail party on the 26th."

The officers who gathered in Santiago on November 26 were several ranks above street-level operational agents like Rawson and Arancibia. These were the superiors of the superiors of people like them. They were the men who developed the strategy and gave the orders. Contreras, based on what we know about his approaches to Venezuela and Paraguay, conceived of the meeting as bringing together the command officers or their deputies for the top military intelligence organizations of each country. Police commanders with intelligence and antiterrorism responsibility were also included in each country's contingent, which numbered at least three official representatives, plus lower ranking staff. In the underground world of competition and mutual suspicion, the Santiago meeting was a unique and unprecedented event, a summit of historic importance.

Before going on, I want to put on the record the names of the men who are known to have participated in the meeting that created Operation Condor or were otherwise associated with its subsequent operations.

The head of Argentina's delegation was a navy captain,* Jorge Demetrio Casas, deputy chief and head of international operations for SIDE. Casas later became head of naval intelligence on his promotion to rear admiral in 1977. He was accused of human rights crimes and was pardoned in the blanket amnesty of 1986.

For Paraguay, the delegation of police and military officers was led by Colonel Benito Guanes Serrano, head of G-2, the intelligence department of the General Staff of the Armed Forces. Police Chief Francisco Britez declined the invitation delivered by Colonel Jahn in early October.

Uruguay had created a combined intelligence command of all branches of the armed forces, called Defense Intelligence Service (SID—*Servicio de Inteligencia de Defensa*). Two subdirectors, representing the army and the air force, were sent to Santiago. Army Colonel José Fons was the head of the delegation. Fons was later refused entry to the United States because of a CIA report linking him to a death threat against Congressman Ed Koch the following year. (See Chapter 13.)

Bolivian President Hugo Banzer, perhaps reflecting his skepticism about the enterprise, sent the lowest ranking officer, Major Carlos Mena Burgos, of SIE (*Servicio de Inteligencia del Estado*). Mena was named in a report by European human rights investigators as a torturer.

Brazil, according to U.S. intelligence reports and the source who was present, sent an observer delegation, but no names could be learned. What is known is that the original recipient of the Condor invitation—according to Colonel Mario Jahn—was SNI director, General Joao Batista Figueiredo, who later became president.

Manuel Contreras, of Chile's DINA, hosted the meeting in the grand hall of the War Academy, in western Santiago, where two years before he had created

---

* A Navy captain is equivalent in rank to an Army colonel.

Chile's new intelligence force and trained its elite group of officers. We know which of those officers were assigned tasks in Contreras's international venture: Air Force Colonel Mario Jahn, in charge of the internationalization project as a whole; Lieutenant Colonel Pedro Espinoza, in charge of liaison with Brazilian intelligence and later chief of operations; Major Raul Eduardo Iturriaga Neumann, chief of DINA's Exterior Department (and the officer carrying out the day-to-day correspondence with Arancibia in Buenos Aires); and finally Captain Cristoph Willeke, a young officer who had accompanied Contreras and Espinoza to Washington and would take over the Exterior Department in 1976.

It was an upbeat meeting. The headlines were the recent attacks and intelligence gains against the JCR. Each country, starting with Chile, was allotted one and a half hours for a report about "their intelligence organization, the current situation of subversion and how it is being combated." Available documents allow us to reconstruct the kind of intelligence information the various agencies were sharing with one another around the time of the Condor meeting. These documents, including a CIA report dated November 26, the first day of the meeting, provide a contemporary picture of how the intelligence agencies perceived their enemies as they launched Operation Condor to combat them internationally.

The documents confirm that the security forces had ample and elaborate information on the JCR military strategy—gathered from sources we now are familiar with: the Fuentes and Santucho interrogations, the ninety-seven microfilms found on the courier Claudet, and DINA's raid on MIR headquarters in Malloco. A four-page secret cable from the embassy in Santiago summarized U.S. intelligence: "In July 1975, the JCR drew up a plan for a major guerrilla operation targeted against Argentina, Chile and Bolivia, with the MIR portion to be initiated in November-December 1975 with the assassination of four senior government personalities, whose identities were given in code."

Argentina's knowledge about the JCR is revealed in a ten-page report dated October 28, 1975, a month before the Condor meeting. The Argentine report has a detailed and accurate account of one of the most secret founding meetings of the JCR, in Santiago in early November 1972, including direct quotation from MIR's Miguel Enríquez and a list of decisions taken. The JCR's strategic vision of Marxist revolutionary war is becoming "increasingly important" among other leftist groups in Latin America, the report says, and it lists eleven other countries, including the United States, whose militant organizations "have sought contact with this continental revolutionary organization."

A long report found in the Paraguay Archive, from late 1975, devotes eight pages to a description of the JCR's recent activity, especially its network in Europe. Both the Argentine and the Paraguayan reports lump together the guerrilla organizations allied in the JCR with solidarity and human rights organizations in Europe and elsewhere. It portrays the "defense of human rights" by two organizations, the Russell Tribunal operating out of Belgium, and the International Council of Jurists in Paris, as providing a front for the JCR.

The intelligence reports, without exception, make little attempt to distinguish between the armed guerrilla forces of the JCR and their allies in political, solidarity, and even church-related organizations. Contreras set the tone in the Condor Agenda:

> Subversion has developed a leadership structure that is intercontinental, continental, regional and subregional. As examples we can list the Tricontinental Conference of Havana, the Revolutionary Coordinating Junta for South America, etc., all of which are given a pleasing face by all kinds of solidarity committees, congresses, Tribunals, Meetings, Festivals and conferences, etc.

Even as the JCR's continent-wide subversion was portrayed as the principal threat, the intelligence documents also report the devasting recent defeats suffered by the leftist organizations. A CIA document, sent to Washington the day the Condor meeting opened, takes stock of MIR after the Malloco raid:

> . . . [T]he MIR estimates about 10 to 15 percent of its total hard-core militancy is left intact in Chile. The MIR calculates that about 900 militants of all levels have been either killed, arrested or have disappeared.
>
> [redacted] reported . . . what remains of the party leadership hopes to begin restructuring the organization in Argentina, with the help of the Revolutionary Coordinating Junta (JCR). . . .
>
> [redacted] opined that the MIR has been effectively eliminated within Chile. They maintain that despite the MIR's brave front and talk of retreating to reorganize and form a united national resistance command (CNR) in Chile, the fact is that the MIR no longer has a leadership group with sufficient credentials to maintain and attract the necessary support for continued activity.

The Uruguayans also were shifting their focus to international enemies. A U.S. embassy cable quoted an intelligence communiqué on the success of the new joint forces commando in smashing two Tupamaro infiltration efforts, in May 1974 and June 1975. It continued: "This germ of the seditious organization . . . is a warning about the tireless activity of the Marxist-Leninist conspiracy which uses all types of international organizations with pretensions to seriousness in order to trick people who are not well informed. These international organizations have carefully chosen titles like tribunals, Amnesty, commissions, etc . . ."

This was the shared information base out of which arose Operation Condor. The bottom line was that domestically the leftist organizations had been decimated in every country except Argentina, where the military had only recently launched a full country-wide offensive. The security agencies' main concern now was outside their own borders, and they were especially obsessed with the JCR, which was functioning underground in Argentina and openly in Europe. Defeating this new, internationally organized threat was a complex, multinational task. It involved tracking underground and public organizations, Marxist extremists along with pro-democracy moderates, political groups, church groups, and human rights groups. All of this had to be confronted on three continents, in Latin America, Europe, and the United States—even elsewhere if needed.

It was a challenge Colonel Contreras relished. His remedy was drastic, and he described it bluntly. We have two statements. To a CIA counterpart, he said: "We will go to Australia if necessary to get our enemies." The second was his speech to the gathered security chiefs, paraphrased by the Uruguayan representative:

> Chile proposed operations to eliminate enemies all over the world, . . . to eliminate people who were causing harm to our countries, people like Letelier.

What role did General Pinochet play in this historic meeting? At a minimum, it is likely that he was present to greet the delegates in the formal opening session. Colonel Jahn said the meeting was a priority at the highest level of the military junta and has raised the possibility of a more hands-on role by

Pinochet. "I don't remember who presided over the conference . . . ," Jahn said in still-secret testimony to Judge Juan Guzman in October 2003. "It is possible that it was presided over by General Pinochet or by one of the members of the junta because of the importance they wanted to give to this meeting." Jahn had been intimately involved in the organizational phase of the conference and of Operation Condor, and he probably knows more details than his vague answer reveals. It was he who met in September with Pinochet to discuss an increased budget for DINA's international activities, and he then had personally delivered Chile's invitation to each of the intelligence chiefs to attend the meeting.

The first day of the meeting ended with a gala dinner hosted by Contreras. The party was held at a DINA installation in the small town of Melipilla, a few miles west of the city—not far from the site of the recent battle between DINA and MIR. Whiskey was flowing freely. A female DINA officer had been assigned to bring a group of attractive young Chilean women to entertain the men—and another DINA agent took pictures of the festivities.

By Friday evening, agreement was reached. The chiefs of the five delegations signed the final "Acta" or resolution and decided to call the new system "Condor" in honor of the host country's national bird.

The feature of Condor most openly described in the founding documents, and acknowledged by Contreras in interviews, was the establishment of a central data bank to which all member countries would contribute intelligence. The data bank was located in the headquarters' Coordinating Center in Chile, designated as "Condor One." The data bank was designed to gather in one place the best information from each country, and from countries outside the system, about "people . . . organizations and other activities, directly or indirectly connected with subversion." The model Contreras had in mind for this data bank was the Interpol system of international police communication, without the formalities of charges, warrants, extradition, or any sort of judicial oversight. Contreras claimed the FBI and CIA participated in the information bank. He said, in little known court testimony, that the FBI's Robert Scherrer was in "permanent contact [with Condor's representative in Buenos Aires] and received the information that he asked for, with regard to records that he requested on numerous occasions. . . . Also the CIA knew about the Condor Organization, and in many opportunities contributed information in this regard," Contreras said.

Computers were almost nonexistent in South America in the mid-1970s, and Contreras's promise that the data bank would be computerized was itself a revolutionary step forward. Intelligence files in police stations and military installations were typed and copied using carbon paper. Cross-indexing required laborious systems of card files with mechanical sorting techniques.

FBI Agent Scherrer said he learned that the CIA provided DINA with the computer systems and training that he presumed were used in the Condor data bank. Several U.S. intelligence documents refer to computer use in Condor. A diagram in the Condor Agenda of the "System of Coordination" indicates the information center was to be organized in four divisions: data bank, police records, microfilm, and computers.

The intelligence services were to communicate by telex* and by a continent-wide radio network—infrastructure elements that also were provided by the United States. The telex system was given the name "Condortel," a label that is found on several documents. Member organizations using the telex system referred to one another by number: Condor one (Chile/Condor headquarters), Condor two (Argentina), Condor three (Uruguay), Condor four (Paraguay), and Condor five (Bolivia). Brazil, Ecuador, and Peru joined later as Condor six, seven, and eight.

The telex messages were at first transmitted in a primitive code, which consisted of a simple exchange of letters.† Later, an automatic encrypting device was installed in all Condortel telex terminals. A Bolivian security agent, quoted by author Gerardo Irusta, revealed the existence of the machines and claimed that the devices were provided by the CIA. The agent, Juan Carlos Fortun, said, "The chief of our department, generally an Army liaison officer, had access to a special machine, which was kept locked, that served to encode and decode the messages that were sent to and received from each of these countries."

The telex system was the most common method of communication among the agencies. Contreras provided funds to set up a telex terminal for the use of Lieutenant Colonel Osvaldo Rawson in Buenos Aires, one of several indica-

---

*Telex is a point-to-point text communication system that was widely used until it was rendered obsolete by fax and e-mail. Sender and receiver each needed special equipment, similar to a large typewriter, and communication was established via a dedicated telephone line.

†In one of the documents, Contreras gave an example of the code using the message "I will travel tomorrow":
Message in the clear: viajare manana
Message in code: NXDBD TCADJ DJD

tions that Rawson may have been operating as an agent on Contreras's payroll independent of his work in his own intelligence service, Battalion 601.

A powerful military radio network provided by the U.S. military, whose central transmitter was located in the Panama Canal Zone, was also used for Condor communications. Paraguayan General Alejandro Fretes Dávalos revealed Condor's use of the system in a conversation with U.S. Ambassador Robert White in 1978 and reported in a declassified cable. A U.S. military intelligence officer who served in Latin America confirmed the existence of the network in an interview. The U.S. military installed transmitters in countries where U.S. trainers were operating, usually in local military facilities. He said a common use of the radio system was for Latin American officers studying at the School of the Americas in the Canal Zone to talk to their fellow officers and families back home on personal business. It was a way to avoid expensive long-distance calls. There were no restrictions, however, on the use of the radio transmitters by the Latin American military, and he acknowledged that intelligence agencies would have access to the system and with simple codes could have used it as the infrastructure for a continent-wide communication system.

As subversives and their allies moved from country to country, information about their whereabouts and activities was to be fed by each service to the central data bank. The agreement, for example, specified that there should be "very rapid and immediate contact when someone is expelled from a country or when a suspect travels so as to alert the Intelligence Services." Each country contributed, and each country retrieved information, using the communications system.

In addition, the system called for members to use their liaison relationships with agencies "outside the member countries, especially those outside the continent, to obtain information about subversion." This provision—5i—in the agreement, was intended to greatly enhance the Condor information base with material provided by friendly agencies in the United States and Europe. The full extent of such information exchange is not known, but my investigation has revealed specific examples of exchanges involving the FBI and the CIA in the United States, and the West German Bundesnachtrichtendienst (BND).

Condor was not just an information exchange. Perhaps its most tradition-breaking aspect was the establishment of close personal relationships among top officers, whose agencies in the past had looked on one another as targets of counterintelligence rather than as collaborators. Part of the Contreras plan was regular meetings and personal visits. The next meeting of all members of Condor was scheduled for the following June, in conjunction with the U.S.-sponsored Conference of American Armies meeting in Santiago. The founding documents also talk of encouraging bilateral meetings—evidence of four such meetings involving intelligence planning and information exchange have been found in the Paraguay Archive.

The heart of the system was the capacity of each agency to station its agents with permission to actually operate in other countries. Until Condor, each country's military presence in another country was limited to the formal military attachés located in foreign embassies. There had been covert espionage as well. Contreras began stationing DINA officers covertly in each country, using embassy cover, after July 1974, to recruit friendly officers in the host country to conduct surveillance on Chilean exiles.

Condor allowed for much more extensive and officially sanctioned operational capability. The Condor agreement, in section 5g, called for "the establishment in the embassies of our countries of the presence of National Intelligence personnel, . . . for direct and personal liaison, who will be fully accredited by the Services." In other words, each country's Condor service would have at least one intelligence official from each other country permanently stationed and working alongside the local service. It was an idea that Contreras borrowed from the CIA, which had its personnel installed inside the Venezuelan intelligence service. Contreras, in an interview, insisted he turned down a similar arrangement offered by Vernon Walters to station CIA officers inside DINA.

In addition, according to the Condor documents, each country had the right and obligation to provide "technical staff" to man the Coordinating Center, the headquarters and data base in Chile. Personnel working there from other countries enjoyed diplomatic immunity.

The system thus created an elaborate multilateral intelligence infrastructure with a central office in Chile and branch offices in each country. These elements—information, communications, and the stationing of operational personnel—created enormous potential capacity for international activity. There could be no illusions about the intended use of this capacity. Contreras made it clear in his opening speech to the meeting that Condor was being created to capture and interrogate his leftist enemies still in Latin America, and to "eliminate" those living as exiles in other parts of the world. These were the operational phases about which the founding documents gave few specifics—Phase Two for joint operations in Latin America, Phase Three for missions to Europe and the United States. Details about those phases would emerge as they were put into action, and detected by U.S. intelligence agencies.

For the moment, the signing of the final Act of Closure of the First Inter American Meeting of National Intelligence concluded the work of the officers from Chile, Argentina, Uruguay, Paraguay, and Bolivia. They had finished one day ahead of schedule. They had before them a weekend of recreation—dining and gambling at casinos in the lush seaside city of Vina del Mar, then an afternoon of horseback riding at the Quillota military base in the coastal plains to the north.

They returned to their home countries having embarked on an enterprise of colossal hubris. The Condor alliance was born from the aggressive instincts of military leaders who saw themselves facing a conflict of world scope. They used the term World War III without irony or qualification. More even than a war of irregulars extinguishing guerrilla uprisings as they occurred, the Southern Cone axis was equipped to project its power abroad, to create "extraterritorial capability." The forces now united to preserve the vaguely defined "Western way of life" were prepared to go even to the European and American capitals to root out the subversive cells there that those governments, softened by democracy, were unwilling to eradicate.

8

"THE OLD MAN DOESN'T WANT TO DIE"

Contreras considered himself . . . "capo" of the anti-Marxist movement . . .
— MICHAEL TOWNLEY

There was a reason Manuel Contreras's ideas for international operations were so well developed and so convincing to his fellow intelligence commanders: by the time the five agencies signed the Condor agreement, DINA's Exterior Department was already up and running and had almost a year's experience in on-the-ground operations in Europe and the United States. The new organization would provide a multinational umbrella for many operations already underway.

The Prats assassination in Buenos Aires—successful despite false starts, intelligence leaks, wasted money, and an awkward combination of military and civilian actors—had been the inauguration of Contreras's international team. The DINA operatives used in that assassination were still an intact unit and would continue to carry our similar operations for the next two years. The DINA Exterior Department would be expanded and trained and tested in dozens of trips abroad. The full extent of those operations may never be known—one agent bragged he had traveled to Europe eighty-four times.

Much of what we know has been obtained from the sources who have testified, principally the Chilean-American Michael Townley. Townley was clearly at the center of DINA's foreign operations, and participated in a long string of assassinations and assassination attempts. It would be a mistake, however, to circumscribe DINA's Exterior Department and Condor only to what we know about and from Townley. But if the details obtained from Townley, who claims to have had only a vague notion of his role within Condor, are the tip of the iceberg, his testimony is evidence that the iceberg itself—DINA operations abroad—was truly enormous.

"Contreras considered himself a focal point or a 'capo' of the anti-Marxist movement and of the groups scattered throughout Europe and in the United States," Townley testified to an Italian judge. "One of the things that Contreras most wanted to accomplish was the creation of an alliance—maybe that term is too fancy—of various movements and various groups which he knew he could trust, and obviously which he could manipulate at his pleasure."

Contreras was building a monster with several heads and many arms. Condor was official, multilateral, and embedded in the institutions of military intelligence. As a military alliance it had enormous resources and operational capacity but also was encumbered by its own military bureaucracy. Contreras meant it to complement his other international operations: the Exterior Department had created a network of civilians recruited from right-wing terrorist groups in Europe and the United States. This "civilian" network was already in place and was to be one of Condor's assets—perhaps its most powerful asset—available for espionage, propaganda, assassinations, and any manner of dirty tricks, for pay or for ideological devotion to Pinochet. DINA's private network was informal and able to respond with maximum flexibility to Contreras's instructions. What it lacked in professionalism and institutional credentials it made up in improvisation, fanaticism, and energy.

General Pinochet himself had a direct role in setting up this network. His overthrow of Allende had made him a hero in the networks of fascist extremists left over from World War II in Europe. One of the most famous, Prince Junio Valerio Borghese, a naval officer in Mussolini's fascist regime, made a pilgrimage to Chile in May 1974 to pay homage to Pinochet and pledge his assistance. Borghese's followers had formed underground organizations that had carried out some of Italy's most spectacular acts of terrorism of the time, including a bank robbery in Milan in 1969 that left sixteen people dead. The general strategy was to provoke chaos and a military coup that would bring Borghese to power. The coup scenario never materialized, giving the aging Borghese even more reason to admire Pinochet for accomplishing the kind of anti-Communist takeover in Chile that had eluded Borghese in Italy.

The meeting with Pinochet cemented a relationship that would extend to

Borghese's followers. He brought with him to Chile his younger lieutenant, Stefano Delle Chiaie, who headed the group *Avanguardia Nazionale*—National Vanguard—and had masterminded the bloody bank assault. Delle Chiaie had earned the name "the Black Bomber." Recognizing an asset for his plans in Europe, Manuel Contreras immediately incorporated Delle Chiaie into DINA, where he was known by the code name "Alfa."

The second group of extremists were Cuban exiles who, a decade after the failure of the CIA-sponsored Bay of Pigs invasion of Cuba, were increasingly resorting to terrorist tactics to unseat Fidel Castro. A small group—Guillermo Novo, José Dionisio Suárez, and Orlando Bosch, names that would soon become infamous—also made the pilgrimage to Santiago in December 1974.

Building on those contacts, Contreras was able to create a makeshift team for operations in both the United States and Europe. In early 1975, he activated the network. Townley was dispatched to Miami, and several other DINA officers from the Exterior Department were sent to Europe. Their mission: conduct surveillance on the Chilean exiles traveling around the world to organize resistance and persuade democratic governments to repudiate Pinochet. For several exiles under surveillance, the orders included assassination.

Townley arrived in Miami in early February with $25,000 in his money pouch and a list of potential collaborators given to him by DINA. One of the organizations that had sent a delegation to Chile, the Cuban Nationalist Movement, assigned a young, sometime used car salesman named Virgilio Paz to work with Townley on his mission, which he called Operation Open Season.

DINA's new international strategy coincided nicely with that of the Cuban movement, which its leaders expressed as "war throughout the roads of the world." Translated, the slogan meant a terrorist campaign against Castro's institutions outside Cuba—against supporters in the United States, Cuban diplomatic posts, and Cuban airlines. (In the most ferocious attack, masterminded by Orlando Bosch, a bomb exploded aboard an Air Cubana airplane bound from Caracas to Havana, killing all seventy-three passengers and crew.)

Townley's first assigned targets were in Mexico City, where a meeting of the International Commission of Inquiry into the Crimes of the Military Junta in Chile was about to start. Carlos Altamirano—the principal target—would be arriving from East Germany. Other important Communist and Socialist leaders would also be there. Orlando Letelier would be arriving from Washington, D.C., where he had recently relocated. Communist Leader Volodia Teitelboim was also on the list. Townley gathered the makings for a remote-control bomb, similar to the one he had used to kill Prats in Argentina a few months earlier. Paz bought a high-powered rifle with a telescopic sight. Townley's wife, Mariana, was the third member of the team.

Townley would later testify he was supposed to kill as many of the top leaders as he could, but in fact the would-be assassins never got close to their targets. Driving incongruously through Mexico, patching together a bomb with C4 plastic explosive in the rear of their rented American Traveler camper, they arrived too late for the meeting.

He reported the bungled mission back to Santiago, to Raul Iturriaga, the chief of DINA's Exterior Department. Iturriaga instructed Townley to return to Chile and then to continue to pursue Altamirano in Europe. The priority was always Altamirano. "Contreras had a personal resentment against Altamirano. I don't know why," Townley recalled.

Arriving in Frankfurt in July, Townley, Mariana, and Paz linked up with other DINA Exterior Department teams that had been carrying out similar missions in the capitals of Europe. One of the teams was headed by Major Cristoph Willeke, Iturriaga's deputy and a German speaker. His primary mission was to follow a prominent Christian Democrat making the rounds of European capitals, Patricio Aylwin, the former senator who in 1990 would be elected president of Chile. Townley and Willeke were also building Contreras's anti-Marxist network. Willeke established liaison with the West German intelligence, the BND (Bundesnachtrichtendienst), a contact that, according to Townley, had been arranged by leaders of a crypto-Nazi German colony in Chile, known as Dignity Colony. BND and DINA exchanged lists of suspected MIR and JCR operatives in Europe, with special attention to those thought to be working with the German terrorists, the Baader-Meinhof gang. Townley also established contact with two unidentified right-wing groups in Germany to incorporate them into Contreras's network.

Another DINA team was working in Paris. It included familiar names: Lieutenant Colonel Pedro Espinoza and Lieutenant Armando Fernández Larios, who would later participate in the Letelier assassination. That team also traveled to Madrid, Germany, and Rome. Some of the assignments involved arms sales and propaganda operations, in addition to espionage and surveillance of dissidents.

There was an element of spy versus spy. At least three European intelligence agencies—French, West German, and East German—knew of the presence of DINA's operatives in Europe. East Germany's Stasi service developed accurate advance information about assassination plans against General Prats in 1974, and against Altamirano later. Several assassination attempts against Altamirano appear to have been averted by quick action of the French intelligence service, DST. Twice, DST agents placed Carlos Altamirano under special round-the-clock protection during visits to Paris and told him that teams of assassins had been detected. In another instance, DST agents detained three DINA agents at Orly Airport and refused them entry to France. Altamirano, who resided in East Berlin, said he depended for his safety on the protection and advice of his friends in the Communist intelligence service. Traveling almost constantly at the time, Altamirano frequently changed his travel plans at the last minute, seldom staying in the same hotel or house two nights in a row.

The DINA missions had done little more than make the European exiles nervous. One of the DINA agents had a near-miss: he located Altamirano and approached him with his weapon, but lost his nerve and failed to fire, according to Townley. Frustrated at the lack of success, Townley called DINA headquarters in Chile for more instructions, asking for "Luis Gutiérrez," which meant his call was for the officer in charge of the Exterior Department, Iturriaga.

Iturriaga added a new name to Townley's hit list: Bernardo Leighton, the grandfatherly Christian Democrat who was working in Rome to forge an alliance between his party and the remnants of Allende's forces. Iturriaga followed up with detailed instructions in a letter that arrived via a Chilean Airlines pilot. Iturriaga ordered Townley to drive to Rome and make contact with DINA's most important Italian asset: Stefano Delle Chiaie, the terrorist known as "Alfa," who had been on DINA's payroll for a year. Iturriaga's instructions were "very clear and precise," Townley said in later testimony: he was to enlist Delle Chiaie's organization in an operation to kill Leighton.

Delle Chiaie was on the Italian police "most wanted" lists because of his alleged involvement in a series of terrorist bombings, including the Milan bank assault. Nevertheless he operated boldly in Rome, from a comfortable apartment on Via Sartoria. He was using a false passport, in the name of Alfredo di Stefano, that had been provided by DINA. The apartment where he received Townley, Mariana, and Paz was a gathering place for members of his group,

Avanguardia Nazionale. Other DINA team members also had been recent guests in the same Rome apartment.

Stefano Delle Chiaie was an intense fireplug of a man, his colorless eyes framed by a broad forehead and thick black mustache. Like Contreras, Delle Chiaie had the commanding presence that sparked Townley's admiration. They had dinner. Delle Chiaie was full of ideas and ready for action. He had the men, experience, and determination to give Pinochet some return on his investment in the Italian fascist groups. He gave Townley some advice. Forget about exiles like Altamirano, he said. They are too well protected, and the risk is too great. Leighton was a better, and easier target. The widely respected elder statesman of the Christian Democratic Party, Leighton had been a vice president in Chile and moved easily in the international circles of the conservative Christian Democratic movement, which was the ruling party in Italy and Germany. Not only was he trying to unite Chileans against Pinochet, he was working hard to create consensus among the Europe's conservative Christian Democrats and leftist Social Democrats to oppose Latin American dictatorships like Pinochet's.

Even more so than killing a leftist bogeyman like Altamirano, the death of a revered figure like Leighton would strike terror in the hearts of exiles everywhere and demonstrate not only DINA's international power but its utter ruthlessness. Leighton lived in Rome with his wife, Anita Fresno, with no apparent security. A former Chilean labor leader living in Frankfurt had been spying on Leighton for DINA and had provided Leighton's address in Rome and information about his activities. After several meetings, Delle Chiaie informed Townley that *Avanguardia Nazionale* would provide the men and weapons to carry out the assassination.

Townley cleared the plan with Iturriaga and gave Alfa the go-ahead. Delle Chiaie organized the operation with a fascist comrade, Pier Luigi Concutelli, who was to be the shooter. Another member of Delle Chiaie's group, Guilio Crescenzi, was sent to find a gun and brought back a nine-millimeter Beretta pistol.

A few days later, October 6, Concutelli was waiting on the quiet Via Aurelia, near the Vatican, where the Leightons had an apartment. Just after 8 P.M., Bernardo Leighton and Anita got off a bus and walked arm in arm, returning from a late-afternoon shopping trip. Concutelli crossed the street toward them, passed them, then pulled the gun and shot Leighton in the back of the head. His wife spun around, and a second bullet caught her in the side, passed through her chest, and nicked her spine. The assassin looked at his victims crumpled on the sidewalk, then ran, neglecting to deliver further shots.

The Leightons both survived. Bernardo miraculously recovered fully from the bullet that passed completely through his skull, exiting above his left ear. Anita Fresno was never able to walk normally because of the spinal injury. Townley would later reproach the Italians for not using a .22 pistol, the weapon of choice for professional close-in work.

Townley and the Italians celebrated with dinner at Delle Chiaie's apartment, thinking that the Leightons were dead. Then they got in their rented car and drove north to join other DINA operatives in Frankfurt, where there were further congratulations all around—tempered by learning of the Leighton's survival. Still, the shootings had the desired effect. Leighton, though recovering quickly, was never active politically again. Exiles were on notice that even Europe was not safe.

The blatant assassination attempt remained unsolved for more than a decade. When Townley was arrested in connection with the Letelier case, it was assumed from his travel documents that he was involved. But the identities of the assassins were not established until a crusading judge, Giovanni Salvi, took up the case in the 1980s, and started a dogged ten-year investigation.

In a deposition in Salvi's investigation, one of the members of Delle Chiaie's group, Vincenzo Vinciguerra, linked the assassination to Pinochet:

> The order was issued directly by General Pinochet. . . . I'm speaking about what I know personally. The order was issued directly by General Pinochet, who later on deplored that they had remained alive. He said, "Too bad, the old man doesn't want to die—*Lástima, este viejo no quiere morir.*" That was the comment Pinochet made when, some time afterwards, he met with Delle Chiaie and he was referring to the episode. The decision to eliminate certain opposition political leaders was precisely the decision of the Chilean military junta and in particular of Pinochet.

The quid pro quos for doing DINA's wet work were not lavish. The Cuban Paz was allowed to give secret details of the Leighton attack to his comrades in Miami, who put out a press release claiming credit. DINA eventually paid the

Italians $5,000, described as a loan that was never repaid. But the main benefit, in the logic of underground right-wing terrorists, was association with Pinochet's Chile and the stamp of special status that that conferred.

Pinochet did not shy away from expressing open gratitude to his terrorist allies. A few weeks after the Leighton attack, on November 20, 1975, Spanish dictator Francisco Franco died after thirty-six years in power. Pinochet flew to Madrid to pay his respects to his own anti-Communist hero and role model. DINA accompanied him in force: Contreras commandeered an entire airplane for his most important staff officers, including almost the entire Exterior Department. The DINA group numbered at least fifty, almost as many as all the other Chilean government officials combined.

Contreras arranged for Delle Chiaie to come to Madrid with several of his Avanguardia Nazionale comrades. Fresh from committing the Leighton attack, an act of terrorism that had dominated the European papers for weeks, Delle Chiaie was given a private audience with Pinochet in his hotel room. Contreras also presented Delle Chiaie with the $5,000 payment.

According to one of Pinochet's civilian staff, Contreras also arranged for Pinochet to meet with others described as "patriots"—Croatian terrorists and extremists from other parts of Europe. The staffer said he had to outmaneuver Contreras to prevent one of the meetings from taking place in a public hotel salon in front of photographers.

In retaliation, during a drinking session at the hotel later that day, a DINA officer grabbed the staffer and put a gun to his head. To Contreras, the officer said, "Whenever you give the word, my colonel. We'll wrap him up in that rug and get him out of here without a trace." It was the kind of thing that passed for horseplay in DINA.

The regal funeral ended, Pinochet, Contreras, and his DINA officers flew back to Chile, just two days before the gathering, on November 26, of the intelligence chiefs convened for the creation of Operation Condor. Delle Chiaie, two other Italians from his group, and Paz arrived about the same time in Chile, where they functioned as a DINA operational cell.

Townley lamented that he was overworked from his many missions. "It was a period of much physical and mental activity, with some days or weeks with no activity at all. When I returned to Chile in 1975, at the end of the year, I found myself in very, very deteriorated physical condition and extraordinarily tired. And I weighed almost 40 kilos less than I weigh now."

With the creation of Condor, there were now two networks in operation to defeat the military governments' leftist enemies. Their areas of operations were the United States, Europe, and Latin America. In the early months of 1976, the focus shifted to the new Condor apparatus and to a concerted campaign against perceived enemies still residing in Latin America.

9

DEATH IN ARGENTINA

Chilean leftist leader Edgardo Enríquez, who was arrested by Argentine security forces on April 10, was subsequently turned over to the Chileans and is now dead.

— CIA REPORT

I'm the only one who talks to everybody . . . I talk with the communists, with the Tupamaros. I talk with all the forces, and they all respect me."

— EXILED SENATOR ZELMAR MICHELINI

The agreement to form Condor was most likely entered into behind the back of the struggling government of Isabel Perón in Argentina. In late 1975 and early 1976 the civilian regime trembled on the verge of disintegration, ceding more and more autonomy to the military. The creation of the Condor alliance was one of the first steps in the military strategy to deal a death blow to the political chaos and terrorism that, in the military's view, Peronism had brought to Argentina. On Condor's map of future action, Argentina was to be the first and largest arena for multicountry operation.

In March 1976, coup plotting was an almost open secret. Admiral Emilio Massera, chief of the navy, had coffee with U.S. ambassador Robert Hill on March 16 to prepare the ground for the inevitable. Speaking in conditional phrases, Massera informed the ambassador the coup was coming. "He said that it was no secret that the military might have to step into the political vacuum very soon," Hill reported in a cable to Washington a few hours later. The military had a clear choice between military intervention and "total chaos leading to the destruction of the Argentine state," both because of the incompetence of the presidency of Isabel Perón and the "terrorist" threat. Somewhat incongruously, Massera asked Hill for help in hiring a Washington-based public relations firm to help shape the new military government's image in the United States. Massera promised, according to Hill's report, that the "military intervention if it comes, will not follow the lines of the Pinochet takeover in Chile. Rather, he [Massera] said, they will try to proceed within the law with full respect for human rights."

Time was short. "Political counselor and I had the distinct impression Admiral Massera was talking about a coup that will probably come within the next few days, possibly even before the weekend," Hill reported.

The meeting was on a Tuesday. Exactly one week later, U.S. Army Colonel Lloyd Gracey, a military intelligence trainer, was about to leave his office at Army Command Headquarters at Campo de Mayo. An Argentine officer he considered one of his most reliable sources came in his office and closed the door. "Lloyd, tonight there will be a coup against Isabelita," he said. The advance information was intended, Gracey felt, to give the United States a chance to express objections, if there were any. The country team—ambassador, political counselor, CIA and DIA chiefs—met and cabled Washington. No reservations were expressed. Within twelve hours the coup was a reality. U.S. recognition of the military government was immediate.

True to Massera's promise, the coup avoided the Pinochet model. There were no bombings, no mass shootings, no bodies in the streets on the day of the coup. It was described as a total, efficient, and airtight takeover of all centers of power. And to judge by what was known publicly, it was virtually bloodless. A dispassionate intelligence summary of the coup signaled the U.S. attitude in a cable to all embassies in Latin America the following day.

> US interests are not threatened by the present military government. The three service commanders are known for their pro-US, anti-communist attitudes . . . Investment problems will be minimized by the Junta's favorable attitude toward foreign capital. . . . Human rights is an area in which the new government's actions may present problems from the US perspective. Several thousand alleged subversives are already being held under a state of siege declared in November 1974, and that figure will mount as the security forces intensify their counterterrorist efforts. The military's treatment of these individuals has been less than correct in the past, and will probably involve serious human rights violations in the future.

Unlike the Pinochet coup, the military takeover in Argentina was not viewed worldwide through the prism of anti-Communism. The Peronist government was universally reviled and had no consistent defenders either on the right or the left outside Argentina. The Argentine left, unlike the defenders of Allende's Socialist experiment in Chile, disliked the government almost as much as the military did. The ERP, and to a lesser extent the Montoneros, had as their goal the overthrow of the government and installation of their own radical alternative.

The new military leaders, in a junta comprising the chiefs of the army, navy, and air force, successfully portrayed themselves as reluctant moderates, especially Army Commander General Jorge Videla—a seemingly innocuous, gangling man whose scarecrow visage was in stark contrast to the sinister image of dark cloaks and opaque sunglasses affected by Pinochet when he took power.

The military's "terrorist" enemies, to whose eradication the coup was dedicated, also garnered little sympathy either inside or outside Argentina. It might have been a different story if the guerrillas had limited their activities to the attacks on military installations, propaganda strikes, and the mountain campaign in Tucumán, with its echoes of the freedom fighter struggles of Che Guevara and Fidel Castro. But both ERP and Montoneros had indulged the worst instincts of their extremist members, carrying out a long and tedious string of kidnappings and killings, often against people with no connection to the military and no particular ideology. Several highly publicized killings became symbolic of the egregious cruelty of which the guerrillas were capable: ERP chief Santucho ordered his men to execute military men in the streets in equal number to the sixteen ERP fighters who had been executed by the military after a battle. An ERP squad gunned down an army captain crossing a street with his three-year-old daughter, killing both the soldier and the little girl. Santucho expressed regret for the girl's death, but the responsible guerrilla commander was not punished.

The Montoneros had kidnapped and executed a former president, General Pedro Eugenio Aramburu, and in another famous case murdered an army general with a bomb planted by a girl who had infiltrated the general's home by befriending his daughter. Foreigners also had been targeted, usually for kidnappings for ransom—such as the ERP kidnapping of Victor Samuelson of Exxon. Two U.S. foreign service officials in the provincial capital of Cordoba were shot, one fatally, in separate kidnapping attempts by Montoneros and

ERP commandos. Several plots against officers of the U.S. military advisory group were discovered, one of which was attributed to the JCR. Inside the U.S. embassy the identification of leftist guerrillas as the enemy was personal as well as ideological.

The military government was welcomed not as an anti-Communist crusader as in Chile but as a legitimate intervention to restore order and stop the violence. Respected and moderate newspaper editors such as Robert Cox of the English language *Buenos Aires Herald* and Jacobo Timerman of *La Opinión* approved the takeover in their editorial columns, even while issuing cautions about human rights abuses. The political parties, with the exception of the Peronist Justicialist Party, lined up to endorse the coup. Even the Soviet-aligned Communist Party did not oppose it.

The new junta adopted the unthreatening title "Process of National Reorganization" for their enterprise. Even before hiring image builders in Washington, the military seemed to have won the first battle of public relations.

The underground reality was starkly different, but for the first few weeks it remained underground and out of sight. What had already begun, even before the coup, in a growing network of secret prisons, was incalculably more brutal than the junta's public image. Behind the mild faces of the new military rulers was a dictatorship far worse—by several orders of magnitude—than Pinochet's experiment in anti-Communist eradication. A nationwide underground extermination system had been operating since the military had taken over the anti-subversive war the previous October. With almost no public notice, the military had kidnapped and disappeared at least 522 people in the five and half months leading up to the coup. Then the disappearances more than tripled to a steady rate of 350 per month for the remaining months of 1976.

It was almost as if the reality of the repression was in inverse proportion to its publicity. The previous year, 1975, was portrayed as the worst year of violence in Argentina's history, with wide coverage of the war in Tucumán, battles between police, military, and the guerrilla groups, and the activities of the Triple A, a Peronist-sponsored death squad.

As the military tightened its grip in late 1975 and pushed aside the Peronist death squads like so many amateurs, the already-high body count escalated. Of the hundreds of people sucked up into the secret prisons every month, almost all—one former agent of the army's 601 intelligence battalion estimated 85 percent—were executed and their bodies secretly disposed of. There was little

Mass Killings in Argentina: CONADEP and Battalion 601 Calculations 1973–1983

	CONADEP List	INTELLIGENCE BATTALION 601 Count †
1973	17	
1974	42	
1975	326*	903
1976	3,792	10,251
1977	2,979	8,207
1978	958	2,639
1979–83	975	no data
Total	9,089**	22,000

Sources: National Commission on the Disappeared (*Comisión Nacional de Desaparición de Personas*—CONADEP), a list of names of detained-disappeared. The list, later updated, was published in 1983 as part of the CONADEP report and contains a small number of obvious duplications.

†Intelligence Battalion 601 count, October 1975–July 1978, Arancibia document V/238. Arancibia's report on the Battalion 601 count lists names of several hundred people, mostly from 1976. I estimated the number of deaths per year by distributing the 22,000 deaths over the four years according to the yearly percentage distribution found in the CONADEP list.

*The CONADEP list excludes killings where bodies were found, which was a considerable number in 1975 and 1976. The *New York Times* reported in December 1975 that a total of 1,100 people had been killed on all sides in political violence in that year—a number that may be assumed not to include the disappearances, which were not known in detail until years later. In 1976 a similar number of publicly known deaths were reported.

**The total is higher than the number of 8,961 published by CONADEP in 1983 because of subsequent addition of new cases.

public outcry about the many arrests at first and family members still harbored hope that those captured eventually would reappear alive as legally sanctioned prisoners under the national security laws.

A candid secret document, from DINA agent Arancibia, describes a two-track system of legal prisoners and secret executions. Reporting to Santiago, he said, "The Army is attacking the subversion 'with the right hand and with the left hand.' That is to say, some of those captured are passed on to the executive power [legally sanctioned] and the rest are RIP. Just this week, SIE [Army Intelligence Battalion 601] eliminated 25 subversive delinquent elements, all 'with the left hand.' " The same language is used in a U.S. intelligence document reviewing the early period of repression: " 'Left handed operations' in the vocabulary of the trade means anything that is extra-legal. 'Ultra left handed' means an operation authorized and or run by a junior unit commander without higher permission or knowledge."

The total death toll would not be officially counted until years later, and even then the numbers were considered to be significantly lower than the actual number killed. The National Commission on the Disappeared documented 8,961 disappearances through the end of the military government in 1983.* Intelligence Battalion 601 itself was keeping a secret count with a much higher number, according to a document in Arancibia's files. Noting that he received his information directly from Intelligence Battalion 601, Arancibia reported to his superiors in Chile: "They have counted 22,000 between dead and disappeared, from 1975 to the present date [July 1978]."

Public perception lagged behind the reality in 1976 because the military established elaborate systems to keep the killing secret. The Argentine military eschewed the most high-profile actions taken by Chile. There were no mass roundups, no stadiums, or visible concentration camps filled with tens of thousands of prisoners. A minority of prisoners were held under "executive power" and thus were judicially acknowledged and publicly known. Few of those prisoners ultimately disappeared. The secret system fooled the U.S. embassy. An embassy cable three weeks after the coup reported that the number of judicially acknowledged prisoners increased from 1,500 before the coup to about 3,000 after the coup. "The general consensus is that the arrests so far, with few exceptions, have been carried out within legal framework," the cable noted. About twenty-five death squad–style killings had occurred, with bodies dumped in ditches, but that was attributed to "off-duty policemen without the knowledge or authorization of senior army officers."

---

* The CONADEP total remains the most reliable, as a minimum number of disappeared, because it is based on an actual list of names of people whose disappearance has been reported to the commission. New cases added after 1983 brought the total to 9,089 (see Table, p. 139). A widely quoted figure of 30,000 disappeared is based on extrapolations made in the early 1980s by human rights activists. The Battalion 601 calculation of 22,000 is important new evidence to support the claim that the true number is far higher than the CONADEP figure, although still lower than the estimate of 30,000.

These sanguine assessments were shared in the early weeks after the coup by moderate Argentine politicians such as Radical Party leader Ricardo Balbín. Actually, hundreds were being exterminated and the secret system of violence was intensifying. It was not until mid-May that the terrifying reality set in: the coup leaders' moderate image was a cruel sham.

For the United States embassy, the wake-up call came with a handful of spectacular attacks against international targets. Those killings we now know were part of Operation Condor.

MOPPING UP THE JCR

With the coup, a combined DINA-601 Intelligence Battalion operation moved quickly to mop up JCR operations in Argentina. The main targets were MIR leader Edgardo Enríquez and ERP leader Roberto Santucho. In May 1975, JCR couriers Jorge Fuentes and Amílcar Santucho had been captured in Paraguay. Then, Jean Yves Claudet, arriving in Buenos Aires with JCR documents on microfilm and a suitcase full of cash, fell into a trap set by 601 operative Osvaldo Rawson. The captured documents showed Enríquez was still operating out of Buenos Aires. A DINA letter in late December—just three weeks after the Condor founding meeting, names several MIR suspects and asks that they be captured and "delivered to Chile."

Only days after the coup in March, 601 and DINA got an important break in their search for Enríquez and ERP leader Roberto Santucho. Despite the military's stranglehold on the city, Santucho decided to go ahead with a large secret meeting of his entire central committee plus members of the JCR executive commission, including Enríquez. At least fifty people were gathered for the two-day meeting, starting March 29, in a house in the Moreno district on the outskirts of Buenos Aires.

Topic A was the analysis of the recent coup. Santucho and Enríquez were close friends and usually saw eye-to-eye on political strategy, but they disagreed strongly on the current situation. Enríquez advocated a strategic retreat, following MIR's example after the coup in Chile.

To the contrary, Santucho saw the coup as opportunity. On the morning of the second day he gave a speech to the gathered revolutionaries that laid out a strategy of accelerated offensives against the military. The coup, he argued, "closes off definitively all possible electoral and democratic solutions and marks the beginning of a process of open civil war." It was, he proclaimed, "a qualitative leap in the development of our revolutionary struggle."

It was instead a leap of such colossal self-will and arrogance that its folly was almost instantaneously revealed. The group adjourned for lunch and began the one-hour siesta that was a tradition in central committee meetings, no matter how clandestine. As the leaders slept, shooting broke out in the walled garden around the house. A military squad of about a dozen men was attacking the house, apparently unaware that there was a superior guerrilla force inside. ERP guards easily held the attackers off while most of the assembled leaders made their escape into the surrounding neighborhood. Enríquez and Santucho, as the top leaders, were among the first to leave. But when army reinforcements arrived and surrounded the entire area, Enríquez was forced to hide in an irrigation ditch in a cornfield for two days.

Twelve guerrilla leaders were killed, some of them captured alive and able to give information before they were killed. One of those captured alive was the ERP intelligence chief. The guerrillas' underground network was fatally compromised. Enríquez apparently made his way to another safe house designated for the JCR, where other officers had taken refuge. That house had also become known to the military. On April 10, Enríquez and a young Brazilian woman, Regina Marcondes, were captured as they left the house.

Enríquez was sighted inside a secret army detention center. Argentine intelligence reported the capture to Chile's DINA using the new Condor telex system. At DINA's Villa Grimaldi compound, Luz Arce, a former Mirista turned collaborator, was working as staff assistant to one of the DINA officers. She opened a folder in her in-box and discovered a secret cable that she knew was not meant for her eyes. It was a telex from Argentine intelligence, marked "*via Cóndor*," giving notice that Enríquez was in custody and was being placed at Chile's disposal. She quickly closed the misfiled folder and gave it to her boss.

U.S. intelligence was closely following the capture of Enríquez, using both Argentine and Chilean military sources. DINA sources told a CIA officer that when Enríquez was captured, he was preparing to smuggle himself back into Chile, with ERP help, to assume the leadership of MIR, which had split into two factions. CIA and Embassy cables quoted an "impeccable Chilean Navy source" who informed the U.S. officers on May 7 that Enríquez was dead. The embassy in Argentina also reported Enríquez's death. French and Brazilian officials later made inquiries with the Argentine government on behalf of the Enríquez and Marcondes families and were told the same thing: Argentina had turned them over to Chile. A later CIA report stated it as an established fact: "Chilean leftist leader Edgardo Enríquez, who was arrested by Argentine security forces on April 10, was subsequently turned over to the Chileans and is now dead."

An investigation by Chile's National Truth and Reconciliation Commission also concluded in 1991 that Enríquez and Marcondes were transported to Chile under the Condor system and executed there. In 1998, when Spanish Judge Baltasar Garzón was looking for a case epitomizing Condor's methodology to document his request for the extradition of General Augusto Pinochet from London, he chose the Enríquez capture.

Enríquez was what the military called *un pez gordo*—"a big fish." His capture effectively ended any semblance of a reliable MIR and JCR infrastructure in Argentina, at least one that could be depended on to support and protect the hundreds of smaller foreign fish who had been working in Argentina since going into exile from their own countries. The intelligence systems of five countries, with Argentina's eager cooperation, combined their resources to dry up the system of safe houses, financial support, and aboveground employment the foreign guerrilla activists depended on.

As the JCR was being eradicated in the weeks following the Argentine coup, it became frighteningly clear that underground guerrillas were not the only, or even the principle, targets of Condor.

In addition to the activists actually involved with the underground organizations, thousands of political refugees from the surrounding countries were living in Argentina at the time of the coup. Many of them were registered with the United Nations High Commission for Refugees, which was headquartered in a Catholic church facility. The UNHCR estimated there were 15,000 such refugees; 10,000 were Chileans, and most of the rest were Uruguayans. In a confidential briefing to the U.S. embassy after the coup, a UNHCR official gave his assessment that "about 1,000 of the Chileans and 300 to 400 of the others could be considered to be in danger from the security forces or rightist extremists, either of Argentina or their native country." A combined force of Chilean, Uruguayan, and Argentine security forces raided the church office and carted off UNHCR records stored there. Two days later, twenty-four Chilean and Uruguayan refugees, whose addresses were in the stolen files, were arrested, tortured, and interrogated by officers from their own countries.

The Chileans associated with MIR and the Uruguayans linked to Tupamaros or other factions were in the greatest danger. Before the coup, a scramble ensued to evacuate those in most danger. Edgardo Enríquez had given the order to abandon most MIR operations in Argentina. His lieutenant, Patricio Biedma, had already gotten the wives and children of MIR operatives on flights out of the country before the coup. Biedma's wife, Luz, said she got help from an official at the Cuban embassy to arrange her safe departure. The Cubans were part of an informal network, which included prominent democratic political leaders and officials from the Mexican and Swedish embassies, to provide money, airline tickets, and safe passage for the most desperate cases.

In early May, an Argentine task force launched a major operation on behalf of their Uruguayan Condor partners. The first targets were not the active guerrilla fighters, but rather the Tupamaros who had abandoned armed struggle and were cultivating a political relationship with exiled civilian political leaders. They went after former Tupamaro leader Efraín Martínez Platero, who narrowly avoided capture and accomplished a hair-raising escape from Argentina. Martínez Platero was one of the founders of the JCR, and the JCR's emissary to Fidel Castro and to Europe. After receiving a lukewarm reception for the JCR idea of revolutionary war, Martínez Platero had returned disillusioned to Argentina in 1974 and soon resigned from the Tupamaro leadership. He had once been the highest ranking Tupamaro in Argentina, but had been inactive for more than a year.

At the time of the coup, he was living in a working-class suburb of Buenos Aires, doing odd jobs. He and his wife had two small children and she was nine months pregnant. He was planning to get out of the country but had hoped to wait until the baby arrived. One day returning home to his apartment, he turned away just as he was about to enter, indulging the survival instincts he had honed over a decade of clandestine life. He later learned that security agents were waiting for him in the apartment. They had already kidnapped his brother.

His wife and children, by a stroke of luck, were visiting at his father's house in the city of Mar de Plata. Martínez Platero immediately gathered them up and brought them to Buenos Aires to try to find a way out of the country. Arriving in a city under total military control, they feared even going to a hotel. They had little money and dubious documents, and Martínez Platero—if his true identity were known—was among the top names on Uruguay's most wanted list. The first day in Buenos Aires, his wife went into labor. She gave birth under emergency conditions in a clinic run by nuns. Terrified, the nuns turned the family out on the street again only hours after the baby was born.

With a newborn, a wife weakened from childbirth, and two small children, Martínez went to an address at Calle Florida and Corrientes Avenue to find a man he knew would help him. Senator Zelmar Michelini had been one of Uruguay's most powerful political leaders when the military closed down parliament in 1973. In exile, he lived in the slightly shabby Liberty Hotel. Since the coup he spent much of his time interviewing people needing help, often using a desk in the lobby. Sometimes there was a line of people waiting to see him. Michelini gave Martínez Platero a contact at the Mexican embassy, to help arrange exit documents and air tickets. And with that bare veneer of diplomatic protection, the family got a room in a nearby hotel and waited. It was the middle of May.

On May 15, Michelini had another visitor at the Liberty, who brought him the news that another Tupamaro veteran had disappeared. William Whitelaw, his wife, Rosario Barredo, and her three small children had been kidnapped two days before from their apartment in Buenos Aires. The news left Michelini profoundly shaken. Whitelaw, like Martínez Platero, was one of the founders of the JCR. He and others had formed a splinter group, Nuevo Tiempo, which had abandoned the Tupamaro's guerrilla tactics in favor of forging alliances with centrist political forces. More importantly, Whitelaw was Michelini's principal channel of communication to the underground Tupamaro groups in Buenos Aires. Since the coup, Whitelaw and Michelini had been working in coordination to get people out of the country. Whitelaw's kidnapping had occurred within twenty-four hours of the unsuccessful operation to capture Martínez Platero.

Zelmar Michelini didn't focus on personal danger to himself and probably would have scoffed at the idea that the Uruguayan government would see him as a target. The father of ten children, he had the kind of Kennedyesque good looks and political charisma that made him one of the top two or three names mentioned as possible presidents should there be a return to democratic government in Uruguay. Indeed, Michelini was part of elaborate maneuvering involving a possible rapid transition to new elections. He and two other prominent Uruguayan leaders—Camara of Representatives President Hector Gutiérrez Ruiz and former presidential candidate Wilson Ferreira Aldunate—were in discussions with a representative of the military government, Minister of Economy Alejandro Vegh Villegas, who had met with them separately in Buenos Aires.

Michelini was a peacemaker, a channel of communication among a broad range of political players, including those who had taken up arms. His daughter quoted him as saying around this time, "I'm the only one who talks to everybody. I talk with Wilson, I talk with the communists, with the Tupamaros. I talk with all the forces, and they all respect me." Ferreira and Michelini also had been exchanging letters and phone calls with members of the U.S. Congress to arrange a visit to Washington to testify about conditions in Uruguay.

In the time since the coup, however, Michelini's priority was to help people like Martínez Platero and their families get out of the country safely. He made little effort to hide his relationships with current and former Tupamaros like Whitelaw, and had acted as a go-between to get small amounts of money, airline tickets and papers from the network of embassies. His own personal business activities were consistent with his status as a prominent but penurious political exile. He worked full-time as a journalist, writing columns on international issues and editing wire copy for *La Opinión* newspaper.

He lived rent-free in the Liberty Hotel, thanks to his friendship with the owner, Benjamin Taub. There was a sinister side to the Liberty Hotel and its owner. Taub ran a legitimate currency exchange business across the street from the hotel, which was a cover for illegal and far larger money trafficking activities. The Liberty was a favorite stopover point for visiting leftists attracted by its moderate prices and central location. Only six months earlier, JCR courier Jean Yves Claudet had taken a room at the Liberty after arriving from Paris with messages and cash, and had been kidnapped and killed.

The owner Taub appeared to survive by doing business on both sides of the ideological divide. A former Argentine intelligence operative said federal police officers used Taub to launder the large sums of illegal cash they stole from criminals and political prisoners. And, as described in Chapter 4, in early 1974, Taub was given the risky but profitable task of handling the $14 million ransom collected from Exxon manager Victor Samuelson—undoubtedly one of his biggest deals ever.

At 5:30 A.M. on May 18, three Ford Falcon automobiles without license plates pulled up outside the Liberty Hotel. Armed men took positions around the lobby. They exhibited no urgency, communicating loudly with one another and a remote headquarters with radios. Others took the elevator to Room 75, where Michelini and two of his sons were sleeping. "We're here to get you. Your hour has come," one said as the men forced their way into the room.

Three hours earlier a similar scene had taken place at the apartment where Congressman Héctor Gutiérrez Ruiz lived with his family. Both men were forced into cars and taken away. For two days, family members and friends from as far away as Boston and Washington, D.C., tried to reach contacts inside the new Argentine government to save the two men. But police refused to take a report or even come to the hotel to examine the crime scene, which was replete with fingerprints and other evidence. A government minister attempted to shift the blame by telling two foreign correspondents privately it was an "Uruguayan operation."

Two days later, a federal police patrol car was told by radio to investigate a car parked under a bridge. The policeman discovered a Ford Torino with the bodies of four people who had been executed with shots to the head and neck. They were identified as Zelmar Michelini, Héctor Gutiérrez, William Whitelaw, and Whitelaw's wife, Rosario Barredo. Barredo's three children—Gabriela, age four, and twin one-year-olds Maximo and Victoria—were missing for two weeks, then showed up at a police commissary and were recovered by their grandparents. Gabriela was able to talk about what had happened. "*Sabés, abuela, que yo vi cuando mataban a mamá?*" "Did you know, Grandma, that I saw when they killed mommy?"

The other intended victim of the roundup, Efraín Martínez Platero, under protection of the Mexican and then the Swedish embassies, was eventually evacuated from Argentina with his wife and children.

No serious judicial investigation has ever been conducted to prosecute those who carried out the murders, despite the abundance of evidence available at the time and from testimony gathered over the years. In a relatively short investigation of the case, I was able to find two sources with what appeared to be firsthand information about those who gave the orders in Uruguay and those who carried out the executions in Argentina. The first source was Hugo Campos Hermida, the former head of the intelligence unit of Uruguayan police. His aggressive and successful campaigns against the Tupamaros in 1972 led to accusations that he headed a police death squad and had committed multiple human rights crimes. Campos was in a unique position to know the inside details of repressive operations even after his police unit was replaced by an even more aggressive army intelligence organization. He talked to me for three hours in October 2001, and expressed his willingness to testify about the murders in an Uruguayan court. A little more than a month after the interview, however, Campos died of complications from lung cancer surgery.

Campos said an Uruguayan army major gave him a firsthand account of the operations that led to Michelini's and Gutiérrez's murders. He said the orders came from the commander in chief of the Uruguayan military, General Gregorio Álvarez. The plan initially was to kidnap the two political leaders with the help of Argentine security operatives and bring them back to Uruguay. Álvarez then changed the order, sending a liaison officer to request that the Argentines kill them in Argentina.

Campos Hermida said the military thought that Michelini and Gutiérrez were providing "support" for the Tupamaros in Argentina. He said the Uruguayan team in Buenos Airges was also involved in the kidnapping and murder a few weeks later of two men from the Cuban embassy who were Michelini's "contacts" with the embassy.

Campos denied that he himself participated in any of the Argentine operations. (His story must be evaluated as self-serving, however, because he faced charges in an Argentine court for participation in other Uruguayan operations in Argentina not linked to the Michelini-Gutiérrez murders.) He said he was able to identify both the officer who participated in the kidnapping and the officer who was sent to transmit the order to kill Michelini and Gutiérrez. He said he wanted to testify in a judicial investigation because he wanted to clear himself and because he considered the murders "a monstrosity."

The other source, who worked for 601 Intelligence Battalion at the time, told the story of the execution of four people in a car that fits many of the circumstances of the Michelini case. He said he was having drinks and exchanging war stories with a federal police officer, Subcommissioner Miguel Angel Trimarchi, who was trying to impress him about how quick he was to follow orders. Trimarchi said he picked up four people and drove them to the enclosed parking lot of Federal Police headquarters. Trimarchi didn't say where he picked them up; presumably it was at other detention centers. He went into the building to ask what he was supposed to do with the four prisoners. The source said he remembered Trimarchi saying, "They said I should kill them, so I went right downstairs. I got in the car, shoved one of them aside"—he makes a gesture with his elbow—"I shot all four."

Another detail coincides with what we know about the murders of Michelini and the others. According to the source, Trimarchi also arranged for the four bodies to be discovered by dispatching a patrol car to the place where the car and the bodies had been left. When the patrolman arrived at the scene, he radioed back that he didn't see four bodies. By radio, Trimarchi told him, "Look in the trunk, you'll find two more." Trimarchi also told the source he was involved in kidnapping "the couple" from their apartment, and that they had just celebrated someone's birthday when the police arrived. The account is intriguing, but must remain in the category of an unconfirmed investigative lead until it can be established that the four people allegedly killed by Trimarchi were the Uruguayans. The source for this account said he is willing to testify about these and other crimes he learned about.

The spectacular murders had the intended effect of sending shockwaves of terror through the large Uruguayan community in Buenos Aires. Indeed, although few realized it, the roundup of Uruguayan leftists had begun within days of the Argentine coup, and involved operations in Bolivia and Uruguay as well as Argentina. The sweeps targeted not only Tupamaros and moderates like Michelini and Gutiérrez, but members of a new organization, the Party for the Victory of the People (*Partido por la Victoria del Pueblo*—PVP), and its armed wing, usually referred to as the OPR-33. The PVP, with anarcho-syndicalist roots, had been overshadowed by the Tupamaros in Uruguay, but in exile in Argentina had gained in members, money, and audacity. Financed by a $10 million ransom from a successful kidnapping of a businessman, the group was on the cusp of launching a major offensive to reestablish guerrilla opposition in Uruguay when the Argentine coup occurred. A few days after the coup, three Uruguayan PVP activists attempted to enter Uruguay from the north driving a camper. They were captured at the border. Within days the arrests began in Argentina, with clear signs that the actions in Argentina were being coordinated with intelligence gained by security forces in Uruguay. Scores of PVP activists were rounded up in the coming weeks, including several of the top leaders who had been living underground. Michelini's daughter, Margarita, a member of the PVP, was arrested in early July. Survivors later reported that a unit of at least five Uruguayan officers was operating for weeks at a time in Argentina, taking part in interrogations and supervising kidnapping operations that were carried out by Argentine commandos. There could be no doubt that the combined actions of Uruguayans and Argentines had penetrated the network of safe houses that sheltered the underground organization and were kidnapping people almost at will.

THE BOLIVIANS

The Bolivian left also had its center of operations in Argentina around former president General Juan José Torres. Torres had brought revolution to Bolivia during his brief ten-month government in 1971, channeling a broad coalition of radical miners, peasants, and progressive military officers in an attempt to end the domination of Bolivia's landowners and mining companies. Some of the military around Torres had been radicalized by their experience of tracking down and capturing Che Guevara and his guerrilla force in 1967. Officers told stories of staying up all night in intense political discussions with the captured guerrillas, knowing that many, including Guevara, would be executed the following day. Guevara's guerrillas, the National Liberation Army (ELN), were defeated militarily, but survived as the enduring symbol of possible revolutionary victory in the future. In exile in Argentina General Torres, likewise defeated militarily and ousted by rightist military leader General Hugo Banzer, remained the single unifying figure around which the opposition was organized.

A short, square man whose indigenous features attracted the loyalty of Bolivia's majority Aymara population, the soft-spoken and gentle Torres was nevertheless an authoritarian who had little confidence that traditional democratic politics would be able to solve Bolivia's problems. He was organizing on two levels: leading a public coalition of opposition groups called the Alliance of the National Left (*Alianza de la Izquierda Nacional*—ALIN), while at the same time working underground to ignite an armed uprising among miners and peasants. In this clandestine strategy, Torres was working closely with the revived ELN and the JCR. The ultimate aim was to set off a military coup to return Torres to power.

His chief political and military aide was Major Rubén Sánchez, who had served with him during his government and followed him into exile first to Chile and then to Argentina. Sánchez had participated in the founding of the JCR, as the representative of the ELN. As one of the few people with formal military training, Sánchez was valued as an instructor at the JCR training camps that were set up in Chile and Argentina. Like Torres, Sánchez had little patience for ideology and the fine points of Marxist theory that stimulated so much debate among the would-be guerrilla fighters. An Argentine trainee re-members Sánchez cajoling them to spend more time learning to read maps and less time formulating grand strategies.

The Bolivians had been among the most successful in actually implement-ing their part in the JCR's plan for continental revolutionary war. In mid-1975, the ELN had reestablished itself in Bolivia as the armed wing of a new organi-zation, the PRT-B—the Revolutionary Workers Party of Bolivia, with a nod to the Argentine ERP's political wing, the PRT. Major Sánchez led a small group of guerrilla leaders back into Bolivia with the goal of preparing for General Torres's return. "At that moment, we all were in favor of taking power through armed action," Sánchez said in a 1996 interview. His leadership corps was in-ternational: he was accompanied by ERP veteran Luis Stamponi from Ar-gentina and Tupamaro Enrique Lucas and their wives, both of whom were guerrilla operatives as well. According to the JCR strategy, agreed upon at a meeting in May 1975, the Bolivian guerrilla offensive was timed to coincide with the Argentine military campaign, already underway, in the mountains of Tucumán Province. MIR's long-planned offensive in the south of Chile was supposed to begin late that same year. By May 1976, both the Chilean and Ar-gentine efforts had fizzled, but the Bolivian campaign organized by Sánchez was gathering strength among miners and peasants in Cochabamba Province.

Sánchez and his group had 150 men under arms, and had organized a larger group of committed and tough miners ready to fight with a lethal weapon that combined ancient Inca and modern technology: sticks of dynamite launched from slingshots. Torres received word that the moment was fast arriving for him to return to Bolivia to lead the uprising. The miners union was threatening a general strike in defiance of the military dictatorship and demanding pay raises of more than 200 percent to offset rampant inflation. Torres had also been meeting secretly with retired Bolivian military officers in an attempt to lay the groundwork for a military coup in response to the planned uprising in Cochabamba. According to the investigative account of these events by journalist Martín Sivak, Torres decided to make his move around the time of the Argentine coup. Torres sent a secret letter to Sanchez saying that he planned to get his family out of Argentina to Venezuela. He then intended to travel to Peru and enter Bolivia clandestinely by crossing the scantily guarded border of desert and mountains in Peru's Tacna Province. Once in Bolivia, he would use the ELN intelligence and security network to establish a clandestine command center in the Siglo XX mining complex of Cochabamba, where he could count on the protection of the powerful mining union.

In late May, according to Sivak, Torres discussed the situation with a Bolivian comrade. "They are insisting that they are well organized in the mines; I want to get in there however I can," the friend quoted Torres as saying.

But it was not to be. Coordinated action by Bolivian and Argentine intelligence forces had already detected the guerrilla infiltration and operations were underway that would lead to its defeat, and ultimately to Torres's death. The Bolivian operational links to Operation Condor are exceptionally well documented. Bolivian author Gerardo Irusta obtained a file of coded and decoded telexes and telegrams, some of which were labeled *"Sistema Cóndor."* One such telex, dated May 3, 1976, was sent from Bolivia to Chile, informing the Chilean service that Colonel Carlos Mena Burgos had become the chief of military intelligence, SIE *(Servicio de Inteligencia del Estado).* Mena's promotion was important to the new Condor System because in November 1975, Mena—then the number two man in SIE—had been Bolivia's representative in Santiago at Condor's founding meeting.

In the first week of April, security forces raided a safe house in Oruro, Bolivia, where the Tupamaro leader Enrique Lucas—who went by the guerrilla name "Guilli"—lived with his Argentine companion, Graciela Rutila, and their infant daughter, Carla. The raiders missed Lucas by only a few hours. He had departed for Cochabamba to work on the preparations for the miners' uprising with Sanchez and other leaders, including the Argentine JCR representative Luis Stamponi. A Bolivian agent interviewed by Irusta said Rutila's capture was an important step in their operation. "It's true that Graciela Rutila was severely tortured because we were trying . . . to locate the whereabouts of Guilli and in that way cause the fall of the whole urban network of the ELN. That was our objective."

It is not known how much information Rutila provided under interrogation, but U.S. documents demonstrate that the Bolivian government was convinced it was under attack by internationally organized Communist forces. Banzer's Interior Minister, Colonel Juan Pereda Asbun, met twice in early May with U.S. Ambassador William P. Stedman and asked for help. He said Argentine intelligence had informed the government that "fifty armed guerrillas are being prepared to penetrate into Bolivia." In a secret cable May 11, Stedman reports, "Minister Pereda said that unbeknownst to the local press, Bolivian authorities have captured many subversive documents, broken up safe houses, and taken subversive elements into custody. They believe these are forerunners of a growing attack on Bolivia inspired by Communism from the outside." (In later cables, Stedman specified that the Bolivians believed the JCR, with its bases of operations in Latin America and Europe, was the source of the international threat.) Asbun asked for an increased flow of U.S. intelligence information, and Ambassador Stedman recommended that Washington approve the request. "I believe the minister's request for a greater flow of information from us about world-wide Communism would be in our best interests. If it were possible for one of our leading specialists on international Communism to visit Bolivia for conversations with the minister I think that would be highly useful for us."

Earlier the same day Asbun and Ambassador Stedman met in La Paz, a team of gunmen in Paris shot and killed Bolivia's ambassador to France, General Joaquin Zenteno. The assassinated general had been Banzer's partner in overthrowing the leftist Torres regime, but in the ensuing years had been transformed into Banzer's chief rival for power. Banzer had dumped him as chief of the armed forces and assigned him the Paris ambassadorship as a kind of golden exile. A group calling itself the International Brigade Che Guevara claimed responsibility for the attack, saying the assassination was in retaliation for Zenteno's role in the capture and death of Che Guevara. A caller to the newspaper *Libération* said the attackers were French leftists who created the brigade after the Chilean coup to retaliate against the Latin American military. The caller provided accurate information, later confirmed by French police, about the gun used in the Zenteno killing. The same gun was used in another assassination attempt in October 1975 against the Spanish military attaché in Paris representing the fascist Franco government. The group also claimed responsibility for the assassination of Uruguayan military attaché Colonel Ramón Trabal in December 1974. French police have never solved any of the assassinations. No evidence was ever developed to settle the lingering question of whether the Paris assassinations were the work of leftist or rightist terrorists.

A short time later in Buenos Aires, Banzer's most public enemy was eliminated. On the first day of June, Juan José Torres said good-bye to his wife and walked with a friend toward his office. The two men went their separate ways at a downtown street corner. Torres never arrived at his office or at an appointment he had made with an Argentine politician. The next day, on a country road seventy-five miles outside of Buenos Aires, the former president's body was found under a bridge. He had been shot once in the head and twice in the neck. A blindfold was still wrapped around his head.

The Argentine government denied knowing anything about the crime, as did the Bolivian government. Argentine economics minister José Alfredo Martínez de Hoz called U.S. Ambassador Robert Hill to assure him of the government's innocence and to say "he considered that killing was work of leftist extremists killing 'one of their own' " so that the blame would fall on the military government. It was not the first or last time this kind of "martyr theory" would be used to shift blame for international assassinations typical of Operation Condor.

Inside the U.S. embassy it was not an explanation that held water. Legal Attaché Robert Scherrer quickly developed information that the Torres murder was part of the new security force cooperation among the military governments. The embassy's initial optimism about a moderate military government was dashed on the bloody reality of mounting repression and the assassinations of three prominent figures—Michelini, Gutiérrez, and Torres—who had sought protection in Argentina.

Reporting to Washington the day Torres's murder was confirmed, Hill wrote that the embassy would reserve judgment pending further information about the crimes, and concluded: "There is no question, however, that it will be widely assumed in Argentina and abroad that the killing was work of GOA [government of Argentina] security forces acting officially, or at least that of semi-official 'death squad' which has tacit approval of GOA. Coming on heels of murders of the Uruguayan exiles Michelini and Gutiérrez, it will be taken as indication of campaign to eliminate leftist exile leadership in Argentina and probably to intimidate exile communities here."

Slowly, among those reading the most secret intelligence traffic about Latin

America—in the embassies, in the CIA, in the Defense Intelligence Agency, the FBI, and the State Department—there was an awakening to a flow of hard evidence that was soon to become a flood: that the government of Argentina was committing human rights violations on a massive scale never before seen in Latin America, and the six military governments of the Southern Cone were cooperating to assassinate one another's opponents.

10

GREEN LIGHT, RED LIGHT

My evaluation is that you are a victim of all left-wing groups around the world, and that your greatest sin was that you overthrew a government which was going communist. . . . In the United States, as you know, we are sympathetic with what you are trying to do here.

—Henry Kissinger to General Pinochet

We are behind you. You are the leader.

—General Pinochet to Kissinger in the same meeting

On June 8, 1976, in the midst of Chile's and Argentina's underground offensive against radical and moderate enemies of the region's military governments, Secretary of State Henry Kissinger arrived in Santiago. On his agenda: a speech on human rights and a meeting with General Augusto Pinochet.

Henry Kissinger didn't become one of the most powerful men in the world as an advocate of human rights. Yet it was on his watch as secretary of state that human rights entered the central lexicon of U.S. foreign policy and became enshrined in U.S. laws and government institutions. Human rights was run on two separate and often contradictory tracts, leading to a Manichean gulf of moral ambiguity in the record of U.S. foreign policy under Kissinger's stewardship. Nowhere are these separate tracks more visible—now that the previously secret documents have been released—than in U.S. actions surrounding Operation Condor and human rights atrocities in the Southern Cone.

It was Kissinger, as national security adviser, who in 1970 chaired the 40 Committee, the secret body of high officials charged with reviewing and approving the covert action program to subvert Chile's democratic election, and then organizing a military coup to prevent the Socialist candidate Salvador Allende from being inaugurated. The CIA reported only to Kissinger in the White House about its most extreme actions—those so secret they were concealed from the other 40 Committee members and even from the U.S. ambassador—such as the supplying of "grease guns" (submachine guns) to groups plotting to kidnap General René Schneider, the chief of the Chilean armed forces, who stood in the way of a coup. When one of the groups botched the kidnapping and killed the general, Kissinger and the CIA gave contradictory versions of the U.S. role. Kissinger claimed he ordered the coup operation stopped before the kidnapping, but the CIA insisted no such "stand-down" order was received. A Chilean court convicted the leaders of both groups and concluded they were working together throughout the coup plotting, including the kidnapping of Schneider.

The various plans to oust Allende were referred to as "Track I" and "Track II," depending on their level of secrecy and degree of criminal activity. This duality of approach, with its accompanying elements of confusion, obfuscation, and cover-up, would continue to characterize Kissinger's actions during later years. When General Pinochet finally accomplished the U.S. policy goal by overthrowing Allende in 1973, Kissinger and the CIA became personally invested in the success of General Pinochet's government. As secretary of state after September 1973, Kissinger sent signals to his subordinates that advocacy of human rights was a low priority, and discouraged reports from Santiago about Pinochet's abuses. When the new ambassador to Santiago, David Popper, reported to Washington that he had initiated a discussion of human rights in a high-level meeting, Kissinger scrawled on the cable, "Tell Popper to cut out the political science lectures."

Embassy officers in Santiago and desk officers in Washington learned quickly the danger of passing negative news about Pinochet up to the Secretary of State. When two embassy political officers wrote a description of empty streets in Santiago during the second anniversary celebration of Pinochet's coup, the report was excised from cables sent to Washington. An officer's eyewitness account of a concentration camp met a similar fate. State Department officers learned to use "weasel words" in writing about Chile, according to one key officer. Another officer working on Chile from State Department headquarters summed up Kissinger's policy toward Pinochet in three words: "Defend, Defend, Defend."

Yet even Henry Kissinger had to face the rising international pressure on human rights. During questioning in his confirmation hearings to be President Nixon's secretary of state, Kissinger framed human rights as a value to be subordinated to strategic goals: "In our bilateral dealings we will follow a pragmatic policy of degree. If the infringement on human rights is not so offensive that we cannot live with it, we will seek to work out what we can with the country involved in order to increase our influence. If the infringement is so offensive that we cannot live with it, we will avoid dealing with the offending country." Kissinger drew a distinction between "aggressive totalitarianism"—the Communist nations and their allies—and the governments who were trying to resist Communism. Chile and Argentina under anti-Communist military rule were clearly in the category of regimes the United States could "live with" because they were engaged in a higher struggle whose ultimate goal—in Kissinger's view—was the preservation of freedom.

By early 1976, however, Kissinger's "see-no-evil" approach to Pinochet had become untenable in the wake of worldwide condemnation of Chile and rising outrage inside the United States over abuses of the new military governments in Latin America. Congressional leaders such as Senators Ted Kennedy and Alan Cranston and Representatives Donald Fraser of Minnesota, Tom Harkin of Iowa, and Edward Koch of New York were accomplishing in Congress what the Executive Branch refused to do: use the leverage of U.S. economic and military aid to put pressure on human rights violators. The congressional pressure was holding up the planned sale to Chile of a fleet of U.S. F-5E fighter airplanes Pinochet had ordered as part of his military buildup against his neighbor to the north, Peru, which was threatening to reopen a century-old territorial dispute.

Thus Kissinger had human rights on his mind as he prepared for his first visit to South America, a region he privately disparaged as culturally irrelevant and economically insignificant. Only on the strategic canvas of the struggle against the Soviet Union did the Latin countries merit his attention. Pinochet had done an enormous service, in Kissinger's view, by stopping the advance of Allende's democratic but pro-Communist movement before it could become a showcase for non-capitalist solutions to social problems in the region. Now,

Pinochet needed Kissinger's help. Kissinger had been working hard, devoting extraordinary Saturday morning briefing sessions to the Chile problem. Ever pragmatic, Kissinger had decided that human rights was to be a tool toward the goal of breaking the barriers to the airplane sale and to improving Pinochet's image.

The occasion of Kissinger's visit to Chile was the annual meeting of the Organization of American States (OAS). At Kissinger's behest, the United States and its allies had lobbied to hold the prestigious meeting in Santiago as a way of raising Pinochet's profile among the few non-military governments still remaining in the northern tier of the continent, Central America and Mexico.

The OAS meeting was held in the massive conference center that had been built by Allende's government for the 1972 world meeting of the United Nations Commission on Trade and Development. Having bombed Chile's traditional presidential palace in the 1973 coup, Pinochet took over the conference complex as his government headquarters, rechristening it for a nineteenth-century military hero, Diego Portales.

Kissinger commented on the "beautiful building" when he arrived at noon on Tuesday, June 8 at Pinochet's office on the twenty-second floor. Pinochet began by saying he was "grateful" that Kissinger had come to the conference.

The account of what was said at the meeting between Pinochet and Kissinger was shielded in secrecy for more than twenty years until a transcript was finally declassified in 1998. These excerpts are from that document:

> *The Secretary:* It is an honor. I was touched by the popular reception when I arrived. I have a strong feeling of friendship in Chile.
>
> *Pinochet:* This is a country of warm-hearted people, who love liberty. This is the reason they did not accept Communism when the Communists attempted to take over the country. . . .
>
> *The Secretary:* . . . In the United States, as you know, we are sympathetic with what you are trying to do here. I think that the previous government was headed toward Communism. We wish your government well.
>
> At the same time, we face massive domestic problems, in all branches of the government, especially Congress, but also in the Executive, over the issue of human rights. As you know, Congress is now debating further restraints on aid to Chile. We are opposed. . . .

I am going to speak about human rights this afternoon in the General Assembly. I delayed my statement until I could talk to you. I wanted you to understand my position.

We want to deal in moral persuasion, not by legal sanctions. It is for this reason that we oppose the Kennedy Amendment.*

In my statement, I will treat human rights in general terms, and human rights in a world context. I will refer in two paragraphs to the report on Chile of the OAS Human Rights Commission. I will say that the human rights issue has impaired relations between the U.S. and Chile. This is partly the result of Congressional actions. I will add that I hope you will shortly remove those obstacles.

I will also call attention to the Cuba report and to the hypocrisy of some who call attention to human rights as a means of intervening in governments.

I can do no less, without producing a reaction in the U.S. which would lead to legislative restrictions.

The speech is not aimed at Chile. I wanted to tell you about this. My evaluation is that you are a victim of all left-wing groups around the world, and that your greatest sin was that you overthrew a government which was going communist.

It would really help if you would let us know the measures you are taking in the human rights field. None of this is said with the hope of undermining your government. I want you to succeed and I want to retain the possibility of aid.

If we defeat the Kennedy Amendment—I don't know if you listen in on my phone, but if you do you have just heard me issue instructions to Washington to make an all-out effort to do just that—if we defeat it, we will deliver the F-5E's as we agreed to do. . . .

Pinochet: We are returning to institutionalization step by step. But we are constantly being attacked by the Christian Democrats. They have a strong voice

---

*The Kennedy Amendment, to cut off future military aid to Chile, was passed June 16. Aid already approved and "in the pipeline" was allowed to be delivered, however. The weapons Kissinger was trying so hard to obtain for Pinochet were intended to counterbalance a feared arms buildup in neighboring Peru, which was receiving aid from the Soviet Union. Pinochet brought up the subject, and began a long discussion about the possibility of Chile launching a pre-emptive strike against Peru. He probed Kissinger about the conditions under which the U.S. would intervene militarily to support Chile. Kissinger made it clear that Chile would be on its own if it were the aggressor, but agreed with Pinochet that there would be one exception: if Cuba were to side with Peru, the U.S. would side with Pinochet.

in Washington. Not [with] the people in the Pentagon, but they do get through to Congress. Gabriel Valdés [a former Christian Democratic foreign minister living in New York] has access. Also Letelier.

The Secretary: I have not seen a Christian Democrat for years.

Pinochet: . . . Letelier has access to the Congress. We know they are giving false information. . . . On the human rights front, we are slowly making progress. We are now down to 400 [prisoners]. We have freed more. . . .

The Secretary: If you could group the releases, . . . have a bigger program of releases, that would be better for the psychological impact of the releases. . . .

My statement and our position are designed to allow us to say to the Congress that we are talking to the Chilean government and therefore Congress need not act.

We want an outcome that is not deeply embarrassing to you. But as friends, I must tell you that we face a situation in the United States where we must be able to point to events here in Chile, or we will be defeated. . . .

Pinochet: We are behind you. You are the leader. But you have a punitive system for your friends.

The Secretary: There is merit in what you say. It is a curious time in the U.S.

Kissinger ended the meeting by trying to nail down Pinochet on more prisoner releases and constitutional reforms. Pinochet sidestepped by saying he couldn't do anything during the OAS meeting or it would appear he was acting under pressure. "We might be able to do it in thirty days," Pinochet said.

Kissinger went almost directly from Pinochet's office to the cavernous meeting hall downstairs where he delivered his address to the OAS General Assembly. It was the first formal pronouncement by Kissinger on human rights, and it made the front page of the *New York Times* and other papers. It was a tough public statement that was seen as significantly raising the profile of human rights in U.S. diplomacy. "One of the most compelling issues of our time, and one which calls for the concerted action of all responsible peoples and nations, is the necessity to protect and extend the fundamental rights of humanity," he said, and proposed that the OAS give its fledgling Inter-American Human Rights Commission an enlarged budget and greater authority to investigate abuses. The commission had presented a 191-page report on continuing abuses in Chile, carefully documenting hundreds of cases of mass arrests, torture, and disappearances.

Then Kissinger delivered what sounded like a stark assessment of relations with Chile. "In the United States, concern is widespread in the executive branch, in the press, and in the Congress, which has taken the extraordinary step of enacting specific statutory limits on United States military and economic aid to Chile. The condition of human rights . . . has impaired our relationship with Chile and will continue to do so. We wish this relationship to be close, and all friends of Chile hope that obstacles raised by conditions alleged in the report will soon be removed." Chile and Cuba were the only countries signaled out for specific criticism in Kissinger's speech.

It was a strong statement, especially coming from Kissinger. Yet the public words had already been discounted by Kissinger's private assurances of friendship, admiration, and support in his meeting with Pinochet. Kissinger made it clear that the public statement was tactical, not a matter of principle, and that Pinochet's real problems were with Congress, not with the administration. And Kissinger did nothing to dispel Pinochet's paranoia about his exiled enemies, such as Orlando Letelier, who had "access to Congress."

Kissinger's private meeting with Pinochet was the green light track, followed by the public red light warning on human rights. Only perhaps in Kissinger's mind were the contradictory tracts reconciled as principled, effective policy.

Pinochet's comment after the meeting to his inner circle indicated that Kissinger's remarks on human rights hadn't made much of an impact. "He asked a lot, but offered little," was the paraphrase of Pinochet's reaction by one aide who heard him. Most important to Pinochet was the fact that Kissinger had come to Santiago. Kissinger's presence, Pinochet said, was an important contribution to his image.

The CIA quickly gave a rosy assessment, in a secret report circulated in Washington, that the Pinochet government was "gratified" and derived "badly needed respectability" from the OAS meeting in Santiago. The meeting also provided an occasion for Pinochet and his allies to strengthen what the CIA described as an emerging "anti-Marxist bloc."

If it was Kissinger's intention to dissuade Pinochet from the pattern of killings and kidnappings that had characterized his regime until June 1976, events immediately following the OAS meeting and in the months ahead showed that exactly the opposite happened.

DINA chief Manuel Contreras was in a period of intense activity. DINA was in charge of security for the OAS conclave, an activity that brought Contreras into regular contact with U.S. intelligence agents. With MIR and the Socialists now soundly defeated, Contreras had redirected his agents against the Communist Party, which at that time was pursuing a non-violent strategy. At a time when Pinochet was reassuring Kissinger that he was releasing prisoners, Contreras was secretly rounding up hundreds of new prisoners in the Communist Party strongholds of the northern mining region and in Santiago. Of those captured in the latest sweep, forty-seven people disappeared, including Communist party chief Victor Diaz and other top members of the party leadership.

Contreras had already turned his focus beyond Chile's borders. The enemies doing most damage to Chile were now outside the country. DINA had been developing what it called "extraterritorial capability" in two operational entities: the network of Italian terrorists and anti-Castro Cuban exiles that had been operating in Europe, and the new Condor system agreed upon at the founding meeting the previous November.

DINA's exterior department had recruited a new Cuban agent, Rolando Otero, who had arrived in Santiago on the lam from the FBI for bombing attacks in Miami. DINA gave Otero some money and sent him to Costa Rica with a mission: assassinate Andrés Pascal and his companion Mary Anne Beausire. The two MIR leaders had been granted asylum by the Costa Rican embassy after escaping the DINA attack on their Malloco headquarters. They had been allowed safe passage out of Chile and had flown to Costa Rica. Otero's mission was to follow them and kill them with the help of other Cubans who would fly in from Miami.

The plan misfired, however. Otero was actually a double agent, working for Venezuelan security police DISIP as well as DINA. Instead of going directly to Costa Rica, Otero flew to Caracas and reported the plot to DISIP. Venezuelan president Carlos Andrés Pérez quickly alerted the president of Costa Rica, Daniel Oduber Quirós, who ordered protection for Pascal and Beausire. Two Cubans arriving from Miami were arrested at the border. Otero, against the advice of his DISIP handlers, returned to Santiago and was thrown in a DINA prison cell and tortured.

The failed operation did not deter Contreras's plans for the Cuban-Italian network. At least two Cubans and three Italians, including Stefano Delle Chiaie, were living in Chile and working for DINA in 1976. There is evidence in secret intelligence files that Contreras planned to use the Cubans and Italians in future operational roles in the multinational Condor system that was just getting started.

Condor was next on Contreras's agenda after ensuring the safety of the OAS meeting. As scheduled in the founding *"Acta Final"* of the first Condor meeting, Contreras convened the heads of security services and their staffs from the six Condor member countries for a second Condor meeting in June. DINA defector Luz Arce said a large group of DINA officials—she was able to name eleven, including Contreras and operations chief Pedro Espinoza—attended the ceremonial inaugural session, held in a large meeting room at DINA headquarters in Santiago. She was able to identify the nationalities of participants from Brazil, Argentina, and Uruguay. The Argentine contingent included the enthusiastic "Rawson"—Lt. Colonel José Osvaldo Riveiro, of Argentina's 601 Intelligence Battalion, who had been so instrumental in recent Condor actions against MIR.

At the meeting, the Condor security forces made a momentous decision. Phase One—intelligence exchange, the data bank, and communications system—and Phase Two—joint operations in one another's countries—had been working well. The joint operations had all but wiped out the JCR leadership and infrastructure in Chile, Bolivia, Uruguay, and Argentina. Now Chile, Argentina, and Uruguay—the three most militant countries—agreed to move to Phase Three: joint operations outside of Latin America to track down and assassinate enemies who were operating from exile.

How U.S. officials learned of Condor's Phase Three assassination plans, and how they reacted, is perhaps the most important discovery of this book's investigation.

The meeting marks the beginning of a broad stream of intelligence about Condor's plans and operations. Unlike the first Condor meeting, about which not a single contemporaneous declassified U.S. document exists, the second meeting apparently was thoroughly penetrated by U.S. intelligence, perhaps due to the frequent contact between DINA and U.S. intelligence officers around that time regarding Kissinger's visit and the OAS meeting.

The intelligence about Condor, and the threat it contained about coordinated terrorist attacks outside of Latin America, became a matter of greatest urgency among a small group of U.S. officials who had access to the top-secret information. In later years, in what appears to be an an exercise in damage control, some of those officials, including Kissinger, claimed to have known little about Condor at the time, and to have remembered less after the fact. Thus the contemporaneous documents—those written during the days and weeks the events were unfolding—become the most important record of U.S. officials' knowledge and actions. It becomes a question, once again, of what did they know and when did they know it. In this case, the facts in dispute concern a series of events leading up to the most egregious act of terrorism involving Condor, the assassination in Washington, D.C., of Orlando Letelier.

In reconstructing the record of U.S. knowledge, based on the now-declassified documents, we find early discovery of planned assassinations, an apparently serious and at first energetic attempt by Kissinger and his lieutenants to warn Chile and the other countries to stop the Condor assassination plans, and finally an inexplicable failure to follow through with the warnings. It is my judgment that such a warning probably would have prevented the assassination of Orlando Letelier, an act of terrorism by a country allied to the United States.

At least one of the State Department officials who knew about the events concerning Condor in the summer of 1976 shared that haunting sense of missed opportunity, and expressed it in a biographical interview before his death.

In my investigation I have found thirty-seven U.S. documents dated prior to the Letelier assassination that relate to Condor directly or to the security coordination later identified as Operation Condor. All were kept secret for at least twenty-five years, until declassification by executive order began in 1999.

The earliest U.S. documents are in reaction to the quick succession of deaths of major exile leaders in Argentina: Edgardo Enríquez of MIR, Uruguayan political leaders Zelmar Michelini and Héctor Gutiérrez, and former Bolivian president Juan José Torres. The embassy–State Department exchanges, occurring just before and during Kissinger's trip to Santiago in June, discuss the immediate and obvious question of whether the various Southern Cone governments are cooperating in killing one another's enemies. The question was raised at first with caution and with obvious skepticism.

Ambassador to Argentina Robert Hill was apparently first to raise a red flag. After reporting in detail on the capture of Edgardo Enríquez and the murders of the Uruguayan politicians, he concluded that hopes for a "moderate Videla government" had been dashed and that strong U.S. action was called for. On May 25, three days after the Uruguayans' bodies were discovered, Hill presented a "démarche"—a diplomatic warning—without Kissinger's authorization to the military government "on the worsening human rights situation."

Kissinger received an intelligence memo on the situation on June 4, the day Bolivian leader Torres was found murdered. The memo discusses the possible "existence of an intergovernmental assassination program," but says "there is no evidence to support a contention that Southern Cone governments are cooperating in some sort of international 'Murder Inc.' aimed at leftist political exiles resident in one of their countries."*

Exchanges of information and training by the Southern Cone governments, however, are "logical," the memo says, because of the international character of the leftist organizations, whose "terrorists" are organized in the Revolutionary Coordinating Junta (JCR) and "move back and forth across Southern Cone boundaries."

Despite the memo's skepticism about international assassinations, Kissinger's deputy sent an "immediate action" cable to the embassies, ordering the ambassadors to provide more information and reply to him by June 7, the day he was to leave for Santiago. Titled "Possible International Implications of Violent Deaths of Political Figures Abroad," the cable included these questions:

> Do you believe that the deaths of political refugees or asylees from your country abroad could have been arranged by your host government through institutional ties to groups, governmental or other, in the country where deaths took place?
>
> Do you have evidence to support or deny allegations of international arrangements among governments to carry out such assassinations or executions?

Quick responses from Santiago and Buenos Aires reinforced the mounting concern. "We believe these arrangements are possible, and that it is also possi-

---

*Congressman Edward Koch, the New York Democrat who later became mayor of New York City, had recently made such a charge. In a confidential letter to the State Department, citing a June 3, 1976, cable (State 136607), Koch said, "It is alleged that these murders [of Michelini and Gutiérrez] indicate that elements within the Argentine military are cooperating with the military dictatorships of Chile and Uruguay to eliminate troublesome exiles." In leftist and exile circles, charges that the dictatorships were cooperating in an assault on one another's enemies had been common since the Prats and Leighton assassinations.

ble Chilean agents have been involved in killings abroad, possibly in cooperation with foreign governments," Santiago reported. "Possible but not proved," said Buenos Aires.

Soon after the OAS meeting in June, probably within days of the Condor meeting conducted by Contreras at DINA headquarters in Santiago, the CIA obtained new, solid information about Condor. A CIA informant provided a detailed account of the Condor meeting, concluding that a conspiracy did exist and for the first time gave its name, "Condor." The intelligence is contained in two heavily redacted CIA reports about the Santiago meeting.

CIA, July 2: [words blacked out] [I]ntelligence representatives from Bolivia, Uruguay, Paraguay, Brazil, Chile and Argentina decided at a meeting in Santiago early in June to set up a computerized intelligence data bank—known as operation "Condor"—and to establish an international communications network. In a separate agreement, Uruguayan intelligence [blacked out] agreed to operate covertly in Paris with its Argentine and Chilean counterparts against the Revolutionary Coordinating Junta and other leftist Latin American subversive groups.

[line blacked out] these security services are already coordinating operations against targets in Argentina. In May armed men ransacked the offices of the Argentine Catholic commission on Immigration and stole records containing information on thousands of refugees and immigrants . . . Two days later, 24 Uruguayan and Chilean refugees, many of whom were the subjects of commission files, were kidnapped and tortured for several hours. Some of the refugees later said their interrogators were security officers from Chile and Uruguay. . . .

There are also several reports that Chilean subversive leader Edgardo Enríquez, who was arrested by Argentine security forces on April 10, was subsequently turned over to the Chileans and is now dead.

The State Department's intelligence and research office, INR, dispatched a report summarizing the CIA information to all U.S. embassies in Latin America, and in France, Portugal, Sweden, Italy, and Norway—the European countries harboring the greatest numbers of exiles. The INR has no independent intelligence sources of its own, but distills and analyzes intelligence from embassies, military and CIA intelligence, and prepares reports for State Department use. The report is clearly based on the CIA reports, but plays down the CIA conclusion about security cooperation. Evidence for "an intergovernmental assassination plot" is "scanty," it said. The report hangs its skepticism on the distinction between intelligence exchange, which was the explicit purpose of Condor, and international assassinations, which had not yet been proven as part of Condor's activities.

An unusual debate ensued among the Condor country ambassadors, at the prompting of Kissinger's recently appointed top Latin American officer, Assistant Secretary Harry Shlaudeman. A career diplomat with a reputation inside the State Department for cold toughness and close relations with the CIA, Shlaudeman had served in Chile as deputy to the ambassador during the two-track coup plotting against Allende in 1970.

Shlaudeman had initiated the original queries to ambassadors on the killings and roundups of refugees, and now sent a third query. He said he intended to draft a formal "Trends Report" on the military governments, and asked the ambassadors in the Southern Cone countries for more information and opinions about security coordination, the seriousness of the "subversive threat," and human rights.

The ambassadors weighed in with long, sometimes passionate, cables. Reading the cables decades later, one can still palpate the deep ambivalence of these career foreign service officers. U.S. policy dictated support for dictatorships whose methods were profoundly at odds with American democracy and moral values, and they struggled to square loyalty to policy with basic common sense ethics. Lacking hard evidence or a pattern of criminal activity, no hard decisions were called for. As long as each ambassador was looking only at his own country, no one was compelled to look for international patterns. It was a system that subjected evidence of criminal conspiracy by governments to the strictest scrutiny but accepted at face value the military governments' disclaimers and professions of good intentions.

Shlaudeman's insistence that the embassies exchange views on security coordination, however, had the effect of bringing the evidence out in the open. Seeing one another's cabled assessments, the ambassadors found it more and more difficult to avert their gaze. The embassy in Buenos Aires showed barely concealed disdain for the overly cautious INR assessment of "scanty" evidence. Granted, the embassy wrote, the conspiracy to eliminate exiles has not been confirmed. "It should be emphasized, however, that local governments have motivation and opportunity to do so, and it would be equally erroneous to conclude that such conspiracy is unlikely." To conceive of Operation Condor as limited to its relatively innocuous activities such as intelligence exchange underestimates the degree of cooperation, the cable said. In fact, the cable said, security officers from Chile and Uruguay have been operating inside Argentina since the coup, and "appear to be acting as advisors to the Argentine forces in connection with nationals of their own countries supposed to be involved in the subversion."

> We consider that the evidence is heavily weighted in favor of the conclusion that both Chilean and Uruguayan security personnel are joining in operations of the Argentine security forces. . . . Without question regional governments have recognized and responded in kind to "internat[ion]alization" of terrorist/subversive effort, represented in Southern Cone by the JCR.

One ambassador said the United States should go along with the new development, not criticize it. From Montevideo, Ambassador Siracusa argued that the "increasingly coordinated approach to terrorism" was a logical response to the international threat confronting the regimes, and should not be viewed with hostility by the United States.

> "That these nations face a regional, coordinated terrorist threat is fact, not fiction," he continued. "The ERP, MIR, ELN, MLN-Tupamaros, and possibly others, have regionalized their operations through the JCR. Their coordination is not only regional, but now inter-continental. The most rational approach to deal with a coordinated regional enemy is to organize along similar lines. The U.S. has long urged these countries to increase their cooperation for security. *Now that they are doing so our reaction should not be one of opprobrium.* We must condemn abhorrent methods, but we cannot condemn their coordinated approach to common perceived threats or we could well be effectively alienated from this part of the world." [Emphasis added.]

It was an argument that would echo through the coming months: These are our friends; we share their goals if not their methods in fighting terrorism. If we express our qualms too loudly, we risk offending them and losing our effectiveness in guiding events in the region.

The ambassadors appear to have based their assessments on incomplete intelligence. Until this point, no report had said explicitly (at least in the portions that have been declassified) that Operation Condor was involved in assassinations outside Latin America, and the State Department's intelligence arm, INR, had taken pains to cast doubt on that possibility. CIA reports also skirted the issue, except to say that Edgardo Enríquez had been returned to Chile and killed.

Finally the debate was resolved. On Friday, July 30, the top Latin American officials for the CIA and the State Department sat down in the same room and exchanged intelligence on Operation Condor. For the first time, CIA laid out in plain language that Condor was set up to assassinate exile leaders and that an operation had already been planned for Europe.

According to a heavily redacted State Department memorandum, the CIA representative, whose name is blacked out,

> spoke about the growth of this organization of security services of the Southern Cone countries and of accompanying disturbing developments in its operational attitudes. Originally designed as a communications system and data bank to facilitate defense against the guerrilla Revolutionary Coordinating Junta, the organization was emerging as one with a far more activist role, including specifically that of identifying, locating and "hitting" guerrilla leaders. This was an understandable reaction to the increasingly extra-national, extreme and effective range of the [JCR] Junta's activities. [Nine lines blacked out.]

The State Department officials were shocked. Details about the location and targets of the Condor "hits" are blacked out in the declassified documents, but other documents specify Paris and Lisbon.

Shlaudeman's deputy, William Luers, who had served in the Soviet Union and prided himself on his impeccable anti-Communist credentials, said he left the meeting upset. Fighting terrorist guerrillas in South America was part of the strategic struggle against the Soviet Union, and he supported it. But sending assassination squads to other countries, especially to a U.S. NATO partner like France, was beyond the pale. Shlaudeman's other deputy, Hewson Ryan, had recently been the State Department's point man in opposing congressional efforts to cut off military aid to Uruguay. In hearings on Capitol Hill, he had launched an energetic defense of Uruguay's military government and assured the congressmen there was no evidence the military had anything to do with

Michelini's and Gutiérrez's deaths. He now knew he had been misled, and had misled Congress.

Shlaudeman was a man of action who rarely shared his emotions, even years later. He and his deputies agreed they had to act immediately on the new information. Kissinger would have to be brought into whatever they proposed. How widely was the intelligence about Condor's assassination plans distributed in the Ford administration? Unquestionably the information went directly to Kissinger, who briefed President Ford daily on national security matters. The intelligence is summarized in two daily intelligence reports, called the INR Afternoon Summary, which was distributed to officials with top secret clearance at State, the White House, and the Pentagon.

A veteran CIA official, Sam Halpern, who was an assistant to CIA director Richard Helms in the early 1970s, examined the reports at the request of the author. "This kind of report would have been highlighted right away," he said. "It would go right to the president [in the document known as the PDB, or President's Daily Briefing], particularly because of the Western Europe part. It would mean you have to assume they will do it [commit assassinations] in the U.S. as well. It is direct action against U.S. interests. If it didn't [go to the president], something was wrong in the system."

Shlaudeman had already been working on a long report to Kissinger on the Southern Cone military governments, based on the queries to the embassies on security coordination and human rights. Now, in the manner of a reporter on the trail of a big story, he had a new lead.

He finished the report (drafted by Luers) over the weekend and sent it to Kissinger on Tuesday, August 3. He gave it a title that would grab the attention of a strategic thinker like the secretary of state: "The 'Third World War' and South America."

He borrowed the title from Uruguayan foreign minister Juan Carlos Blanco, who said the Southern Cone governments were engaged in a Third World War against the terrorist left. To fight this war, Shlaudeman said, the military governments are coalescing in an alliance that involves both political solidarity and international security actions.

> They are joining forces to eradicate "subversion," a word which increasingly translates into non-violent dissent from the left and center left. The security forces of the southern cone

—now coordinate intelligence activities closely;

—operate in the territory of one another's countries in pursuit of "subversives";

—have established *Operation Condor* to find and kill terrorists of the "Revolutionary Coordinating Committee" [*sic*] in their own countries and in Europe. Brazil is cooperating short of murder operations.

Shlaudeman emphasized that the enemies in this war were so broadly defined that they could include "nearly anyone who opposes government policy." The problem is then compounded when police pursue these dissidents into foreign countries where they have sought refuge, he wrote, citing the cases of the Uruguayans killed in Argentina, perhaps as a "favor."

The term "Third World War" was significant as a description of the antiterrorist campaign, Shlaudeman said, because it "justifies harsh and sweeping 'wartime' measures [and] . . . the exercise of power beyond national borders."

Shlaudeman's report keeps the human rights aspects at a cool remove, avoiding moral commentary or alarmist characterizations. Instead, he casts the problem presented by the Condor alliance as the danger that the United States will lose influence as the dictatorships band together.

On the world scale, which he calls "the main East-West stage," the United States would be a "casual beneficiary" of the formation of a right-wing bloc, since it will be a sure ally against the Soviets and Cubans. But it would be a mistake to be lulled into complacency.

> We would expect a range of growing problems. Some are already with us. Internationally, the Latin generals look like our guys. We are especially identified with Chile. It cannot do us any good. Europeans, certainly, hate Pinochet & Co. with a passion that rubs off on us.

He ticked off the problems: human rights is becoming more and more a problem for international diplomacy; the bloc might be an obstacle to a "natural" alliance between the United States and Brazil; democratic countries in the north might start feuding with the dictatorships in the south. The most serious problem, he says, is the danger of spreading terrorism.

Over the horizon, there is a chance of serious world-scale trouble. This is speculative, but no longer ridiculous. The Revolutionary Coordinating Junta now
seems to have its headquarters in Paris, plus considerable activity in other European capitals. With terrorists being forced out of Argentina, their concentration
in Europe (and possibly the U.S.) will increase.

The South American regimes know about this. They are planning their own
counter-terror operations in Europe. Argentina, Chile, and Uruguay are in the
lead; Brazil is wary but is providing some technical support.

The next step might be for the terrorists to undertake a worldwide attack on
embassies and interests of the six hated regimes. The PLO has shown the way.
[Underlining in original.]

In response to this critical problem, Shlaudeman recommended the U.S.
should continue to exert a "moderating influence" while demonstrating support and understanding for the military regimes. The State Department
should have a balanced strategy of persuading the South American regimes
that the "Third World War" idea is exaggerated and dangerous and that they
need not fear a gradual return to democracy. On the other hand, the State Department should continue to defend the regimes against criticism in the U.S.
Congress and help them prove the terrorist threat they face.

On human rights, Shlaudeman said only that Secretary Kissinger's speech
in Santiago provided the framework for policy: a multilateral approach
through the OAS to avoid charges of U.S. intervention, while launching parallel attacks on Communist violators "to make clear that authoritarian regimes of
the right have no monopoly on abuses."

Shlaudeman's strategy paper to Kissinger is an articulate but ultimately self-
defeating statement. It attempts to accommodate human rights into the narrow range of options available to U.S. policy as defined by Kissinger. The goal
of preserving the anti-Communist alliance was seen to trump any action to
stop the military regimes' increasingly evident human rights crimes. Having
led with the alarming news of military assassination plans in Europe, the paper
ends with policy recommendations that are anemic by comparison. It carefully
parallels Kissinger's actions in Santiago only a few weeks before: Even as a red
light is flashed to stop human rights abuses, a green light of encouragement
and defense of the military's war on terrorism is placed beside it.

The strategy's weakness was almost immediately demonstrated. Some quarters at State favored taking direct action to stop the Condor assassination plans. Shlaudeman and Luers enlisted Kissinger's chief deputy, Undersecretary for Political Affairs Philip Habib, in an effort to persuade Kissinger to approve a plan of action. The goal was to warn the military regimes that the United States was aware of their assassination plans. The basic strategy was laid out at a meeting on August 3. Habib strongly supported the idea of confronting the governments directly to force them to abort their ongoing plans.* This time, at least in the minds of those drafting the policy materials, the red light would be bright, unequivocal, and would remain on until Operation Condor's plans were stopped.

As they deliberated, a Condor operation was already underway. It was not the one detected against targets in Europe. It was assassination in Washington, D.C.

---

* Habib had used a similar tactic before, with notable success. As ambassador to South Korea's military dictatorship in 1973, Habib confronted a remarkably parallel human rights drama. Korean security forces, the KCIA, had kidnapped dissident leader Kim Dae Jung. The embassy's CIA chief of Station, Donald Gregg, quickly confirmed that Kim was in the hands of the KCIA and was in danger of being executed. Habib acted immediately, ordering his embassy officers to contact every Korean official of any importance, and he personally met with the Korean prime minister to give an unequivocal message: "If Kim doesn't come back alive, you are in deep trouble." Kim was saved. He had been chained to concrete blocks and was being taken on a ship out to sea when the word came to abort his assassination. Kim became the architect of Korea's return to democracy and served as president from 1998 to 2003. See Donald A. Ranard, "Kim Dae Jung's Close Call," *Washington Post*, February 23, 2003.

11

A PREVENTABLE ASSASSINATION

Government planned and directed assassinations within and outside the territory of Condor members has most serious implications which we must face squarely and rapidly.

—Kissinger cable on Operation Condor one month before
Letelier assassination

We knew fairly early on that the governments of the Southern Cone countries were planning, or at least talking about, some assassinations abroad in the summer of 1976 . . . Whether there was a direct relationship or not, I don't know. Whether if we had gone in, we might have prevented this [the Letelier assassination], I don't know. But we didn't.

—Deputy Assistant Secretary Hewson Ryan

Michael Townley got his orders to kill Orlando Letelier in late June 1976, perhaps two weeks after Kissinger had his conversation on human rights with Pinochet, and a week after the Condor meeting that gave the go-ahead for Phase Three, "third country" assassinations. Four of the main actors—Townley, DINA chief Contreras, operations chief Espinoza, and Captain Armando Fernández Larios—have said directly or indirectly that Pinochet personally authorized the assassination. Contreras, in a court statement after his conviction, left no doubt that he was following orders: "In my role as representative of the President and Executive Director of DINA, I carried out strictly what he ordered me to do . . . I did not act on my own and whatever mission had to be carried out had to have come, as it always did come, from the President of the Republic."

That Letelier was very much on Pinochet's mind in June 1976 is evident from the transcript of his meeting with Kissinger. "Letelier has access to the Congress. We know they [Letelier and other exiles] are giving false information," Pinochet complained. Pinochet rightly worried that Letelier's access was an important factor in marshaling support for the cutoff of military aid to Chile.

Letelier's influence was well grounded. He was a veteran of more than a decade of Washington's high-stakes games of lobbying, money, and power. In the 1960s he worked as an economist at the Interamerican Development Bank. When Allende came to power, he was a natural choice for ambassador to the United States. He was a member of Allende's Socialist Party. His high-profile mission in the U.S. shielded him from the contentious in-fighting that was rampant in Allende's Popular Unity coalition of Marxist and non-Marxist parties. One of his main tasks was to negotiate compensation for American companies whose copper mines had been expropriated.

In 1972, Allende called Letelier back to Chile to serve as foreign minister. At the time of the 1973 coup he was defense minister, which meant that Letelier was Pinochet's most direct civilian boss. Arrested on the day of the coup, Letelier was imprisoned with other high-ranking prisoners in a concentration camp on frigid Dawson Island in the Strait of Magellan, one of the southernmost inhabited spots on the globe. Kissinger was one of several prominent international figures who lobbied for Letelier's release in September 1974. And Kissinger was among those who gave Letelier access when he arrived back in Washington to begin his new life as exile leader and international lobbyist against Pinochet. "I knew him. I liked him personally . . . And I saw him, I think, two or three times when he was in Washington as an exile," Kissinger said in a previously unpublished interview. The conversations with Letelier undoubtedly had little impact on Kissinger's attitudes toward anti-Communist dictators, but Kissinger chose not to mention the meetings when Pinochet raised the subject of Letelier in their conversation in Santiago.

Not surprisingly Letelier's most effective influence was among liberal congressmen such as Senators Frank Church, George McGovern, Edward Kennedy, and Hubert Humphrey. He had worked hard to provide evidence and coherent arguments for cutting off military aid to Chile. When the aid cutoff, known as the Kennedy Amendment, passed on June 16, Letelier was already off on another mission against Pinochet. He traveled to Holland, and his meetings there were followed by announcements that major Dutch investments planned for Chile had been cancelled.

Pinochet's fury was further inflamed by intelligence reports that Letelier was plotting with other exiles to launch a government in exile. No such plot existed, but there was no question that by mid-1976, Letelier had positioned himself as a powerful and unifying figure in Chilean politics. He was one of the few leaders, especially since the shooting of Bernardo Leighton in Rome the previous year, who bridged the political gulf between Allende supporters on the left and the centrist Christian Democrats, who had supported Allende's overthrow but now opposed Pinochet. On the short list of possible presidents in a post-dictatorial Chile, Letelier was among the youngest, smartest, and most broadly appealing.

The plot to kill Letelier in Washington was, in the words of the chief FBI investigator Robert Scherrer, a "modified stage three Condor operation." The complex operation put in play a conglomeration of DINA's Condor and non-Condor assets. Over a three-month period it involved missions to Buenos Aires, Asunción, Paraguay, and Washington. Participants included an American, Cuban exiles from DINA's civilian terrorist network, personnel from DINA's Exterior Department, and Condor partners in Argentina and Paraguay. Condortel, the encoded communications system, was also used.

On the last Saturday in June, Operations chief Colonel Pedro Espinoza summoned Michael Townley to an early morning meeting on a sparsely traveled road on the outskirts of Santiago. He ordered Townley to prepare for another mission, this time to Washington.

"Elimination?" asked Townley.

"Yes."

Townley was to work with Lieutenant Armando Fernández Larios, a diligent officer who, though still in his early twenties, was a veteran of a long list of major operations since the coup. He had entered La Moneda Palace immediately after it was captured on September 11, 1973, to carry out intelligence-gathering activities. He was along on the so-called "Caravan of Death," in which a team of officers traveled to five provincial cities after the coup to execute groups of captives. Assigned to DINA's Exterior Department at its creation, Fernández Larios was in Buenos Aires as part of the preparations for the Prats murder in 1974. And in 1975 and 1976 he was a member of the DINA teams operating in Europe.

(Contreras, again on the cusp of a major operation, in early July once again traveled to Washington to meet with the CIA. His conversations with Deputy Director Walters are secret, although Walters confirmed the meeting took place. Contreras also met with former CIA operatives who helped him buy weapons and high-tech surveillance equipment in violation of the Congressional ban.)

Fernández Larios was immediately dispatched to Buenos Aires. Townley followed the next day. They made contact with SIDE, the umbrella intelligence service that was DINA's Condor partner in Argentina, to arrange for false documents for the trip. But SIDE, which was immersed in the massive task of overseeing the kidnapping and disappearance of more than 300 people every month, declined DINA's request.

Back in Santiago, Townley learned his target was to be the former foreign minister, Orlando Letelier, and that he was to enlist the help of the Cuban exiles who had worked on previous missions and had recently spent time in Chile. Fernández Larios and Townley were to fly to Paraguay to get false passports and U.S. visas. Espinoza briefed Townley on Operation Condor. Paraguay was a member, and getting the false documents was going to be a good test of their cooperation, he said. The contact there was Colonel Benito Guanes, head of military intelligence and Paraguay's chief of delegation to the Condor founding meeting.

On July 17, Guanes's office received an encrypted telex, using the Condortel system. It read:

TO: GERMAN (D-2)
FROM: GUILLERMO (SUB-DIRECTOR OF FOREIGN INTELLIGENCE)
SERIAL NUMBER V/500   X-S GH171950JULIO76
FROM: CHILE
TEXT: TO ADVISE THAT TOMORROW, 18 OR 19 JULY, WILL BE ARRIVING
IN THAT COUNTRY FROM BUENOS AIRES ALEJANDRO RIVA DENEIRA
WITH COMPANION. FLIGHT NUMBER WILL BE FORWARDED FROM CON-
DOR ONE.* I WOULD APPRECIATE ASSISTANCE IN THE PERFORMANCE

---

* Condor One is Condor headquarters in Chile. In this case, according to what Guanes told the FBI, the use of the first person indicated the message was a personal request from DINA chief Contreras. Alejandro Rivadeneira was the false name used by Fernández Larios.

OF THE MISSION IN ACCORDANCE WITH REQUEST TO BE MADE BY THE
ABOVE-NAMED PERSON.

Townley and Fernández arrived as scheduled in Asunción. Guanes arranged for them to receive false Paraguayan passports, in the names of Juan Williams and Alejandro Romeral. Also as requested, Paraguayan officials presented the passports to the U.S. Embassy, which stamped visitors' visas in the passports allowing the two men to enter the United States. But there was a hitch: a Paraguayan official, eager to curry favor, informed the U.S. ambassador that the passports were false and that the two men were actually Chilean agents on their way to carry out a secret intelligence mission in Washington. On July 27, Ambassador George Landau informed the CIA. His message began the paper trail of U.S. information on the mission that would ultimately solve the crime.

At the State Department, an extraordinary and intense period of activity focusing on secret police operations got underway. There were two streams of information. One involved the CIA's revelation of Condor's plans to assassinate exiles outside of Latin America. The other stream concerned the discovery by Ambassador Landau in Paraguay that a secret DINA mission was actually on its way to Washington, D.C. Information from both streams, conveyed through the special "Roger Channel" communications system, swirled around many of the same officials at the CIA and the State Department.

As described in the previous chapter, CIA and State Department officials met July 30 to discuss the shocking new developments in Operation Condor. CIA revealed that Condor was going beyond mere information exchange to begin "hitting" guerrilla leaders abroad. Operations were being planned for targets in Paris and Lisbon. State's Latin America chief Harry Shlaudeman reported the information to Henry Kissinger on August 3, in a long memo on strategy. He stressed that the Condor targets include not only violent guerrillas but peaceful political exiles as well.

Two days later, on Thursday, August 5, Shlaudeman received a Roger Channel message marked "Eyes Only for Asst Secretary Shlaudeman from Ambassador Landau." The cable from Asunción says, "I want to bring to your attention the following matter, which in my view has troublesome aspects." Landau laid out the details of the visas granted to the two Chilean officers using false Paraguayan passports to enter the United States. He said a Paraguayan official had assured him that the Chilean mission was being coordinated with the CIA and that the officers would be meeting with CIA deputy director Vernon Walters in Washington. Landau had gotten suspicious, however, and ordered the passports and visas photocopied, including the photographs of the two men. He then had checked the story with CIA and found out, from CIA director George Bush, that Walters wanted nothing to do with the Chileans' mission.

Shlaudeman replied late that same day: "If there is still time, and if there is a possibility of turning off this harebrained scheme, you are authorized to go back through Pappalardo [the Paraguayan official who had arranged the visas] to urge that the Chileans be persuaded not, repeat, not to travel."

The photographs of the passports and visas were pouched to CIA, which passed them on to the State Department. Shlaudeman issued an alert to the Immigration and Naturalization Service to stop the men bearing the passports at the border should they try to enter. A few days later, the visas were officially revoked.

Three new CIA reports were filed the following week, adding additional detail to the Condor plots, and demonstrating how closely CIA was monitoring Condor developments. The new facts: Chile, Argentina, and Uruguay will hold a training course in Buenos Aires to prepare teams for assassination operations in Europe, to be centered in France, which has the highest concentration of exiles. The plans and the identities of the targets are so secret, they will not be revealed to some of the government leaders. Brazil decides it will not participate in the European operations.

For the State Department officials, it was time to move from information to action. Based on this information, a reasonable person could elaborate a simple and disturbing syllogism: Condor countries are planning assassinations of exile leaders abroad. There is specific evidence they plan to send teams of agents to Paris and Lisbon on collaborative assassination missions. There is separate evidence that Paraguay and Chile, both known to be Condor members, are collaborating to send a team of agents to Washington, D.C. Conclusion: the mission to Washington might be an assassination mission, and urgent measure should be taken to prevent such an act of terrorism in the capital of the United States.

If any official executed the syllogism outlined above and wrote it down, that document has not been released. If such a conclusion was indeed recorded before the assassination and not acted upon, its continued secrecy constitutes an official coverup of a devasting intelligence failure.

It is hard to believe that the officials didn't add two and two (Paraguay and Condor) and come up with four (a possible act of terrorism in Washington). There is no record in the declassified documents, however, to show that those privy to both streams of intelligence connected Condor to the DINA officers in Paraguay. In interviews, Shlaudeman, Luers, and Ambassador Landau say they did not make the connection. Shlaudeman's other deputy, Hewson Ryan, the one official known to have connected the events, as described below, is deceased. Nevertheless, whatever the conclusions there is ample evidence that Shlaudeman and his deputies took the warnings about Condor assassination plans very seriously at the time.

What action, then, was taken?

ARA chief Shlaudeman and his deputy William Luers knew that any effective action had to come from "the seventh floor"—the suite of offices occupied by Kissinger, his senior deputies, particularly undersecretary for political affairs Phillip Habib, and the senior policy staff. Habib had a track record of standing up to foreign dictators. Doing nothing was not an option, at least not for the officials informed about Condor. But they shared a two-pronged anxiety. First, they feared Kissinger might be hostile to anything that smacked of "human rightsy" criticism—a term of derision Kissinger had more than once used to brush aside reports from the Latin American desk. Second, and more ominously, there lurked just beneath the surface, never expressed in writing, the fear that the CIA may have a strong interest in Condor that went beyond gathering intelligence about it. The CIA guarded information about Condor with the highest "codeword" classification, and it was parceled out to State in dribbles. No one really believed that the CIA was involved in the assassination plans, but the CIA had encouraged assassinations before and it would be naive to rule it out. Less than a year earlier, the U.S. Senate had issued its report on CIA involvement in assassination plots in Cuba, Africa, and, most relevantly, in Chile.

Shlaudeman and Luers, both former ambassadors in Venezuela, knew well the peculiar competition between ambassadors and CIA station chiefs. Shlaudeman by all accounts was close to the CIA and had worked without friction with the CIA station. Luers had resisted CIA actions in Venezuela and felt long-lasting scars from his battles there. A common complaint, repeated often but off the record by former State Department officials, is "the CIA has its own policy for Latin America," separate from State.

Most of the negotiations about trying to head off the planned Condor assassinations took place in person and by phone between ARA and the seventh floor. The basic idea was simple and obvious: the United States government should tell each of the Condor governments that it knew about the assassination plans and was unequivocally opposed to them. In diplomatic language, such an official course of action is called a "démarche."

The devil in the details, of course, involved how to frame the warning, how strong it should be, to whom it should be addressed, and—of particular concern to Kissinger—how to signal that the United States understood and sympathized with the goal of fighting terrorism, even as it admonished the countries to change their methods. The actions must conform to Kissinger's Green Light–Red Light approach laid down by the secretary in his Santiago meetings and elaborated by Shlaudeman in his "Third World War" memo.

The process took two weeks and multiple drafts. Luers did the writing, as he had done on Shlaudeman's first long report to Kissinger on Condor. Undersecretary Habib was Kissinger's point person on the seventh floor. He also acted as go-between with the CIA, which had to sign off on the action. No record of Habib's conversations with CIA has been declassified, however. Habib died in 1992.

Kissinger initialed a final draft, titled "Operation Condor," on Wednesday, August 18. Another week passed before the four-page cable was dispatched via the Roger Channel, addressed for "immediate" action to U.S. ambassadors in Buenos Aires, Montevideo, Santiago, La Paz, Brasilia, and Asunción:

SUBJECT: OPERATION CONDOR
   YOU ARE AWARE OF A SERIES OF [CIA] REPORTS ON "OPERATION CONDOR." THE COORDINATION FOR SECURITY AND INTELLIGENCE IN-FORMATION IS PROBABLY UNDERSTANDABLE. HOWEVER, GOVERN-MENT PLANNED AND DIRECTED ASSASSINATIONS WITHIN AND OUTSIDE THE TERRITORY OF CONDOR MEMBERS HAS MOST SERIOUS IMPLICATIONS WHICH WE MUST FACE SQUARELY AND RAPIDLY.
   . . .

FOR BUENOS AIRES, MONTEVIDEO AND SANTIAGO: *YOU SHOULD SEEK APPOINTMENT AS SOON AS POSSIBLE WITH HIGHEST APPRO- PRIATE OFFICIAL-PREFERABLE THE CHIEF OF STATE*—TO MAKE REP- RESENTATIONS DRAWING ON THE FOLLOWING POINTS:

A. THE USG [U.S. GOVERNMENT] IS AWARE FROM VARIOUS SOURCES, INCLUDING HIGH GOVERNMENT OFFICIALS, THAT THERE IS A DEGREE OF INFORMATION, EXCHANGE AND COORDINATION AMONG VARIOUS COUNTRIES OF THE SOUTHERN CONE WITH REGARD TO SUB- VERSIVE ACTIVITIES WITHIN THE AREA. THIS WE CONSIDER USEFUL.

B. THERE ARE IN ADDITION, HOWEVER, RUMORS THAT THIS COOPER- ATION MAY EXTEND BEYOND INFORMATION EXCHANGE TO INCLUDE PLANS FOR THE ASSASSINATION OF SUBVERSIVES, POLITICIANS AND PROMINENT FIGURES BOTH WITHIN THE NATIONAL BORDERS OF CER- TAIN SOUTHERN CONE COUNTRIES AND ABROAD.

C. WHILE WE CANNOT SUBSTANTIATE THE ASSASSINATION RUMORS, WE FEEL IMPELLED TO BRING TO YOUR ATTENTION OUR DEEP CONCERN. IF THESE RUMORS WERE TO HAVE ANY SHRED OF TRUTH, THEY WOULD CREATE A MOST SERIOUS MORAL AND POLITICAL PROBLEM.

D. COUNTER-TERRORIST ACTIVITY OF THIS TYPE WOULD FURTHER EXACERBATE PUBLIC WORLD CRITICISM OF GOVERNMENTS IN- VOLVED. [EMPHASIS ADDED.]

The basic message of the démarche was unequivocal. It was a direct order, an immediate action instruction. It not only had Kissinger's signature at the end, there was a rarely seen annotation at the top "approved by the secretary." The ambassadors would understand that the instructions had Kissinger's full backing. Moreover, the cable had the effect of transforming the intelligence in- formation on Condor into an official finding—information on which action must be taken. For the ambassadors, the existence of "government planned and directed assassinations" was presented as a given, whose factual confirma- tion was as strongly established as is ever possible in the murky world of espi- onage. Assassinations had already occurred—Michelini, Gutiérrez, Torres, and dozens of other Condor country exiles only weeks ago in Argentina. And the new reports put previous terrorist attacks—Prats in Buenos Aires and Leighton in Rome—in a new and more ominous context.

The language suggested to the ambassadors was clear but couched in diplomatic escape clauses. Rather than accuse the governments directly, the ambassadors were to inform them that the United States was aware of and deeply concerned about "rumors." The message was clear: if nothing happened, if no assassinations occurred, the rumors would remain rumors. But if there was "any shred of truth" to the rumors, the governments were forewarned of moral and political consequences that could follow.

There was no threat of U.S. retaliation or sanction, only the general admonition that carrying out such assassinations would worsen the already deteriorated reputations of the military governments on the world stage. The most serious threat was unspoken but unmistakable: you have been found out; the U.S. government—including your counterparts in the CIA—oppose what you are doing; we want you to halt these plans.

The greatest potential impact was in Chile. Ambassador David Popper was a professional's professional. In being named as ambassador to Chile only three months after the coup, he had been given one of the toughest assignments in the U.S. diplomatic corps. With Chile's civilian leaders, he had to contend with the conviction that the United States had sold out the democratic political parties in favor of the right-wing military. With the military, Popper's challenge was to carry out Kissinger's mandate to support and defend, while attempting to convey a message that human rights was also a value to the United States. Popper presided over an oftentimes deeply divided embassy. On one side were the Cold War hawks in the military and CIA missions who advocated uncritical obeisance to Pinochet for dealing a death blow to Communism in Latin America. On the other were the more liberal foreign service officers who kept in touch with the Catholic Church's human rights organization and were appalled at Pinochet's rejection of democracy and the atrocities of his secret police. Popper let the debate rage in his embassy. The open environment earned him the near-universal respect of every officer who worked under him, even while exposing him to occasional rebukes from Kissinger, such as the "stop the political science lectures" note. Perhaps no other U.S. official so exemplified the Manichaean moral dilemmas facing those charged with executing U.S. policy in the Condor years.

And for Popper, the arrival of Kissinger's cable presented a dilemma of classic proportions. What follows is based on the declassified documents and the recollections of Popper's then deputy-chief of mission (DCM), Thomas Boyatt.

The U.S. embassy was located just off Constitution Plaza, where the bombed and burned Moneda Palace stood as a blackened monument to Pinochet's entry on the pages of Latin American history. When Popper arrived at the embassy that Tuesday morning, Kissinger's cable was his first order of business. As a Roger Channel communication, it was received through the most secure CIA radiotelegraph facilities controlled by the CIA station on the top floors of the embassy, and would have been delivered to Popper personally by CIA Station Chief Stewart D. Burton. Typical of his open style of leadership, Popper called in his two top political officers, DCM Boyatt and political counselor Charles Stout.

They all read the cable, focusing on a paragraph addressed specifically to their embassy: "For Santiago, discuss [with CIA station chief] the possibility of a parallel approach by him." The suggestion made sense: if Condor was operating out of DINA then one way to stop the assassinations was for CIA Chief Burton to go directly to Contreras.

But Popper's dilemma was about whether to confront Pinochet directly. Boyatt's account:

"My memory is that the station chief, the ambassador, myself and Charlie [Stout], we looked at this and we said, 'Now what the hell do we do.' " The obvious question—what did CIA in Chile know about this and when did they know it—went unasked. Burton said little in the meeting, and Boyatt assumed the ambassador already had an answer in his one-on-one meetings with Burton. Popper ran a tight embassy and insisted on regular briefings on what CIA was learning from its contacts with Contreras. Boyatt:

> Here's the ambassador, he's been ordered to do something. The question: is what the State Department is ordering us to do the best way to handle this problem? Essentially what we did was we sat down and talked about it. And a lot of arguments were made. The two main ones were, if you do this, you can forget the channel between the ambassador and Pinochet. That will be over. The ambassador will be frozen out, and as for the other 250 items the State Department wants us to raise at the highest levels of government we won't be able to do that. It would have burned him.

The real argument—we didn't put this in the cable—was, if we go to Pinochet, we will never know if he in fact is going to call Contreras in and make this point to him. He may just ignore it. He may never speak to Contreras. So if we want to get the message to DINA, we've got to take the message direct to DINA. And the ambassador is not the person to do that. The person to do that is his counterpart—the CIA station chief.

Popper ended the meeting. He quickly drafted a cable and had it sent out by the Roger channel before lunch. He recommended that he be allowed to drop the meeting with Pinochet.

> SECSTATE WASHDC IMMEDIATE
>
> IN MY JUDGMENT, GIVEN PINOCHET'S SENSITIVITY REGARDING PRESSURES BY USG, HE MIGHT WELL TAKE AS AN INSULT ANY INFER-ENCE THAT HE WAS CONNECTED WITH SUCH ASSASSINATION PLOTS ... IT IS QUITE POSSIBLE, EVEN PROBABLE, THAT PINOCHET HAS NO KNOWLEDGE WHATEVER OF OPERATION CONDOR, PARTICULARLY OF ITS MORE QUESTIONABLE ASPECTS.

Popper wrote that he agreed with Station Chief Burton's alternative approach, that Burton carry the message directly to DINA Chief Contreras.

Then he closed the cable with a sentence that can only be read with tragic irony after the fact:

> I NOTE THAT THE INSTRUCTION IS CAST IN URGENT TERMS. HAS DE-PARTMENT RECEIVED ANY WORD THAT WOULD INDICATE THAT ASSAS-SINATION ACTIVITIES ARE IMMINENT? THE ONLY SUCH INFO WE HAVE SEEN IS ONE REPORT FROM [ONE WORD REDACTED] UNCONFIRMED BY OTHER SOURCES. PLEASE ADVISE.

Popper's assessments that Pinochet was probably uninformed about Condor, and his question about the imminence of assassination, should not be judged with the hindsight we enjoy twenty-six years later. As Boyatt commented, this was an ambassador at work, responding to an official instruction in less than twenty-four hours. We have to believe that had the State Department replied as quickly to his request to "please advise," Popper would have acted immediately: Burton would have delivered the message to Contreras—at least within a day or two—and history perhaps would have been different. But that was not the way it happened.

Other ambassadors also reacted immediately. Ambassador William P. Stedman replied by Roger Channel on August 26. Bolivia was not suspected of participation in the Condor assassinations abroad, so Stedman had a very different message to deliver, one more in line with Kissinger's Green Light approach. In the Condor cable, Kissinger authorized Stedman to propose intelligence exchanges on terrorism. Stedman had for weeks been seeking authorization to provide U.S. intelligence on international terrorism to the Bolivian government, which felt particularly targeted because the Bolivian military had executed the guerrilla hero Ernesto "Che" Guevara. Now, Stedman was able to report that he had already had a meeting with a two high officials. "Both [names redacted] were pleased at the positive U.S. response and look forward to a fruitful interchange of information. [One of the officials] noted that the intelligence services of several countries are more closely cooperating than heretofore. However, there is still a desire on the part of the GOB [Government of Bolivia] to enter into a more productive interchange of information with the USG."

The intelligence sharing was offered to Argentina as well. "We are prepared to undertake periodic exchanges with the government of Argentina of information on the general level and mode of communist and other terrorist activity in the hemisphere and elsewhere if the GOA would be interested." The offer of U.S. intelligence on the military governments' enemies shows once more the dual nature of U.S. policy. Even as the United States was warning governments not to assassinate their enemies, it was offering information on them. A disclaimer at the end of the Kissinger cable demonstrates that the contradiction may have been noted: "You should of course be certain that no agency of the U.S. government is involved in any way in exchanging information or data on individual subversives with host government. Even in those countries where we propose to expand our exchange of information, it is essential that we in no way finger individuals who might be candidates for assassination attempts."

In Asunción, Paraguay, Ambassador George Landau also acted immediately on the instruction. Even though Stroessner's government had not been identified in the CIA reports as participating in Condor's extracontinental assassination plotting, Landau saw his job as preventive. "The approach was a warning that we were aware of it and we wanted to make sure that Paraguay does not get involved in this," he said in an interview. Stroessner received Landau alone in his office early in the morning, as he almost always did. He heard Landau out on Condor, said nothing in reply, then changed the subject. A few weeks before, Landau had handled the messy situation of the Chilean officers asking for U.S. visas under false pretenses, yet when the Condor démarche cable came in, he didn't connect the two issues.

Those three actions—Popper's request for further guidance, Stedman's reporting on new intelligence exchanges, and Landau's meeting with Stroessner—are the totality of the known embassy responses to Kissinger's August 23 instruction on Operation Condor. As far as is known, only one ambassador—Landau in Asunción—actually delivered the warning about U.S. disapproval of Condor's plans. There are no messages from the embassies in Buenos Aires, Montevideo, or Brasilia. Ambassadors Hill (Argentina) and Siracusa (Uruguay) are dead, and senior diplomats in those embassies at the time said they were never informed about the Condor telegram and know nothing about how their ambassadors carried out Kissinger's instructions. One thing is universally agreed: it is inconceivable that an ambassador in Henry Kissinger's State Department would ignore a direct order from the secretary of state. That is the unanimous and categorical judgment of every foreign service officer I interviewed.

So far as we can now determine, in the twenty-seven days between the sending of Kissinger's cable and the assassination of Orlando Letelier in Washington, Kissinger's instructions to warn Chile, Uruguay, and Argentina—the countries thought to be planning international assassinations—were not carried out.

Shlaudeman and Luers met with their CIA counterparts in Washington for their regular intelligence briefing on Friday, August 27. The declassified record of the meeting, dated August 30, is almost obliterated by redactions—only sixty-eight words can be read in a twenty-five-line typewritten section on Operation Condor containing approximately 250 words. Shlaudeman says, "we are not making a representation of Pinochet as it would be futile to do so."

The message seems to endorse Ambassador Popper's recommendation to avoid an approach to Pinochet that would be taken as an insult. The second part of Popper's recommendation, to send the CIA station chief directly to DINA chief Contreras, is not mentioned in what can be read of the memo.

Neither decision was conveyed to Santiago. DCM Boyatt says he remembers distinctly that no message endorsing Popper's alternative approach was received at the Santiago embassy:

> This says Shlaudeman has decided by August 30 not to go to Pinochet. So what's the big secret? Why couldn't we be put into action on August 31? And I don't know the answer to that. . . . But going to Contreras on August 31 would have made a difference, I think. Or at least it might have.

Three more weeks passed. In that period, ambassadors to both Argentina and Uruguay had opportunities to meet the heads of state in their respective countries. Ambassador Siracusa met on September 14 with General Aparicio Méndez, whom the military junta had recently named president. Siracusa discussed human rights in the context of recent U.S. legislation cutting off military aid to Uruguay, but nothing that could be construed as a warning on assassinations.

Ambassador Robert Hill had finally obtained his first audience with Argentina's top military leader and junta president, General Jorge Videla. The meeting was scheduled for September 21.

The day before, a message was received that seemed to put an end to the entire effort to warn the three countries about Condor. Shlaudeman, writing from the U.S. embassy in Costa Rica, where he was visiting, sent a secret cable to his deputy Luers to be conveyed to U.S. ambassadors to Argentina, Chile, and Uruguay:

> FOR ARA-LUERS FROM SHLAUDEMAN
> SUBJECT: OPERATION CONDOR
>   UNLESS THERE IS SOME COMPLICATION I AM UNAWARE OF, THERE WOULD SEEM TO BE NO REASON TO WAIT MY RETURN. *YOU CAN SIMPLY INSTRUCT THE AMBASSADORS TO TAKE NO FURTHER ACTION,* NOTING THAT THERE HAVE BEEN NO REPORTS IN SOME WEEKS INDICATING AN INTENTION TO ACTIVATE THE CONDOR SCHEME. [EMPHASIS ADDED.]

In fact the plan was well underway. Michael Townley had been in the United States almost two weeks. Lieutenant Armando Fernández Larios had come and gone. His part of the operation was to conduct surveillance on Letelier in Washington. He had handed Townley the surveillance report as they crossed paths in JFK Airport. Townley had all the information he needed—Letelier's address, car description, daily routine, and the route Letelier drove daily to his office in downtown Washington. Fernández and Townley had started the mission together as a Condor operation with the trip to Paraguay to obtain false passports and U.S. visas. But the gringos had gotten suspicious. The Paraguayan passports were worthless; the Paraguayans' bumbling had ruined the plan to use the Condor system to cover DINA's tracks. Instead, Townley and Fernandez traveled to the United States on official Chilean passports identifying them as government employees. It was a greater risk, but Townley intended to delegate the killing to the Cubans.

On September 16, Townley went to New Jersey to meet the Cuban members of DINA's network. Virgilio Paz had worked with Townley in Mexico, then in Europe the previous year as he crisscrossed the continent in futile pursuit of Socialist leader Carlos Altamirano. He had been in Rome before the assassination attempt against Bernardo Leighton, and had conducted spying missions for DINA in a variety of countries. He was the young operations man; his political leader was Guillermo Novo, chief of the Cuban Nationalist Movement, northern division, based in the large Cuban exile community around North Bergen and Union City, New Jersey. The CNM members' hatred of Fidel Castro had led them to embrace terrorism in the United States and to make common cause with Chile's Pinochet. Both Paz and Novo had spent time in Chile, most recently the previous June, when they received DINA training and solidified their relationship with the group of right-wing Italian fugitives hiding out in Chile. Among other things, Townley had taught Paz to build remote control bombs. Now Paz and Novo had accepted another DINA mission.

It was after midnight when Paz and Townley pulled up to the Union City house. Novo and another Cuban, Dionisio Suárez, were in the house with the supplies they needed: detonating cord and a fist-sized chunk of the putty-like explosive known as plastique, or C-4. There was also some TNT. Paz brought the radio paging device Townley had helped him modify at Townley's workshop in Santiago.

On Saturday, September 18, Paz, Suárez, and Townley gathered at a seedy motel room in northeast Washington to assemble the bomb inside an aluminum baking tin. When it was late and dark, they drove across the city to the well-appointed suburb where Letelier lived. They had driven by earlier to verify the address and confirm other details of Fernández's surveillance report. Letelier's Chevy Chevelle was parked in the driveway on the quiet cul-de-sac as expected. It was Chilean Independence Day. Orlando Letelier and his wife, Isabel Margarita Morel, had attended a party with other members of the large Washington-area Chilean community, and had arrived home about 11 P.M.

For Townley, it was familiar work. He walked down the street, quickly turned into the driveway, and slid under Letelier's car. Using black electrician's tape, he positioned the bomb under the driver's seat, the explosive shaped to direct its force upward. The Cubans had insisted that he, the DINA agent, have a direct role in the assassination. When morning came, Townley took an early plane to Newark and then spent part of the day with his sister, Linda, who lived in Tarrytown, north of New York City. Then he flew to Miami, where his father lived.

On Tuesday morning, September 21, Letelier drove down Massachusetts Avenue on his way to his office near Dupont Circle. With him were Michael Moffitt and his wife of four months, Ronni. Both worked at the Institute for Policy Studies—Michael as an economist assisting Letelier in writing projects, and Ronni as a fund-raiser. They lived near Letelier and were catching a ride because their car had broken down.

The bomb exploded just as the car entered Sheridan Circle, on a stretch of road known as Embassy Row. Letelier's legs were blown off, and he died almost immediately. Ronni Moffitt, in the front seat, caught a piece of shrapnel to the neck, which severed her carotid artery and windpipe. She drowned in her own blood. Michael Moffitt, riding in back and shielded from the main force of the blast, suffered cuts but survived.

The assassins escaped undetected. Investigators believe Dionisio Suárez, following Letelier's car in his own, used a remote-control device fashioned from a pager to detonate the bomb. Michael Townley got the news in Miami and flew back to Chile the next day, after visiting his parents and buying souvenirs for his children.

The bombing on Sheridan Circle was in 1976 the most egregious act of foreign-inspired terrorism ever committed in the U.S. capital. The crime was aggravated by the fact that it was organized and carried out not by an enemy of the United States but by a government that was a firm ally, and by a security force trained and with intimate ties to the U.S. military and to the CIA.

In inside-the-office exchanges, few U.S. officials doubted that Chile's hand was behind the crime. Officers at the State Department's Latin America bureau expressed the common assumption that Chile's DINA was the most likely perpetrator. One officer remembered someone bursting into his office and proclaiming, "DINA killed Letelier."

Connections to Condor and the Paraguayan incident were also made. CIA Director George Bush told an assistant he remembered the communications about the Paraguay passports. The assistant checked it out and wrote a memo to Bush, saying:

> You have an excellent memory and recalled Amb. Landau's efforts to involve Gen. Walters in doing something about the Paraguayan issuance of official passports to two Chilean army officers . . . The entire matter was turned over to State, which informed the FBI, in early August. In addition, after the Letelier killing, we told Schlaudeman's deputy Bill Luers, to review the case. . . . [word blacked out] speculates that, if Chilean govt did order Letelier's killing, it may have hired Cuban thugs to do it.*

The CIA also quickly made the connection to Operation Condor. In a meeting with Justice Department officials on October 4, Bush was told "the killing had been professionally executed . . . , and may well have been planned by DINA or may have been a CONDOR operation." On that basis, Bush approved CIA participation in the investigation as part of its "counterintelligence activities abroad."

The CIA immediately produced intelligence information pointing to Pinochet himself. In a October 6 "Intelligence Information Cable," a field official, probably in Chile, reported that "[source blacked out] believes that the Chilean government is directly involved in Letelier's death and feels that investigations into the incident will so indicate. . . . [Source] has pointed to comments made by Chilean President Augusto Pinochet Ugarte to the effect that Letelier's criticism of the Chilean government was 'unacceptable.' "

---

* This intriguing note has been overlooked until now because it is incorrectly dated as August 23, 1976. An internal reference to an article in "today's" *New York Times*, established the real date as September 23—two days after the assassination. The note is addressed "To: DCI [Director of Central Intelligence—Bush's title], Subject: Two Chilean Army Officers and Paraguayan Passports" (Chile Project).

That was in private, however. The story that received unofficial public sanction was the idea that leftist terrorists had committed the crime to discredit the Pinochet government and create a martyr of Letelier. This "martyr theory" found its way into early newspaper accounts, sourced to the CIA and unnamed government officials. One story said "the FBI and the Central Intelligence Agency had virtually ruled out the idea that Mr. Letelier was killed by agents of the Chilean military junta. . . . The intelligence officials said a parallel investigation was pursuing the possibility that Mr. Letelier had been assassinated by Chilean left-wing extremists as a means of disrupting United States relations with the military junta."

The leaked stories were deeply at odds with what was actually known about Chile, DINA, the Paraguay passports episode, and the three-month debate over Operation Condor. So deeply at odds that it must raise the possibility of an intentional effort in some quarters of the U.S. government to divert attention away from evidence pointing to Chile, DINA, and Condor. We will not be able to resolve the question of whether the deception was intentional and approved by high officials. In any case, the false trails were ultimately overwhelmed by the massive and determined investigation launched by the FBI and the Justice Department with the cooperation of the State Department. That investigation, described in *Assassination on Embassy Row*, solved the case after some delay, once it began to focus on the Paraguayan passport photos of DINA agents Townley and Fernández, which had been in CIA and State Department files for weeks before the assassination.

Our concern here is the story of what the officials knew *before* the assassination and what they did about it when the assassination occurred. Declassified documents now available tell a very different story from what officials led the public to believe in the official version of the Letelier assassination presented in court documents and testimony.

I have raised the question in this book: why didn't the officials privy to intelligence about Condor's assassination plans make the connection to the DINA mission thought to be on its way from Paraguay to Washington, D.C.? The context is the devastating possibility that a chance was missed to avert the act of terrorism in Washington.

The answer put out twenty-five years ago was that no connection could have been made, because Condor's international assassination plans were not discovered until *after* the Letelier assassination. For more than two decades, the only source of information on Condor was a cable from Robert Scherrer, the FBI's legal attaché in Buenos Aires, who has played a central role in many of the events in this book. Scherrer's cable, a week after the assassination, is still the most detailed description of the working of the three-stage Condor system.

Scherrer, in interviews with the author in 1979, said he learned about Condor on September 28 from an Argentine intelligence officer who complained that the Letelier assassination was "a wild Condor operation" by Chile's DINA. The head of Argentina's Army Intelligence Service (*Servicio de Inteligencia de Ejército—SIE*) had actually been in Santiago for consultations with DINA Chief Contreras during the week the assassination took place, the source said.* Argentina was concerned that the high-profile assassination in the U.S. capital would ruin Condor's plans for other ongoing operations in Argentina and abroad.

Scherrer said he had heard about intelligence sharing, data banks, and other kinds of cooperation among the countries of the Southern Cone, but nothing like this. That is only Phase One, the source said, and proceeded to reveal what Scherrer thought was the first information about Condor's international assassination plans.

A THIRD AND MOST SECRET PHASE OF "OPERATION CONDOR" IN-VOLVES THE FORMATION OF SPECIAL TEAMS FROM MEMBER COUN-TRIES WHO ARE TO TRAVEL ANYWHERE IN THE WORLD TO NON-MEMBER COUNTRIES TO CARRY OUT SANCTIONS UP TO ASSASSI-NATION AGAINST TERRORISTS OR SUPPORTERS OF TERRORIST ORGAN-IZATIONS FROM "OPERATION CONDOR" MEMBER COUNTRIES. FOR EXAMPLE, SHOULD A TERRORIST OR A SUPPORTER OF A TERRORIST ORGANIZATION FROM A MEMBER COUNTRY OF "OPERATION CONDOR" BE LOCATED IN A EUROPEAN COUNTRY, A SPECIAL TEAM FROM "OPER-ATION CONDOR" WOULD BE DISPATCHED TO LOCATE AND SURVEIL THE TARGET. WHEN THE LOCATION AND SURVEILLANCE OPERATION HAS TERMINATED, A SECOND TEAM FROM "OPERATION CONDOR" WOULD

---

* Colonel Alberto Alfredo Valín was the head of SIE, which was operating since the October 1975 reorganization as Intelligence Battalion 601 and Scherrer once mentioned that his source in SIE was a colonel. Airfare receipts establish that three other Argentina intelligence officers were also in Santiago in September, including the known Condor operative, José Osvaldo Riveiro, aka Osvaldo Rawson, of Battalion 601 (Arancibia II/122–123).

BE DISPATCHED TO CARRY OUT THE ACTUAL SANCTION [ASSASSINA-
TION] AGAINST THE TARGET. SPECIAL TEAMS WOULD BE ISSUED
FALSE DOCUMENTATION FROM MEMBER COUNTRIES OF "OPERATION
CONDOR" AND MAY BE COMPOSED EXCLUSIVELY OF INDIVIDUALS
FROM ONE MEMBER NATION OF "OPERATION CONDOR" OR MAY BE
COMPOSED OF A MIXED GROUP FROM VARIOUS "OPERATION CONDOR"
MEMBER NATIONS. TWO EUROPEAN COUNTRIES SPECIFICALLY MEN-
TIONED FOR POSSIBLE OPERATIONS UNDER THE THIRD PHASE OF "OP-
ERATION CONDOR" WERE FRANCE AND PORTUGAL.

 ... IT SHOULD BE NOTED THAT NO INFORMATION HAS BEEN DE-
VELOPED INDICATING THAT SANCTIONS UNDER THE THIRD PHASE OF
"OPERATION CONDOR" HAVE BEEN PLANNED TO BE CARRIED OUT IN
THE UNITED STATES; HOWEVER IT IS NOT BEYOND THE REALM OF POS-
SIBILITY THAT THE RECENT ASSASSINATION OF ORLANDO LETELIER
IN WASHINGTON, D.C., MAY HAVE BEEN CARRIED OUT AS A THIRD
PHASE ACTION OF "OPERATION CONDOR."

Scherrer told the author he thought he was the first U.S. intelligence officer to develop information about Condor's international assassinations, and that the information emerged only after the Letelier assassination. The same view is expressed by Letelier case prosecutor Eugene Propper. According to Scherrer and Propper, what was known about Condor before Letelier was murdered was that it was conducting intelligence exchange, not assassinations.*

That, we now know, was not true.

Detailed knowledge about Condor assassination plans went back several months before the Letelier assassination, as I have demonstrated in this and previous chapters. An effort endorsed by Secretary of State Kissinger was launched to stop Condor by warning the member governments. The effort was called off on September 20, even as the bomb had already been affixed to Letelier's car. The day it exploded and killed Letelier and Ronni Moffitt, the State

*In the course of his investigation, Propper received briefings on Condor from the CIA and State Department and was told they knew about Condor's European assassination plans before Letelier was killed (Chile Project). Yet his 1982 book *Labyrinth* portrayed the CIA as ignorant of the Condor assassination plans: "... the CIA station in Buenos Aires had previously reported something similar about Condor as an intelligence operation. But the Agency had not mentioned assassinations."

Department's INR Afternoon Summary contained yet another item about Condor, describing it as designed for the "covert elimination of subversives," but not mentioning the elimination of Letelier that same morning.

ARA chief Shlaudeman had issued the order for the ambassadors of Chile, Argentina, and Uruguay to "take no further action" on the Condor démarche. Then, in one of the strangest episodes in this perplexing saga, Shlaudeman again reversed himself and reinstated the cancelled order. Here is what is known from available documents and interviews.

On September 25, four days after the assassination, Shlaudeman reported on the Condor connection to Kissinger's Political Undersecretary, Philip Habib, who had handled liaison with CIA and Kissinger during the drafting of the Condor démarche cable:

> Operation Condor
>
> My CIA counterpart tells me that all the reports we have on this subject have been disseminated to the FBI. . . . My friend also told me that the security services in the Condor countries now know that we know about the proposed Paris* operation.

Then, Shlaudeman sent a Roger Channel cable to Santiago that is truly bewildering in the context of what has preceded it. You must recall that Kissinger's démarche cable was sent August 23, and Ambassador Popper answered immediately, asking for authorization to skip the approach to Pinochet and go directly to DINA's Contreras. For more than a month, Popper received no clarifying instructions. Then, on October 4, two weeks after the assassination in Washington, Shlaudeman abruptly replies by Roger Channel to Popper's six-week-old question:

> OPERATION CONDOR
> REFERENCE A) STATE 209192 B) SANTIAGO 8210
> WE AGREE THAT OUR PURPOSE CAN BEST BE SERVED THROUGH [CIA STATION] APPROACH TO CONTRERAS AND THAT THE ISSUE SHOULD NOT REPEAT NOT BE RAISED WITH PINOCHET. [CIA STATION

---

* I will return to the Paris operation in Chapter 12.

CHIEF] IS RECEIVING INSTRUCTIONS TO CONSULT WITH YOU ON MAN-
NER AND TIMING OF APPROACH.

Contreras answered predictably. DINA had nothing to do with any assassination plots, in Europe, Washington, or elsewhere.

Former Assistant Secretary Shlaudeman, in correspondence with the author about the declassified documents, called the argument based on the documents "speculative." But he said, "I simply do not remember the Condor affair
and have no idea what caused the delay in the telegram to Popper. . . . On my
side, I have no doubt that démarche or no démarche, Contreras's operatives
would have gone ahead and murdered Letelier." Shlaudeman declined to elaborate on the basis for that conclusion.

Other officials did remember and were disturbed by the missed opportunity
to act. CIA official Charles Bertram Dickens had been station chief in Paraguay
until 1973. He was working at CIA headquarters in Langley, Virginia, in later
years and discussed the cable traffic about both Condor and the Paraguay passports with FBI official Robert Scherrer. According to Scherrer, Dickens said he
looked up the traffic from the weeks before the assassination and was "appalled
by the way the cables were handled." The CIA should have taken action, but
didn't. "We should have called the attention of the Chileans on this, and said,
Hey, if anything happens to anyone with [connections] in Chile, we'll hold you
responsible."

Another U.S. official also has addressed the devastating implications of the
botched Condor démarche. He is Hewson Ryan, who was Shlaudeman's second
deputy and was present at the briefing on Condor that led to the démarche.

In an oral history interview in 1988, a few years before his death, he made
this comment, apropos of State Department shortcomings in human rights:

I think that we were remiss in some ways. I know of one case, which has never
come to public attention, of the fact that we knew fairly early on that the governments of the Southern Cone countries were planning, or at least talking about,
some assassinations abroad in the summer of 1976. I was Acting Assistant Secretary at the time and I tried to get a cable cleared with the 7th Floor instructing
our ambassadors to go in to the Chiefs of State, or the highest possible level in
these governments to let them know that we were aware of these conversations

and to warn them that this was a violation of the very basic fundamentals of civilized society. Unfortunately that cable never got out* and about a month later former Chilean Ambassador Letelier was assassinated on the streets of Washington. Whether there was a direct relationship or not, I don't know. Whether if we had gone in, we might have prevented this, I don't know. But we didn't.

We were extremely reticent about taking a strong forward public posture, and even a private posture in certain cases, as was this case in the Chilean assassination.

---

* Speaking from memory twelve years after the event, Ryan was mistaken on this detail but otherwise accurately characterizes the sequence of events. In fact, the cable was sent, but the instructions it contained were not carried out.

12

KISSINGER AND ARGENTINA'S
"TERRORIST PROBLEM"

[Argentine foreign minister] Guzzetti went to the U.S. fully expecting to hear some strong, firm, direct warnings on his govt's human rights practices. Rather than that, he has returned in a state of jubilation, convinced that there is no real problem with the U.S. over this issue.

—AMBASSADOR HILL IN CABLE CRITICIZING KISSINGER

"He [Kissinger] explained his opinion [that] GOA [Government of Argentina] had done an outstanding job in wiping out terrorist forces."

—CABLE ON KISSINGER'S VISIT TO ARGENTINA, 1978

"More and more is being heard about 'Operation Condor' in the southern cone. Military officers who heretofore had been mum on the subject have begun to talk openly about it. A favorite remark is that 'one of their colleagues is out of the country because he is flying like a condor.'"

—DEFENSE INTELLIGENCE AGENCY REPORT

It would be a mistake to assume there was a nefarious plot in the State Department to encourage the dictatorships to violate human rights, and that the plethora of cables to the contrary was some sort of elaborate fabrication. In fact, both message tracks were authentic, the ones putting up a green light as well as those displaying a red light.

Those who believe—out of ideology or cynicism—that there was no sincere effort by many U.S. diplomats to encourage respect for human rights during this time of terror do so in defiance of the obvious and abundant record now available to us. Such simple condemnation misses the deeper story, with much more disturbing significance for ongoing U.S. policy in contemporary wars on terrorism. There is a clear conclusion to be drawn from U.S. actions during the Condor Years: dictators will not understand a two-track moral message on human rights with the subtlety intended by its authors, however carefully crafted the message. The U.S. message will instead be grasped as a single, muddled endorsement of the brutal tactics in which our unsubtle allies are already engaged.

Sometimes the red light is from one institution, the green light from another—as in the roles the CIA and the State Department adopted in some cases. Sometimes it was one official who showed the green light even as another tried to put up a red light. This is the case with the various ambassadors in the Condor countries—with Siracusa in Montevideo and Stedman in La Paz tending to show an encouraging green light to the dictators, while Landau and Hill in Paraguay and Argentina tended to show red.

Sometimes—too often—both red and green lights are shown side by side in the same document or in the same official. This was the case of the Condor telegram a month before the Letelier assassination. Even as it tried to stop planned assassinations known to be underway, it went to great lengths to emphasize U.S. understanding and endorsement of the goals of the antiterrorist fight. Likewise, Ambassador David Popper's reporting from Chile combined criticism of human rights violations with condemnation of the extremist left. Yet he flinched when faced with the challenge of confronting Pinochet with a clear warning on Condor. Instead of decisive action, he undertook to fashion a compromise that would avoid offending General Pinochet. In Washington, officials dithered over details and ultimately lost the chance to stop Condor.

It would be naive to suggest that it was entirely within the power of the U.S. government to prevent the military governments of the Condor countries from killing and torturing their own citizens in their own territory, even if that were an unambiguous policy goal. Likewise, the failure to deliver a clear message to Chile was not the cause of the unprecedented act of terrorism on U.S. soil. But it was certainly the responsibility of U.S. officials to try to stop or limit the ongoing slaughter when the opportunity presented itself.

In this chapter our investigation will reveal cases in which quite the opposite happened. In the first case, Secretary of State Kissinger directly undercut the human rights efforts of his ambassador to Argentina. In the second case, U.S. intelligence agencies treated a Condor torture center not as a human rights crime but as a source to glean intelligence information about Cuba.

Ambassador Robert Hill was an unlikely human rights hero. He married into the enormously wealthy W. R. Grace family, whose vast investments and un-abashed manipulations of political power in Latin America had made it the stereotype—for Latin Americans—of Yankee imperialism. He was a Republi-can Party activist who had served in Congress and in several political appoint-ments in the State and Defense Departments under Presidents Nixon and Ford. As ambassador to Spain, he was known as an inveterate defender of Gen-eralissimo Franco.

As Argentina sank deeper into violence in 1976, however, Ambassador Hill responded not with anti-Communist ideology and pro-business instincts but with simple moral outrage at the mounting evidence of mass murder surround-ing him. When the military coup took place in March, Hill had been in con-versations with prospective coup leaders, and had been encouraged by assurances that the new government would avoid the atrocities of the Pinochet takeover in Chile. Indeed, for the first weeks, that seemed to be the case, and the scattered killings that occurred were able to be explained as the work of death squads outside the control of the military junta. In line with official U.S. policy, Hill endorsed the military's goals to bring order and defeat leftist ter-rorism.

As described in Chapter 9, neither human rights observers nor U.S. intelli-gence were aware that the military had already begun a program of secret ex-terminations of hundreds of suspected enemies in the months before the coup. It would be months before the extent of the mass killing would be discovered. The events that destroyed the illusion of a "moderate" military junta were the killings of foreign leaders in Argentina—crimes now known to be linked to Operation Condor—the murders of Uruguayan leaders Zelmar Michelini and Héctor Gutiérrez, followed quickly by the assassination of former president Juan José Torres of Bolivia.

Hill cabled the State Department in late May that "the time has come for a démarche at the highest level" to call attention to the worsening human rights

situation. He received authorization for an urgent meeting with the new foreign minister, Admiral César Guzzetti, and gave him a strong message of U.S.
concern. Those who killed Michelini and Gutiérrez and others, Hill said,
"seem to operate with impunity and are generally believed to be connected
with the Argentine security forces. Whether they are or not, their continued
operation can only be harmful to the GOA [government of Argentina] itself
and cause consternation among Argentina's friends abroad."

The killings only escalated, despite Hill's imprecations. At a subsequent
meeting with Guzzetti, Hill got an inkling that his tough message on human
rights may have been undermined by a different message from Washington,
even before he delivered it. At his September 17 meeting, Hill brought up the
murders several weeks earlier of several priests and the discovery of a pile of
bodies of suspected guerrillas at the locality of Pilar north of Buenos Aires. Yet
Foreign Minister Guzzetti seemed to dismiss Hill's concerns, according to
Hill's cable to Washington:

THE FOREIGN MINISTER SAID GOA HAD BEEN SOMEWHAT SURPRISED
BY INDICATIONS OF SUCH STRONG CONCERN ON THE PART OF THE USG
IN HUMAN RIGHTS SITUATION IN ARGENTINA. WHEN HE HAD SEEN
SECY OF STATE KISSINGER IN SANTIAGO,* THE LATTER HAD SAID HE
"HOPED THE ARGENTINE GOVT COULD GET THE TERRORIST PROBLEM
UNDER CONTROL AS QUICKLY AS POSSIBLE." GUZZETTI SAID THAT HE
HAD REPORTED THIS TO PRESIDENT VIDELA AND TO THE CABINET, AND
THAT THEIR IMPRESSION HAD BEEN THAT USG'S OVERRIDING CON-
CERN WAS NOT HUMAN RIGHTS BUT RATHER THAT GOA "GET IT OVER
QUICKLY."

Hill said he tried to explain that Secretary Kissinger surely was not implying
insensitivity toward human rights and that "murdering priests and dumping 47
bodies in the street in one day could not be seen in context of defeating terrorists quickly. . . . What USG hoped was that GOA could soon defeat terrorists,
yes. But do so as nearly as possible within the law. I said if any other meaning had
been placed on the secretary's remarks, I was sure it was a misinterpretation."

---

* Kissinger met with Foreign Minister Guzzetti during the OAS meeting in Santiago, after
Kissinger's meeting with Pinochet described in Chapter 10.

Hill was hopeful he had corrected misconceptions he believed Guzzetti had taken away from his Santiago conversation with Kissinger. There would be another opportunity soon to drive home the message on human rights. Guzzetti said he was traveling to Washington in October, and Hill helped set up a series of high-level meetings, including separate meetings with Kissinger and Vice President Nelson Rockefeller. Human rights would be high on the list of talking points.

But when Guzzetti returned from Washington, Hill learned that no such thing had happened. Far from appearing chastened, Admiral Guzzetti was "euphoric" and greeted Hill with an effusive and uncharacteristic hug when they met. The meetings had been a grand success, and Guzzetti had already delivered an enthusiastic report to President Videla. He had encountered barely a word of criticism about human rights but rather "consensus . . . to get the terrorist problem over as soon as possible."

From Rockefeller, he said he heard, "finish the terrorist problem quickly . . . the US wanted a strong Argentina and wanted to cooperate with the GOA."

From Kissinger: "The secretary, he said, had reiterated the advice given to him at the Santiago meeting, had urged Argentina 'to be careful' and had said that if the terrorist problem was over by December or January, he (the secretary) believed serious problems could be avoided in the US."

His open-arms reception in Washington "had gone far beyond his expectations." Guzzetti "expressed appreciation that high officials in our government 'understand the Argentine problem and stand with us during this difficult period.'"

Ambassador Hill reported the conversations to Washington on October 19 in a long cable in which he barely controlled his fury.

GUZZETTI WENT TO THE U.S. FULLY EXPECTING TO HEAR SOME STRONG, FIRM, DIRECT WARNING ON HIS GOVT'S HUMAN RIGHTS PRACTICES. RATHER THAN THAT, HE HAS RETURNED IN A STATE OF JUBILATION, CONVINCED THAT THERE IS NO REAL PROBLEM WITH THE U.S. OVER THIS ISSUE. BASED ON WHAT GUZZETTI IS DOUBTLESS REPORTING TO THE GOA, IT MUST NOW BELIEVE THAT IF IT HAS ANY PROBLEMS WITH THE U.S. OVER HUMAN RIGHTS, THEY ARE CONFINED TO CERTAIN ELEMENTS OF CONGRESS AND WHAT IT REGARDS AS SLANTED AND/OR UNINFORMED MINOR SEGMENTS OF PUBLIC OPIN-

ION. WHILE THIS CONVICTION EXISTS, IT WILL BE UNREALISTIC AND
INEFFECTUAL FOR THIS EMBASSY TO PRESS REPRESENTATIONS TO
THE GOA OVER HUMAN RIGHTS VIOLATIONS. HILL.

Hill's angry cable was a rare example of an ambassador daring to criticize Secretary of State Kissinger in an official communication, and his effrontery was not missed in Washington. Assistant Secretary Shlaudeman put the matter on Kissinger's desk within hours. "Bob Hill has registered for the record his concern for human rights in a bitter complaint about our purported failure to impress on Foreign Minister Guzzetti how seriously we view the rightist violence in Argentina," he wrote to Kissinger. "I propose to respond for the record."
Kissinger approved Shlaudeman's response to Hill, which began:

AS IN OTHER CIRCUMSTANCES YOU HAVE UNDOUBTEDLY ENCOUN-
TERED IN YOUR DIPLOMATIC CAREER, GUZZETTI HEARD ONLY WHAT
HE WANTED TO HEAR. HE WAS TOLD IN DETAIL HOW STRONGLY OPIN-
ION IN THIS COUNTRY HAS REACTED AGAINST REPORTS OF ABUSES BY
THE SECURITY FORCES . . . GUZZETTI'S INTERPRETATION IS STRICTLY
HIS OWN.

Shlaudeman's clarifications, however, referred explicitly only to his own meeting with Guzzetti. His cable did not challenge Guzzetti's version of remarks attributed to Kissinger and Rockefeller. He seemed to throw up his hands.*

---

* Shlaudeman, referring to the episode in an oral history interview in 1993, when asked about the controversy over human rights policy, replied: "It really came to a head when I was Assistant Secretary, or it began to come to a head, in the case of Argentina where the dirty war was in full flower. Bob Hill, who was Ambassador then in Buenos Aires, a very conservative Republican politician—by no means liberal or anything of the kind, began to report quite effectively about what was going on, this slaughter of innocent civilians, supposedly innocent civilians—this vicious war that they were conducting, underground war. He, at one time in fact, sent me a back-channel telegram saying that the Foreign Minister, who had just come for a visit to Washington and had returned to Buenos Aires, had gloated to him that Kissinger had said nothing to him about Human Rights. I don't know—I wasn't present at the interview." Association for Diplomatic Studies and Training Foreign Affairs Oral History Project, interviewed by William E. Knight, May 24, 1993.

IN ANY EVENT, YOU AND WE HAVE LAID IT OUT AS BEST WE COULD. IN
THE CIRCUMSTANCES, I AGREE THAT THE ARGENTINES WILL HAVE TO
MAKE THEIR OWN DECISIONS AND THAT FURTHER EXHORTATIONS OR
GENERALIZED LECTURES FROM US WOULD NOT BE USEFUL AT THIS
POINT.

The futility of the ambassador's lectures could not have been clearer as the
toll of atrocities by the Argentine military mounted in the waning months of
1976. Kissinger's State Department was sending both a red light and a green
light, and the green light was coming from a higher authority—Kissinger himself. Hill described a "discouraging" meeting with President Videla several
weeks before in which the Argentine president put the embassy officials in
their subordinate place. Videla repeated Guzzetti's version of his friendly visit
with Kissinger and contrasted it to the ambassador's pressing attitude on
human rights. Videla then said, according to Hill, "He had the impression senior officers of USG understood [the] situation his government faces but junior
bureaucrats do not."

If there were lingering doubts about Kissinger's real sentiments about Argentina's war on terrorism, they were dispelled after the secretary of state left
office and was welcomed by the junta in a private visit in 1978. According to a
cable by the new ambassador, Raul Castro, Kissinger met alone with Videla to
offer suggestions about how to improve relations with the U.S. government
under President Jimmy Carter, who had placed unprecedented emphasis on
human rights. In open meetings with prominent Argentines, Kissinger lavishly
praised the Videla government. "He explained his opinion [that] GOA [Gov-
ernment of Argentina] had done an outstanding job in wiping out terrorist
forces. But also cautioned that methods used in fighting terrorism must not be
perpetuated."

Indeed, Argentina's military leaders had followed Kissinger's recipe for
quick, intensive victory in the war on terrorism. The government had moved
with all speed. Roberto Santucho and the top ERP leadership were killed in a
raid in July. By the end of 1976, the ERP had been eliminated as a guerrilla
force, and Montoneros were fleeing the country. More than 4,000 people had
disappeared into the military network of secret torture camps. Another 1,000
people were killed in military actions in which bodies were left behind and
could be identified. Not surprisingly, however, the Argentine military had ig-

nored Kissinger's advice to change their "methods" once the war was won. The secret mass killing continued throughout 1977 and 1978, resulting in 3,937 additional disappearances, according to the conservative count of the Sabato commission, and did not stop completely until the military left power in 1983.

Condor's coordinated offensive against foreign leftist groups still in Argentina reached its greatest intensity in the period from July to October 1976. The center of operations was a nondescript building with a large metal door in the middle-class neighborhood of Floresta in Buenos Aires. A battered sign reading AUTOMOTORES ORLETTI remained from its former existence as an automobile repair shop. Since June it had been taken over by SIDE, the *Secretaria de Informaciones del Estado.* Orletti was one of an estimated 300 such secret prisons in Argentina. It had the distinction, according to later investigations, of headquartering the operations of foreign intelligence forces working in Argentina. Argentine military intelligence set aside this detention center for joint operations involving Argentina's Condor partners. Orletti was run by a civilian SIDE employee with a record for armed robbery, Anibal Gordon, and staffed by a squad of civilians and military known inside SIDE as Taskforce 18 or simply as "the Gordon Gang." The overall commander was SIDE chief General Otto Paladino. Orletti had an additional distinction: of the hundreds of prisoners interrogated there, only a handful survived.

Orletti was called *El Jardin*, "The Garden," by the security force squads that used it. Prisoners were kept on the first floor, in spaces once used for changing oil and overhauling engines. A few hulks of old cars still remained. Interrogations and torture took place on the second floor, where Gordon and the military interrogators had offices. During the day, from their filthy cells and the interrogation rooms, the prisoners could hear the sounds of classroom bells and children playing. There was an elementary school on the other side of an adjoining wall.

One of the few survivors, José Luis Bertazzo, who spent almost two months in Orletti, said in confidential testimony that he was able to identify Chileans, Uruguayans, Paraguayans, and Bolivians among the prisoners. They told him they were being interrogated by security officers from their own countries. Two prisoners from Chile's MIR also told Bertazzo that two Cuban "diplomats" had also been tortured at Orletti.

The two Chileans and two Cubans are at the center of our first story about Condor operations in Orletti, an episode that establishes that the CIA was receiving detailed, up-to-the-minute reports based on interrogations inside Orletti.

One of the Chilean activists was Patricio Biedma, who was MIR leader Edgardo Enríquez's right-hand man in Argentina. Since the March coup, his main function was to organize the escape of the remaining MIR elements from Argentina. Biedma had also been one of the MIR operatives staffing the JCR headquarters in Buenos Aires, and was in charge of moving money and messages back and forth to Chile. Biedma had been born in Argentina but lived most of his life in Chile. He had successfully arranged for his wife, Luz, and their child to leave Argentina before the coup.

The JCR war chest having been exhausted, money was short for the Chileans, Uruguayans, and even the Argentines operating in the JCR underground. And money was the key to obtaining the airline tickets, visas, and false documents needed to escape the rapidly tightening noose created by the military offensive and the accelerating Condor operations. Biedma and some of the Uruguayans turned to the Cubans for help. The Cuban embassy in Argentina was one of the few in Latin America. President Juan Perón, in defiance of the United States, had reinstated diplomatic relations with Cuba in 1973 and signed a lucrative trade agreement that included a $1.2 billion line of credit. It was because of this mutually beneficial relationship that Fidel Castro had turned a cold shoulder to the ERP emissaries who had asked his support for their guerrilla campaign in Tucumán.

In mid-1976, the Cubans were in a bind. They needed to keep the trade relations with Argentina, even as their ideological comrades from MIR and Tupamaros were being swept up. According to several sources, the Cubans began to provide clandestine financial support to help the various groups organize what was in effect an underground railroad for guerrillas and their families to escape from Argentina. Biedma was one of the intermediaries through whom the Cubans passed relatively small amounts of money to the fugitives.

Biedma was rounded up with other suspects in July, and when his captors learned he was Chilean, they delivered him to Orletti. On August 9, two young Cubans who worked as drivers and bodyguards at the Cuban embassy were walking to a bus. Clean-cut and muscular, Jesús Cejas Arias and Crescencio Galañena resembled in age and training the marine guards at the American embassy. They were part of a team of specially trained commandos brought in to guard ambassador Emilio Aragones, who had already survived one attempted kidnapping, and other Cuban diplomats. They also did odd jobs and messenger tasks as needed.

Because it was their day off, Arias and Galañena had been shopping for gifts to take home to Cuba and were unarmed. Witnesses said a detachment of thirty-five to forty armed men shut off both ends of the street where the two Cubans were walking. They put up a tremendous fight—both were trained in hand-to-hand combat. The Argentine commando didn't fire their weapons, clearly under orders to take the Cubans alive. They were taken to Orletti, where they were interrogated by both Argentine and Chilean officers.

Bertazzo, a nineteen-year-old bank clerk who by all accounts had no connections with guerrilla activity, arrived at Orletti on August 23 and was put in the same room with the MIR operative Patricio Biedma and another Chilean he knew only as "Mauro." In conversations, Biedma told Bertazzo about the two Cubans. He said he had been interrogated with them and that he could hear the Cubans (recognizable for their distinctive accents) being tortured upstairs.

The CIA's Buenos Aires station learned from its intelligence sources about this potential bonanza of information about the JCR and the Cuban connection in Argentina. The CIA station had been following closely the growing threat. A May cable expressed concern about the guerrilla alliance's continuing strength in Argentina, and its ability to organize effective propaganda operations in Europe against the military governments. The cable said JCR documents captured in Paraguay, Bolivia, and Argentina indicated "the *Junta [Coordinadora Revolucionaria]* has already achieved a status and operational capability that exceeds past efforts by Latin American revolutionaries to form an intra-hemisphere terrorist organization."

The interrogations of Biedma, Mauro, and the Cubans linked two areas of major U.S. intelligence interest: Cuba and the JCR. Both the FBI and the CIA were informed about the arrests and interrogations. Robert Scherrer, the FBI's man in Buenos Aires, said he was told, "It was a SIDE operation. The Argentines said the two Cubans were a *chofer* [driver] and a DGI [Cuban intelligence] agent. They were identified as having passed funds to MIR/ERP contacts. They said there had been in a meeting with the guerrillas."

Scherrer also pointed out that DINA agent Michael Townley had traveled from Santiago to Buenos Aires several days after the Cubans were captured. He suggested that Townley, who handled DINA's contacts with anti-Castro Cubans, may have been tasked to help with the interrogation of the Cubans in Orletti.

The U.S. embassy's CIA station received a briefing on the Orletti interrogations within days and reported the news to CIA headquarters. The CIA Directorate of Operations field report provides a rare window into the CIA's intimate knowledge of the Argentine security forces and their most secret repressive operations. The source of the report is not revealed, of course, but the information could only have come from SIDE or other Argentine intelligence contacts working at Orletti. The report is dated September 22, 1976—when the two Cubans and two Chileans were still alive and under interrogation inside Orletti. The text is as follows:

SECRET
Argentina-Cuba: Castro Support for Local Subversion?
Two leftist subversives in the hands of Argentine Authorities have detailed what they claim is Cuban support for terrorism in Argentina.

Argentine security forces last month captured Patricio Biedma and Mario Espinosa, Chileans who for some time had been working for the terrorist cause in Argentina. Biedma says he was both the leader of Chile's Leftist Revolutionary Movement (MIR) in Argentina and that group's delegate to the Revolutionary Coordinating Junta (JCR), a loose coalition of regional terrorist organizations. Espinosa claims also to have been a MIR member and most recently a combatant for the Argentine Peoples Revolutionary Army (ERP).

Biedma states that he met frequently with an officer of the Cuban embassy in Buenos Aires who "on a regular basis" provided funds for the JCR as well as for the ERP and Montoneros. [four lines blacked out]

Espinosa echoes the assertion that Cuba's embassy provides funds to Argentine leftists and says that he himself was trained in Cuba and then introduced to the ERP by a Cuban contact in Argentina.

"Mauro" and "Mario Espinosa" are clearly two false names for the same person Bertazzo saw with Biedma and the Cubans in Orletti. In their final conversation, Biedma told Bertazzo he thought he and Mauro were going to be transferred to Chile. Both men and the two Cubans disappeared.

Biedma, Mauro, and the Cubans were four human beings about whose illegal capture, imprisonment, and torture the CIA was informed in time to have intervened to save their lives. In the case of Mauro, the CIA information provided details that eventually allowed the author to establish his probable identity and to inform his family about a long-lost son. Mauro, in all likelihood, is Homero Tobar Aviles, the half brother of a famous guerrilla, Elmo Catalán, who fought with Che Guevara in Bolivia in the 1960s. Tobar received military training in Cuba and is known to have arrived in Argentina in the 1970s before his family lost track of him. The family never brought his disappearance to the attention of Chile's human rights organizations.

A second major Condor operation revolved around Orletti. A team of officers from Uruguay's SID, the newly consolidated defense intelligence service, began operating inside Argentina around the time of the coup. The Uruguayan operations in Argentina resulted in the largest group of disappearances carried out by Operation Condor. Indeed, more Uruguayans disappeared and were assassinated in Argentina—135—than in Uruguay itself as a result of security police operations.

Later investigations put names to the Uruguayan officers. They were led by then-Major José Nino Gavazzo, operations chief of Uruguay's Defense Intelligence Service (SID—*Servicio de Inteligencia de Defensa*), the centralized security force. SID deputy director was Colonel José Fons, who had led Uruguay's delegation to the Santiago meeting at which Condor was founded in late 1975. During much of 1976, Major Gavazzo was stationed almost exclusively in Argentina, returning home on weekends to visit his family. Several U.S. intelligence documents refer to an Uruguayan major, whose name is blacked out, operating in Argentina in coordination with Argentine security police.

There were three groups of politically active exiles in the large Uruguayan community in Buenos Aires. Prominent political leaders such as Senators Zelmar Michelini and Wilson Ferreira Aldunate and Camara of Representatives president Héctor Gutiérrez were pursuing a return to democracy. The second group, the deeply divided Tupamaros, had all but ceased guerrilla activity. The assassinations of Michelini, Gutiérrez, and Tupamaro leader William Whitelaw in May scattered these two groups into exile. That left a more recent third group, with anarcho-syndicalist roots, called the Party for Victory (Partido por la Victoria del Pueblo—PVP).

The newer PVP network was less known and more deeply hidden. It was better organized than the Tupamaros and flush with money. And Party for Victory included a small but capable military apparatus often referred to as the OPR-33. The military unit had carried out a quiet but successful kidnapping of a wealthy Argentine businessman in 1974, which netted a $10 million ransom. The PVP was seeking to supplant the dormant Tupamaros movement by launching a bold campaign of publicity and armed actions inside Uruguay. For the Uruguayan security forces and their Argentine partners, the PVP was an inviting target—as much for its subversive plans as for the prospect of confiscating the multimillion-dollar ransom thought to be stashed in a PVP safe house in Buenos Aires.

The operations against the PVP were relentless, and included waves of kidnappings in Buenos Aires from May to November 1976. Scores of captured Uruguayan PVP activists were packed into the small rooms on the first floor of the Orletti detention center. They included Michelini's daughter, Margarita, and the two most important PVP leaders, Leon Duarte and Gerardo Gatti. One of the women, Sara Méndez, was kidnapped with her twenty-day-old baby, Simon. Two other woman were in advanced stages of pregnancy. The prisoners were interrogated by Major Gavazzo, who made little secret of his identity and spoke openly with the captives, sometimes allowing them to remove their blindfolds.

The ransom money was the principal target of the interrogations of the Uruguayans in Orletti. Their story was told in dramatic detail by a survivor, Washington Pérez, a newsstand vendor. Pérez was allowed to enter and leave Orletti in order to establish contact with the remnants of the underground organization. His mission was to persuade the PVP underground to turn over the remains of the ransom money (thought to be at least $2 million) in exchange for the lives of the top PVP leaders, Gatti and Duarte. The mission failed, and the two leaders, who witnesses said were savagely tortured, disappeared.

Gavazzo, however, arranged for the transfer of a group of twenty-two captives back to Montevideo, thus saving them from the fate of virtually all the other prisoners who entered Orletti. His plan was to orchestrate a staged "invasion" of guerrillas into Uruguay and announce their capture. The idea was to use the incident to magnify the continuing threat of leftist violence, especially in view of the mounting human rights legislation from the United States Congress aimed at cutting off military aid. The U.S. embassy reported that the incident constituted "clear evidence of cooperation between GOA and GOU [governments of Argentina and Uruguay] authorities in such matters and, presumably, agreement on a 'cover story' to explain appearance here of persons disappeared in Argentina."

In September, Argentine and Uruguayan commandos rounded up another large group of Uruguayans. The twenty-eight captives included virtually the entire military apparatus of the PVP. Witnesses have established that nineteen of the captives were seen inside Orletti. Others were seen in other interrogation centers. None of the second group of PVP captives was ever seen alive again. They joined the ranks of the disappeared.

U.S. intelligence—both the FBI and the DIA—detected the secret roundups, and they were immediately linked to the emerging body of information about Operation Condor.

Contemporary U.S. embassy and CIA documents demonstrate that U.S. intelligence knew soon after the Argentine coup that a team of Uruguayan intelligence officers had set up shop in Buenos Aires and had launched a dragnet against exile leaders. The presence of the Uruguayan team was one of the arguments raised early on in embassy reports to support the suspicion that the military governments were coordinating their security activities across national borders. The August 23 Kissinger cable ordering the démarche to stop Condor assassinations cites the disappearance of thirty Uruguayans from the first roundups in June and July.

Just before and after the Letelier assassination in Washington, U.S. intelligence agencies reported on intensified Condor activities in the Southern Cone. A Defense Intelligence Agency report from Buenos Aires in late September noted that high-ranking Argentine intelligence officials traveled to Montevideo and Brasilia in mid-September to discuss intelligence coordination. A source told the DIA officer how the countries worked together:

...MUCH OF THE SUCCESS ENJOYED RECENTLY IN THE BATTLE AGAINST SUBVERSION CAN BE ATTRIBUTED TO STREAMLINED INTEL-LIGENCE ORGANIZATION AND PROCEDURES. [LINES REDACTED]... WHEN INTELLIGENCE INFORMATION IS RECEIVED BY THE POLICE IT IS RAPIDLY DISSEMINATED TO THE ARMY, NAVY AND AIR FORCE AND VICE-VERSA. [WORDS REDACTED] DESCRIBED THE SPEED OF DISSEM-INATION BY SAYING THAT INFORMATION "LITERALLY FLIES" FROM

ONE HQ TO ANOTHER. THEN, OPERATIONS ARE MOUNTED, SOMETIMES
IN A MATTER OF HOURS TO EXPLOIT LEADS BEFORE THE TERRORISTS
HAVE TIME TO REACT.

Information on Condor operations was also flying quickly into the hands of
U.S. intelligence officers. Uruguay's joint operations with Argentina in rounding up and disappearing the PVP and OPR-33 militants was a typical Phase
Two Condor operation, such as that described in the cable. Another DIA cable,
dating its information to September 28, showed that U.S. intelligence learned
within twenty-four hours about the roundup of the Uruguayan members of the
PVP and their military apparatus, the OPR-33.

DURING THE PERIOD 24-27 SEPTEMBER 1976, MEMBERS OF THE AR-
GENTINE STATE SECRETARIAT FOR INFORMATION (SIDE), OPERATING
WITH OFFICERS OF THE URUGUAYAN MILITARY INTELLIGENCE SER-
VICE, CARRIED OUT OPERATIONS AGAINST THE URUGUAYAN TERROR-
IST ORGANIZATION, THE OPR-33 IN BUENOS AIRES. AS A RESULT OF
THIS JOINT OPERATION, SIDE OFFICIALS CLAIMED THAT THE ENTIRE
OPR-33 INFRASTRUCTURE IN ARGENTINA HAS BEEN ELIMINATED. A
LARGE VOLUME OF US CURRENCY WAS SEIZED DURING THE COM-
BINED OPERATION.

MORE AND MORE IS BEING HEARD ABOUT "OPERATION CONDOR" IN
THE SOUTHERN CONE. MILITARY OFFICERS WHO HERETOFORE HAD
BEEN MUM ON THE SUBJECT HAVE BEGUN TO TALK OPENLY ABOUT IT.
A FAVORITE REMARK IS THAT "ONE OF THEIR COLLEAGUES IS OUT OF
THE COUNTRY BECAUSE HE IS FLYING LIKE A CONDOR."

13

ED KOCH AND CONDOR'S ENDGAME

In the aftermath of the assassination of Orlando Letelier in Washington, DC, U.S. officials questioned their assumption that other countries would not conduct assassinations in the U.S.

—CIA LETTER TO EDWARD KOCH.

Because throwing bodies in the River La Plata is creating problems for Uruguay, such as the appearance of multilated cadavers on the beaches, crematorium ovens from the state hospitals are being used for the incineration of conquered subversives.

—BRAZILIAN AIR FORCE DOCUMENT, 1977

The CIA had also discovered another plot. This one fit the description of Condor's top secret Phase Three capability—in which one country's assassination team targeted another Condor country's enemy outside Latin America. In this case, confirmed by exclusive CIA, Justice Department, and State Department documents obtained by the author, the intended victim was a prominent U.S. politician: Democratic Congressman and soon to be mayor of New York City, Ed Koch.

Koch was one of a small group of congressmen who began to focus fiercely in 1976 on human rights violations in the Southern Cone. He had entered Congress as a flamboyant liberal among the growing group of left-liberal congressmen elected in reaction to the Watergate scandal. He was looking for a way to make his mark on an issue of international importance. While most of the human rights attention in Congress was directed at Chile, Koch and Representative Donald Fraser of Minnesota wanted to put the spotlight on Uruguay because of its large prison population and many documented cases of systematic torture. The hearings began in June with the dramatic appearance of Uruguayan Senator Wilson Ferreira, only a few weeks after the assassinations of his colleagues Senator Zelmar Michelini and Representative Héctor Gutiérrez. The hearings continued through the summer, amassing evidence of fresh human rights violations by Uruguay. Koch used the evidence to draft legislation calling for the immediate cutoff of all military aid to Uruguay. The amount of aid—about $3 million—was among the smallest in Latin America. Koch picked such a small target on purpose. He expected he could win a significant symbolic victory for human rights without provoking the full juggernaut of opposition from the Republican administration. His strategy was well wrought, and Koch's amendment was signed into law on October 1, bolstered by outrage over the Letelier assassination only a week earlier.

As Koch was holding hearings and preparing his amendment in July, however, the CIA was picking up reports of assassination plans. The Uruguayan military, furious about Koch's targeting of their country, was prepared to back their anger with action. In late July, CIA station chief Frederick Latrash learned that two Uruguayan intelligence officers had made a death threat against Koch. Latrash reported the threat to CIA headquarters, with the caveat that it should not be taken seriously because the two officers were at a cocktail party and had been drinking heavily. The CIA did nothing. Latrash, in violation of basic chain-of-command procedures, did not report the information to his superior in the Montevideo embassy, Ambassador Ernest Siracusa.

Siracusa, a consistent defender of the Uruguayan military government, was in the midst of a State Department campaign to turn back Koch's amendment before it could become law. He flew to New York in August on a special trip to try to persuade Koch that he was wrong about Uruguay. After spending two hours with Koch, thinking he had made some progress, Siracusa invited Koch to come to Uruguay as his guest to see for himself. In his oral history interview, Siracusa recounted the incident: "He asked whether I thought he would be safe," Siracusa said. "I replied that he would be as safe as I was, as, to the extent he wished, I would be at his side at all times and that my guards would protect him as they did me."*

Koch said he considered going to Uruguay, but couldn't find the time. He was already preparing his next political move—to leave Congress to run for mayor of New York City. He now considers himself lucky. In September, the Letelier assassination radically changed the way the CIA looked at Operation Condor and its capability to conduct operations outside the borders of Latin America. On September 27, the CIA resurrected the death threat report and transmitted it to the FBI for possible action. It also informed the State Department.

The information about the threat was almost two months old, but it caused a small, secret earthquake inside the U.S. government. Sometime in early October, CIA Director George Bush took on the task of personally informing Koch about the threat. Koch took the call at his New York congressional office. He remembers Bush, a former and still friendly colleague from Congress, telling him that his amendment to cut off aid to Uruguay had provoked a threat and a plan of action to kill him. According to Koch, Bush said the security forces of another country, "I think he said Chile—I know it wasn't Uruguay—had put a contract out for you."

Koch was understandably worried. His amendment had been signed into law on October 1, ending all Fiscal 1977 military sales and aid to Uruguay. He wondered if he should have protection. Bush said the CIA was not in the business of providing security guards and suggested he contact the local police. Over the next few weeks, Koch was contacted by the FBI, who told him the Uruguayan officer who made the threat was quoted as saying to a CIA officer, "Maybe we would have to send someone to the U.S. to get Congressman Koch." Koch also received a mollifying visit from Assistant Secretary for Latin America, Harry Shlaudeman. In an interview, Shlaudeman said that Chile was named in the threat as the country that allegedly had been enlisted to assassinate Koch.

Ambassador Siracusa was beside himself when he learned what had happened. During a visit to Washington, he was informed that Latrash had known about the threat as early as July and had not informed him. "It was deeply em-

---

* Koch and another State Department source remember a different version: that Siracusa said Koch would be as safe in Uruguay as he was on the streets of New York—a not-too-subtle jab at the city's then rampant muggings and high murder rate.

barrassing to Siracusa," recalled his deputy chief of mission James Haahr. It had put the ambassador in the position of inviting a prominent American to visit a country whose military had said it intended to have him killed.

As soon as Siracusa returned to Uruguay, he called CIA station chief Latrash into his office and demanded to know why he had put the ambassador in an untenable situation by keeping the threat secret. The explanation that the threat was drinkers' braggadocio was not an acceptable excuse to expose a U.S. congressman to danger, no matter how unlikely it was considered inside the CIA. Shortly thereafter, Latrash was removed from the embassy. He had lost the confidence of the ambassador.

Who were the officers who made the threat? Latrash knew at least one of them personally. He was Colonel José Fons, deputy director of SID, the defense intelligence service, and Uruguay's representative to Condor. Fons considered Latrash a friend. They drank together, told war stories together, and sometimes Latrash gave him money for information. "I treated him like one of the family. Then he betrayed me," Fons said in an interview. The other officer was Major José Nino Gavazzo, SID's chief of operations on the ground in Argentina, whom we met in Chapter 12.

This is how it happened. In late July 1976, there had been what in the Southern Cone is called a "well-irrigated" cocktail party. From available documents it appears to have been the farewell party for the U.S. Army Attaché, Colonel Raul Garibay. Koch's amendment to cut off aid had been made public but had not yet been passed in Congress. Fons started to shoot his mouth off about Koch, about how the United States had trained the Uruguayans for decades to fight Communism, then the liberals came in and said the Communists were the good guys. Americans who understood Spanish had no trouble picking up what he was saying when he said he could arrange for Chile's DINA to go to Washington to kill Koch. Latrash heard him, and Latrash knew about Condor. It was a hot topic in July 1976, especially at CIA stations in the Condor countries. Most likely Latrash had done some of the reporting on Condor. He may even have known that Colonel Fons was Uruguay's representative to the first Condor meeting.

Fons was wrong about Latrash. It wasn't his CIA friend who had betrayed him. Latrash had reported the threat with no recommendation for action. It was someone at the CIA who had put two and two together after the Letelier assassination and had dug out Latrash's report, setting in motion the events that followed. In the dry language of an agency required to tell the minimum truth after the fact, the CIA eventually wrote to tell Koch how they had come to take the threat more seriously.

> The Agency's initial analysis of these comments was that they represented nothing more than alcohol-induced bravado. In the aftermath of the assassination of Orlando Letelier in Washington, D.C., U.S. officials questioned their assumption that other countries would not conduct assassinations in the U.S.

In other words, three months late, the CIA decided to do something about a an assassination threat against a U.S. congressman. There is another recognizable pattern of U.S. inaction: Congressman Koch wrote to Attorney General Edward Levi with the common sense suggestion that the U.S. government should put the Uruguayan government on notice "that it will be held responsible in the event of an assault upon him or his staff." Levi, in a declassified letter, passed the buck to Henry Kissinger, saying he should take "any action you deem appropriate." As far as the declassified record shows, no démarche on the Koch threat was ever presented to Uruguay, by any U.S. agency.

Fons and Gavazzo paid a small price for the incident. Both officers now had a record that could not be ignored in U.S. intelligence and State Department files. Those records were brought out when, in December 1976, the Uruguayan government attempted to reward both officers with plum assignments to represent the Uruguayan military in Washington, D.C. Fons was to become vice president of the Inter-American Defense Board, and Gavazzo was named defense attaché in the Uruguayan embassy. Both assignments required agreement by the U.S. government.

Assistant Secretary Shlaudeman, in a heavily redacted memorandum to Undersecretary Habib, explained the threat against Koch and named Fons and Gavazzo as the two officers linked to the threat. He noted that "Gavazzo is apparently a dangerous type." The appointments should be blocked, he said. "The fact alone of the threat against Koch seems to me sufficient grounds." Habib agreed and the two officers were refused visas. The only public reason ever given until now, however, was that Fons and Gavazzo might be subject to "unpleasant publicity" if they came to the United States because of their connection to Uruguay's controversial human rights record.

The Condor countries had at least one more Phase Three operation in advanced stages of preparation. Condor was planning to assassinate three leftist "terrorists" in Europe. The CIA had detected the plans as early as June. One of the Condor member services was leaking operational details of the mission to CIA officers. The targets were two JCR leaders in Paris, where the JCR was headquartered after it abandoned its base of operations in Buenos Aires. The plan also called for another assassination to be carried out about the same time in Lisbon. Brazil, known to have reservations about the plan, ultimately backed out, deciding that its participation in Condor would be limited to operations within Latin America.

The three most hardline Condor countries, Chile, Argentina, and Uruguay, began to put the operation into action around the time of the Letelier assassination, in September 1976. A CIA report three days after the assassination was titled "Operation Condor goes Forward," and stated, "With the Brazilian decision to confine its activities to the territorial limits of the Condor nations, training has begun in Buenos Aires for Argentine, Chilean and Uruguayan agents, who will operate in Western Europe."

FBI legal attaché Robert Scherrer also learned about the Paris and Lisbon plans, and about the training activities in Buenos Aires. The Condor team was made up of members of Argentine Army intelligence (SIE-601 Intelligence Battalion) and the state information service (SIDE), and included Uruguayan and Chilean participants. A DIA report based on Scherrer's information said, "They are reportedly structured much like a US Special Forces Team with a medic (doctor), demolition expert, etc. They are apparently being prepared for action in Phase Three."

In Chile, Michael Townley had been assured he would be allowed to lie low until the furor about the Letelier assassination blew over. Nevertheless, in November, DINA chief of operations Colonel Pedro Espinoza—the same officer who had given him the order to kill Letelier—told him he was being sent to Paris on another mission. In a handwritten letter in Spanish later obtained by a Chilean court, Townley described the mission as "an operation that we were going to carry out in Paris in combination with the Argentines and the 'Condor' network . . ." The targets, according to Townley, were René "Gato" Valenzuela, the MIR leader who ran the JCR office in Paris, and his companion, Silvia Hernández, the daughter of a prominent Chilean journalist.

Valenzuela had never been a high-profile leader of MIR during the Allende government, when demonstrations, speeches, and public debate were at the top of the revolutionary agenda. But in the time since the coup, he had proven an invaluable underground operative. He handled the day-to-day business of keeping the underground organizing functioning. Seldom a decision maker, he was the one doing the dangerous street work, running the network of couriers moving messages and documents among the safe houses, meeting in person with MIR militants to transmit the leadership's strategies and plans, and to impart instructions for operations. His distinctive facial features had gained him his nickname *"El Gato"* ("The Cat"), and he was careful to regularly change his appearance.

DINA brigades hunted obsessively for Gato Valenzuela. Tortured captives frequently talked about his central role, but he always eluded capture. In late 1974, he moved to Argentina to work with Jorge Fuentes and Patricio Biedma in the fledgling JCR. They worked under the direction of Edgardo Enríquez. After Fuentes was captured in Paraguay in mid-1975, Enríquez stayed in Argentina, and Valenzuela moved again, to run MIR and JCR headquarters in Paris. After living underground for two years in the most dangerous countries of South America, he considered Paris a safe haven. Still, he kept away from public events and never called attention to himself, living quietly with Silvia, who later became his wife. From Paris, he managed the flow of men, money, intelligence, and documents from JCR's growing European support network to the people in the underground in Chile and Argentina. He was meticulous about secrecy, keeping all his records in code, based on Soviet methods learned from East German intelligence.

In late 1976, his job had become damage control, as the coordinated security forces systematically obliterated the final traces of the MIR and JCR network in Argentina. Among his responsibilities was the debriefing of survivors who began to arrive in Europe, many having passed through DINA prisons. It was assumed that few had been able to resist the torture. His task was to evaluate the information they had delivered to assess how much damage had been done and what, if anything, of the decimated underground network could be reactivated.

The third major Condor target in Europe was the Venezuelan terrorist Ilich Ramírez Sánchez, also known as Carlos the Jackal. Condor's international mission, in the mind of its designer Manuel Contreras, was to rid the world of all manner of terrorists, such as Carlos, that the European governments were unable or unwilling to catch. Townley in testimony to an Italian court described an "intense" hunt for Carlos, and said that DINA was pursuing radical leftist groups in Europe, including the Baader Meinhof gang, the Irish Republican Army, and the ETA in Spain. Other confirmation that Carlos was a target is found in the still-top-secret Senate report, "Activities of Certain Foreign Intelligence Agencies in the United States." After describing Condor's Phase Three, the report says, "Condor thereupon planned an operation aimed at assassinating three well-known European leftists, one of whom was the notorious terrorist Carlos." A possible scenario for the operation was that Carlos had been located in Lisbon—the other city mentioned in CIA documents as the site of Condor's European operation.

It was an extremely complex mission, involving Townley and his wife; two other DINA Exterior Department agents, Cristoph Willeke and Ingrid Olderock; two Argentine military officers; and two Uruguayan officers. At one point in late November or early December, at least six of the eight members of the Condor team arrived in Paris. The size of the team would seem to indicate that the plan called for the creation of a permanent Condor headquarters in Europe. Two CIA documents refer to plans for such an ongoing presence.

But Condor was leaking badly. Reaction to the Letelier assassination started a flow of information that so severely compromised Condor that it caused the Paris-Lisbon mission to be aborted, and by the end of the year, Condor's Phase Three operations were dismantled entirely. Within a short time after the assassination, information about the European Condor mission appears to have become an almost open secret in intelligence circles. The notorious and spectacular nature of the assassination was a major factor in the decision by an Argentine intelligence officer to give detailed information about Condor to FBI legal attaché Robert Scherrer. The Argentine officer, who was most likely involved in the Paris and Lisbon Condor plans, said he considered Condor "ruined" by Chile's audacity in commiting such a crime in Washington, D.C.

Many documents showing the detailed flow of information about Condor after the Letelier assassination are still secret. But we know this much: On September 25—four days after the assassination—a CIA officer informed the State Department, "the security services in the Condor countries now know that we know about the proposed Paris Operation." Then, at an undisclosed date, the CIA informed French and Portuguese intelligence that assassinations were being planned in their cities. The French and Portuguese services did not dither or hesitate or debate the diplomatic implications. They went directly to their contacts in Chilean, Argentine, and Uruguayan intelligence and told them bluntly to stop the operations.*

Townley, who was waiting in Frankfurt, received word he was to abandon the operation against Valenzuela and Hernández. There had been *infidencias*—"disloyalties"—by the Argentines, and the operation was compromised. Townley was sent to Madrid, with yet another assignment: to team up with an Italian terrorist to try one more time to kill Socialist leader Carlos Altamirano, who was to attend a political meeting there. Again, nothing came of it, even though Townley says he located Altamirano and at one point physically bumped into him in the concourse of Barajas Airport in Madrid.

Another assassination plan, possibly part of the same Condor mission, was also aborted. Around the same time as the Paris operation, Scotland Yard contacted Uruguayan senator Wilson Ferreira in London, where he had begun his life in exile. Ferreira had survived the roundup in Argentina that had resulted in the assassinations of his colleagues Zelmar Michelini and Héctor Gutiérrez. He had testified before Congress in Washington in June, then gone to London to begin an exile of many years. The Scotland Yard agents told him they had detected a plot to kill him, and they provided protection.

A few weeks later, the six Condor security agencies assessed the damage, meeting in Buenos Aires in what was to be their final plenary meeting. Condor, in the argot of the intelligence services, was blown. The elaborate Phase Three scheme to carry the war against the left to the farthest corners of the world was collapsing under the weight of Chile's arrogance and Condor members' own inability to keep its secrets. The CIA had a source at the meeting who later provided a full report.

Argentina took the blame for the leaked operation in Europe, the CIA source said.

REACTION TO THIS PARTICULAR BREACH OF SECURITY WAS EX-TREMELY HARSH IN ARGENTINA WHICH RESULTED IN THE FIRING OF

---

* The Senate Report on Activities of Certain Foreign Intelligence Agencies states, "The plot was foiled . . . The CIA warned the government of the countries in which the assassinations were likely to occur—France and Portugal—which in turn warned possible targets (the CIA was aware of the identity only of Carlos) and called in representatives of Condor countries to warn them to call off the action. They did—after denying that it had ever been planned."

THE THEN DIRECTOR OF THE ARGENTINE STATE SECRETARIAT FOR IN-
TELLIGENCE (SIDE)...HE ADDED THAT THE FOREGOING INCIDENT
MADE CONDOR REPRESENTATIVES REALIZE THAT THE OTHER INTEL-
LIGENCE SERVICES ARE PROBABLY AWARE OF THEIR ORGANIZATION
AND, THEREFORE, EVERYTHING IS HANDLED ACCORDINGLY, I.E. WITH
A MAXIMUM OF CAUTION.

Condor's botched Phase Three operations were discontinued. Condor was
far from over, however. The cable continues:

CONCERNING CURRENT CONDOR OPERATIONS, [THE SOURCE] BE-
LIEVED THE EXCHANGE OF INFORMATION ON SUBVERSIVES AND TER-
RORISTS WAS BEING CONDUCTED MOSTLY BILATERALLY BETWEEN
INTELLIGENCE SERVICES OF MEMBER COUNTRIES. IN THE COVERT
ACTION FIELD, [HE SAID] THAT BOTH ARGENTINA AND CHILE WERE
MAKING EXTENSIVE USE OF THE COMMUNICATIONS MEDIA FOR PRO-
PAGANDA PURPOSE...

Going forward, the cable portrays an organization in the process of scaling
back the elaborate systems that held the six-country alliance together. A meeting on "Psychological Warfare Techniques Against Terrorists and Leftist Extremists" planned to be held in Asunción in early 1977 was cancelled because
Paraguay was no longer willing to participate. Finally, the cable said,

A NEW DATE FOR THE NEXT CONDOR MEETING HAD NOT BEEN SET.

The scaling back of Condor coincided with another security disaster in Argentina. The Orletti interrogation center, where many of the Phase Two Condor operations were carried out, had to be shut down in early November after
two prisoners managed to escape. The Orletti Taskforce 18 team had just
begun another joint operation with Bolivia, and Orletti housed several prisoners recently transferred from Bolivia in addition to the Uruguayans who remained. Publicity about the escape revealed for the first time the existence of
the Orletti prison in the middle of a quiet neighborhood. With the exception of
the two escapees, none of the final group of Bolivian, Uruguayan, and Argentine prisoners in Orletti survived.

The four-day Condor member meeting ended on December 16. On one of the evenings during the meeting, SIDE chief Otto Paladino, threw a large and loud party for the assembled intelligence officers. The occasion was his own dismissal as head of SIDE. It was a *despedida*—a farewell party, for him and other officers being transferred out of the intelligence service to other posts. One of the SIDE officers present described the party in secret testimony to an army tribunal in 1977. He said Uruguayan and Chilean officers were present. The party was held at Los Años Locos, a riverside restaurant, which had long been a favorite hangout for the men carrying out the dirtiest operations of the dirty war.* The name was appropriate: "The Crazy Years."

The Dirty War would continue with brutal intensity in Argentina, but in the other Condor countries the levels of repression never again approached those of the period from 1973 to 1976. As an apparatus for international assassination outside Latin America—Phase Three operations—there is no evidence of any Condor activity after December 1976.

Condor's deadly operations inside Latin America continued, however. Intelligence exchanges expanded, and at least two new members—Peru and Ecuador—joined the Condor System in 1978. The Condortel communications network was fully operational at least through that year. The final intelligence document mentioning ongoing Condor activity is a report from Paraguayan police intelligence chief Pastor Coronel, dated April 13, 1981. The CIA and U.S. military intelligence kept tabs on Condor activity, but U.S. officials—assured by their sources that Condor no longer ventured outside of Latin America—never again attempted to stop any Condor operations or express disapproval of Condor activities.

The security services employed the methods developed under Condor for several years to eliminate perceived enemies of the military governments.

---

*Leandro Sanchez Reisse, a civilian employee for Intelligence Battalion 601, said he had spent many nights drinking with security officers at Los Años Locos. Since most of the kidnapping operations occurred after midnight, the agents spent a lot of time at the bar drinking before the operations, and then would return to continue drinking and trading war stories after the operations were finished. Some nights, he said, he saw agents drinking at the restaurant with blood splatters on their clothes.

Many of the deaths and disappearances were seen as isolated actions at the time, but now can be more clearly seen as fitting the pattern of Condor Phase Two joint operations. Some of the operations can be linked by documentary evidence directly to Condor; in other cases we can only draw reasonable conclusions from the modus operandi. Here are a few of the most prominent examples among the many that could be listed in which adversaries of a Condor member were captured outside their own countries and killed.

Paraguay continued to track down its neighbors' enemies living in Paraguay, and received reciprocal help in capturing Stroessner's two most prominent enemies, who were operating from Argentina. One case is documented in detail in the Paraguay Archive. On March 29, 1977, Paraguayan intelligence police picked up two Uruguayans and three Argentines on suspicion of subversive activity against their home countries. The group was attempting to obtain false documents to send back to Argentina to help large numbers of Montoneros and Uruguayan PVP fugitives escape to Europe. Paraguay's Condor chief Colonel Benito Guanes notified his Argentine and Uruguayan intelligence counterparts, and a group of officers came to Asunción to participate in the interrogation of the suspects. Then, on May 16, the two Argentine SIDE officers returned with an airplane and took the five suspects to Argentina, where they disappeared.

The Condor transfers went in the other direction as well. In February 1977, at Paraguay's request, Argentine agents kidnapped exile leader Dr. Augustín Goiburú, a former Colorado Party ally of Stroessner's who had masterminded the botched attempt to assassinate the Paraguayan dictator in 1974. Goiburú was living in the Argentine provincial city of Paraná, where he was a practicing physician. Paraguay Archive documents establish that he was delivered across the border into the hands of Paraguayan intelligence police, and disappeared. Another prominent Paraguayan exile, Epifanio Mendes Fleitas, was also arrested in Argentina, but was released alive after several months.

One of the most complex Phase Two operations involved the roundup and disappearances of sixteen people in two countries, the extortion and confiscation of tens of thousands of dollars, and an elaborate three-country coverup scheme. A Chilean Communist with a Swiss passport, Alexei Jaccard Siegler was transporting a suitcase of cash from Europe for delivery to party contacts in Santiago. He landed in Buenos Aires on May 16, 1977, and was picked up in the street the next day. Argentine agents immediately rounded up twelve Argentine Communists and two other Chileans linked to Jaccard. It was one of the rare instances of deadly repression against members of the Argentine Communist Party, which had not openly opposed the military.

In Santiago, DINA agents kidnapped two Communist Party operatives thought to be the intended recipients of the money Jaccard was carrying. Within a few days of these arrests, two other Chileans, wealthy currency trader Jacobo Stulman* and his wife, Matilde, were taken into custody as they arrived from Santiago to Buenos Aires Ezeiza Airport. All seven Chileans and nine of the Argentines picked up were never seen again and are listed as disappeared.

The Swiss government and U.S. Jewish organizations made aggressive efforts to investigate the disappearances. To cover their tracks, the intelligence agents faked the departure of Jaccard and the Stulman couple from Argentina, using airline manifests, forged hotel registrations, and falsified immigration documents. The false documents showed Jaccard traveling to Chile a few days after his arrest, and then departing Santiago to Uruguay. False records also purported to show the Stulman couple's arrival in Montevideo. In the vain hope of rescuing the couple, family members paid tens of thousands of dollars in ransom to unknown persons. The extortion scheme intensified in the weeks following the kidnapping. Stulman's banks received payment orders with Stulman's authentic signature authorizing the transfer of a total of $127,000.

Brazil had kept an arm's length relationship with Condor, but its security force swung into action in 1980 to help Argentina smash an attempted guerrilla counteroffensive. Montonero leader Mario Firmenich, in exile in Spain, recruited a group of young exiles, who were trained in the Arab countries and organized as "Special Infantry Troops"—TEI in Spanish. Converging in Southern Cone countries in early 1980, they tried to smuggle themselves back into Argentina to renew the fight against the military.

But the 601 Battalion had penetrated the operation with informers and collaborators. The agents learned that two top Montonero leaders were about to fly from Mexico to Rio de Janeiro. One was Horacio Campiglia, the commander of the TEI operations. A U.S. security official got the whole story from his 601 source: "The Argentine military intelligence [601] contacted their Brazilian military intelligence counterparts for permission to conduct an oper-

---

* Also spelled Stoulman in court documents.

ation in Rio to capture two Montoneros arriving from Mexico. Brazilians granted their permission and a special team of Argentines were flown under the operational command of Lt. Col. Roman to Rio aboard an Argentine air force C130. Both of the Montoneros . . . were captured alive and returned to Argentina aboard the C130."

Then, as they had done in the Jaccard and Stulman cases, the 601 agents created a false paper trail in Rio showing that the two Montoneros had registered at a hotel, checked out, and departed Brazil on a commercial flight. In fact, the Montoneros were taken to one of the secret prisons at Campo de Mayo army base in Buenos Aires. Another Montonero was captured in the southern Brazilian city of Uruguayana about the same time and turned over to Argentina. In a short time virtually the entire counteroffensive force was captured. Almost all disappeared.

Following the failed counteroffensive, according to the well-informed U.S. officials, Argentina dispatched "three teams operating abroad with the specific mission of killing Firmenich."

Peru had shed its left-leaning military government and in 1980 was Condor's most recent member. In June 1980, a 601 Battalion team traveled to Peru to track down a group of Montoneros residing there. Again, U.S. officials in Buenos Aires received detailed information about the operation. The agents brought with them a Montonero collaborator to identify the suspects in Peru, three of whom were captured at their homes in a joint operation with Peruvian security forces. The captives were savagely tortured inside a Peruvian military installation, according to the eyewitness account of a Peruvian Army intelligence agent, Arnaldo Alvarado, to journalist Ricardo Uceda. After a few days the captives were transported to Bolivia with the intention of transporting them back to Argentina. "Once in Argentina, they will be interrogated and permanently disappeared," a U.S. official reported.

The operation blew up in the Peruvian press, however, and the Peruvian government was forced to acknowledge the detentions and "expulsions" to Bolivia. The U.S. embassies in Peru, Bolivia, and Argentina as well as Amnesty International and the United Nations Human Rights Commission were immediately involved in tracking the case. Some of the captives had recently been in Europe, and one was a well-known human rights activist, Noemi Gianotti de Molfino, one of the founders of the "Mothers of the Plaza de Mayo" group. With all the publicity about the operation and the knowledge that some of the captives were in Bolivia, U.S. officials expected "the media spotlight will provide a continuing measure of protection" and that the transfer to Argentina would be aborted. The scandal was still in the air in mid-July when U.S. ambassador Raul Castro had a meeting with Argentine Army Commander Leopoldo Galtieri. Ambassador Castro, according to his report to Washington, prodded him so much about the issue that Galtieri waved his hand and said, "enough is enough."

Despite the pressure and publicity, Battalion 601 proceeded with what appears to have been a far-reaching plan that included transporting the captive Noemi Gianotti secretly to Madrid. Judging from past 601 international operations, the plan may have been to use the woman, a prominent Montonero, to trap other Montoneros in exile in Europe. Whatever the plan, it resulted in Gianotti's death. Her body was discovered in an apartment in Madrid on July 21. Two men had rented the apartment only a few days before, in the name of one of the other captives in Peru, Julio César Ramírez.

No other bodies were ever found. Both Peru and Argentina were pilloried in the local and European press, and Peru was deeply embarrassed by its foray into Condor cooperation. Like the Letelier assassination, it was a Condor operation that had a diplomatic cost. Peru cancelled its invitation to President Videla to attend inauguration ceremonies of Peru's new president, Fernando Belaunde Terry. The episode caused wonderment in the U.S. embassy in Buenos Aires that the military government was continuing to sponsor such seeming counterproductive international operations.

The bloody yet damaging Peru operation is the last joint operation with a clear Condor trademark. It betrayed the disarray into which Manuel Contreras's grandiose scheme had fallen. Chile had ceased joint operations with Argentina in 1978 when the two countries fell into near warfare over a territorial dispute. Contreras was no longer the leader of DINA, much less of the international alliance. The Letelier assassination in Washington had exposed the existence of Condor and put a stop, for all practical purposes, to its Phase Three operations outside of Latin America. Contreras, the mastermind of the secret multicontinent war on terrorism and the most powerful man in Chile next to Pinochet, was suddenly vulnerable inside Chile. The FBI investigation of the Letelier murder, following the paper trail of the false Paraguayan passports, was leading directly to Contreras and DINA. Pinochet cut his loses in August 1977 and dissolved DINA. Contreras resigned from the army in March of 1978, a few weeks before a U.S. grand jury indicted him for the Letelier murder and the U.S. government officially asked for his extradition.

The wreckage left by Operation Condor would leave scars for decades to come. State-sponsored terror had eviscerated the nonviolent political opposition, creating an entire generation of political exiles forced to look over their shoulder wherever they were in the world, haunted by the specter of the assassination attempts against leaders like Letelier, Michelini, Gutiérrez, Torres, Prats, and Leighton—and even Paraguay's Goiburú. When other democratic and military leaders died, if the circumstances were at all uncertain, the possibility of assassination was inevitably raised even if no overt connection to Operation Condor could be shown. In a short span of years, so many prominent opponents of the dictators—civilian and military—died of natural or unnatural causes that questions have to be raised and investigations continued. Such are the cases of three Brazilians, all perceived as possible alternatives to the military: former president Joao Goulart died of a heart attack at fifty-eight at his exile home in Argentina in December 1976); former president Juscilino Kubitchek died in an automobile accident a few months earlier; and perennial "presidential hopeful" Carlos Lacerda died suddenly in the same year. There were never-solved assassinations in Paris that eliminated the most prominent dissident military leaders of Bolivia and Uruguay, Colonel Ramón Trabal in 1974, and General Joaquin Zenteno in 1976. Despite claims of responsibility by leftist-sounding groups, the doubts persisted. Chile's respected former President Eduardo Frei died at 71 from a massive infection after routine surgery in 1982.

A Paraguayan general was willing to talk frankly about the effectiveness of Condor. "There had been cooperation of one sort or another before," said retired General Alejandro Fretes Dávalos, who was chief of the Paraguayan general staff during the Condor years. "The difference was it [Condor] worked. It was very successful. It made short work of the international subversion. Otherwise we might have had communist governments in all our countries."

14

THE PURSUIT OF JUSTICE AND
U.S. ACCOUNTABILITY

The Condor years demonstrated, two decades after the fact, that unresolved crimes of the past do not remain in the past. Operation Condor returned like a painful, inflamed carbuncle to plague the old age of those who conceived it and the officers who carried it out.

Condor's success turned out to be ephemeral. A decade later, none of the military governments was still in power. The Condor regimes' secret campaign to eliminate their democratic and guerrilla adversaries eventually was replaced by another kind of pursuit, to bring the military leaders themselves to justice. This time it was a campaign carried out in the light of day and in the arenas of international law.

The pursuit of justice, begun while the crimes were still being committed, would continue and gain strength for more than two decades. It was at first a slow and tedious process that for long years seemed doomed to futility by lingering military influence, legal setbacks, and national indifference. But as this is written, human rights prosecutions were reaching a crescendo, resulting in hundreds of extradition petitions, indictments, and imprisonment for many of the military officers who had enjoyed years of court-protected impunity.

The crimes of Operation Condor became the catalyst for an intense international prosecution that mirrored Condor's three-continent arena of activity. The cross-border Condor activities had been a relatively small portion of the mass violations of human rights committed by the military governments. Nevertheless, Condor took on unique significance, both symbolically and legally, in the effort to bring the military leaders to justice. The Condor crimes, by targeting high-profile public figures, especially military leaders and democratic politicians, attracted the extraordinary attention of zealous human rights lawyers, crusading judges, and persistent investigative reporters.

The international nature of the crimes expanded the jurisdictions that could prosecute them. The military leaders left behind amnesty laws, often negotiated with their civilian successors, but Condor presented a special problem. Because the military governments did not admit the existence of the international operations, the amnesty laws were drafted to cover only internal human rights abuses. The Letelier murder, for example, was explicitly excluded from Chile's amnesty law, passed in 1978. Thus in many cases the Condor operations left military leaders exposed to prosecution in neighboring countries for crimes protected by amnesties at home.

Condor's operations also left a trail of potential witnesses and other evidence in dozens of countries in Latin America, Europe, and the United States. While the Condor countries were fairly systematic about eliminating incriminating evidence about their own military activities, they were far less efficient in protecting their Condor partners, especially after the alliance had ended and civilian governments were in power. The evidence was of less importance to the country where it was discovered than to the countries it implicated in criminal activity. Thus pursuing investigators were able to uncover rich veins of evidence, including caches of documents in some cases.

Because of its nature as a massive intelligence undertaking, Condor generated a broad paper trail in the U.S. government as well. Condor involved at least six governments' intelligence services, and as such it was of immediate and crucial interest to the CIA and U.S. military intelligence. While there was no systematic U.S. attempt to gather information on human rights abuses or to place obstacles in the way of those committing them (at least until the Carter administration), intelligence reporting on Condor alliance enjoyed a high priority. It was relevant not only to U.S. policy but to overall counterintelligence and military liaison goals as well. Reporting on Condor was protected at the highest "codeword" level of classification.

To be sure, this is not to say that Condor was the only factor in unleashing of the recent breakthroughs in human rights prosecutions. It is my task here, however, to complete the account of the Condor years by showing how the international crimes of the military governments gave way to an increasingly successful campaign to document the crimes of the past in courts of law and to bring charges against the authors of those crimes.

No step was easy in the search for evidence and the pursuit of eventual justice.

Still, the first step was gigantic. The FBI investigation of the Letelier assassination led not only to indictments but to the gathering and eventual declassification of an enormous body of evidence about the Pinochet government's secret police and its international activity. That evidence, contained in thousands of pages of trial transcript and evidentiary documents measured in linear feet, was the first detailed exposure of Chile's secret apparatus of repression. It was that evidence, in particular the investigative work by the FBI's man in Buenos Aires, Robert Scherrer, that first publically revealed the existence of Operation Condor, in 1979. We now know, however, as described in Chapter 11, that the evidence was carefully selected to conceal crucial details about U.S. intelligence on Condor. Chile maintained an iron wall of silence about its own military crimes as long as Pinochet remained in power, refusing extradition of those indicted in the United States.

Argentina was the first country to attempt real investigations and real trials. The junta generals tumbled from power after an abortive invasion in April 1982 to wrest the bleak Falkland Islands off the southern coast from Great Britain. The armed forces that had pursued so relentlessly the war against terrorism against Argentina's own citizens were routed when their bluff was called by Britain's counterattack. Thousands of ill-equipped and badly led Argentine troops were captured with barely a fight, and at least 1,000 were killed. Junta president Leopoldo Galtieri resigned in disgrace. The new military leader, General Reynaldo Benito Bignone, was forced to begin the process of restoring civilian rule.

There was an immediate campaign, fiercely resisted by the military, to prosecute the crimes of what everyone now called the Dirty War. The newly elected president, Raúl Alfonsín, who had been a courageous human rights activist during military rule, created a commission, headed by writer Ernesto Sábato, to investigate the fate of the disappeared. The Sábato Commission conducted a hurried investigation and delivered its report, titled *Nunca Mas*— Never Again—in less than a year. It listed 8,961 names of disappeared, the bedrock minimum of documented victims of the regime's network of secret prisons and extermination centers.

The task of naming and trying the perpetrators was left to the courts. The Alfonsín government pushed through legislation sweeping aside the military government's "Self-Amnesty" decree enacted just before leaving power. Trials of the members of the military juntas lasted from April to December 1985 and ended in the conviction of the five top leaders, including Videla and Navy chief Emilio Massera, who received sentences ranging from life to five years in prison. The trials created explosive anger among other military officers, who understandably concluded that they might be next to face trials. In fact, at least 1,700 additional prosecutions were in preparation in the months following the conviction of the top leaders.

For the next several years, the country roiled in unresolved conflict, including four armed rebellions by military units known as the *carapintados* for the camouflage paint they used on their faces. Alfonsín was forced to back down on prosecuting the lower ranking military. He agreed to set a deadline—called the *Punto Final*—after which no further charges could be filed against the military for human rights atrocities. Finally, in 1989, after a final bloody military revolt, Alfonsín's successor, Peronist President Carlos Menem, bought peace with the military by issuing presidential pardons for Videla and the other junta members.*

In the midst of the turmoil surrounding the trials and pardons, a young Chilean investigative reporter, Mónica González, arrived in Buenos Aires in pursuit of information about Chile's most famous unsolved murder: the 1974 assassination of Pinochet's predecessor, General Carlos Prats. There had been a perfunctory judicial investigation at the time that was quickly squelched by pro-military judges. González, a freelance reporter for a weekly magazine, wanted to study the Prats case files for a book she was writing.

After a frustrating week roaming the hallways of the majestic federal court building in downtown Buenos Aires, she had managed to read the official file of the case, but learned little. Most of the court employees and judges were holdovers from the military era, and the atmosphere in the court offices was unremittingly hostile.

By making herself and her quest visible, she finally got a break. A man she assumed was a court employee approached her in the hallway. "Señora, if you

---

* Menem also pardoned 277 other officers who had been convicted for human rights crimes, misconduct in the Falklands War, and participation in the military revolts.

want to find something, don't waste your time [with the Prats case file]," he said. "Just look for the espionage trial of Enrique Arancibia Clavel, for when they arrested him in 1978. Just get ahold of those files."

González knew the name. Enrique Arancibia was a notorious right-wing civilian who had fled Chile in 1970 because of involvement in terrorist bombings around the time of the elections that brought Allende to power. After the coup, he had gotten a job in the Buenos Aires branch of the Chilean Banco de Estado. There had been a brief flurry of publicity surrounding his arrest as a spy in 1978, during a tense period in which Chile and Argentina had both mobilized their forces in a military standoff over disputed territory in the southernmost tip of the continent, known as the Beagle Channel. But when the crisis between Chile and Argentina abated, thanks to papal mediation, the charges were dropped, and Arancibia resumed what appeared to be a quiet life as a restaurant owner. He was one of the people González had on her list to interview.

González learned that at the time of his arrest, Argentine police had searched Arancibia's apartment and his bank office and confiscated extensive files documenting his work as a Chilean agent. González looked up the case and located the judge in charge. The court files were supposed to be public records, but the judge had absolute control over who would be allowed to see them. He refused to give her access to the archive, or even to talk to her.

González had been ignored, brushed off, lied to, and threatened on this reporting trip, and she was no longer willing to take no for an answer. She decided to make herself a nuisance. She found out where the judge lived and set up a vigil, arriving by bus at 7 A.M. each morning on the street outside his house. For a week, she was there as he left his house in his chauffeur-driven car, trying to get his attention. The judge's wife came out and surveyed the spectacle with irate impatience.

"I heard her tell him, '*Nada mas*'—'No more.' This has to stop," González recalled. "Finally he had his driver pull up beside me. He just said, 'Get in,' and never said another word to me." The judge took her to his office and instructed a secretary to show her where the Arancibia documents were archived. She was allowed to read the documents, but she couldn't make copies.

The court archive was a sea of disorder. Ringed binders with ancient labels were arranged haphazardly on shelves. Boxes full of filings from long-forgotten cases covered most of the floor. The room appeared not to have been cleaned in years. The secretary located three closed boxes with files labeled *"Causa 949, Enrique Arancibia Clavel y otros . . . ,"* and left González alone.

González jerked the lid off one of the boxes, and let some of the loose contents spill out onto the floor. One of the first things that caught her eye was a small stack of Chilean identity cards. She recognized some of the names. They were Chilean political prisoners who had disappeared. In other boxes there were hundreds of pages of correspondence—original letters received from Santiago, and carbon copies of letters from Buenos Aires to Santiago. The correspondence started in October 1974, only a few days after the Prats assassination, and was arranged in chronological order up to the time of Arancibia's arrest in November 1978.

Note taking was too slow. González took out her tape recorder and spent the rest of the day reading the documents verbatim onto cassette tapes. She returned the next day and continued recording. It was astounding material of the kind few reporters or human rights investigator had ever seen. Arancibia had served as DINA's man in Buenos Aires for almost four years. The letters contained the day-to-day instructions from his superiors in Santiago as well as his intelligence reports back to DINA. There were code names and aliases, references to operations in Chile, Argentina, and Europe. There were long lists of names of people who had been kidnapped in Argentina and Chile. Some of it made sense. Much of it was uncharted territory. She didn't have time to record every document before time ran out.

Back in Chile, still under Pinochet's rule, she transcribed the material and turned it over to the Catholic Church's human rights organization, the Vicariate of Solidarity, which presented it as new evidence to keep the courts from closing the investigations of hundreds of cases of disappeared persons. González's most important story, in *Analysis* magazine and later in *La Nación* newspaper, was an exposé of one of DINA's pre-Condor propaganda operations, called Operation Colombo.

The operation, organized by DINA's Exterior Department in 1975, was intended to create a cover story for disappearances in Chile. In July 1975, two obscure publications, one in Buenos Aires and the other in the provincial Brazilian city of Curitiba, published lists of 119 Chileans with stories saying they had been killed in guerrilla activity in Argentina or infighting between leftist groups. Other stories showed pictures of dead bodies found in Argentina with placards saying they were MIR members. The ID cards with the bodies were Chilean, but the bodies were not. They belonged to Argentine victims of the AAA death squad. The stories were provided by an equally obscure Argentine news service and were picked up by Chile's pro-Pinochet press. One Chilean newspaper headlined its story "Chileans Exterminated like Rats."

All but four of the names appearing in the stories were of disappeared persons whose cases had been presented in a group habeas corpus filing by the Chilean Catholic Church in early 1975. The lists published in Buenos Aires and Brazil even reproduced the spelling errors contained in the Church's presentation to the court.

González's stories cited documents establishing that Arancibia, on DINA orders, had arranged for the publication of the false stories and lists, and that DINA Exterior Department officers had provided identity cards to be planted on the scene where the bodies were discovered. "Operation Colombo" was DINA's own name for the scheme.*

The Arancibia documents provide exclusive internal information on the whole range of security force activities from 1974 to 1978, and constitute a virtual road map of the joint operations between Chile, Argentina, and Paraguay that led to the formalization of Operation Condor. The documents were known publicly only in the form of González's transcripts for many years. Alerted to their existence, however, a Roman judge, Giovanni Salvi, traveled to Buenos Aires and obtained a complete copy from the court as evidence in his investigation of the assassination attempt against Bernardo Leighton. The author also obtained a complete set of the documents for use in this investigation—the only copy available outside judicial archives.

Uruguay, Bolivia, and Brazil all returned to civilian government in 1984 and 1985. In 1989, Paraguay's army unceremoniously dumped General Stroessner in a bloodless coup and called elections. Pinochet was also on his way out. He called a plebiscite designed to extend his presidency for eight more years, but was delivered a resounding "No" by the Chilean people. He tried to stop the vote count and reverse the result, but his own fellow junta members refused to go along with what in effect would be another military coup to prolong the dic-

---

* Operation Colombo was primarily a propaganda operation that should be included among the precursors to operation Condor. Arancibia and other Chilean participants in Colombo later had roles in Condor operations, but there is little evidence of formal participation by Argentine security forces.

tatorship. The loss meant that free elections were allowed to go forward in December 1989, and Christian Democrat Patricio Alywin, backed by a coalition of parties that including Allende's Socialist Party, won a decisive victory.

Finally, all the Condor countries had shaken off the long military nightmare. Still, none had grappled successfully with the legacy of the past. Like Argentina, Uruguay had briefly attempted to investigate the crimes of the military junta, in a congressional commission, but the effort was aborted by an airtight amnesty law, ratified by majority vote in a national plebiscite. Uniquely among the Condor countries, Uruguay's Amnesty, called *"la ley de caducidad,"* renounced the right even to conduct criminal investigations of the human rights crimes.

Paraguay was the scene of the next major breakthrough in the pursuit of truth about the past.

Martín Almada was an accidental human rights hero. He was a teacher and fervent Colorado Party activist with a bright future. He studied at the University of La Plata in Argentina, and became Paraguay's first PhD in education. He returned to Paraguay in 1974 with the well-founded expectation he would advance in the small world of Paraguayan politics. He headed the local chapter of the teachers association, and was able to dispense minor patronage through his control of a government-funded project to provide subsidized housing to teachers. He was already asked to be an educational consultant for the government. There was talk of a ministry of education job.

In late 1974, when their lives changed forever, Almada and his wife, Celestina Pérez, were running a small private school in the town of San Lorenzo just outside of Asunción. On November 24, a squad of Paraguayan police came to his house and placed him under arrest. At the office of police intelligence chief Pastor Coronel, he was tortured and interrogated. There had been a car bomb attempt on President Stroessner's life, and the police had traced the plot to a group of young people, some of whom had studied at the University of La Plata at the same time Almada was there. The group had received training and support from the ERP, and Stroessner's archenemy, Dr. Augustín Goiburú, had obtained the bomb from JCR contacts in Argentina and smuggled it into Paraguay himself.

Almada was totally innocent, according to those who were involved. One participant said they knew Almada in La Plata but decided not to approach him because he was on a government scholarship and was considered a loyal Colorado. "It was our fault he was arrested," said Dimas Piris Da Motta, who was the group's liaison between Argentina and Paraguay. But innocence was no protection in Stroessner's jails. Almada was savagely tortured for weeks. At one point he was placed on display in Pastor Coronel's office in front of a large group of officers, including foreigners, which he later would describe in public speeches as a "Condor tribunal."

During one of the torture sessions, the police called Almada's wife, Celestina. They questioned her and held the phone so that she could hear her husband's groans. A few days later, she collapsed and died of a heart attack. Almada's torture and his personal tragedy transformed a small-town schoolteacher into one of the most relentless pursuers of the military leaders of the Condor countries. Almada's experience gave him a unique vision of the inner workings of Operation Condor. He was in the same prison as JCR couriers Jorge Fuentes and Amílcar Santucho, and heard the story firsthand of their interrogations by Argentine and Chilean officers, and of Fuentes's transport back to his death in Chile. One of the Chilean officers, Colonel Jorge Otaiza, interrogated Almada at one point.

In 1978, after almost four years in prison, Almada was released and made his way into exile first in Panama, then in Paris, where he got a job as an education specialist in UNESCO. Determined to document what had happened to him and especially to find out how his wife had died, he began to research the personnel and structures of Stroessner's armed forces and police. When Stroessner fell in 1989, Almada was among the first exiles to return home, and he accelerated his quest for information.

Unlike the other Condor countries, there were no amnesties or special laws to protect the military. Stroessner fled into exile in Brazil and was joined by some of his followers. The most notorious torturers were put on trial and imprisoned, including Pastor Coronel, Police chief General Francisco Alcibiades Brítez, and intelligence chief General Benito Guanes, who had been Paraguay's representative to Condor. But Almada wanted the truth more than he wanted the punishment of his tormentors. Using a provision called "habeas data" of the newly passed constitution, Almada petitioned the courts for all public records concerning his arrest and imprisonment and the death of his wife. Habeas data was similar to the Freedom of Information Act and Privacy Act in U.S. law. It provided that any citizen could have access to any public document about himself or herself. Almada's petition was the first time the law had ever been used. In the hands of a sympathetic judge, it was a powerful tool.

Almada filed his request with a lower level criminal court judge, José Augustín Fernández, who sent a court order in December 1992 to the Paraguayan police. The police responded that the police archives containing records of Almada's arrest and imprisonment had been destroyed at the time of the coup against Stroessner.

Almada knew his country well and was undaunted. Among the vast network of people compromised by their work for Stroessner there were many who were jockeying for position with the new power holders, and there were many scores to settle. Almada put out the word in the press. A prominent human rights activist and Liberal Party congressman, Francisco de Vargas also got involved in the search. Within a few days they had some solid leads. A woman who was a friend of de Vargas brought her companion, a former policemen, to see him. The policeman knew where some documents had been hidden after the coup. They were in an obscure police facility outside Asunción, called the "Department of Production," he said. He had a small quid pro quo in mind. He needed a job for one of his sons. De Vargas was glad to oblige.

The woman also went to see Almada, and gave him a hand-drawn map. Almada arranged with Judge Fernández to go to the facility, in the town of Lambaré, just outside Asunción. The map showed which building at the site housed the hidden documents. Almada alerted a group of reporters and television cameramen, and they drove in a caravan to the police station, arriving at 10:30 in the morning of December 22, 1992. De Vargas lagged behind, nervous that nothing would be found.

With the press crowded behind him, Judge Fernández confronted the police official in charge of the facility. Policemen in Paraguay were used to taking orders only from their military superiors, not from judges. "I am the judge. At this moment I am empowered with the authority given to me by the Constitution, and I order you to let me enter," Fernández said. "I am your guarantee that nobody will harm you."

Once inside, Almada followed the map to a room on the second floor at the rear of the the complex of buildings. There was a formidable padlock on the door. Fernández ordered someone to get a crowbar. They broke the lock and pushed open the door, against the weight of something piled against it.

They were amazed by what they found inside. It was a medium-sized office with almost no furniture. Every horizontal surface was covered with stacks of papers. There were hundreds of ringed archive binders, bound chronological volumes of police interrogation reports, boxes of surveillance tapes and photos, jailhouse log books recording the arrival and departure of thousands of prisoners, correspondence with security forces from Chile, Bolivia, Argentina, Uruguay, Brazil, and the United States, "rap sheet" summary reports in alphabetical order with photos and fingerprints of thousands of Paraguayan and foreign prisoners, many of them on the lists of disappeared. Almada's rap sheet was there, and he also found interrogation reports and numerous other documents on his case.

Acting on another tip, searchers dug up other boxes of documents that had been buried in the courtyard. Among the findings were the yellowed and moldy remains of scores of ID cards of political prisoners who had been executed. The archive was so vast, it had to be transported in borrowed trucks to the Palace of Justice court building, where Judge Fernández had his office.*

Press reports at the time called the collection "The Archive of Terror" and the name stuck. Reporters estimated the weight of the documents at three or four tons. When years later the collection was microfilmed, the number of document pages was put at 593,000. It was quickly determined that the papers were the nearly complete records from the Department of Investigation of the Capital Police (DIPC), headed by Pastor Coronel. They were from Coronel's DIPC headquarters and jail located on a downtown street only blocks from Parliament. It was the jail where Jorge Fuentes and Amílcar Santucho were held and interrogated after their arrest in 1975, and their case is recorded in dozens of documents. Several telegrams and intelligence reports from 1976

---

* The complete archive is housed in the eighth floor of the Palace of Justice in Asunción and is maintained by a small, dedicated staff, under the supervision of the Paraguayan Supreme Court. Its official name is Centro de Documentación para la Defensa de los Derechos Humanos, directed by Luis María Benítez Riera and Rosa Palau Aguilar. The author initiated contact with the archive in 1999 and, with National Security Archive analyst Carlos Osorio, conceived of a project to catalog, microfilm, and digitize the complete collection. The project, in collaboration with Paraguay's Catholic University, received funding from AID and was launched in 2001. When completed, a catalog of 60,000 key documents will be available over the Internet. A preliminary Web site, sponsored by UNESCO, is:

http://www.unesco.org/webworld/paraguay/documentos.html

and 1977 were labeled for distribution to "Condor." The researchers eventually found Manuel Contreras's original invitation to Paraguay to attend the founding Condor meeting, with the only copy anywhere of the agenda for the meeting. Many of the most important Phase Two Condor operations and prisoner exchanges are documented in dozens of memos and letters exchanged among all the Condor member countries.

Almada's* discovery is by far the largest collection of previously secret security force documents from any of the Condor countries. The Paraguay Archive forms a major part of the documentary backbone of this book, together with the Arancibia documents discovered by Mónica González and the declassification of Chile and Argentina documents ordered by the Clinton administration. Without these documents, the history of the Condor years could not be written.

The document collections and the dogged investigations of pursuers like González, Almada, and human rights researchers in each of the countries laid the groundwork for an unprecedented series of human rights victories beginning in the mid-1990s. The first was in Rome. Investigating Judge Giovanni Salvi had been working since the early 1980s on the assassination attempt that left Bernardo Leighton and his wife seriously injured. Among the early leads was a 1979 article by the author, based on DINA sources in Chile, revealing for the first time that DINA had harbored a group of Italian terrorists, one of whom was identified as Stefano Delle Chiaie, who had organized the Leighton assassination attempt. Judge Salvi prosecuted Delle Chiaie and the Chilean suspects through three trials over more than a decade. His was the first judicial investigation of DINA's European network, and he persuaded several of Delle

---

* Martín Almada was awarded the 2002 Right Livelihood Award, often referred to as "the Alternative Nobel Prize," ". . . for his outstanding courage and persistent efforts to expose and bring to account the torturers and to set his country on a new course of democracy, respect for human rights and sustainable development." Almada has traveled extensively in recent years and has testified in all of the major Condor investigations, including those in Spain, Rome, Paris, and Argentina described in this chapter and in Chapter 3. The prize committee said "the 'Archive of Terror' has proved the most important collection of documents of state terror ever recovered. It is important not just for Paraguay but for the whole of Latin America and, indeed, for the world."

Chiaie's rightist comrades to testify. He also traveled to Chile and Argentina. In Chile, he interviewed more than a dozen DINA personnel. In Buenos Aires, he became the only judge to enter SIDE headquarters, and came away with a complete copy of the Arancibia papers. The first trial, against Delle Chiaie, was premature—it was attempted without direct testimony from Michael Townley—and resulted in acquittal. Finally, Salvi reached an agreement with U.S. authorities to allow Townley to testify; during several days of secret depositions in 1992 and 1993 and personal testimony in Rome in 1995, Townley identified Delle Chiaie and his other coplotters in court for the first time. In June 1995, the court convicted Manuel Contreras and Exterior Department head Raúl Iturriaga Neumann in absencia and sentenced them to twenty and eighteen years respectively.

Chile refused the Italian extradition request, as it had done in response to earlier petitions from the United States in the Letelier case. But with a civilian government in power in Chile, the situation was changing quickly. After intense negotiations, the United States agreed to drop its extradition requests, dating from 1978, and Chilean courts began the first serious prosecution of the assassination case in Chile. The Letelier murder was the sole explicit exception to the amnesty law Pinochet's government had left in place. The trial, conducted by prosecuting Judge Adolfo Bañados, relied heavily on the evidence developed by the FBI, the testimony of Townley, and new evidence developed in Italy. In response to a Chilean *exhorto*—a request for cooperation—Judge Salvi delivered the voluminous body of testimony and documentary evidence he had gathered. The trial in Chile lasted four years, ending in spectacular public hearings in May 1995 and convictions of Contreras and operations chief Pedro Espinoza. Pinochet, still commander in chief of the armed forces, had rattled sabers against the civilian government before to prevent civilian action against the military, but this time he turned his back. After a few dramatic days of hiding out in military bases, Contreras gave himself up and began to serve a seven-year sentence in a special prison facility. Espinoza was locked up in the same facility to serve a six-year sentence. The prison was comfortable, but it did not mask the reality: for the first time, two of Pinochet's closest collaborators were serving time behind bars.

The Leighton and Letelier prosecutions were major tremors opening up cracks in the fortresses of military impunity, but the real shifting of the tectonic plates of international justice came with the arrest of retired general Pinochet in London in October 1998. That event is examined in detail in Chapter 3. Although Pinochet himself was able to slip away from personal accountability by claiming advanced age and mental disability, the Spanish case was followed quickly by other energetic prosecutions, first in Europe and finally in South America.

Judges in Rome and Paris fashioned investigations around carefully selected cases of binational victims—those with French or Italian passports in addition to their Latin American citizenship. The French judge, Roger Le Loire, centered his investigation, opened less than three weeks after Pinochet's arrest, on the disappearance of Jean Yves Claudet Fernández, one of the earliest Condor victims and part of the string of Condor kidnappings that started in Paraguay and included the capture in Argentina of MIR leader Edgardo Enríquez. Le Loire issued international arrest warrants for Pinochet and seventeen other Chilean and Argentine officials, including Batallion 601 operative José Osvaldo Riveiro, the "Colonel Osvaldo Rawson" of the Arancibia documents. Le Loire worked hand in hand with two other pursuers, lawyers William Bourdon and Sophie Thonon, representing the families of the victims. The judge brought his wide experience in espionage and terrorism prosecution to the investigation. He earlier had handled the questioning of Ilich Ramírez Sánchez—Carlos the Jackal—after his capture in Sudan in 1994. In May 2001, Le Loire served papers on Henry Kissinger, who was in Paris for a meeting, asking him to testify about his knowledge of Condor. Kissinger refused, but subsequently curtailed his international travel to avoid additional subpoenas.

Operation Condor was also the focus of the Italian case. Judge Giancarlo Capaldo, the Italian federal investigating judge, opened the case at the request of the Italian Justice Ministry within a few months of Pinochet's arrest in London. He was asked to investigate evidence of other crimes against Italians committed by Pinochet, but he soon expanded the investigation to include the top military leaders and security force personnel of four Condor countries—Chile, Uruguay, Argentina, and Brazil. The new case, in effect, was the continuation of Judge Salvi's Leighton assassination case trials, and all of the evidence arduously gathered by Salvi—whose office was in the same court facility—was turned over to Capaldo.

The Rome investigation involved three Phase Two Condor operations: the Uruguayan-Argentine action against leaders of the Uruguayan Party for Victory guerrilla group in Buenos Aires in 1976; the 1977 Paraguayan-Argentine-Uruguayan interrogations of a group of Uruguayans and Argentines captured in Asunción and subsequently delivered by plane to Argentina; and the Argentine-Brazilian operation in 1980 to capture Montoneros trying to smuggle themselves back into Argentina (see descriptions of these cases in Chapter 13). The case was brought on behalf of eleven victims, all of Italian ancestry.

Even before Pinochet arrived back in Chile, courts in Argentina and Chile began to act with unprecedented vigor, resurrecting old cases and finding loopholes in the amnesty laws. The Prats murder investigation, taken over by a politically astute judge, María Servini de Cubria, cast its net across the Andes to Chile for the first time. Servini asked Chile to extradite Contreras and Espinoza, later adding DINA Exterior Department Raúl Eduardo Iturriaga, Iturriaga's brother, and DINA officer José Zara Holger. She included Pinochet in the list of suspects and asked for his extradition as a material witness. Arancibia, who had been in jail on Prats murder charges since 1996, was convicted in late 2001 and was sentenced to life in prison.

Chile's courts, which had hitherto ignored the Prats murder, were thus forced to give the case a fresh hearing. In December 2002, the Chilean Supreme Court ruled that the extradition case presented by Servini had merit. Instead of extradition, however, the court ordered the five defendants to be tried in Chile for the Prats murder. The court also found that the defendants could appeal for protection neither to Pinochet's amnesty law nor to the statue of limitations—referred to as "prescription" in Chilean law. Contreras and Iturriaga were immediately jailed.

By mid-2003, the amnesty in Chile had become an empty shell. The church sponsored human rights organization, FASIC, counted 247 separate ongoing prosecutions on human rights charges and was keeping track day to day on its Web site of which officers were currently in jail. Stopping short of a declaration of victory, the organization proclaimed:

> Chile of 2003 is a profoundly different country in matters of human rights. From FASIC's point of view, the period 2000–2003 has been the most fruitful of the last 30 years. Never before has so much truth been achieved as now, never have there been more trials than now, and never before have we been in the presence of more propitious conditions to advance in the pursuit of justice in cases brought for violations of human rights.

Meanwhile, in Argentina an even bigger case was launched, tailored to investigate the crimes of Operation Condor under organized crime statutes and to prosecute its perpetrators as members of an illegal criminal association. The case, under the direction of federal Judge Rodolfo Canicoba Corral, was far and away the most comprehensive judicial investigation of military crimes that had ever been attempted in Latin America. Its defendants were the top military leaders and intelligence officials of five of the six Condor countries (only Brazil was excepted). The list of victims, initially five, grew to include seventy-two people who disappeared in Condor operations in Paraguay, Chile, Argentina, and Uruguay. The charges went beyond the litany of crimes against humanity—torture, disappearance—to include violations of the right of asylum, extradition laws, and violations of each country's sovereignty. In addition to Argentine law—subject to the *Punto Final* laws restricting prosecution of Dirty War crimes—the Condor case established jurisdiction over the defendants in all the countries by citing the Nuremberg principles and other international precedents establishing universal jurisdiction in human rights cases.

In establishing the basic narrative of the creation of Operation Condor, the judge (citing as his source an article by the author in *La Nación* in August 1999) described the arrest of Jorge Fuentes and Amílcar Santucho in Paraguay in 1975 and how the three-country collaboration in that case can be traced with documents to the meeting in Santiago at which the security forces joined together in the new organization. The case continued to expand, adding the Michelini-Gutiérrez murders in late 2002, which had languished with little or no investigation either in Uruguay or Argentina for more than a decade.

In August 2001, Canicoba submitted an official request to the U.S. Justice Department, in accord with the Mutual Legal Assistance Treaty (MLAT) with the United States, seeking the testimony of Henry Kissinger on Operation Condor. (Kissinger's reply is analyzed below, p. 249.)

By indicating all of the top military leaders and seeking their extradition, the Condor case had the effect of nailing them in place in their own countries. None of the defendants could travel outside their own counties without fear of arrest on international warrants. The case also has a powerful, embarrassing effect on neighboring Uruguay, which was the one country that had conducted no human rights trials. Judge Canicoba demanded the extradition of four Uruguayan officers identified as working inside Argentina, in Condor operations based at Automotores Orletti, but Uruguay refused even to provide information. In addition to the Michelini-Gutiérrez case, the largest group of victims were the members of the Party for Victory who had been kidnapped in mid-1976 in Argentina. In late 2002, an Uruguayan judge finally allowed a criminal investigation of the Michelini and Gutiérrez murders to be opened. These were just the most important international investigations. Several other European countries (including Germany, Belgium, and Switzerland) opened investigations of their own citizens killed in the Condor countries.

The number of international warrants for military officials from the Condor countries had surpassed 200 as this book went to press. Retired military officers, even younger and lower-ranking officers pursuing lucrative business ventures, were at risk whenever they traveled abroad. In a major follow-up to the Pinochet precedent in June 2003, a Mexican court extradited a former Argentine navy officer, Ricardo Cavallo, to face charges of genocide and terrorism in Judge Baltasar Garzón's court in Spain. Cavallo had been running a small business in Mexico until his arrest in 2000. He was identified as a notorious torturer known as "Serpico" at the Navy's ESMA camp in Argentina. The legal procedure for his case was the same as that pioneered by Garzón in Pinochet's arrest in London, except that Cavallo was actually turned over to face trial in Spain. It was the first case in human rights law of a person arrested in one country being extradited to a second country for crimes committed in a third.

Condor, in its new incarnation as the central target of multicountry judicial investigations, had become the vehicle to ruin the peace and prosperity the military leaders were expecting in their declining years. Officers from Uruguay, where impunity still reigned at its most blatant, were prevented from taking the short trip to Argentina, and thus were cut off from their country's most active partner for business, cultural, and family connections. It became hard to keep track of which officials had been indicted in which countries, and who was currently in jail or under house arrest. As the cases advance from investigations to formal indictments, an increasing number of officials have actually found themselves in jail. Those consequences are a measure, albeit imperfect, of justice. In a larger perspective, there is a deep historical irony in the two incarnations of Condor. It once was the primary destroyer of international protections. Now two decades later its legal prosecution is the catalyst for a pioneering new era of international law. As a result of the Pinochet precedents set in Spain, followed by far-reaching prosecutions in the other countries, human rights protections were greatly strengthened, and for the first time since World War II, courts began to routinely honor the concept of universal jurisdiction as the last resort to prosecute the most powerful violators of human rights—those who enjoy impunity in their own countries. Just as Condor was created to mirror the international coordination of the JCR, Condor's international activities made it vulnerable to a multinational legal strategy to prosecute its leaders and operatives.

The Spanish have a saying that fits what happened to the military leaders who created Condor:

Criá cuervos, y te sacarán los ojos.
Raise a flock of crows and they will pluck out your eyes.

The CIA also has a term for it, "blowback"—the unintended consequences of U.S. policies kept secret from the American public. Here in the United States this era is undigested history. Only in the United States, whose diplomats, intelligence, and military were so intimately intertwined with the military dictators and their operational subordinates, has there been judicial silence on the crimes of the Condor years. No prosecutor has opened an investigation into the deaths in Chile of two American citizens, Charles Horman and Frank Teruggi, even after declassified documents produced promising new leads. The Letelier investigation has returned to a state of dormancy. For a while after Pinochet's arrest in London, the U.S. Justice Department began pursuing an energetic new approach to the solving of the still pending elements of the Letelier murder. There was talk of indicting Pinochet for giving the order to kill Letelier, but in the end, especially with the Bush presidency, the investigation seemed to be kept open more as a pretext for continued secrecy about unanswered questions in the case—such as those raised in this book—than a genuine effort to indict additional participants in the plot.

I have tried to establish the historical baseline of truth, at least of documented fact, about the United States government's relationship to the military personnel responsible for these mass international crimes. I have tried to balance my criticism of U.S. complicity with respect for the many U.S. officials who tried to keep their moral compass intact while implementing policies of deep moral ambiguity. Even after all these years, the toughest obstacle to this task continues to be U.S. official secrecy and a continuing will in some quarters to deceive, obfuscate, and even to cover up the extent of official U.S. connections to Operation Condor.

The Letelier assassination in Washington, D.C., was blowback. It was ordered by a close ally, a dictator the United States helped install, maintain, and defend in power; it was planned by an intelligence official who had been on the CIA payroll and who traveled frequently for consultation with CIA officials in Washington; it was carried out by DINA, a newly created security organization whose personnel were trained in Chile by a CIA team; it was detected in its initial operational stages not by alert spycraft but by the very chumminess of CIA officials with those planning the crimes.

Yet the U.S. ally carried out this major act of international terrorism on U.S. soil unimpeded. It is a major conclusion of this book that U.S. officials knew enough to have stopped the assassination, and that they launched a flawed and foreshortened effort to do so, then covered up their failure after Letelier and an American woman were murdered. Records declassified two decades later show that U.S. officials, including Secretary of State Kissinger, knew about Operation Condor's plans to assassinate nonviolent opposition leaders who were living in exile outside Latin America. Those same officials knew that Chile had attempted around the same time to send DINA agents clandestinely to the United States using false Paraguayan passports—one of Condor's standard operating procedures. The exact record of what happened next remains drastically censored, but we can know this much: Condor's assassination plans were taken so seriously that Kissinger himself sent a long cable to the ambassadors in the Condor countries, instructing them to take action to stop the Condor plans. Yet the instructions were not carried out and the assassination plans went forward.

The official story, promulgated at the time, was that U.S. intelligence knew about Condor only as a relatively innocent apparatus for international intelligence exchange. The Phase Three assassination plans were discovered only after Letelier was dead, according to this version. Therefore, U.S. officials could not have concluded an assassination was afoot. That version is starkly contradicted by documents declassified under President Clinton's executive order in 1999. The updated version of the cover story is that the Letelier assassination was not a Condor operation in the first place, that Operation Condor was barely visible on the radar screen of the busy officials surrounding Kissinger in the weeks prior to the Letelier assassination, but that, in any case, Kissinger, with his August 23 cable, spoke out against Condor.

This is the framework of Kissinger's official reply to Judge Canicoba's request for his testimony about Condor. The State Department letter to Canicoba, on behalf of Kissinger, is the most authoritative statement the U.S. government has made about its involvement with Condor.

Some excerpts:

> First, extremely serious crimes were committed in the name of Operation Condor by the Argentine military and security forces from 1976 to 1983. The questions address whether the United States knew of those crimes. The questions, furthermore, are directed to Dr. Kissinger's knowledge and acts while he was secretary of state. It is therefore important to state firmly and unequivocally in response to these questions that the United States was not complicit in Condor, *neither in the last few months of Secretary Kissinger's service as Secretary of State in 1976, nor during the later years of its most intense activity.* The 26,000 [*sic*] documents in the Chile Declassification Project and the newly released 4,700 documents in the Argentina Declassification Project support this fact and clearly demonstrate the opposition of the United States government to the activities of Operation Condor.
>
> Dr. Kissinger became aware of the existence of Operation Condor in 1976. As the documentary record shows, during that same year he spoke out publicly to the OAS General Assembly against human rights violations as a method of suppressing terrorism, and, on August 23, 1976, instructed U.S. ambassadors in the region to make clear to the highest government officials the "deep concern" of the United States over rumors of coordinated assassination plans, emphasizing that "if these rumors were to have any shred of truth, they would create a most serious moral and political problem. [Emphasis added.]

In the manner of U.S. government denials, this one is carefully qualified. "Firm and unequivocal" are strong words, but the denial of U.S. complicity in Condor is restricted to the "last few months" of 1976 and thereafter. That period covers the period after which the Condor countries agreed to implement Phase Three assassination plans (June 1976, just after Kissinger's speech at the OAS meeting). But it excludes Condor's period of gestation in 1975, the founding of Condor at the Santiago meeting, and the early months of its intense Phase Two activity. During that period of more than a year, there were frequent contacts between Condor mastermind Manuel Contreras and the CIA, including at least three trips to Washington (January and July 1975 and July 1976) and a CIA payment to Contreras. There is also direct evidence of CIA and FBI access to interrogations under torture by Condor agents (the June 1975 letter from FBI officer Robert Scherrer concerning Fuentes and Santucho and the CIA report on two Chileans being held in Condor's secret Orletti detention center).

It is my argument, based on the declassified evidence, that the CIA and other U.S. agencies encouraged and supported the integration of the security forces of Chile, Argentina, Brazil, Uruguay, Paraguay, and Bolivia. This activity was applauded in Washington, not criticized, and was seen as a needed response to "international terrorism," especially the growing international organization of the JCR. The United States maintained liaison with Condor operations, provided training and material support to the Condor data bank and communications system, and received and disseminated intelligence generated by Condor kidnappings and torture. It is highly probable that Contreras informed his CIA contacts, including the Santiago station chief and CIA deputy director Vernon Walters, of his plans before convening the Santiago meeting, and that the CIA was immediately informed about the formation of Condor. I have established, based on the account of one of the intelligence officers present, that international assassinations were discussed at that meeting. Intelligence exchange and cross-border prisoner transfers (Phase One and Two) began immediately, and there is no evidence of U.S. "opposition" to those activies. Cooperation, liaison, acquiescence, and even complicity are words that would seem to accurately describe the relationship prior to the latter months of 1976.

The U.S. attitude changed from support to opposition, however, when our agents learned in June 1976 that Phase Three operations were being planned outside Latin America. Adding to the U.S.'s second thoughts were the assassinations in Argentina around the same time of prominent Bolivian and Uruguayan exiles, Juan José Torres, Zelmar Michelini, and Héctor Gutiérrez. The United States was not willing to support, even by acquiescence, the assassination of democratic, nonviolent leaders or to tolerate the launching of terrorist killings in Europe.

It was these Condor activities and plans that created a stir in the State Department when Latin American bureau officials learned about them from CIA reports. Kissinger's cable of August 23 did indeed order a strong expression of U.S. opposition to the Condor assassination. The obvious question left by Kissinger's response is why his instructions were not carried out. Why was his "deep concern" not conveyed to any of the three heads of state—Pinochet, Videla, and Alvarez—or to the security force chiefs who were planning the assassinations? It is inconceivable that lower-ranking State Department officials or ambassadors in the field would disobey a direct order from Kissinger. Yet the record shows that the order was not carried out, with tragic consequences.

I interviewed the principals in the Latin American bureau who handled the Condor matter for Kissinger. William Luers says he remembers being greatly concerned about Condor and personally pushed to try to stop it, but he was not able to consult still classified records to refresh his memory about why the warnings were not delivered. Harry Shlaudeman, the chief of the bureau at the time and the official whose name is on dozens of pages of documents about Operation Condor, now says he did not consider Condor important and does not remember why he sent word to the ambassadors to "take no further action" on Kissinger's instructions. Another Kissinger aide involved in Latin matters, William Rogers, said, "I don't have any recollection now of anything with regard to pulling our punches with respect to that cable." Both Shlaudeman and Rogers* asserted that the Kissinger warning, even if it had been delivered, would not have deterred Pinochet and Contreras from carrying out the assassination in Washington. No one knows the answer to that hypothetical question, but in my judgment such a supposition defies common sense. Contreras and Pinochet were American allies, not our enemies. They were running a terrorist organization, but they considered that Washington shared their strategic goals, to defeat world Communism. They were grossly mistaken to believe the United States government would tolerate the killing of a leftist exile leader in Washington, as shown by the persistent U.S. prosecution of those responsible. I find it impossible to believe they would have not called off the Washington

---

* Rogers, of the powerful Washington law firm of Arnold and Porter, represents Kissinger in fending off a lawsuit brought by the family of assassinated General René Schneider. As assistant secretary for Latin America, he was with Kissinger in the meeting with Pinochet in June 1976. In a statement seemingly at odds with the declassified record and other officials' statements, he said it was "not at all" U.S. policy to support and defend Pinochet at that time.

operation if U.S. officials had told them in no uncertain terms, as Kissinger's démarche required, that their European assassinations plans were known and the United States officially opposed such activities.

The strongest evidence, of course, is what actually happened when the CIA got around to informing the French about the planned Paris operation. When French intelligence confronted the tri-national security forces (of Chile, Argentina, and Uruguay) planning the operation, they immediately called it off.

Kissinger's sidetracked expression of opposition to Condor should be seen in light of another series of events I have been able to document. At the same time Kissinger was sending the Condor démarche, the Argentine foreign minister was claiming that Kissinger had told him, not once but twice, that Argentine should step up its war on terrorism. Similar, though less blatant, messages were conveyed to Bolivia, Uruguay, and Chile. In the end, the red lights of opposition to atrocities were always dimmer than the green lights egging the military governments on in their war on terrorism.

The military governments were not only led to believe, they were told explicitly in secret meetings that U.S. human rights policy was public and tactical only and that United States sympathies were with the regimes that had overturned democracies and were killing thousands of their own citizens.

I do not believe the United States set out to encourage the mass killings or the international terrorist missions carried out by our military allies in South America in the Condor Years. I believe that individual officers took courageous actions to lessen the violence and save lives in some cases. Our overall policies and actions on human rights, however, were so burdened by caution and ambiguity as to be meaningless to military leaders, such as Pinochet, Videla, and others. The result was in the end the same. "You are our leader," Pinochet said to Kissinger in the same month in which he, Pinochet, gave the go-ahead to commit an assassination in Washington, D.C. Looking to the United States for leadership, the military rulers found unequivocal support and public justifications for their war on Communism and terrorism. They therefore pursued that war in the way they thought was most effective.

What happened during the Condor Years was the first formalized international alliance to fight a war on terrorism. As such, they provide a template of pitfalls and tragedies that should be examined honestly and understood if we are to avoid complicity with similar human rights violations in future alliances and future antiterrorist campaigns. The cautionary lesson of Operation Condor and the massive military repression against their countries' own citizens is to be found in the way the United States exercises its leadership of the countries it gathers into its coalition against terrorism. The echoes of the past are already to be seen in the current war on terrorism: the massive pooling of intelligence, the compromised intelligence relationships, the gleaning of intelligence from the torture centers run by our allies, and even targeted, cross-boarder assassinations. Add secrecy, demands for internal loyalty among U.S. citizens and officials, and the dismantling of mechanisms of accountability. Combine with good intentions, high moral language, and the implacable will to prevail in a world struggle in which America's place in the world is perceived to be at stake. The echoes cannot be mistaken by those who care to listen.

All of these elements were present in the U.S. alliance with Condor countries in their war on terrorism. We aligned ourselves with our ideological, geopolitical allies. We divided the world into those who are with us or who are with the terrorists. We ended up in intimate embrace with mass murderers running torture camps, body dumps, and crematoriums, and who brought their terrorist operations to our own streets.

The history of the Condor Years is not one we are condemned to repeat.

AFTERWORD: A DICTATOR'S DECLINE

"Las violaciones de los derechos humanos nunca y para nadie pueden tener justificación etica." ("Violations of human rights never and for no one have ethical justification.")

—GENERAL JUAN EMILIO CHEYRE, COMMANDER IN CHIEF OF THE CHILEAN ARMED FORCES, ACKNOWLEDGING THE ARMY'S "INSTITUTIONAL" RESPONSIBILITY FOR TORTURE AND DISAPPEARANCES, NOVEMBER 2004

At midmorning on January 4, 2005, a representative of investigating judge Juan Guzman Tapia and two policemen entered the walled compound surrounding the former dictator's estate on the Pacific Coast. The visit took only five minutes. The official read out loud an order from Guzman placing Augusto Pinochet under house arrest on charges of aggravated kidnapping and murder in connection with his leadership of Operation Condor.

From that moment forward, even after a subsequent court order granting bail, Chile's Pinochet was subject to the jurisdiction of the court. Additional appeals were likely in the complicated Chilean judicial system, but never before had criminal charges against Pinochet advanced so far.

Pinochet had escaped previous prosecutions—first in London on charges from Spain, and then in an earlier separate case brought by Judge Guzman—on grounds of his advanced age and mental fragility. This time a trial seemed inevitable, and with it the opportunity at long last for the evidence against

Pinochet compiled over long years by many investigators to be tested in the official crucible of Chilean justice.

Judge Guzman began the Condor investigation that led to Pinochet's indictment without fanfare and without even naming Pinochet as a suspect in 2003. It was intended as perhaps the final human rights case the crusading judge would bring before his planned retirement. At the age of 63, the energetic Guzman would have preferred an appointment to the Supreme Court to retirement, but his relentless pursuit of one human rights case after another had made him too controversial.

It had been Guzman who had enunciated the legal doctrine in 1999 that resulted in the shattering of the amnesty protection Pinochet had created for those who had implemented his policy of systematic torture and disappearance in the period 1973–1987. Guzman reasoned, and obtained Supreme Court endorsement for his doctrine, that disappearance—capture and presumed execution of a dissident whose body was never recovered—was in reality a "continuing crime" of aggravated kidnapping ("sequestro calificado" in Guzman's terminology), and therefore not covered by the Amnesty period.

By the end of 2004, Guzman and other judges had used the doctrine to bring charges against 160 officers in 365 separate cases. It was the "military parade" before the court that Pinochet's supporters began to denounce shortly after Pinochet returned from his seventeen-month house arrest in London. Until the Condor investigation, however, the doctrine had never been used successfully against Pinochet.

Guzman's Condor investigation also at first excluded Pinochet, naming only DINA chief Manuel Contreras, his director of operations Pedro Espinoza, and chief of the Exterior Department Cristoph Willeke. The case was built around the most important Chilean victims of Operation Condor, including MIR and JCR leaders Edgardo Enriquez, Jorge Fuentes, Jean Yves Claudet Fernandez, and others whose stories are told in this book. (Judge Guzman requested a copy of the freshly published book *The Condor Years* as soon as it was available. In January 2004, and again in April, he interviewed the author several times about the book's investigative conclusions.)

Then in May, instead of retiring as he had told colleagues he would, he brought his investigation to a head and filed charges against Pinochet himself. The first step was to request that the higher court remove Pinochet's "fuero," or immunity from prosecution as a former head of state. Guzman outlined the charges in a long filing in late May. He stated that Pinochet's immunity should be removed so that he could be indicted for the creation of the "criminal conspiracy" that was Operation Condor, which included crimes of aggravated kidnapping and torture.

Guzman argued that he had evidence that "all the victims of the so-called Operation Condor were illegally detained in foreign countries, kidnapped as part of a vast operation of international coordination of the secret services of the military dictatorships of the Southern Cone, . . . on the basis of explicit and secret agreements adopted by these regimes at the initiative of the dictatorship headed by the accused." He said it was "impossible" that such high-level meetings and agreements could have taken place without the authorization of Pinochet.

The Appeals Court approved Guzman's request. The Chilean Supreme Court, by a vote of nine to eight, ratified the lifting of immunity. Guzman immediately ordered medical and psychiatric exams for Pinochet, who was approaching his 89th birthday. In a previous case that had reached this point, involving the Caravan of Death killings in the weeks after the military coup (see page 30), charges against Pinochet were dismissed on health grounds, and Pinochet's lawyers were confident the same would happen in the current case.

But in early December, Guzman reviewed the examinations and ruled that Pinochet was fit to stand trial. The higher court, again by a closely-split verdict, ratified Guzman's finding. What had changed since the decision two years prior? Pinochet had decided to give a valedictory interview to a Spanish language television station in Miami known for its conservative politics. In the November 2003 interview, Pinochet held forth with subdued eloquence about his career, his success in defeating his leftist enemies, and his conviction that he had done no wrong.

"Everything that I did, I would do again, everything was thought through," Pinochet said. He had nothing to apologize for. If anyone should apologize, it should be the Marxists. "I'm a good person, I feel like an angel," he concluded.

It was an action of extraordinary hubris, and one that made a decisive impression on the courts. The interview was introduced as evidence, allowing Guzman and the higher court to hold that, "It can be observed, without doubt, [that Pinochet possesses] perfect discernment and ability to discriminate clearly between the important and the useless, . . . between good and evil and, finally, between what incriminates him and that which does not incriminate him."

The formal indictment, dated December 13, was attached to the finding of fitness. Pinochet was charged with the disappearances of eight people captured by Condor in Paraguay, Argentina, and Bolivia, and in the murder of a tenth whose detention was linked to other cases but whose body was found in Santiago.* Pinochet's formal arrest and arraignment followed after the holidays.

Almost as devastating to Pinochet, certainly in terms of his reputation with his supporters, were the revelations of a committee of the U.S. Senate linking him to a money laundering investigation against Riggs Bank in Washington, D.C. The bank had allowed Pinochet to deposit large sums using false names and had helped him transfer money out of London at the time of his arrest, thus thwarting the efforts of the Spanish court to sequester his assets. Deposit records and other documents revealed that Pinochet had had at least $8 million in deposits at Riggs, clearly vastly more than he could have saved on his salary as an Army general. The origin of Pinochet's fortune had not been explained at the time of this writing, but some documents presented by Pinochet to Riggs indicated he received the multimillion-dollar transfers of money from the Chilean Defense Ministry.

An investigating judge was appointed to examine the case for possible criminal charges. In its early stages, the investigation determined that Pinochet had not declared the income on his tax returns, and tax evasion charges seemed likely. In another precedent-shattering development, Riggs bank agreed to pay $9 million to the families of Pinochet's victims out of the bank's own funds.

Pinochet was thus stripped of the reputation he had always maintained among his supporters: that he had run a corruption-free government, whatever

---

* The victims in Judge Guzman's Operation Condor case, with date and place of detention: Jorge Fuentes Alarcon, May 16, 1976, Asunción, Paraguay; Manuel Jesús Tamayo Martínez, Luis Gonzalo Muñoz Velásquez, and Juan Humberto Hernández Zazpe, April 3, 1976, Mendoza, Argentina; Edgardo Enríquez Espinosa, April 10, 1976, Buenos Aires; Alexei Vladimir Jaccard Siegler, May 16, 1977, Buenos Aires; Jacobo Stoulman Bortnik and his wife Matilde Pessa Mois, May 29, 1977, Ezeiza airport, Buenos Aires; Julio Valladares Caroca, detained July 2, 1976, in Bolivia, turned over to Chile, November 13, 1976; Ruiter Correa Arce, May 27, 1977, body found in Santiago, Chile. See pages 88–89 (Fuentes), 142–143 (Enríquez), 225–226 (Stoulman, Pessa, Correa, Jaccard).

his record on human rights. For those willing to wink at the human rights crimes, the exposure of apparently ill-gotten gains from his presidency was the unkindest cut of all.

Meanwhile, other investigations were advancing. A case charging top DINA officers under the aggravated kidnapping doctrine was brought to completion with the conviction and sentencing of Manuel Contreras to twelve years imprisonment. The other officers, Miguel Krassnoff, Fernando Laureani, Marcelo Moren Brito, and Gerardo Godoy, were also convicted and got similar sentences. The landmark case involved the disappearance of a single MIR activist, Miguel Angel Sandoval. It was the first time military officers were completely stripped of amnesty protection, convicted, and jailed for human rights crimes. The four turned themselves in to the court to start serving their sentences on January 28, 2005. But Manuel Contreras refused to go quietly. He denounced the leadership of the Army for failing to protect him, and drew a gun when policemen went to his house to take him into custody. At one point he shouted, "¡Soy un general!, ¡traidores!" ("I'm a general! Traitors!")

Finally surrendering, he was taken to begin serving his sentence at the Penal Cordillera, a prison located in the hilly eastern outskirts of Santiago, within walking distance of DINA's most notorious torture camp, Villa Grimaldi, now converted into a memorial park commemorating human rights victims. It was the second time Contreras had seen the inside of a prison cell. Contreras had served a seven-year sentence in the 1990s, for his conviction in the Letelier-Moffitt murders. Then, the weak civilian government had been forced to accept the building of a comfortable detention facility for Contreras and other special prisoners.

This time there was to be no special treatment for the increasingly embittered Contreras. In a series of interviews before his arrest, Contreras pointed the finger at his former chief, Pinochet, who had consistently maintained that any abuses during his government were the work of his subordinates without his knowledge or approval. Contreras declared Pinochet should have accepted responsibility for what happened under his government, "as corresponds to his rank of general and his position as president of the republic."

"I'm disappointed that he has not done so," Contreras said in an interview with Reuters news agency. "Because it would have been logical for him to do it. A military man must always count on his honor, on his dignity, and to maintain them always."

With the DINA command in prison and Pinochet facing trial, it seemed that the tide had definitively turned in Chile. First the courts, with gradual shifts in personnel and cautious adoption of new legal doctrines, such as the continuing crime thesis and acceptance of norms of international human rights law, had engineered a sea change in jurisprudence. The Chilean government, under Socialist Party president Ricardo Lagos, stayed out of the court cases but contributed to the new climate by careful negotiations with the new military command. Lagos created a commission headed by Bishop Sergio Valech to produce an official report on illegal arrest and torture. Released in May 2004, the report was meticulously documented with some 36,000 interviews with surviving prisoners. The report certified that 27,255 of those who offered testimony had suffered torture, and were eligible for modest government reparations—an annuity of approximately $300 per month for the now aging victims.

The Army, under the leadership of a new generation of officers, signaled it was ready to abandon the stonewalling on human rights of the past. Commander in Chief Juan Emilio Cheyre, in a speech a few days before the Torture Commission report was released, acknowledged for the first time that the Army as an institution was responsible for the abuses of the past, and that the human rights crimes could not be explained as the individual "excesses" of soldiers acting alone. Nor could the tortures and killings be justified by the geopolitical circumstances of the Cold War, he said. His condemnation was unequivocal: "Violations of human rights never and for no one have ethical justification." He stopped short of what many thought was the next logical conclusion: that under Pinochet, the deaths, tortures, and disappearances were explicit policies of state and were implemented as military doctrine through the Army chain of command.

The statements of Cheyre nevertheless signaled that the Army had in effect abandoned its past efforts to deny, minimize, and justify the actions of its officers and soldiers. After Cheyre's statement there could be no doubt that the military would no longer defend its former commander in chief, Pinochet, as it had done in the past, even with threats of military intervention. When it came time to arrest Contreras, the Army not only failed to come to his aid, but instead participated in the effort to persuade Contreras to drop his resistance to serving his sentence.

In other Condor countries there was modest but significant progress, associated with the coming to power of left-of-center presidents. In Argentina, President Nestor Kirchner declared he intended to annul the laws his predecessors had used to pardon the former military leaders and limit investigations. Hundreds of cases continued to proceed through the courts.

Uruguay elected leftist president Tabaré Vásquez, who put together much the same coalition of centrist and leftist parties that ran in the 1970s before the military takeover. A coalition of partners included the Movement of National Liberation-Tupamaros. The Vasquez government was unlikely to find a way around the ironclad "ley de caducidad" which prevented human rights prosecutions. But he vowed to open newly vigorous investigations of past crimes to arrive at the truth of the events of the period of dictatorship.

Why in the final analysis does it matter to put Pinochet or other dictators on trial? Why do we care about what happens in the last years of an increasingly frail ex-dictator? It is a question that should be explored.

As far as is known, Pinochet did not apply the electric pincers to anyone himself. He did not hold the prisoners' heads underwater in the torture known as "the submarine" (a method later sanctioned by the Bush administration for use in Afghanistan and Iraq). He did not tie the pieces of iron railroad track to prisoners and throw them from helicopters or tugboats to their deaths in the sea. It was not Pinochet who traveled to Argentina or Paraguay to pick up Condor prisoners for transport back to Chile.

Most simply put, the argument for the trial of Pinochet is that without his leadership the systematic commission of crimes against humanity in the Southern Cone would not have happened. Military regimes undoubtedly would have used repressive measures as they had in the past, but the systems of torture and mass murder can be seen as originating with Pinochet. The case can be most forcefully made in consideration of the dramatic facts of Operation Condor.

As expressed in the case developed by Judge Guzman, the international military alliance that is Operation Condor could only have been the product of planning and authorization at the highest level of the government, and of necessity involved the head of state himself. Condor provides the strongest evidence that the assassinations were the actions of an institution and cannot be explained as the excesses or abuses of individual military personnel who "went too far." A subordinate officer cannot authorize and organize an international alliance of security forces in six countries.

I argue further that without the authorship of Pinochet, the Condor alliance of six countries would never have come into existence. Pinochet epitomized the turning back of the anticommunist threat. With the clear endorsement of the United States, which was widely perceived as having helped him come to power and was unquestionably supporting his hardline offensive against his adversaries, Pinochet was in a unique historical position to unite his neighbors in what they called "The Third World War."

While Pinochet's DINA did not kill as many people as their counterparts in Argentina, Pinochet stands as a giant in historic and symbolic importance. His was the first military government to introduce systems of mass murder, disappearance, prison camps, and torture calculated to eliminate for generations the radical political movements that—in his analysis—democracy had allowed to flourish. (Even Brazil's dictatorship, already nine years old when Pinochet came to power, fell far short of Chile's system both in quantity and totalitarian thoroughness.) Pinochet's success in Chile legitimized his extreme methods. And Argentina, facing even more intense guerrilla resistance than Chile, used Pinochet's system as a model for its own repressive apparatus. Argentina endeavored to "improve" on the Pinochet model by relying almost exclusively on secret detention centers and disappearance to avoid the adverse publicity Pinochet had attracted in the early months of his regime. Even today, Argentina's minimum 22,000 victims evoke far less international outrage than Pinochet's 3,197 dead and disappeared.

There are thus right reasons and wrong reasons to advocate Pinochet's trial and conviction (if the evidence is found to be sufficient). The wrong reason is political payback, in a word revenge, for the overthrow of Chile's progressive, democratic government of Salvador Allende. The examination of the Allende period, and what can serve as a model or lesson for future experiments should go forward independent of Pinochet's fate in the courts—likewise, the debate over how much credit Pinochet's government can claim for Chile's remarkable economic success.

The right reason to try Pinochet is to delegitimize once and for all the Pinochet rationale for a state policy of systematic repression, torture, and mass killing. If only officers are to go to jail, and the evidence against Pinochet is never to be tested at trial, Chile's final accounting with its past will remain unresolved. And Pinochet's grand idea will stand: that the threat of terrorism and extremism is sufficient reason to justify torture, murder, and the derogation of judicial systems protecting individual liberties.

We should care, even three decades later, because Pinochet and the Condor era he shaped and presided over represents the very darkest side of South America's darkest era. History's final word on Pinochet and that era should not be ambiguous, a continuation of the on-the-one-hand, on-the-other-hand discussion of his legacy, as if crimes against humanity can be put in a scale with economic development statistics to see which comes out ahead.

A final verdict should instead come from society's highest and only mechanism to judge matters of fact and morality: the courts. As imperfect as that system may be, it has the power to accept or reject the notion that the legacy of dictatorship shall be impunity.

In the streets of Santiago a popular verdict is already being shaped in the hard facts of bricks and mortar. Last October, a construction crew dismantled the most grandiose symbol of the military government, the so-called Altar of the Fatherland (Altar de la Patria), that dominated La Alameda in front of La Moneda presidential palace. The centerpiece, a constant fire called "the Flame of Eternal Liberty," meant to memorialize the actions of September 11, 1973, was moved and relighted in a less public place—behind the walls of a military installation. How long it will continue to burn there, along with the ideas that inspired it, will be the quandary of a future generation.

BIBLIOGRAPHY

BOOKS

Martín Almada. *Paraguay: la carcel olvidada, el pais exiliado* (Panama: Asunción, 1978, 1993).

Martin Edwin Andersen. *Dossier Secreto: Argentina's Desaparecidos and the Myth of the "Dirty War"* (Boulder, Col.: Westview, 1993).

Ariel C. Armony. *Argentina, The United States, and the Anti-Communist Crusade in Central America, 1977–1984* (Athens, Ohio: Ohio University Press, 1997).

Samuel Blixen. *El vientre del Cóndor: Del Archivo del terror al caso Berrios* (Montevideo: Brecha, 1994).

Samuel Blixen. *Sendic* (Montevideo: Trilce, 2000).

Alfredo Boccia Paz, Myrian Angélica González, and Rosa Palau Aguilar. *Es mi informe: Los archivos secretos de la policia de Stroessner* (Asunción-CDE, 1994).

Alfredo Boccia Paz, Miguel H. Lopez, Antonio V. Pecci, and Gloria Gimenez Guanes. *En los Sotanos de los Generales: Los Documentos Ocultos del Operativo Condor* (Asunción, 2002).

Stella Calloni. *Los Años del Lobo: Operación Cóndor* (Buenos Aires: Ediciones Continente, 1999).

John Dinges and Saul Landau. *Assassination on Embassy Row* (New York: Pantheon, 1980).

Mónica González. *La Conjura: los mil y un dias del golpe* (Santiago: Ediciones B Grupo Zeta, 2000).

Seymour Hersh. *The Price of Power: Kissinger in the Nixon White House* (New York: Summit, 1983).

Gerardo Irusta. *Espionaje y Servicios Secretos en Bolivia* (La Paz: Todo Arte Servicio Gráfico, 1995).

Peter Kornbluh. *The Pinochet File: A Declassified Dossier on Atrocity and Accountability* (New York: The New Press, 2003).

Paul Lewis. *Guerrillas and Generals: The "Dirty War" in Argentina* (Westport, CT: Praeger, 2002).

Nilson Cézar Mariano. *Operación Cóndor: Terrorismo de Estado en el Cono Sur* (Argentina: Lohlé-Lumen, 1998).

Francisco Martorell. *Operación Cóndor: El Vuelo de la Muerte* (Santiago: Lom, 1999).

Pedro Alejandro Matta. *Cuartel Terranova: El Palacio de las Risa* (unpublished manuscript, 1998).

Luis Mattini. *Hombres y Mujeres del PRT-ERP (La Pasión Militante)* (Buenos Aires: Editorial de la Campaña, 1990).

Gladys Meilinger de Sannemann. *Paraguay y la Operación Cóndor en los Archivos del Terror* (Asunción, 1993).

Carlos Prats González. *Memorias: Testimonio de Un Soldado* (Santiago: Pehuen, 1985).

Eugene M. Propper and Taylor Branch. *Labyrinth* (New York: Viking 1982).

Lars Schoultz. *Human Rights and U.S. Policy toward Latin America* (Princeton, NJ: Princeton University Press, 1981).

Maria Seoane. *Todo o Nada: La Historia Secreta y la Historia Publica del Jefe Guerrillero Mario Roberto Santucho* (Buenos Aires: Planeta, 1991).

Martin Sivak. *El Asesinato de Juan José Torres* (Argentina: Serpai, 1997).

Alfred Stepan. *Rethinking Military Politics: Brazil and the Southern Cone* (Princeton, NJ: Princeton University Press, 1988).

Pilar Urbano. *Garzón: El Hombre que Veía Amanecer* (Madrid: Plaza James Editores S.A., 2000).

CONGRESSIONAL REPORTS

"Covert Action in Chile 1963–1973: Staff Report of the Select Committee to Study Governmental Operations with Respect to Intelligence Activities." U.S. Senate, December 18, 1975.

"CIA Activities in Chile." A report by the CIA to Representative Maurice D. Hinchey (Democrat, NY) and to the House and Senate Select Committee on Intelligence, unclassified, September 18, 2000.

"Alleged Assassination Plots Involving Foreign Leaders: Interim Report of the [Senate] Select Committee on Intelligence Activities." November 1975.

"Senate Foreign Relations Committee, Activities of Certain Foreign Intelligence Agencies in the United States," January 18, 1979. Still classified "Secret." The report was written by committee staff counsel Michael Glennon for a subcommittee chaired by Senator George McGovern. Document in author's possession.

DECLASSIFIED DOCUMENTS

Argentina Project. A collection of approximately 4,000 State Department documents that were released in September 2002 in accordance with an order dating from two years before from Secretary of State Madeleine Albright. Hereafter, Argentina Project.

Arancibia Collection. Documents confiscated from Enrique Arancibia Clavel by Argentine authorities in 1978 and archived in the Federal Court of Buenos Aires. They are identified by date, folder number and document number as assigned by the court. Documents are arranged in "Carpetas" or folders, IA, IB, II, III, IV, and V, each containing approximately 300 pages of documents in reverse chronological order.

Argentine military documents declassified as part of trials of Junta leaders in 1980s, including: Roberto Viola, *Anexo 1 (Inteligencia) A la Directiva de Comandante General del Ejército Nro 404/75 (Lucha Contra la Subversion)*, October 28, 1975; Jorge Videla, *Directiva del Comandante General de Ejército Nro 404/75 (Lucha contra la Subversión)*, October 28, 1975; and Apendice 1 (*Síntesis de su origen y evolución. Doctrina—OPM PRT-ERP y JCR) al Anexo 1 (Inteligencia) a la Directiva del Comandante General del Ejército Nro 404/75 (Lucha contra la subversión)*, October 28, 1975. These documents are archived at the CELS offices in Buenos Aires.

Paraguay Archive. A room full of documents from Paraguayan police intelligence units was discovered by a Paraguayan judge in 1992 and made available to the public. The collection, known in Paraguay as the Archive of Terror, contains approximately 600,000 pages and is housed on the eighth floor of the Palace of Justice in Asunción. References include document title (if available), date, and number of microfilm. There is no consistent catalog of the documents to date. The author has copies of approximately 3,000 pages of documents selected from the archive.

Dinges FOIA Releases. U.S. government documents released in response to requests by the author under the Freedom of Information Act (FOIA). I received approximately 2,000 pages of documents from the State, CIA, DIA, and FBI that had not been included in the Chile and Argentina declassification projects.

Chile Declassification Project. Starting in 1999, the U.S. government in response to an executive order by President Clinton released 24,000 previously secret documents, including 18,000 from the State Department, 2,200 from the CIA, and the rest from the Pentagon and other government agencies.

Primera Reunión de Trabajo de Inteligencia Nacional. Santiago, October 29, 1975 (Paraguay Archive 22:0155–0165).

Acta de Clausura de la primera reunión interamericana de inteligencia nacional. November 28, 1975. Among documents obtained by *La Nación* newspaper, Santiago. Chilean Foreign Ministry documents.

HUMAN RIGHTS REPORTS

Argentina: Nunca Mas: The Report of the Argentine National Commission on the Disappeared (New York, 1986). The Spanish edition of the same name was published in 1984.

Chile: Corporacion Nacional de Reparación y Reconciliación, *Informe Sobre Calificación de Victimas de Violaciones de Derechos Humanos y de la Violencia Política* (Santiago, 1996).

Chile: *Informe de la Comisión Nacional de Verdad y Reconciliación:* Tomos 1, 2, 3 (Santiago, 1996). The report was first issued in 1991.

Uruguay: Raul Olivera, *El Contexto Represivo*, of PIT/CNT. This electronic document consists of a seventy-five page chronology with hyperlinks to the transcriptions of testimonies of almost one hundred witnesses.

Uruguay: *Uruguay Nunca Mas: Informe Sobre la Violación a los Derechos Humanos 1972–1985* (Servicio Paz y Justicia Uruguay, 1989).

JUDICIAL INVESTIGATIONS

Spanish case against Pinochet: *Procesamiento* (Indictment), December 12, 1998. *Sumario Terrorismo y Genocidio, "Operativo Cóndor,"* Juzgado Central de Instrucción Numero Cinco, Audiencia Nacional, Madrid. This document, 239 pages long, is the statement of the indictment against Pinochet and a summary of principal evidence.

Leighton Investigation. Testimonies to Judge Giovanni Salvi in the Leighton investigation, Tribunale di Roma. Those used in this investigation include: Stefano Delle Chiaie, Vincenzo Venciguerra, Aldo Stefano Tisei, Cristoph Willeke, Mariana Inés Callejas Honores, Alejandra Damiani, Marcia Alejandra Merino Vega, Luz Arce Sandoval, Ingrid Felicitas Olderock Bernhard, Wolff H. Von Arnswaldt, Enrique Arancibia Clavel, Marcia Merino, Mario Ernesto Jahn Barbera, and Carlos Labarca.

Prats Investigation. Sentencing document, thirty-five pages, was filed September 25, 1995, and contains summaries of evidence.

Prats Investigation. *Autos de procesamiento: Introducción y Pruebas*, June 26, 2001. "Indictment: Introduction and Evidence" against Chilean and Argentine officers for murder of Carlos Prats, issued in case investigated by Judge Maria Servini de Cubria. This 35,000-word document summarizes testimony of scores of witnesses interviewed by Servini.

Prats Investigation. *Autos de Sentencia*, November 27, 2000. This document is 63,000 words and contains more extensive summaries of evidence.

Letelier Investigation. Contreras statement to Chilean Supreme Court in his defense against extradition to the United States, 1979. Undated transcript in author's possession.

Letelier-Moffitt assassination investigation, Washington, D.C. Documents include January–February 1979 trial transcript, grand jury testimonies of witnesses appearing, evidence and exhibits sent to Chile to support the request for extradition, FBI "302" interview reports of Michael Townley and dozens of other sources. The "Extradition Packet" lists 157 such statements and other exhibits.

Michael Vernon Townley. Testimony in Prats case, November 9, 1999, Alexandria, Virginia, in closed session before Argentine Judge María Servini de Cubria and Justice Department official John Beasley. This testimony has never been declassified either in the United States or in Argentina.

Michael Vernon Townley. Testimony in Leighton case to Italian Judge Giovanni Salvi, Alexandria, Virginia, November 24, 1992, February 24–25, 1993, and July 9, 1993.

"Condor" Investigation, Argentina: *Procesamiento* (Indictment), in case *"Videla, Jorge Rafael y otros s/ Privación Ilegal de la Libertad Personal,"* Juzgado Nacional en lo Criminal y Correccional Federal numero 7, July 10, 2001. This is a 177-page statement of charges and summary of principal evidence. The main investigating judge is Rodolfo Canicoba Corral, assisted by his judicial secretary Oscar Aguirre.

ORAL HISTORY

The Association for Diplomatic Studies and Training. *Foreign Affairs Oral History Project.* Histories consulted include: Harry Shlaudeman, Hewson Ryan, Ernest Siracusa, Thomas Boyatt, George Landau, William D. Rogers, William P. Stedman, Robert W. Zimmermann.

NOTES

12 *Documents and sources:* Condor founding documents. The first, found in the Paraguay Archive, is an eleven-page agenda for the meeting, apparently distributed in advance to participants: *Primera Reunion de Trabajo de Inteligencia Nacional,* Secret, Santiago, October 29, 1975. Paraguay Archive 22:0155-0165, hereafter Condor Agenda. The second is the concluding document of the meeting: *Acta de Clausura de la primera reunión interamericana de inteligencia nacional,* November 28, 1975, hereafter Condor Acta. This document was found in the Chilean Foreign Ministry and delivered to the newspaper *La Nación,* which first wrote about the document on June 16, 1999. Thanks to editor Ascanio Carvallo for providing copies to the author.

13 *CIA contributed information:* Contreras statement to Chilean Supreme Court in his defense against extradition to the United States on charges of assassinating Orlando Letelier and Ronni Moffitt, undated transcript, ca 1979, in author's possession.

15 *Chile proposed operations:* Telephone interview, Montevideo, October 2001, with retired Colonel José Fons.

15 *Condor name:* Condor Acta. Air Force colonel's suggestion: interview with Fons. Later CIA and FBI reports said Brazil's military government sent a delegation but remained in observer status. Thus its representative is not listed on the final document.

19 *Helms informed:* CIA, "Special Mandate from the President on Chile," July 15, 1975 (Chile Declassification Project), 24,000 previously secret documents on Chile declassified by executive order of President Clinton, 1999–2000, hereafter Chile Project.

20 *Schneider murder:* CIA Activities in Chile, a report by the CIA to Representative Maurice D. Hinchey (Democrat, NY) and to the House and Senate Select Committee on Intelligence, unclassified version, September 18, 2000. The section on

Schneider relies heavily, at times in verbatim quotation, on the July 15, 1975, CIA memorandum cited in the previous note.

20 *CIA payment to kidnappers:* Hinchey Report, 11.

23 *Last day in La Moneda:* Interview, e-mail correspondence with Garcés.

25 *Miravet court filing:* The charges name all those who served in the junta between 1973 and 1978: Army General Augusto Pinochet Ugarte, Navy Admiral José Toribio Merino Castro, Air Force General Gustavo Leigh Guzmán, General (Carabineros) César Mendoza Durán, Air Force General Fernando Matthei Aubel, and Carabineros General Rodolfo Stange Oelckers.

26 *Garcés cites Condor:* Court document filed July 5, 1996, by Joan Garcés.

26 *Condor cable:* John Dinges and Saul Landau, *Assassination on Embassy Row* (NY: Pantheon, 1980), 238–39. Scherrer wrote the cable one week after the assassination of Letelier. I obtained a verbatim transcription in 1979. The three-page cable was declassified in 1981.

26 *Not a single investigation:* Miravet filing, July 1, 1996.

27 *Investigating judges:* In most European and South American court systems, judicial investigations leading up to indictment are conducted by an investigating judge, who supervises the gathering of evidence as well as evaluates it in view of the final decision to indict the accused or dismiss the charges. In contrast, the prosecutor, or *fiscal,* is the representative of the State, and has much less power. The investigating judge has many of the powers we associate with the prosecutor in the U.S. judicial system, usually an assistant U.S. attorney, who conducts the investigation, presents the evidence to a grand jury, and has considerable flexibility in defining the severity of charges. In both of the Spanish cases, for example, the *fiscales* at various points tried to block the proceedings from going forward but were overruled by the investigating Judges Garzón and García-Castellón.

27 *Universal jurisdiction:* See Nigel S. Rodley, "Breaking the Cycle of Impunity for Gross Violations of Human Rights: The Pinochet Case in Perspective," *Nordic Journal of International Law* 69: 11–26, 2000, for an account of the legal path connecting the Nuremberg principle to the Pinochet prosecution. For the proceedings and Spanish laws surrounding the Pinochet case, see Richard J. Wilson, "Prosecuting Pinochet: International Crimes in Spanish Domestic Law," *Human Rights Quarterly* 21 (1999), 927–79. The Spanish court laid out the basis in Spanish law for its claim of jurisdiction in a 1997 petition sent to the U.S. Justice Department: "After those serious facts were brought before the court, on July 29th, 1996 it was decided Spanish Jurisdiction exists over the defendants for the allegations of the complaint and for this Court to conduct a complete inquiry of the facts alleged in the criminal complaints. Articles 65.1. (e), 88, 21.1, and 23.4 of the Law of Judicial Power (*Ley Orgánica del Poder Judicial*) confer to the National Court of Justice jurisdiction and competence to prosecute and judge crimes of genocide or terrorism committed by Spaniards or non-Spaniards outside the territory of Spain, as

well as any other offenses that according to international treaties or conventions should be prosecuted in Spain."

29   *Letters rogatory:* Confidential court documents in author's possession.

29   *Don't declassify:* Justice Department reticence was described by Morton Halperin, a Clinton administration official in the National Security Council, in a talk at the Latin American Studies Association meeting in Washington, September 6, 2001. Several officials and former officials described the "reversal of roles."

29   *Promised publicly: New York Times,* June 27, 1997. This short article was one of the rare reports in the U.S. press about the ongoing Spanish case.

30   *Headlines on Pinochet:* "hero . . . ," *Toronto Star,* November 6, 1997; "National Father . . . ," *Washington Post,* December 8, 1997.

31   *Discreet visitor:* "Pinochet in Plan for UK Arms Office," *Financial Times* (London), November 19, 1997.

31   *Amnesty law:* The main effect was to allow Chilean military and civilian courts to dismiss without further hearing hundreds of cases against military personnel accused of human rights crimes. The law had a single exception: the 1976 assassination in Washington of Orlando Letelier. The law also had the effect of pardoning several hundred leftists who had been sentenced by military tribunals. They were immediately expelled from their prison cells into foreign exile.

32   *Garzón adds Pinochet:* Criminal complaint, March 30, 1998, submitted by Joan Garcés as lawyer for the Association of Families of Disappeared Prisoners of Chile.

33   *Rumors:* "Pinochet in London Clinic," *The Independent* (London), October 12, 1998.

33   *Whatever measures necessary:* Joint petition submitted to Garzón and García-Castellón, dated October 13, 1998.

33   *Fax from London:* Garzón's actions and thinking are described in Pilar Urbano, *Garzón-El hombre que veía amanecer* (Madrid, 2000), 515–19.

36   *"That communist Garcés":* Cf. Urbano, 519, which renders this statement as "that communist Garzón." Indeed, Garzón was told by the interpreter, in the presence of several other people, that Pinochet had named him. She corrected herself, however, after she learned there was another person with a similar name, Garcés, whom Pinochet was much more likely to know and accuse of Communist associations. All descriptions and statements are based on the recollections of one of those present.

38   *U.S. sides with Chile: Washington Post,* December 6, 1998, quoting Albright statement made a few days earlier. Albright's statement about prosecutions of Yugoslavs and Rwandans illustrated the "victor's justice" line of demarcation the United States was hoping to preserve: Prosecutions in international tribunals for atrocities by those countries' officials were among the important advances in human rights jurisprudence. Yet they were much closer to traditional "victor's justice" re-

strictions in that the Yugoslav government was not a U.S. ally in the Cold War, and the accused Rwandan government was on the losing side of a civil war. In June 1999, the State Department restated the U.S. position with a nod to the British proceedings, which had reaffirmed Pinochet's extradition. "We're committed to the principles of accountability and justice and we strongly condemn the abuses of the Pinochet regime when it was in power. We respect the British judicial process, which is underway and continues. We also believe it's important, consistent with the principle of accountability, to support countries like Chile that, over a sustained period of time, have made significant efforts to strengthen democracy and promote reconciliation and the rule of law." State Department briefing, June 13, 1999.

38 *Marathon meeting:* An account of the meeting was provided by Morton Halperin, of the National Security Council staff, who was present.

43 *Proved them right:* Castro strongly supported Allende's movement, spending several weeks in Chile in 1971, but he considered the Allende revolution an exception and did not waver from his commitment to armed struggle. At a 1970 ceremony honoring Lenin in Havana, he said, "Cuba has never denied, nor will it ever deny, support to the revolutionary movement. . . . Revolutionaries like Che willing to struggle to the final consequences, willing to fight to die—they will always be able to count on Cuba's help." See State 48656, March 16, 1973, document released to author in response to Freedom of Information Act requests, hereafter Dinges FOIA Release.

43 *"Non-commissioned officers":* Speech by Enríquez, July 12, 1973, in Caupolican Theater, quoted by Mónica González, *La Conjura: Los mil y un dias del golpe* (Santiago: Ediciones B Grupo Zeta, 2000), 203.

44 *"Central force":* Interview with Andrés Pascal, June 22, 2000.

44 *Pinochet had come late:* This is the main thrust of González, *La Conjura,* op. cit., a thoroughly documented book based on interviews with officers who began the coup plotting long before Pinochet was a participant in the plans.

45 *Concentration camp population:* Confidential report (mimeographed) of the Committee for Peace (COPACHI), no. 778, ca 1975, *"Servicios de inteligencia del gobierno militar."* From dates mentioned, the document appears to have been prepared no later than early 1975.

46 *Counterinsurgency training:* CIA DO, Western Hemisphere Brief, October 3, 1973 (Chile Project).

46 *Brazilian training:* CIA DI, September 6, 1974 (Chile Project): ". . . it is known that the security services have been sending officers to Brazil for intelligence training and that Brazilian officers were in Chile as advisors during the first months of the junta government." Brazil's military intelligence had been helping their Chile intelligence counterparts "in the efforts to remove Allende," according to a U.S. intelligence officer who was serving in the region.

46 *"Although the CIA did not instigate . . .":* Hinchey Report, 5.

46 *U.S. support before the coup: Covert Action in Chile 1963–1973: Staff Report of the Se-*
   lect Committee to Study Governmental Operations with Respect to Intelligence Activities,
   U.S. Senate, December 18, 1975 (hereafter Church Committee Report). The report contains other details about this period, including the compilation of "arrest
   lists"—presumably of leftists to be rounded up in the event of a coup:

   > The Station/Headquarters dialogue over the use of the intelligence net-
   > work paralleled the discussion of the deception operation. In November
   > the Station suggested that the ultimate objective of the military penetration
   > program was a military coup. Headquarters responded by rejecting that
   > formulation of the objective, cautioning that the CIA did not have 40 Com-
   > mittee approval to become involved in a coup. However, Headquarters ac-
   > knowledged the difficulty of drawing a firm line between monitoring coup
   > plotting and becoming involved in it. It also realized that the U.S. govern-
   > ment's desire to be in clandestine contract with military plotters, for what-
   > ever purpose, might well imply to them U.S. support for their future plans.
   >   During 1970–73, the Station collected operational intelligence neces-
   > sary in the event of a coup—arrest lists, key civilian installations and per-
   > sonnel that needed protection, key government installations which need to
   > be taken over, and government contingency plans which would be used in
   > case of a military uprising. According to the CIA the data was collected only
   > against the contingency of future Headquarters requests and was never
   > passed to the Chilean military.

47 *CIA discussion of coup support:* CIA Director of Operations, documents dated November 3, 1971, November 9, 1971, November 12, 1971, and December 1, 1971
   (Chile Project), provide a fascinating and rarely seen window into the CIA's covert
   action planning process. The latter two are cited in the text.

48 *CIA activity:* Hinchey Report, 2, 5. The report's hedging is not directly related to
   the point being made here, but should be included for completeness: The first sentence continues: ". . . but did not assist Pinochet to assume the Presidency. In fact,
   many CIA officers shared broader US reservations about Pinochet's single-
   minded pursuit of power." The Church Committee Report made a similar point:
   "After the coup, the CIA renewed liaison relations with the Chilean government's
   security and intelligence forces, relations which had been disrupted during the Allende period. Concern was expressed within the CIA that liaison with such organizations would lay the Agency open to charges of aiding political repression;
   officials acknowledged that, while most of CIA's support to the various Chilean
   forces would be designed to assist them in controlling subversion from abroad, the
   support could be adaptable to the control of internal subversion as well."

49 *War Academy: La Conjura*, 409–410, 431–33. Mónica González described the
   makeup of the War Academy planning group based on interviews with military
   sources in Chile, many of whom are named in her book. Several young officers
   who were students at the Academy, including Raul Wenderoth, Raul Eduardo

Iturriaga Neumann, and Armando Fernández Larios, would became Contreras's chief subordinates in DINA's foreign operations, which reached full fruition in Operation Condor.

49 *Best and brightest:* Interview with retired Colonel Lloyd Gracey, who served in the U.S. Embassy milgroup, the military advisory group.

50 *"Best moments . . ."*: Luis Mattini, e-mail of March 27, 2002.

51 *JCR training and early meetings:* Interviews with Andrés Pascal and Tupamaro leader Luis Efraín Martínez Platero, October 2001. The military trainers were often the veteran Tupamaros, who had gained experience on the ground during years of urban guerrilla activity in Uruguay.

51 *Creation of the JCR:* Interviews with Andrés Pascal, Enrique Gorriarán Merlo, Luis Efraín Martinez Platero, and Luis Mattini (whose real name is Arnol Kremer). Very little has been written about the JCR. Argentine sociologist Horacio Vennera, who is writing a PhD thesis on the history of the JCR provided a rare copy of the first issue of the JCR magazine, *Che Guevara: Junta de Coordinación Revolucionario.* The men listed all participated in some or all of the early founding meetings. Memories differ about what was decided at each meeting, but there is general agreement that the JCR was formed before the Chilean coup and was already holding regular meetings, which two sources said took place as often as every two weeks.

52 *JCR's continental role:* Interviews with Gorriarán, Mattini, and Pascal. The ideological underpinnings of the organization and its role as the Latin American or "Fifth International" was explained by Luis Mattini and Gorriarán. See also Luis Mattini, *Hombres y Mujeres del PRT-ERP* (La Pasión Militante) (Buenos Aires: Editorial de la Campaña, 1990), 159. Mattini said in an interview that Santucho never used the term "Fifth International" in referring to the JCR, but he saw it as replacing the overly centralized Third and Fourth Internationals for Latin America.

53 *JCR declaration:* Published in the clandestine newspaper *El Tupamaro: Organo del Movimiento de Liberación nacional,* Tupamaros, March 1974. The first issue of *Che Guevara,* the official JCR press organ, appeared in Spanish in November 1974 and reprinted the JCR declaration and call to arms.

54 *We were in diapers:* Interview with René Valenzuela.

56 *Castro statements:* Interview with Martínez Platero, October 2001.

58 *Samuelson kidnapping:* Exxon produced a full internal report of the kidnapping negotiations, see *Wall Street Journal,* December 2, 1983. Other negotiation details, including chess playing, are from interviews with ERP leaders involved: Luis Mattini and Enrique Gorriarán. Exxon avoided dealing with the Argentine police in negotiating the ransom. See declassified cable, Buenos Aires 1949, and memo by Legal Attaché Robert Scherrer, March 15, 1976 (Dinges FOIA release).

58 *Kidnappings and ransom amounts:* Interview with Enrique Gorriarán. The Firestone executive was John Thompson, kidnapped in July 1973, just following the Buenos

Aires meeting creating the JCR. ERP had profited minimally from two previous kidnappings, Oberdan Sallustro of FIAT (who was killed in a police-ERP shoot-out in March 1972 before ransom could be paid) and Stanley Silvestre, the British consul in Buenos Aires, kidnapped and released in 1971.

58 *Azul attack:* FBIS (Foreign Broadcast Information Service), January 20, 1974. See also Mattini, 255, 274; Paul H. Lewis, *Guerrillas and Generals: The "Dirty War" in Argentina* (Westport, Conn.: Praeger, 2002), 92. Mattini says Gorriarán was criticized inside ERP for his conduct of the retreat and removed as top military commander.

59 *Clandestine press conference:* Interview with Mattini, Gorriarán, and two journalists who were present, *Buenos Aires Herald* reporter Andrew Graham-Yool and *New York Times* reporter Jonathan Kandel. *New York Times*, February 15, 1974. Two other EPR guerillas spoke at the press conference, Domingo Menna and Juan Manuel Carrizo, in charge of propaganda and logistics, respectively.

59 *Money changer:* Gorriarán Merlo identified the money changer as the owner of the Liberty Hotel, Benjamin Taub. Taub's son, Guillermo Luis Taub, who was arrested with his father on money trafficking charges, confirmed the handling of the Samuelson ransom in an interview with journalist Miriam Lewin as part of a joint investigation with the author.

59 *JCR millions:* Interviews with Mattini, Martínez Platero, and Pascal. Several U.S. documents speak of the JCR war chest, notably State 128058 and Santiago 1965, May 25, 1976 (Dinges FOIA Release). The disbursement lead to at least one major dispute. MIR was in the most immediate and urgent need, and the task of smuggling the cash into Chile fell to Tupamaro leaders William Whitelaw and Lucas Mansilla (who used the nom de guerre "Marcelo"). The Uruguayans, with a decade of underground experience, had mastered the tradecraft of cross-border smuggling of men and money. Gorriarán said $1 million was sent, but it never arrived. To this day, the dispute over the missing cash remains a point of contention between the survivors of MIR and Tupamaros. The story accepted by Tupamaros is that Marcelo spent the money on weapons and other infrastructure in Argentina. With such enormous sums circulating in the guerrilla underground, strict accounting was impossible.

60 *Tucumán campaign:* Martin Edwin Andersen, *Dossier Secreto: Argentina's Desaparecidos and the Myth of the "Dirty War"* (Westview, 1993), 127–130; and Lewis, 98–100.

61 *Covert support of Christian Democrats:* Hinchey Report, 8. "Frei's victory on 4 September 1964 was a milestone in the CIA's Chilean election effort." The Church Committee Report also has abundant detail on the funding of the Christian Democrats.

61 *Democracy pro and con:* ARA-CIA weekly meeting, November 23, 1973 (Chile Project). Other documents make clear that some funds were allocated to the Christian Democrats, as Shlaudeman recommended. The party passed into opposition to

Pinochet early in 1974, and soon its leaders were being arrested and its offices raided by Pinochet's security forces.

64 *Decline in deaths:* Contemporaneous mimeographed reports of the *Vicaría de la Solidaridad*, the successor organization to the Peace Committee, and lists of deaths and disappearances provided by the office of Chile's *Comisión Nacional de Verdad y Reconciliación*, as updated in 1996.

64 *Contreras biographical workup:* Department of Defense Biographic Report, May 15, 1974 (Chile Project). The report says Contreras's English was fluent enough in 1968 to act as a translator and interpreter. Contreras spent a year in the United States, September 1966 to September 1967, while attending the U.S. Army engineering course, Fort Belvoir, Virginia. There is no record of Contreras ever receiving training at the U.S. Army School of the Americas, a U.S. military school dedicated to training Latin American officers, many of whom subsequently have been accused of human rights abuses.

65 *Defense attaché reports:* DIA 6 817 0041 74, February 5, 1974 (has reference to KGB); 6 817 0044 74, February 8, 1974 (reference to "Pinochet, God and DINA"); and 6 817 0094 75, April 15, 1974 (interservice rivalries and reference to Gestapo) (Chile Project).

66 *Intelligence officer's description:* Interviews in 1979 with Robert Scherrer, FBI legal attaché covering the Southern Cone.

66 *Brazil relationship:* CIA document dated September 6, 1974 (Chile Project).

67 *Peru violence:* Peru's Truth and Reconciliation Commission concluded in an August 2003 report that approximately 69,000 people were killed in political violence after 1980; more than half were victims of the guerrilla group Shining Path *(Sendero Luminoso)*, a Maoist group. Peru is the only country in Latin American in which the military killed fewer people than did the guerilla groups they were pursuing.

68 *Concept of national intelligence:* Interviews with several U.S. military intelligence officers familiar with South American intelligence operations.

69 *Interview with Contreras for this book:* June 2002.

69 *DINA training needs:* DIA 6817 0041 74, February 5, 1974 (Chile Project).

70 *Senate report:* "Senate Foreign Relations Committee, Activities of Certain Foreign Intelligence Agencies in the United States." January 18, 1979 (draft date). Copy in author's possession was provided by investigative reporter Dale Van Atta, who wrote a series of reports on it in the Jack Anderson column. See *Washington Post,* August 2, 1979, "Six South American Regimes Run Hit-Man Rings in Foreign Lands."

70 *Espinoza corroboration:* Deposition in Chile to Judge Juan Guzmán, ca 2000.

70 *Former DINA agents:* Both asked to remain anonymous. One was a noncommissioned army officer, the other was a civilian. I was able to confirm their DINA affiliation independently. See also González, *La Conjura,* 431–33, for an account of the creation of DINA.

70   *Venezuelan intelligence agency:* Interview April 22, 2002, with Orlando García, General Commissioner of DISIP *(Dirección de Servicios de Inteligencia y Prevención)*. Garcia said that when Carlos Andrés Pérez became president in 1974, he ordered the CIA official removed. The CIA also provided anti-subversive training in Paraguay, according to a Paraguay Archive document, a letter November 22, 1977, from Police Inspector General Antonio Cardozo to Commissioner Alfonso Lovera Cañete. A "CIA expert" was giving a lecture on "identification of false documentation in use by subversive groups," the letter says.

71   *CIA destroyed records:* CIA, "Name Trace Request, Juan Manuel Contreras Sepúlveda, Pedro Espinosa [*sic*] Bravo, et al," memorandum May 21, 1991 (Chile Project). Payment to Contreras is Hinchey Report, 17.

71   *Dealing with disgruntled officers:* CIA memorandum from the office of the Director of Central Intelligence, March 22, 1974, "Aspects of the Situation in Chile." (Chile Project). The memo includes a paragraph justifying and minimizing the human rights violations of the regime: "The government has been the target of numerous charges related to alleged violations of human rights. Many of the accusations are merely politically inspired falsehoods or gross exaggerations—the junta has not been bloodthirsty. The government has given first priority to repressing perceived security threats, however, and respect for human rights has been a secondary consideration."

71   *Coordinated action:* CIA June 23, 1976 (Chile Project); interview with embassy security officer with liaison to police and military.

72   *Prats's book:* Carlos Prats González, *Memorias: testimonio de un soldado* (Pehuen, Santiago, 1985). Other details from 1979 interview with Prats's daughter, Maria Angelica Prats.

73   *Townley CIA overtures:* The CIA had an officer meet with Townley, conducted a name check on him, and approved him on December 23, 1970, for "operational support." CIA memorandum, January 4, 1971 (Chile Project). For a detailed account of Townley's contacts with the CIA, see *Assassination on Embassy Row*, 100–104. At one point, the CIA attempted to contact Townley, but was unsuccessful.

74   *First plot to kill Prats:* The evidence includes dozens of depositions whose transcripts are part of the Servini de Cubria investigation. A central document summarizing much of the relevant evidence is the June 26, 2001, indictment, or *Procesamiento*, naming Contreras, Espinoza, General Raúl Iturriaga Neumann, Jorge Iturriaga Neumann (Raúl's brother, a private businessman), and Brigadier José Octavio Zara Holger, Raúl Iturriaga's deputy. "Evidence Collected" is enumerated 1 through 82, and "Elements of judgment" 1–33. Evidence concerning the first plot is found in sections 34 (payment of $20,000), 75 (Arancibia's role and background), 76 (DINA sources give FBI information on Arancibia's and Townley's role); and "Elements of proof," 28.

74   *Argentine plotters:* SIDE agents became notorious in 1976 for their work as kidnap-

pers and torturers in the Condor interrogation center known as Automotores Orletti. The group's leader was Anibal Gordon (see below). A typewritten intelligence report entered into evidence says an Argentine, Luis Alfredo "Freddy" Zarattini, was the go-between for Townley, Arancibia, and the terrorists they hired in Argentina. "Freddy was the one who put Arancibia in touch with Anibal Gordon through one of the members of the group . . . This group would have been the one that kept the money the Chileans paid to carry out the Prats assassination, but they didn't do it and kept the money, which explains Townley's anger." Document in author's possession.

74 *Stasi intelligence on Prats:* Markus Wolf, with Anne McElvoy, *Man Without a Face: The Autobiography of Communism's Greatest Spymaster,* (New York: Times Books, 1997), 309–14. Wolf wrote that the system used hiding places constructed "in much the same way that escapees from the GDR were secreted in cars to get past the [Berlin] Wall."

78 *Prats passports:* Prats and his wife already had official diplomatic passports, but as a matter of military honor Prats refused to use them improperly on purely personal travel. See Servini, *Procesamiento,* op. cit., Evidence no. 68, testimony of Renato Osório. Another consular official, Eugenio Mujica (Evidence no. 48), testified that he traveled to Chile in a personal attempt to get the passports. He testified he was told just three days before the murders that there was an order, from Undersecretary Claudio Collados Nuñez, saying "those passports are not going to be issued." In March 2003, the Prats murder investigation was finally opened in Chile, and the message from Collados to the Consulate was discovered in ministry files.

78 *Osorio death:* Robert Service memorandum, "Letelier Case—The Death of Guillermo Osorio," March 17, 1978 (Chile Project).

78 *Investigator's conclusion about Townley:* Interview with an Argentine official directly involved in the Servini de Cubria investigation.

78 *Argentine approval:* Testimony of Vincenzo Vinciguerra to Judge Salvi, March 1993, 12.

79 *Eight Chileans:* Arancibia Collection, December 6, 1974, IB/392. Documents confiscated from Arancibia Clavel will be identified by date and document number assigned by the Federal Court of Buenos Aires. Documents are arranged in folders (*carpetas*), IA, IB, II, III, IV and V, each containing approximately 300 pages of documents in reverse chronological order.

80 *Chief of Clandestine Information:* Arancibia Collection, Luis Gutiérrez, ca November 1974, II/220.

80 *Anti-Communist information community:* Arancibia Collection, Memorandum no. 2, October 10, 1974, IB/406–407.

80 *Intelligence on Prats murder:* "Blessings of Pinochet": DIA 6 804 0461 74, September 30, 1974 (Chile Project). CIA sources on Prats: CIA DO (Directorate of Operations), October 25, 1974 (Chile Project).

80 *Precursor to Condor:* Hinchey Report, 6.

82 *Tucumán campaign:* Lewis, 100, 105ff., for control of territory; Maria Seoane, *Todo o Nada: la historia secreta y la historia publica del jefe guerrillero Mario Roberto Santucho* (Buenos Aires: Planeta, 1991), 264, for number of fighters. It is a matter of dispute whether ERP actually controlled territory in Tucumán. See Andersen, op. cit. 129 ff, who says the ERP greatly overestimated their own success, quoting one veteran as saying, "We had already begun talking about liberated zones when we had just begun to fight."

83 *MIR fighters in Tucumán:* Pascal interview. The MIR casualties included a Chilean known as Sargento Dago, and a Swede, Svante Grande.

83 *Liberated zones: El Combatiente,* July 30, 1975, cited in Seoane, 269.

84 *Tupamaro plans:* Interview with Luis Alemany, Luis Nieto, and Amir Kimal.

84 *Penetration of Tupamaros:* Excerpts of the transcription were obtained by Alfonso Lessa, a Uruguayan writer. He describes the events in his book, *Los tupamaros y el fracaso de la vía armada en el Uruguay del siglo XX* (Fin de Siglo, Montevideo 2002).

84 *MIR postponement:* Mattini interview. He said Fidel Castro also had urged MIR to move more quickly to military action. Cf. Mattini, 378.

84 *Bolivia intelligence exchanges:* La Paz 3657, May 11, 1976 (Dinges FOIA release).

85 *Paraguay plot:* Interviews with participants Gladys Meilinger de Sannemann and Dimas Piris Da Motta, and Luis Alberto Wagner. CIA report December 4, 1974, Staff Notes, Latin American Trends (Dinges FOIA release).

85 *Campaign stalled:* Seoane, op. cit., 265. The most carefully documented account of the Tucumán campaign is in Andersen, 128–134, and notes citing internal army documents on guerrilla strength and army operations.

86 *Revolutionary grant making:* Mattini interviews, and cf. Seoane, 380. Mattini says much of the money was wasted: "The Political Bureau, particularly Santucho, acted with magnanimity that sometimes bordered on naivete and in some cases efforts and resources were expended on people who were not very responsible." M-19 interest in JCR: Francisco Martorell, *Operación Condor: El vuelo de la muerte* (Santiago: LOM, 1999), 77. Martorell does not give a source for his information, although he names Alvaro Fayad as the M-19 representative.

87 *JCR Executive Commission:* It was comprised of Enríquez for MIR, Roberto Santucho for ERP, former Bolivian army major Rubén Sánchez for Bolivia, and a shifting cast of the deeply divided Tupamaro leaders, including William Whitelaw.

87 *Trip objectives:* Mattini e-mail interview.

87 *Relocation of JCR:* Interviews with Martín Hernández, a former MIR militant, who mentioned Peru, and Kimal Amir, a Tupamaro leader, who said the JCR was considering relocation to Caracas.

89 *U.S. account of arrest:* Buenos Aires 7936, October 21, 1977. See also Asunción 4318, October 20, 1977, and State 256523, October 26, 1977 (Dinges FOIA releases).

89 *Carrying cash:* Paraguayan human rights activist Francisco de Vargas helped arrange Santucho's release in 1979 and accompanied him on his flight to freedom

in Switzerland. Luis Mattini, in an e-mail interview, said the money was probably about $5,000 and was intended to be given to the Peruvian organization they planned to meet.

89 *Travel documents and Peru mission:* Fuentes arrest record: Document 16:1117–18 (Paraguay Archive).

89 *Role of Amílcar Santucho and Jorge Fuentes:* For Santucho, interviews with Mattini and Gorriarán Merlo; for Fuentes, interviews with Andrés Pascal and René Valenzuela.

91 *Scherrer letter to Baeza:* The author viewed the letter and copied it verbatim in July 2000. After being told of the existence of the letter in the Rettig archive, the FBI released a copy in response to a FOIA request to *New York Times* reporter Tim Weiner.

92 *Story on Scherrer in NYT:* "F.B.I. Helped Chile Search for Leftists, Files Show," by Tim Weiner, *New York Times,* February 10, 1999. "We would be remiss in not checking out these people," one FBI official was quoted as saying.

93 *Sonia Bacicalupo:* Interview. The address in Puerto Rico now houses an office for the Department of Education, and neighbors remember nothing about the occupants in 1975. Several sources, including JCR veterans as well as intelligence documents, confirm that the JCR had representatives in New York, but I was unable to establish if there was a connection between them and the two women listed as living in New York.

93 *Scherrer exchange:* Interview on October 29, 1979. Scherrer said the proposal was made at the meeting of the Conference of American Armies in Montevideo, Uruguay, in October 1975. The meeting was attended by a delegation of high U.S. Army officers led by U.S. Southcom Commander General Dennis P. McAuliffe.

94 *Carlos the Jackal raid:* Coronel included the account of the Paris raid and its connection to the Paraguay arrests in at least three reports found in the Paraguay Archive. The earliest has his name handwritten on the top and is dated "June 1976," and may have been presented at the second meeting of Operation Condor, which occurred in Santiago in that month. Documents containing the description are as follows: *"Sintesis del Proceso de la subversion que se ha pretendido desatar en el pais,"* June 1976, with the notation "De: Pastor Coronel, jefe del Dpto de investigación de la Policia—Asunción, Paraguay," 6 (no microfiche number on my copy); a second document with identical wording is titled *"IV Conferencia Bilateral de Inteligencia entre los Ejercitos de Paraguay y Brasil,"* microfiche 78:1674–86 (no date, but the meeting is referred to in other documents as occurring in May 1976); a third reference is an undated document "Actividades Subversivas Dentro del Pais" (78:1649–68, 13). Internal references place this document in 1977. The account of the Carlos raid is identical in each case (Paraguay Archive).

95 *Carlos photo:* DIPC documents, August 28, 1975 (21: 1560), and April 21, 1976 (21: 1531) (Paraguay Archive).

95 *DISIP account of Carlos raid:* Interview with Orlando García. He said the informa-

tion came from a source in an Algerian extremist organization handled by his boss, DISIP chief Rafael Rivas Vásquez. Rivas Vásquez was proud of his role and listed "The Carlos Affaire, Caracas, Paris, and London, 1975" among his intelligence experience "highlights," in a 1996 copy of his Curriculum Vitae (provided by journalist Don Bohning). The claim is mentioned in his obituary in the *Miami Herald*, November 27, 2000.

95   *Carlos letter:* Handwritten letter, La Santé, March 3, 2001, sent through his lawyer, Isabelle Coutant Peyre (whom he later married). He identifies himself as Ilich Ramirez Sanchez, Ecrou 274630, Q.I.3, and signed the letter "Carlos." He said the apartment where the shootout took place was the residence of "two Venezuelan university students," and did not have a telephone line. "I do not know personally Messrs. Amilcar Santucho, Mario Roberto Santucho, or Jorge Isaac Fuentes Alarcon, even if our comrades did know the ERP in Paris. . . . The Palestinian Joel Al Ardja was the PFLP responsible for South America (excepting Brazil); he was martyred in Entebbe in July 1976." I asked Carlos for any information about the assassination attempt in early 1975 against the Chilean military attaché in Beirut, Lebanon, Colonel Alfredo Canales. He said the attack and three assassinations in Paris in 1974, 1975 and 1976 ". . . were carried out by internationalist revolutionary commandos. I can only disclose the identity of the three members of the Beirut commando: 'El Hajj Mohmoud' . . . ; Ahmed 'Abdallah' Farhan . . . ; and 'Mujahed' [aka] 'Agop Agopian.'" A secret CIA Directorate of Operations document, April 3, 1975, transmits a DINA report on PFLP activity in Santiago. According to the report, DINA arrested two people in March 1975 who were "recruiting Chileans of Arab descent to work for the Popular Front for the Liberation of Palestine (PFLP) to carry out terrorist acts." The last name of one of the PFLP recruiters mentioned in the document, Al Arja, coincides with a spelling variation of the name mentioned by Carlos (Chile Project.)

97   *DICP prison and interrogation:* Author visited the prison in October 2001. Former prisoners who described their experience in interviews included Martín Almada, Gladys Meilinger de Sannemann, and Luis Alberto Wagner.

97   *Santucho interview:* Soon after his release, Santucho gave an interview in Stockholm, Sweden, published in an obscure political magazine, *Denuncia*, November 1979. Santucho gave a more detailed, confidential interview to Amnesty International (AI) in London about the same time, but repeated requests to AI by the author and the Santucho family failed to produce that unique historical document.

98   *Fuentes statements to Pastor Coronel:* DICP documents 28: 1020–21, July 14, 1975; and 46: 1551, July 3, 1975 (Paraguay Archive). The woman named by Fuentes, "Marcia," was a prominent journalist in Chile at the time, with no public connection to MIR. Fuentes is also asked whether a prominent Christian Democratic politician, Belisario Velasco, was the "liaison between MIR and the Christian Democratic [Party]," which Fuentes denies.

98   *Osvaldo letter and materials:* Documents 46:1558–59, 1520–21, and 46:1532 (the

original letter in red ink); 46:1535–37 (letter from "David" in Mexico about Fuentes's arrest, dated June 12, 1975; 24:1754–57 (handwritten questions); 46: 1537 (question and picture about Rubén Sánchez) (Paraguay Archive).

100 *Proportion of deaths:* For specific DINA activity, Chilean researcher Pedro Alejandro Matta, himself a torture victim, has compiled extraordinarily complete day-by-day records of prisoners detained, disappeared, or otherwise killed, and survivors of the principal DINA torture camps, including the largest, Villa Grimaldi. Pedro Alejandro Matta, *Cuartel Terranova: el palacio de la risa* (unpublished manuscript, 1998).

101 *Enríquez death:* interview with Castillo's mother, Mónica Echevarria.

101 *Brazil model:* Cf. Alfred Stepan, *Rethinking Military Politics: Brazil and the Southern Cone* (Princeton University Press, 1988), Chapter 2, for a description of Brazil's intelligence force and the importance of the intelligence school in consolidating its power.

101 *January trip to Washington:* Notes from confidential testimony of various Chilean officers, including Espinoza, to Judge Juan Guzman, 2000. Thanks to Chilean journalist Patricia Verdugo.

102 *Memo to Walters:* CIA document, January 4, 1975 (Chile Project).

103 *Contreras payment:* The $6,000 deposit is mentioned in State 229940, August 31, 1979 (Chile collection). Manuel Noriega, who as head of Panamanian intelligence in the 1970s held a position comparable to Contreras, received monthly payments from the CIA totaling $160,000 and an equivalent amount from the U.S. Army. It is fair to assume, considering Chile's relative importance that Contreras would have received payments at least as large as Noriega. See John Dinges, *Our Man in Panama* (New York: Times Books, 1991), p. ix.

103 *CIA cable on Contreras visit:* Secret, July 10, 1975 (Chile Project). ". . . Little if anything can be accomplished by Contreras in explaining human rights problems, concerns, etc. to senior U.S. officials, given Chilean leadership's distorted views of their own situation. . . . This aspect of planned visit not justified from our standpoint and, if there were publicity, could be counter-productive. On the other hand [name blanked out] recognizes value in maintaining good relations with President Pinochet, who should not be led to believe we are rebuffing his efforts to communicate with us." The name of the person making these judgments is blanked out, but Contreras said in an interview the trip was requested by Ambassador Popper.

103 *Memo on luncheon with Contreras:* CIA document, undated but containing luncheon date. Another CIA memorandum, "Meeting with State Department and Justice Department Officials Regarding Letelier Case," August 22, 1978, refers to a written "summary of Contreras's visits to the United States," which was provided to Letelier case prosecutor Eugene Propper (Chile Project). The CIA has refused to provide any information about Contreras's visits to the United States except the one in August 1975.

104 *North American senators:* Contreras interview with journalist Lilian Olivares, *La Segunda*, September 25, 2000. In the interview, Contreras also said that Walters

arranged for the "clandestine" delivery to Chile of 2,000 LAW antiaircraft missiles, whose sale to Chile had been banned by Congress. Contreras also mentioned, in *La Tercera*, September 21, 2000, the proposal to bribe the U.S. senators.

104 *Contreras information for Kissinger:* Interview with Contreras by journalist Gomez-Pablo from questions provided by the author.

105 *International help to DIA:* The point is made repeatedly in the Church Committee Report, the Hinchey Report, and the Senate Report, Activities of Certain Foreign Intelligence Agencies.

105 *Walters's suggestion:* Gomez-Pablo interview with Contreras.

106 *Caracas visit:* Interviews with Orlando García and Carlos Andrés Pérez. Rivas Vásquez and Orlando García testimony to grand jury of U.S. District Court for the District of Columbia, June 29, 1978. Intelligence about JCR moving to Caracas: 1979 interview with Robert Scherrer. Two former JCR leaders also confirmed that the move to Caracas was under consideration at the time Fuentes and Santucho were arrested.

106 *Request for $600,000:* I have long considered this to be an important document, but one of unconfirmed authenticity. In the course of my current investigation I obtained the corroborating evidence detailed here. The memorandum appears to have a genuine Contreras signature, and its formatting and seals match other available DINA documents. Nevertheless, because it was released by exiles, who were not able to describe how they received it from within the Chilean government, the document should not, by itself, be considered of undisputed investigative value. The letter first surfaced in Mexico in 1977, where it was released to the press by former Chilean Senator Hugo Miranda. I obtained it at that time. I recently learned that lawyer Giovanni Salvi—who later prosecuted Contreras and Espinoza for the assassination attempt in Rome against exile leader Bernardo Leighton, came upon the document in *La República* newspaper, accompanying an article I had written (John Dinges, "Anatomia di un'Anonima Omicidi," *La Repubblica*, May 25, 1975). Salvi passed the document on to a Chilean judge investigating the Letelier murder in Chile in the early 1990s. The letter resurfaced in dubious circumstances in the late 1990s with the mistaken claim that it had been found in the Paraguay Archive. Archive staff and Martín Almada, who discovered the documents in the archive, say the document was never part of the archive. The FBI declined to use it as evidence in the Letelier case because its origin could not be traced to DINA, and Judge Salvi told the author he declined to use it in his case for similar reasons. Contreras described the letter in court testimony as a *montaje*—a montage. See John Dinges, "Dubious Document," *Columbia Journalism Review*, January–February 2000. Judge Salvi interrogated Michael Townley about the document, attributing it to the *La Repubblica* article, in January 1993.

108 *Pinochet advisers opposed to Contreras:* The source named General Sergio Covarrubias, Justice Minister Mónica Madariaga, ideological adviser Jaime Guzman, Colonel René Escairuiga, and Colonel Patricio Ewing (a close friend of the slain

General Carlos Prats). Cf. Dinges, and Landau, op. cit., 329, for account of civilian and military officials who pressured Pinochet to cooperate with the United States on the Letelier case investigation, in opposition to Contreras.

108 *Contreras presidential ambitions:* The Brazilian model again was a factor in this thinking. The leader of the security force, SNI, Joâo Baptista Figueiredo, was a major force in the Brazilian military government as it entered its second decade, and he would eventually rise to the presidency. Several sources among Contreras's group of civilian supporters also talked in interviews about their expectation that Contreras would succeed Pinochet.

108 *Fuentes transfer to Chile:* There is extensive documentation about Fuentes's transfer. Paraguay's Capital Police completed their bureaucratic paperwork to show he had left their custody. His police *ficha* (booking card), found in the Paraguay archive, has this final entry: "By superior order, he was released Sept. 23, 1975 and expelled via Presidente Stroessner Airport." Amílcar Santucho, in an interview in Europe after his release in 1979, said two other Chilean officers, Air Force Colonels Edgar Ceballos and Jorge Otaiza, came to Paraguay to interrogate himself and Fuentes. Santucho also said the two colonels took Fuentes back to Chile, although it is unclear how he would have that information. Ceballos and Otaiza both worked for air force intelligence, SIFA, which at the time was competing with DINA in the pursuit of MIR. How the Ceballos-SIFA operation related to the Krasnoff-DINA operation could not be learned.

109 *Fuentes remained in Villa Grimaldi until January:* When last seen by other prisoners, he was in good spirits and had been given clean clothes for his supposed release. On January 12, he was taken away from Villa Grimaldi and disappeared. There was an erroneous report circulating in human rights circles that he had been killed by being injected with rabies. The story is based on the testimony of Luz Arce, the DINA collaborator. When questioned in detail by the author, Arce corrected the story. She acknowledged the person injected with rabies could not have been Fuentes, because she heard the story before she left Villa Grimaldi in December 1975, and at that time Fuentes was still alive, according to multiple witnesses.

109 *DINA invitation to Paraguay:* Contreras thank-you letter: September 25, 1975, 22:0152; invitation to Police Chief Britez, October 1975, 22:0153; Britez memo about meeting with Jahn, November 6, 1975, 22:0154; meeting agenda, October 29, 1975, no microfiche numbers on document in author's possession. The thank-you note and invitation are on Contreras's personal—and elegant—stationery. They have Contreras's original signature (Paraguay Archive).

110 *Osvaldo identity:* Lieutenant Colonel José Osvaldo Riveiro gave a deposition to federal judge Maria Servini on June 17, 2001, and confirmed his military rank and position in Battalion 601 in 1975 and 1976. He denied being "Rawson," but the court concluded that it had been established that he and Jorge Osvaldo Riveiro Rawson, the person referred to many times in Arancibia's papers, are one and the same person. The name also appears written with b, as Ribeiro, in secondary sources. The

spelling Riveiro is used in the court testimony, which is signed by Riveiro. The Arancibia documents contain a napkin from a Buenos Aires restaurant, Queen Bess, with the handwritten name "Jorge Osvaldo Riveiro Rawson" and the date August 15, 1975. Document II/184–185 (Arancibia Collection). Intriguingly, the Queen Bess is mentioned in another document obtained by the author as the place Michael Townley used to pick up and drop off messages from his contacts in Buenos Aires.

110 *Details about JCR:* In two reports, dated August 21 and 27, Arancibia pours out details he has gathered. Some excerpts:

August 21, Memorandum 57-G:

"A hotel bought by the Tupamaros (Junta Coordinadora Revolucionaria) is the Hotel Roma." [Names of those involved follow.]

"The Atlantic Ferry line from Buenos Aires to Colonia [the Uruguayan port across the Plata River Delta] is used as a weekly mail route by the JCR." (Names of contacts follow.)

"The plot against Chile discovered in June 1975 was coordinated from Switzerland by the JCR after meetings in Paris." [Names of contacts in Paris, including a post office box number.]

"More information about the Junta Coordinadora will go in the next dispatch. Next week, I will make contact with Major Washington Perdomo Diaz, of the 4th Engineers of Colonia Uruguay, who is charge of the 'repression of Tupamaros,' and with the chief of police Jose Do Campo, of Colonia Uruguay. The idea is to coordinate information about the Junta Coordinadora and information exchange in general. All these contacts are clandestine."

August 27, Memorandum 57-G:

"Revolutionary Coordinating Junta:

"The best information that has been obtained on this guerrilla organization was provided to Colonel Podesta [Argentine], military attache in Paraguay, by the number 2 chief of SIE [Army intelligence service—*Servicio de Inteligencia del Ejército*], Lt. Col. Jorge Osvaldo Rawson. This officer will travel to Santiago at the invitation of DINE [Chilean Army Intelligence Department—*Departamento de Inteligencia del Ejercito*].

"He will be accompanied by his wife. He will make the trip directly from Asunción to Santiago. . . .

[A description of JCR operations in France, Belgium, Italy, Portugal, Spain, and Switzerland follows.]

"Lt. Col. Osvaldo Rawson, who will be in Santiago from September 2 on, has offered [to provide us] the complete list from Argentine immigrations of all of the Chileans who have entered Argentina after September 11 [date of the 1973 coup in Chile.] This officer has the idea of forming a center for intelligence coordination among Chile-Argentina-Uruguay and Paraguay (Arancibia Collection).

111 *Rawson requests:* Arancibia Collection, October 10, 1975, IA/184.

111 *Contacts with Rawson:* Arancibia Collection, October 3, 1975, II/172; December 23, 1975, II/165.

112 *Videla statement:* Quoted in *La Opinion*, October 10, 1975 (cited in Seoane).

112 *Intelligence coordination:* Roberto Viola, *Anexo I (Inteligencia) A la Directiva de Comandante Teneral del Ejercito Nro 404/75 (Lucha Contra la Subversion)*, October 28, 1975, 10, which designates the 601 Intelligence Battalion as the center of "reunion" of all other intelligence units; and Jorge Videla, *Directiva del Comandante General de Ejercito Nro 404/75 (Lucha contra la Subversion)*, October 28, 1975, 2. The latter refers to SIDE as an "element under functional control" of the army. See also James Blystone, "Organizational Chart of '601,'" attached to memo dated February 6, 1980 (Argentina Project).

113 *Malloco raid:* Interviews with Pascal, Beausire, and another Mirista present, Martin Hernández. DINA director Contreras described the raid in detail in a January 2, 1976, declaration to a Chilean investigating judge. Document in author's possession.

114 *Boomerang:* DINA released some details of the purported plan but embellished it as a plot to assassinate President Pinochet and other high government officials. MIR leaders deny such a plan called "Boomerang" existed, as described publicly by DINA. How much of the plan was real and how much was DINA propaganda has been difficult to establish. MIR leaders like Andrés Pascal discounted the plan's importance, but a contemporary intelligence report found in the Arancibia files indicates that Argentine and Chilean security forces took it seriously. It is unlikely the intelligence agencies were conveying propaganda to one another in secret reports exchanged among themselves. See "Material de Intercambio y Solicitud de Información," Buenos Aires, August 18, 1976, De: L.F.A./ A: A.D.F. Baires (Arancibia Collection: This document could be found only in González transcription.). See also IA/103, July 23, 1976, which refers to the report. Arancibia also reported earlier in 1975 about a planned MIR, ERP, ELN, Tupamaro offensive "Operativo Altiplano" against Bolivia. Arancibia Collection, February 14, 1975, IB/345–346. The report describes a "summit" meeting of guerrilla leaders in Salta province September 15–18, 1973.

114 *Captured map:* A copy appeared in *El Mercurio*, November 11, 1975.

115 *Argentine coordination: El Mercurio*, November 11, 1975. An Arancibia Collection document, August 18, 1976 (transcription by Mónica González), describes two joint operations between October 15 and November 15, involving DINA and the Argentine army and air force in the southern border area of Lonquimay Pass.

115 *Roundups:* Arancibia Collection document, October 31, 1975, IB/177–178.

115 *Claudet disappearance:* The Claudet disappearance is under investigation in France. In December 2001, French investigating Judge Roger Le Loire requested the extradition of retired Colonel José Osvaldo Riveiro, to face charges in Claudet's disappearance. Riveiro was briefly detained in Argentina, then released. There is

another twist to Rawson's pursuit of Claudet. According to former comrades, Claudet had a girlfriend in Buenos Aires. In 2002, when the case resurfaced because of Judge Le Loire's extradition request, an Argentine reporter tried to interview the girlfriend. To the reporter's astonishment, she found that Riveiro was living with the woman who had been Claudet's girlfriend twenty-six years earlier. The relationship obviously raises the possibility that the woman may have been working as a double agent for Rawson in 1975 and successfully infiltrated the MIR/JCR apparatus in Buenos Aires.

116 *Telex on Claudet capture:* There are three Arancibia Collection documents on the capture, the memorandum (IA/168–170), a draft telegram (IB/171)—both dated November 17—and the undated telegram as sent by the embassy (IB/172). The transcription is from the draft, which is clearer.

116 *Cocktail of the 26th:* Arancibia Collection, Memorandum 74-J, November 21, 1975, IA/165–67.

117 *Carlos Mena:* Documentos del Tribunal de Russell, 1976, p. 327. According to Martín Sivak, *Asesinato de Juan José Torres*, 105, Mena was in Buenos Aires a few days before the assassination of former president Juan José Torres.

118 *Names of those present at Condor meeting:* Casas, Mena, Fons, Guanes, and Contreras are listed as signatories to the final *"Acta de Clausura"* or Final Resolution (document in author's possession). Fons, in a telephone interview, said there were at least fifteen officers present, including the unnamed Uruguayan air force officer.

118 *Chile's report:* The Condor Agenda says the report was to be presented the morning of November 26, 1975 ("Primera Reunión de Trabajo de Inteligencia Nacional": Paraguay Archive 22:0155–22:0165). Arancibia refers to the report as a document that has been delivered to 601 operative Rawson, in Memorandum 78-J, December 11, 1975, IA/159–160 (Arancibia Collection).

118 *U.S. intelligence on JCR plan:* Santiago 1965, March 11, 1976 (Dinges FOIA release). Other U.S. intelligence documents refer explicitly to information obtained from "recent interrogations," which U.S. officials at the time understood to include savage torture.

118 *Argentine report: Apendice 1 (Síntesis de su origen y evolución. Doctrina - OPM PRT-ERP y JCR) al Anexo 1 (Inteligencia) a la Directiva del Comandante General del Ejército Nro 404/75 (Lucha contra la subversión),* dated October 28, 1975. This and other intelligence documents were obtained from military sources during the 1986 trials in Argentina, and are archived at the *Centro* de Estudios Legales y Sociales (CELS). The report quotes Enríquez as comparing the JCR to Lenin's "Zimmerwald" strategy at the time of the Russian Revolution. I talked to three people present at the meeting: Andrés Pascal, Enrique Gorriarán Merlo, and Luis Efraín Martínez Platero. Their recollections of the decisions taken match the information contained in the intelligence report.

119 *Paraguay reports:* "Informe No. 64," October 20, 1975, 21:1578–81; and "Informe No. 65," October 22, 1975, 21:1558–59, both signed by Guanes (Paraguay

Archive). The October 22 document refers to information received from "the Security aide of the US Embassy in our country, Mr. McWade." Report titled *"VIIa Conferencia Bilateral de Inteligencia Paraguay-Argentina: Exposición a Cargo de la Delegación del Ejercito Paraguayo, Año 1975"* (internal references date the document as later than July 1975), 46:1344–77 (Paraguay Archive).

119 *Intercontinental leadership:* Condor Agenda, op. cit.

119 *CIA assessment of MIR:* CIA (untitled), Directorate of Operations, November 26, 1975 (Chile Project).

120 *Go to Australia:* Senate Report Activities of Certain Foreign Intelligence Agencies, op. cit., 15.

120 *Eliminate enemies:* Interview with retired Colonel José Fons, October 2001.

120 *Party:* Contreras mentioned the location of the party in a published interview. The DINA installation bore the name Cuartel Malloco—no relation to the Malloco farm where the MIR-DINA battle occurred. Chilean investigative reporter Mónica González interviewed an officer present at the party, who told her about the girls and showed her pictures of the party. Author's interviews with Mónica González, and her article in *La Nación*, November 13, 1992.

121 *Organization of Condor:* Our knowledge of the structure and operations of Condor, as agreed at the meeting and expanded at two additional meetings in 1976, must be gleaned from a variety of sources, including: the Condor Agenda and Condor Acta, op. cit., the description of FBI agent Robert Scherrer, whose reports and interviews with the author provided the first description of Condor in 1979, and recently declassified documents from the CIA, DIA, and the State Department.

121 *CIA and FBI participated:* Contreras statement to Chilean Supreme Court, 1979.

121 *Computers:* Two former CIA officials who served many years in Latin America said in separate interviews that such support was typical of operations they were familiar with and would have been provided through an outside company under contract with the CIA.

122 *Condor numbers:* Interview with Scherrer; telex message "From Condor 1 To Condor 4," April 4, 1976 (Paraguay Archive 132:2129), CIA document February 14, 1978 (Chile Project) for Ecuador's joining, and Chilean document "Secret" April 14, 1978, letter from Colonel Jeronimo Pantoja, chief of CNI (the organization that succeeded DINA in 1977) to deputy minister of foreign affairs, for Peru's joining Condor.

122 *Encrypting machines:* See Gerardo Irusta, *Espionaje y servicios secretos en Bolivia* (La Paz, 1995, no publisher listed), 301. Irusta's source, Interior ministry official Juan Carlos Fortun, provided copies of coded and decoded telexes from Condortel. Fortun said his boss told him, "It was a machine specially manufactured for the 'Condor System' by the Logistics Department of the American Central Intelligence Agency."

123 *Radio system:* Asunción 4451 (quoted in State 205779, October 20, 1978) (Chile Project). Colonel (R) Lloyd Gracey, who served in the U.S. military training

group in Argentina, confirmed the existence of the radio system and its use by officers. He did not know if it had been used for Condor communications, but said the U.S. military allowed users to transmit in code, which would have made such use possible.

123 *Military attachés:* Letter from Contreras to Foreign Minister, October 3, 1974, Chilean Foreign Ministry documents in author's possession.

127 *Alliance:* Townley testimony to Salvi, November 24, 1992, 36, 42.

128 *Pinochet contact with Italian fascists:* Testimony of Stefano Delle Chiaie, Appeals Court of Rome, December 5, 1995, to Judge Salvi; testimony of Vincenzo Vinciguerra, December 5, 1995, Appeals Court of Rome. Venciguerra said, "Prince Borghese, in his international contacts, going to meet, to interview and visit Pinochet, accomplished the contact of Delle Chiaie [with Chile]. . . . When he [Delle Chiaie] went to Chile, he participated in meetings at the highest level in DINA."

129 *Resentment against Altamirano:* Townley testimony to Salvi, November 24, 1992, 26.

130 *DINA Exterior Department and Europe missions:* Townley testimony to Salvi, November 24, 1992, and July 1993. Testimony to Judge Servini of Carlos Labarca, a DINA driver, in Servini Evidence. Author's interview with Carlos Altamirano, December 2001.

131 *Townley instructions:* Townley testimony to Salvi, July 1993; and in sentencing, September 25, 1995. Delle Chiaie on payroll, passport: testimony of Carlos Labarca, and Townley testimony to Salvi.

132 *Reproach:* Vinciguerra testimony to Salvi. Townley acknowledged his preference for such a weapon but said he didn't remember the conversation with Vinciguerra.

132 *Celebration in Frankfurt:* Testimony in Servini Evidence from Wolf Von Arnswaldt, a Chilean Airlines employee and DINA collaborator based in Frankfurt.

132 *1995 trial:* Townley testified May 19, 1995.

132 *Pinochet gave the order:* Vinciguerra testimony to Salvi, 21. Other details of Townley's European operations can be found in Townley's testimony to Judge Salvi, November 24, 1993, and July 9, 1994. See also Dinges and Landau, op. cit., 160–61.

133 *$5,000 payment:* Statement by Judge Salvi in Servini Evidence, based on his interview with Vinciguerra, who was present in the meeting with Pinochet.

133 *Pinochet's meetings with terrorists:* Interview with one of Pinochet's civilian aides. Townley, in statements to U.S. investigators, provided the first information about Pinochet's meeting with Delle Chiaie in Madrid. Contreras confirmed it in testimony in Chile in 1997.

133 *Townley's lament:* Townley testimony to Salvi.

136 *Massera visit:* Buenos Aires 1751, March 16, 1976, document among collection of approximately 4,000 State Department documents released in September 2002 in accordance with an order dating from two years before from Secretary of State

Madeleine Albright. Hereafter Argentina Project. Argentina eventually hired the public relations firm Burston and Marsteller.

136 *Coup report:* State 72468, March 25, 1976 (Argentina Project).

138 *U.S. officials attacked:* Honorary consul John Egan was killed by Montoneros, and U.S. Information Agency official Alfred Laun was wounded by an ERP commando. Defense Attaché Col. Samuel Stapleton was evacuated after receiving repeated death threats. In August 1976, Battalion 601 captured documents and several ERP operatives, who revealed under torture that they had deeply infiltrated the Army base where the U.S. military group was headquartered and had targeted Lt. Col. Lloyd Gracey, the officer assigned to intelligence training, for assassination. Buenos Aires 5082, August 4, 1976, "Targeting of and collection of Information by ERP on USMILGP Members" (Dinges FOIA Release).

140 *Arancibia talks of the "right" and "left" methods.* He uses the term *"por derecha y por izquierda"* in two documents, December 11, 1975, IA/159, and July 7, 1978, V/238 (Arancibia Collection). U.S. intelligence document: William H. Hallman, Memorandum: "Nuts and Bolts of the Government's Repression of Terrorism-Subversion," August 7, 1979 (Argentina Project).

140 *List of killed and disappeared:* National Commission on the Disappeared *(Comisión Nacional de Desaparición de Personas)*—CONADEP—also known as the Sábato Commission. Major findings were published in a book, *Nunca Mas: The Report of the Argentine National Commission on the Disappeared* (New York: Farrar Straus Giraux, 1986). The Spanish edition, with the same name, was published in Buenos Aires in 1984. The book does not include the list of names of disappeared. I obtained an updated list in digital form with the help of Carlos Libenson, of the human rights research group Nunca Mas.

140 *Battalion 601 total:* Arancibia Collection document V/238, ca July 1978, part of a larger document containing lists of people kidnapped in 1975.

140 *"General consensus":* Buenos Aires 2528, April 16, 1976; Buenos Aires 2288, April 6, 1976 (Argentina Collection). Press reports for the first month after the coup reported sporadic violence and few deaths.

141 *DINA letter:* Luis Gutiérrez to L.F. Alemparte, December 23, 1975 (Arancibia Collection II/165). The letter names, in addition to Enríquez, Fernando Alarcón Ovando, "Daniel"—the code name for Claudet, who was already dead—and Ruy Mauro Marini, the number-two man in MIR, who was thought to be traveling to Argentina to meet with Enríquez.

142 *Santucho speech:* Mattini, op. cit.

143 *CIA report on Enríquez:* National Intelligence Daily, June 23, 1976, Directorate of Intelligence (Chile Collection). The report also says "Argentina has handed over to Chilean authorities a Brazilian political exile wanted by Santiago," an apparent reference to Enríquez's Brazilian colleague Regina Marcondes.

143 *Enríquez capture:* Description of meeting is in Mattini, op. cit., 446–53. Cables on

Enríquez death: Santiago 4325, May 7, 1976; Buenos Aires 3047, May 7, 1976, and CIA Directorate of Operations, "Sec Sit Per DINA," May 20, 1976 (Chile and Argentina Projects, Dinges FOIA Releases); CNVR report, Vol. 2, p. 596. Condor telex: interview with Luz Arce. Evidence of Enríquez presence in Chile is summarized in the CNVR report and in greater detail in a court filing by Enríquez family to the Interamerican Human Rights Commission, October 28, 1998.

144 *UNHCR briefing:* Buenos Aires 3766, June 7, 1976 (Argentina Collection).

146 *Uruguayan transition conversations:* Vegh Villegas revealed the conversations in testimony on October 25, 1985, to the *Comisión Investigadora Sobre Sequestro y Asesinato Perpetrados Contra los ex Legisladores Héctor Gutiérrez Ruiz y Zelmar Michelini,* quoted in the Uruguayan magazine *Postdata,* May 17, 1996. Michelini's statement to his daughter, Margarita, is from the same magazine.

146 *Planned visit to United States:* Referred to in *La Opinión* in stories about Michelini's death. See also Buenos Aires 2425, Montevideo 1165 and State 82853 (Argentina Project).

146 *Taub money trafficking:* See Chapter 4, note p. 267, for transactions with ERP. For transactions with federal police, interview with Leandro Sánchez Reisse. Taub also employed several police officers in his exchange business, according to court documents.

147 *Murder of Michelini and others:* Testimony of witnesses, including the statement attributed to Gabriela, is compiled in court records in the Camara Nacional de Apelaciones en lo Criminal y Correccional Federal de la Capital Federal (Buenos Aires) in connection with the unsuccessful attempt in 1987 to extradite officers suspected of ordering and carrying out the killings.

148 *Uruguayan role in murders:* Campos said the liaison officer, a major who was a protégé (*"ahijado"*) of Álvarez, carried the message directly to General Videla. Another source, former Colonel Fons, said Uruguayan intelligence, SID, knew Michelini was helping Tupamaros escape Argentina.

148 *Campos Hermida was interviewed:* Interview was at his office in Montevideo, October 12, 2001. He died after an operation for lung cancer on November 24.

149 *Trimarchi involvement:* Interview with Leandro Sanchez Reisse, a civilian employee of Intelligence Battalion 601 between 1976 and 1980. He said he did not know the killings described to him by Trimarchi related to the Michelini murder until I pointed out the similarities between his story and the facts of the case, especially the details about the car, the radio call, and the bodies in the trunk. There is a difference in one detail: according to the police report, three bodies were found in the trunk, not two, as Sánchez Reisse remembers Trimarchi saying. Sánchez Reisse later worked as an FBI and DEA informant and testified in 1987 before the Senate Committee on Foreign Relations, Subcommittee on Terrorism, Narcotics, and International Operations. He said his activities in 601 did not involve violence, although he knew many of the police and military personnel carrying out

such operations. He was jailed for several years on charges of participating in a kidnapping for extortion, but in 2003 was exonerated by an Argentine federal court.

152 *Torres political and military organizing:* Interview with Rubén Sánchez in 1996 by Martín Sivak, who provided a transcript to the author. Sivak notes that other Bolivians disputed Sanchez's story that Torres was planning to enter Bolivia clandestinely. However, as Torres's chief aide and the head of his operations in Bolivia, Sánchez would have been directly informed of these clandestine plans. Other accounts also support the fact that Sánchez was plotting against Banzer. See Irusta, 327–32. Quote from colleague, Sivak, 26.

152 *Mena's promotion:* Irusta, 337. Sivak, 105, says Mena was in Buenos Aires at the time of the Torres assassination.

152 *Rutila's torture:* Irusta, 346.

153 *Stedman cables:* La Paz 3254, May 9, 1976, and La Paz 3657, May 11, 1976 (Dinges FOIA Releases). In an earlier cable, La Paz 2779, April 7, 1976, Stedman reported on a series of raids on ELN safe houses in La Paz and Cochabamba, including a raid on April 2, the day Graciela Rutila and her daughter were captured (Dinges, FOIA release).

154 *International Brigade: Liberation* interview with International Brigade spokesman is reported in Paris 14243, May 13, 1976, and Paris 19795, July 7, 1976 (Dinges, FOIA Release). The spokesman said the gun used to kill Zenteno was also used in the attack on Captain Bartolome García Plata, the assistant military attaché of the Spanish embassy. García Plata survived the attack. According to the cable, French police established that the guns used in the two attacks "were of similar make."

154 *Theories of Torres and Zenteno killings:* Martínez de Hoz statement is in Buenos Aires 3664, June 3, 1976 (Dinges FOIA Release). The CIA initially portrayed Torres's murder as "eye for an eye" retaliation for the assassination of Zenteno in Paris, in Senate Report on Activities of Certain Foreign Intelligence Agencies. The author and other investigators lean to the view that both Zenteno and Torres were killed for the same reason: to eliminate them as rivals to Banzer. Cf. Sivak, 131–158; James M. Malloy and Eduardo Gamarra, *Revolution and Reaction: Bolivia, 1964–1985* (New Brunswick, 1988), 95.

154 *Hill cable on murders:* Buenos Aires 3664, "Body of Ex-Bolivian President Torres Found," June 3, 1976 (Argentina Project).

157 *CIA-Kissinger dispute:* "Alleged Assassination Plots Involving Foreign Leaders: Interim Report of the (Senate) Select Committee on Intelligence Activities," 225–27. Kissinger said in an interview with Elizabeth Farnsworth of PBS's *The News Hour,* "As far as we were concerned and the White House, the thing ended on October 15th." The CIA points to a series of documents after that date in which the coup preparations are continuing with CIA help, including the delivery of the submachine guns to one group only a few hours before a second group carried out the fatal kidnapping. Leaders of both groups, General Camilo Valenzuela and retired General Roberto Viaux, were convicted by a Chilean military court for the

coup activity, which found they were working together throughout the coup plotting. Moreover, a machine gun found at the site of the kidnapping was of the same type as those provided to the plotters, although the committee investigators said they were not able to determine if it was one of the weapons supplied by the CIA. The CIA recovered all three guns and dumped them in the ocean, making it impossible to know anything about the guns except what the CIA officers said. See Seymour Hersh, *The Price of Power: Kissinger in the Nixon White House* (New York: Summit, 1983), 293.

157   *Tell Popper: New York Times,* September 27, 1974.

158   *Pragmatic policy:* Kissinger quoted in Lars Schoultz, *Human Rights and U.S. Policy toward Latin America* (Princeton University Press, 1981), 110.

159   *Saturday briefings:* State Department officers called in for those briefings included Chile desk officer Robert Driscoll. Interviews with Driscoll and Rudy Fimbres, who also worked at ARA.

159   *Kissinger-Pinochet meeting:* The transcript was first declassified in response to a request from author Lucy Komisar. Memorandum of Conversation, June 8, 1976 (Chile Collection). Also present at the meeting was William D. Rogers, who was then assistant secretary for American Republic Affairs. Pinochet was accompanied by Foreign Minister Patricio Carvajal, ambassador to the U.S., Manuel Trucco, and Ricardo Claro, a prominent Chilean businessman who pops up regularly in the role of mediator between the United States and Chile on thorny issues. He played a similar role in 1978 when the United States was pressuring Chile to turn over DINA agent Michael Townley in connection with the Letelier assassination.

162   *Kissinger speech: Department of State Bulletin* 75 (July 5, 1976), 4.

162   *Rosy assessment:* CIA Latin Trends, June 28, 1976 (Chile Project).

163   *Round-ups of Communists:* Amnesty International denounced the arrests of 185 people in Antofagasta on May 17–18. The author wrote in the *Washington Post,* August 7, 1976, "A U.S. Dilemma: Chileans Vanish," that 130 people had been kidnapped by DINA in April and May—a figure that did not include the Antofagasta arrests.

163   *Plot to kill Pascal Allende:* Interviews with Rolando Otero, Orlando García, and President Carlos Andrés Pérez.

163   *Otero and DISIP:* Otero provided a boatload of intelligence to DISIP about Chilean operations, including the claim that DINA intended to set up an operation based in Florida using Cuban exiles to conduct operations against Chilean exiles living in the United States. This U.S. installation may have been the "Condor base" the CIA learned the Condor alliance was trying to establish, according to the Senate Report on Activities of Certain Foreign Intelligence Agencies. Otero returned to Chile, which detected his double dealing, detained, and tortured him. FBI legal attaché Robert Scherrer, in Argentina, learned that Otero was being held in Chile, and in personal negotiations with Contreras, obtained his expulsion from Chile into FBI custody. He was imprisoned in the United States and

in 1978 provided information leading to the arrest of Letelier assassin Michael Townley.

163 *Cuban-Italian role in Condor:* The evidence is circumstantial and basically contained in the Arancibia documents. Delle Chiaie was in Chile at the time of the foundation of Operation Condor, and was also there for the second meeting in June. The Italians and Cubans worked closely with Michael Townley and with Enrique Arancibia, and conducted missions to Argentina. DINA sent a German-Chilean, Karl Werner (an alias) to Peru to spy on the military buildup there, a mission that is well documented in the Arancibia papers.

164 *Santiago Condor meeting:* Interview with Luz Arce. Arancibia, in a report June 3, 1976 (IA/111), writes, "I had a meeting with Osvaldo Rawson who informed that the SIE had approved of a direct line of communication with our office, just as he had offered Mamo [Contreras] in the past. They needed to know what type of telex machine the office would be using. Rawson and two service technicians would go to Chile after the 10, when the Conference of Ambassadors of the Organization of American States ends."

165 *Hill démarche:* Buenos Aires 3462, May 25, 1976 (Argentina Project). "I wish authorization to say to him [the Argentine foreign minister] the following: Quote, The US very much sympathizes with the moderate policies announced by President Videla and has hoped to be helpful to Argentina in her process of national reconstruction and reconciliation. We fully understand that Argentina is involved in an all-out struggle against subversion. There are, however, some norms which can never be put aside by governments dedicated to a rule of law. Respect for human right[s] is one of them. The continued activities of Triple A-type death squads which have recently murdered Michelini, Gutiérrez Ruiz and dozen[s] of others and have kidnapped a member of the Fulbright commission, Miss Elida Messina, are damaging the GOA's generally good image abroad. These groups seem to operate with impunity and are generally believed to be connected with the Argentine security forces. Whether they are or not, their continued operation can only be harmful to the GOA itself and cause consternation among Argentina's friends abroad, end-Quote." State 129048, same date, conveys State's authorization for the démarche (Argentina Project).

166 *Intelligence briefing:* Briefing Memorandum, to the Secretary, from INR-Harold H. Saunders, "Murders in Argentina—No Intergovernmental Conspiracy," June 4, 1976 (Argentina Project). Kissinger instruction to ambassadors: State 137156, Immediate Action, Possible International Implications of Violent Deaths of Political Figures Abroad," June 4, 1976 (Argentina Project).

166 *Response to query on conspiracy:* Santiago 5434, June 7, 1976, and Buenos Aires 3766, June 7, 1976 (Chile Project and Dinges FOIA Release). State 141275, June 10, 1976, is a report summarizing responses from the various embassies and is addressed to the U.S. delegation, including Secretary Kissinger, gathered in Santiago for the OAS meeting (Argentina Project).

167   *CIA intelligence on Condor meeting:* CIA, National Intelligence Daily, June 23, 1976 (Chile Project). This report links the new organization to the murders of Michelini and Torres. CIA, Weekly Summary, July 2, 1976 (Chile Project), is the first mention of Condor in the U.S. documents. INR report no. 526, July 19, 1976, quoted without redaction in State 178852, July 20, 1976 (Dinges FOIA Release). A copy of this document released in the Argentine collection in August 2002, after the Bush administration announced a more restrictive FOIA policy, eighteen months after I received it, blacks out all references to the Santiago Condor meeting and joint operations in Paris. The unredacted version also contains a reference to a joint Brazilian-Argentine operation: "A reliable Brazilian source has described a Brazil-Argentina agreement under which the two countries hunt and eliminate terrorists attempting to flee Argentina for Brazil."

168   *Shlaudeman role in Chile:* While Kissinger was in Chile in June, Shlaudeman was called before a Senate confirmation hearing and grilled about his knowledge of the U.S. government's role in the coup plots. In secret testimony, Shlaudeman admitted he had made misleading statements to cover up U.S. participation in the coup plots. Senate Foreign Relations Committee, ca June 1976, undated, unpublished transcript, "Statement of the Honorable Harry W. Shlaudeman, Nominee to be Assistant Secretary of State for Inter-American Affairs."

168   *Trends report:* State 171456, July 10, 1976, "Trends in the Southern Cone," addressed to all embassies in Latin America "for ambassador from Shlaudeman" (Dinges FOIA Release).

169   *Argentine cable:* Buenos Aires 4844, July 23, 1976, "South America Southern Cone Security Practices" (Chile Project).

169   *Uruguayan embassy cable:* Montevideo 2702, July 20, 1976 (Dinges FOIA Release).

170   *CIA-State meeting:* ARA-CIA Weekly Meeting—30 July 1976, "Operation Condor" (Chile Project).

171   *Other reports summarizing Condor intelligence:* There are four reports in all with Condor assassination information between the July 30 briefing and the Letelier assassination. CIA, Latin American Trends Staff Notes, August 11, 1976, "Southern Cone Counterterrorism Plans", CIA, August 12, 1976, "Decision by Condor Countries to Suspend Operations in Europe," INR Afternoon Summary, August 13, 1976, "Latin America: Suspension of 'Condor' Plans," and September 21, 1976, "Latin American Political and Economic Cooperation in Southern Cone" (Chile Project).

174   *August 3 meeting:* The meeting is mentioned in the declassified memorandum of August 30, 1976, "ARA/CIA Weekly Meeting, 27 August 1976 (Chile Project). Habib, whose name is blacked out but was provided by an informed source, "is very concerned about making representations concerning Operation Condor (notes for meeting of August 3)," the memorandum says.

175   *Pinochet personally authorized:* Contreras's statement was in a 300-page statement to the Chilean Supreme Court December 23, 1997, 259–261, after his conviction for

the Letelier murder. Espinoza implicated Pinochet in a notarized declaration known as *Acta de Punta Arenas*, May 2, 1978, signed by Espinoza and notorized. The secret document was obtained by journalist Patricia Verdugo and provided to the author. Espinoza said a superior officer tried to force him, as a coverup, to accept sole responsibility for the "elimination" of Letelier, and that he, Espinoza, wanted to state instead that Contreras gave him the order "on assignment from the President of the Republic" ("por encargo del President de la Republica"). See John Dinges, "Affidavit Links Pinochet to Car Bomb Assassination," *Miami Herald*, March 24, 2000.

Fernández Larios made statements implicating Pinochet after he arrived in the United States as a cooperating witness in the Letelier case in 1987, including an interview with the author February 9, 1987, that was broadcast on National Public Radio. Townley has made general statements in his many court testimonies to the effect that he understood that the orders originated with Pinochet, although he did not have firsthand knowledge.

176 *Kissinger and Letelier:* Kissinger interview with Elizabeth Farnsworth of PBS's *The News Hour with Jim Lehrer*, February 2001.

178 *Contreras visit to Washington:* Walters confirmed the visit in Congressional testimony in 1981. See "U.S. Economic Sanctions Against Chile," House Subcommittee on International Economic Policy and Trade and on Inter-American Affairs, Committee on Foreign Affairs, March 10, 1981, 55–56. Information on the purchases are in Saul Landau and John Dinges, "The Chilean Connection," *The Nation*, November 28, 1981. A dated weapons invoice signed by "Renato Sepulveda," a Contreras pseudonym, places him in Washington July 8, 1976. Walters did not disclose the meetings in his earlier statements to the FBI as part of the Letelier investigation.

178 *Townley's knowledge about Condor:* CIA "Memorandum for the Record," August 23, 1978, is the CIA's record of a meeting with Letelier case prosecutor Eugene Propper, who was seeking CIA information on Operation Condor: "Mr. Propper explained that Townley is knowledgeable about Condor and has mentioned it in connection with the issuance of the Paraguayan passports." The still-classified Senate Report on Activities of Certain Foreign Intelligence Agencies, op. cit., based on CIA documents and testimony, says the DINA officers in Paraguay "might have been operating under the umbrella" of Operation Condor.

179 *Condor One telegram:* The text is transcribed in English as Exhibit 114, included in evidence sent to Chile in 1979 as part of the Extradition Packet. The FBI obtained a copy of the telegram from Guanes in 1978.

180 *Landau to Shlaudeman:* Asunción 3233, August 5, 1976. Shlaudeman to Landau, same date: State 194941 (Chile Project). Paraguayan official Conrado Pappalardo also told Landau that the request for the Paraguayan cooperation came in a phone call from General Pinochet to General Stroessner, the Paraguayan president. U.S. investigators later received the Condor One telegram requesting cooperation and

concluded, after interviewing Pappalardo, that no such call was made. See Asunción 3276, August 6, 1976 (Chile Project).

180 *Three CIA reports:* CIA, Latin American Staff Notes, Southern Cone Counterterrorism Plans, August 11, 1976; CIA, Directorate of Operations, "Decision by Condor Countries to Suspend Operations in Europe," August 12, 1976; INR Afternoon Summary, "Suspension of Condor Plans" (Top secret/Exdis/Codeword), August 13, 1976 (Chile Project). The reports discuss Brazil's reluctance to participate in Condor's European operations, leading to a suspension of the operation until Brazil decided to limit its participation to activities in the Condor countries themselves. This detail is reported in INR Afternoon Summary several weeks later, September 24, 1976, "Operation Condor goes Forward" (Chile Project). ARA head Shlaudeman, however, knew this much earlier. In his August 3 report to Kissinger, he reports Brazil's decision to limit its participation to cooperation "short of murder operations." See above pp. 171–72 (Chapter 10).

181 *Assassination plots:* "Alleged Assassination Plots Involving Foreign Leaders: Interim Report of the (Senate) Select Committee on Intelligence Activities," November 1975.

182 *Phone calls:* Shlaudeman oral history. The Association for Diplomatic Studies and Training, Foreign Affairs Oral History Project, interviewed by William E. Knight, May 24, 1993.

182 *Condor démarche:* State 209192, "Operation Condor," August 18, 1976. Two other versions, with identical wording but more extensive redactions, are dated August 23, 1976 (Chile Project).

184 *Respect for Popper:* The author also must acknowledge a debt of respect and gratitude. In 1977, Popper and Boyatt intervened to prevent the Pinochet regime from executing a decree of expulsion from Chile against the author. I later learned from Chilean officials that the expulsion was ordered by Contreras because of my writing on DINA—much of which at that time was under a pseudonym or without a byline. That an order by Contreras was countermanded was an early sign that Contreras's hold on power was weakening.

186 *Meeting in Santiago:* Interview with Thomas Boyatt. Popper's cable, dated August 24, 1976, bore the identifying number "Santiago 8210" and was in reply to "State 209192," the designation on Kissinger's cable. The numbers become indispensable guides to the paper trail about Operation Condor and the Letelier assassination in the coming weeks.

187 *Bolivia response:* Stedman conveyed Bolivia's request for intelligence in La Paz 3657, "High level Bolivian Concern about World-wide Communist advances and implications for the Southern Cone of South America," May 11, 1976 (Dinges FOIA Release). "Minister [of Interior Colonel Juan Pereda] indicated that he and the president [Hugo Banzer] hope that Washington will provide a global analysis from the U.S. point of view of the actions and plans of world Communism based on our intelligence. The minister also hopes that Bolivia can receive an expanded

flow of information on world communism actions and plans." Stedman recommended that State should provide the information "from INR or others within the U.S. intelligence community." Stedman's response to Kissinger's authorization is La Paz 6758, August 26, 1976 (Chile Project).

188 *Approach to Stroessner:* Author's interview with George W. Landau, September 26, 2001. Landau was named ambassador to Chile in late 1977 and presided over the arduous negotiations leading to the expulsion of DINA agent Michael Townley, whose testimony led to the indictment of Contreras, Espinoza, Fernández Larios, and five Cuban exiles charged with assisting Townley in the Letelier bombing. On the passport episode, he said, "I must say that neither the Department nor I had any inkling that this whole episode was connected to the Letelier murder. Because they wouldn't have sent me to Chile, that would not have made great sense to send me to Chile. They didn't know, and I didn't know. This was the interesting thing. It came as a great surprise to us."

188 *Embassies actions on Kissinger instruction:* Author's interviews with DCM Maxwell Chaplin and political counselor Wayne Smith for Argentina, DCM James C. Haahr for Montevideo.

189 *Siracusa meeting with Méndez:* Montevideo 3451, September 15, 1976, "Meeting with President Aparicio Méndez" (Dinges FOIA Release). Hill meeting with Videla: Buenos Aires 6276, September 24, 1976, "Ambassador Discusses U.S.-Argentine Relations with President Videla" (Argentina Project).

189 *"Take no further action":* San Jose 4526. This document, a key part of the investigation of U.S. actions regarding Operation Condor, has not been included in any of the collections of declassified documents and was not provided in response to any of the authors of more than 60 FOIA requests. It was discovered by National Security Archive senior analyst Carlos Osorio in a search in State Department microfilm archives of past FOIA releases. Apparently, the document was declassified in 1991, as the sole release to an unidentified researcher who requested documents on Henry Kissinger and Operation Condor. William Luers, in several interviews, said he has no memory of the cable exchange. His cable, referenced as State 231654, remains classified.

190 *Cuban exile terrorism:* For a list of terrorist actions, by CNM, Omega 7, Zero, CORU, and other Cuban groups operating at this time, see Dinges and Landau, 240 and 252n.

192 *CIA and Bush actions:* CIA, Memorandum to DCI [Director of Central Intelligence] August 23, 1976 [*sic*]; CIA Memorandum, "Contacts with Justice Department Officials Concerning Letelier Murder," October 12, 1976 (Chile Project).

193 *CIA points to Pinochet:* CIA Directorate of Operations cable 314/02794-76, October 6, 1976 (Chile Project). This document had been released to the Letelier family in 1980, but all references to the source's statements about Pinochet and Chilean involvement in the murder were redacted.

193 *Martyr theory stories:* See Dinges and Landau, 243–44. Stories propound-

ing the theory included *Washington Post*, November 1; *Newsweek*, October 11; *New York Times*, October 12. The martyr theory as an explanation for leftists killing Letelier was suggested in a State Department cable to Secretary Kissinger, who was traveling abroad, recounting a meeting with Chilean Ambassador Manuel Trucco. State 234417, "Exdis for the Secretary through Habib from ARA-Luers," September 22, 1976.

195 *Scherrer knowledge of Condor:* Author's interviews in 1979; Condor cable dated September 28, 1976, the text of which was first published in Dinges and Landau, in 1980, declassified as of March 1981, when a copy is published in "U.S. Economic Sanctions Against Chile," Hearing of Interamerican Affairs Subcommittee, House Committee on Foreign Affairs, March 10, 1981, 63 ff.

196 *Condor connection post-assassination:* Briefing Memorandum, Shlaudeman to Habib, "Operation Condor," September 25, 1976 (Chile Project and FOIA release to writer Lucy Komisar, which contains material redacted in the Chile Project release). In plainer English, the memo means that CIA had already distributed Condor material to FBI at the time of the original CIA reports. It should not be read to mean that the CIA called attention to Condor and its possible relevance after the assassination. Whatever CIA dissemination there may have been before the assassination, the FBI officials in charge of the case said they first learned about Condor from Scherrer's report, not from the CIA.

196 *Reinstatement of démarche:* State 246107, October 4, 1976 (Chile Project). The reference numbers in the cable are important: State 209192 is Kissinger's démarche order August 23, and Santiago 8210 is Popper's request for instructions August 24.

196 *Contreras denial:* Hinchey Report, 17.

197 *Dickens appalled:* Interview with Robert Scherrer, 1989. Dickens died in the late 1980s.

197 *Hewson Ryan interview:* The Association for Diplomatic Studies and Training, Foreign Affairs Oral History Project, interviewed by Richard Nethercut, April 27, 1988.

202 *Hill démarche on human rights:* Buenos Aires 3462, May 25, 1976, "Request for Instructions." State 129048, May 25, 1976, "Proposed Démarche on Human Rights" (Argentina Project).

202 *Guzzetti dismisses concerns:* Buenos Aires 6130, September 20, 1976, "Other aspects of September 17 Conversation with Foreign Minister" (Argentina Project). Kissinger's conversation with Guzzetti in Santiago was first reported by Martin Edwin Andersen, "Kissinger and the Dirty War," *The Nation*, October 31, 1987. Andersen's article was based on a memo by Assistant Secretary for Human Rights Patricia Derian, who was told the story by Hill during a visit to Argentina in March 1977. In response to Andersen's article, William Rogers, a close associate of Kissinger's who served as assistant secretary for Latin America before Shlaudeman, cast doubt on the story by claiming—inaccurately—that Hill had never reported his concern about the Guzzetti-Kissinger conversation to the State

Department. In a letter prepared for Kissinger and sent to *The Nation*, Rogers writes: "Hill never told us during the last six months of 1976, while he was working the human rights issue so energetically, that you had misled Guzzetti, or that the junta was under a dangerously misguided impression about your attitude."

204 *Guzzetti euphoric:* "Foreign Minister Guzzetti euphoric over visit to United States," Buenos Aires 6871, October 19, 1976 (Argentina Project).

204 *Shlaudeman response:* State 262786, October 22, 1976, "Guzzetti's Visit to the U.S." (Argentina Project). There is a further wrinkle to this exchange. I found another version of the same cable, with a different concluding paragraph. The alternate version, released to an Argentine court in response to a request under the Mutual Legal Assistance Treaty (MLAT), instructs Hill to persevere in his representations. "We will continue to impress on Argentina representatives here, as we expect you to do there, that the USG regards most seriously Argentina's international commitments to protect and promote fundamental human rights." About Kissinger's views, this version says that Hill should tell Guzzetti to read a recent speech on human rights given by Kissinger to the Synagogue Council of America. No explanation for the radically differing versions could be learned.

207 *Cuban embassy support:* Cuban officials consulted by the author denied the embassy was supporting guerrilla groups in any way. A variety of other sources with direct information said there is no question that such support occurred. The sources include former Tupamaros and ERP activists in Argentina at the time, who specified that the support was not for guerrilla activity but only to help militants escape. The leftist sources confirmed information from intelligence sources. Biedma's wife said that a Cuban embassy official "Angel" helped her and her son leave Argentina shortly before the family's house was raided by a AAA squad in May 1975.

208 *CIA cable on JCR:* Western Hemisphere Brief CI-WHB 76-097, June 1976 (date obtained from reference in cable to killing in Paris of Bolivian ambassador Joaquin Zenteno "last month") (Dinges FOIA Release).

209 *Cubans' kidnapping:* Interview with Carlos Alzugaray, Cuban consul in Argentina at the time of the arrests. Interview in 1979 with Robert Scherrer. Townley's trip to Buenos Aires on August 12 is confirmed by his passport in the name of Kenneth Enyart. Townley had other Cuban related business as well. He was meeting with Enrique Arancibia Clavel to coordinate the extortion-kidnapping of a Dutch banker to get money for the anti-Castro leader Guillermo Novo and his group, the Cuban Nationalist Movement, which the following month would assist him in carrying out the Letelier assassination in Washington, D.C. See Propper and Branch, op. cit., 321–33. A Miami Cuban exile group with ties to Novo's Cuban Nationalist Movement eventually claimed responsibility for the kidnapping of the Cuban diplomats—an obviously untrue claim that echoed the similar claim in the Leighton assassination attempt.

209   *CIA report on Biedma:* CIA, Directorate of Operations, "Argentina-Cuba: Castro Support for Local Subversion?," September 22, 1976 (Dinges FOIA Release).

210   *Homero Tobar Aviles:* My investigation involved piecing together information from activists in Chile, Argentina, Cuba, and Bolivia who had contact with Mauro/ Tobar. The young revolutionary was a "sergeant" in charge of an ERP guerrilla unit when he was captured.

210   *Uruguayan team:* The group of officers also used the name OCOA, *Organismo Coordinador de Operaciones Antisubversivas.* Those identified by prisoners, in addition to Gavazzo, were Juan Manuel Cordero, Jorge Silveira, and Hugo Campos Hermida. Gavazzo and Cordero were seen by multiple witnesses and have not denied their participation in Argentina operations. Silveira and Campos Hermida, a police commissioner then assigned to narcotics duty, have denied they were in Argentina. Campos Hermida was identified by two prisoners, Washington Perez and Maria del Carmen Martínez. Campos Hermida was the only one of those accused to testified before the 1985 parliamentary commission. He presented alibi evidence that he was in Uruguay and on a trip to the United States during some of the time he was alleged to be in Argentina. In a long interview with the author, he described the Argentine operations in considerable detail, and said he learned about them from an army officer who told him he had used Campos Hermida's identity in interrogating prisoners at Orletti. Campos Hermida's story, while clearly self-serving, contained many concrete leads of major importance to a serious judicial investigation of the Uruguayan Condor activities in Argentina. He said in the interview he was willing to provide information to a judicial investigation, but no such investigation existed in Uruguay until after his death in November 2001.

210   *Uruguayan SID:* Testimony in 1985 to *Comisión Investigadora sobre Situación de Personas Desaparecidas, Camara de Representantes del Uruguay,* of Julio Cesar Barboza Pla, a soldier assigned to SID in 1976, who identified the respective roles of Gavazzo, Fons and other officials participating in SID operations in 1976.

210   *Uruguayan major:* Buenos Aires 4378, July 2, 1976, says that kidnapped refugees after release said they "recognized and could name Uruguayan security officials (plural) who are active in Buenos Aires in joint operations . . ." (Argentina Project). Buenos Aires 4844, July 23, 1976, cites an "Argentine Army source reference to a Uruguayan Army major assigned to the Uruguayan military intelligence service 'who has been in Buenos Aires for the past several weeks cooperating with Argentine security forces in anti terrorist operations' " (Dinges FOIA Release). Thus, according to these documents, the United States had information and identities of Uruguayan officers working in Argentine at the time of the string of murders and kidnappings.

211   *PVP:* Interviews with Hugo Cores, one of the founders of the PVP, who confirmed the kidnapping and ransom amount. The kidnap victim was an Argentine businessman, Federico Hart. Ransom was paid quietly in 1974, without involvement

of the Argentine police and with little public notice. The PVP-OPR-33 activities and organization are described in a book-length military publication, *"El Proceso Politico: Las Fuerzas Armadas al Pueblo Oriental,"* no date (copy obtained from human rights sources).

212 *Clear evidence of cooperation:* Montevideo 4161, November 1, 1976 (Argentina Project).

212 *Uruguayan disappeared:* The testimonies of survivors of the Uruguayan Condor operations in Argentina are excerpted in an elegantly documented summary of evidence, *El Contexto Represivo,* compiled by Raul Olivera, of the union federation PIT/CNT. The electronic document consists of a seventy-five-page chronology, excerpts from key testimony, and hyperlinks to the transcriptions of testimonies of almost one hundred witnesses. A total of forty-six Uruguayans disappeared in Argentina in 1976. Those seen in Automotores Orletti, with date of capture, are:

6/9/76, Gatti Antuña, Gerardo Francisco;
6/15/76, Méndez Donadio, José Hugo;
6/15/76, Rodríguez Rodríguez, Julio;
6/?/76, Candia, Francisco Edgardo;
7/13/76, Duarte Luján, León Gualberto;
8/26/76, Cruz Bonfiglio, Mario Jorge;
9/3/76, Betancourt Garin, Walner Ademir;
9/23/76, Morales von Pieverling, Juan Miguel;
9/23/76, Kleim Lledo de Morales, Josefina Modesta;
9/26/76, Julien Caceres, Mario Roger;
9/26/76, Grisonas de Julien, Victoria;
9/26/76, Mechoso Méndez, Alberto Cecilio;
9/26/76, Soba, Adalberto Waldemar;
9/26/76, Tejera Llovet, Raúl;
9/26/76, Errandonea Salvia, Juan Pablo;
9/27/76, Islas Gatti de Zaffaroni, María Emilia;
9/27/76, Zaffaroni Castilla, Jorge Roberto;
9/28/76, Trias Hernández, Cecilia Susana;
9/28/76, Cram González, Washington;
9/30/76, Prieto González, Ruben;
1/10/76, Lezama González, Rafael;
1/10/76, Moreno Malugani, Miguel Angel;
1/10/76, Rordíguez Mercader, Carlos;
1/10/76, Recagno Ibarburu, Juan Pablo.
1/10/76, Carretero Cardenas, Casimira Maria del Rosario.

List compiled by human rights researcher Anabel Alcaide, *Liga Argentina para protección de los derechos humanos,* based on data on individual cases in CONADEP and PIT/CNT.

212 *DIA cable:* IR 8 804 030076, September 20, 1976. This document in the author's possession was released to Italian investigating Judge Giancarlo Capaldo during a visit to the United States in 2001. It has not been released in any of the document collections.

213 *DIA report on Condor:* IR 6 804 0334 76, October 1, 1976, Buenos Aires (Chile collection). The report contains an annotation "date of information: 1976, Sep 28." Other cables reporting on the kidnapping of Uruguayans in Argentina and the subsequent reappearance of some of them in Uruguay are: Buenos Aires 5661, August 30, 1976; Montevideo 4161, November 1, 1976; State 267364, October 29, 1976; Montevideo 4136, October 29, 1976; Buenos Aires 7203, November 2, 1976; Montevideo 4143, October 30, 1976; Buenos Aires 6884, October 19, 1976; and State 213081, August 27, 1976 (Argentina Project and Dinges FOIA Release).

214 *Brazilian document:* Brazilian Air Force, "Evolution of the Anti-subversive Fight, January to May 1977," discovered in a government archive and published by Folha de Sao Paolo.

215 *Siracusa defense of Uruguayan military:* Montevideo 3095, August 20, 1976, rebuts a human rights study on Uruguay by the Washington Office on Latin America (WOLA) paragraph by paragraph. In clear contradiction to the recent cable traffic on Condor, he asserted there was "no evidence" that GOU (government of Uruguay) ordered the murders of Michelini and Gutiérrez. In rebutting one of the WOLA charges, he contradicted his own cable report, in which he reported that "Michelini was considered by Argentine authorities to be working with the Revolutionary Coordinating Junta (JCR) in Argentina in orchestrating the Propaganda campaign against Uruguay." Montevideo 2238, June 18, 1976 (FOIA Release Carlos Osorio).

216 *Siracusa and Koch:* The Association for Diplomatic Studies and Training, Foreign Affairs Oral History Project, interview with Ernest V. Siracusa, by Hank Zivetz, June 1989.

216 *Bush call to Koch:* Interviews with Edward Koch and his congressional aide Charles Flynn. Neither could remember the date of the call except that it was subsequent to the Letelier assassination. The FBI call to Koch was October 19, according to FBI Memorandum, October 21, 1976, "Irritation of the Uruguayan Military with U.S. Congressman Edward I. Koch (FOIA Release to Koch).

218 *CIA letter to Koch:* Letter to Koch from Robert J. Eatinger, Jr., Chief, Litigation Division, CIA, September 26, 2001. After an interview with the author about the possible Operation Condor implications of the incident, Koch wrote to the CIA in 2001 and filed FOIA requests for documents. The account here is based on five documents released to him and an interview with Colonel Fons, who described his relationship with Latrash but refused to comment about the Koch threat. None of Siracusa's cables on the subject have been released, and other documents released to Koch are heavily censored. Siracusa mentioned the incident to Assistant Secre-

tary for Human Rights Patricia Derian in a meeting in 1977. A memorandum on that conversation was obtained by journalist Martin Edwin Andersen, who included a sentence mentioning Koch in his book, *Dossier Secreto*. It was Andersen's account that led the author to investigate the incident's deeper connections to Operation Condor. See Andersen, 228.

218 *Shlaudeman blocks appointments:* Memo to Philip Habib, December 13, 1976 (Koch FOIA request). The memo refers to two cables on the Koch threat, which the State Department has refused to release to Koch. They are Montevideo 4652, December 2, 1976; and State 292202, December 1, 1976.

219 *Condor goes forward:* INR Afternoon Summary, September 24, 1976 (Chile Project).

219 *René Valenzuela:* Valenzuela remained active in Europe after the dissolution of the JCR. In 1992 he was arrested in Spain on charges of participating in activities of the Basques terrorist group ETA. See Jorge G. Castañeda, *Utopia Unarmed: The Latin American Left After the Cold War* (Knopf, 1993), 67n.

221 *Condor targets in Europe:* This account of the Paris-Lisbon Condor mission is based on multiple sources, cited here and in other notes, each of which provides a piece of the puzzle. The still secret Senate Report on Activities of Certain Foreign Intelligence Agencies mentions Carlos as a target. The CIA appears not to have known the identity of the two targets in Paris. Townley's account also must be pieced together from his statements in several documents. See Townley testimony to Judge Giovanni Salvi, July 9, 1993, 98 (about Valenzuela); testimony to Salvi, November 24, 1992, 65 (Italian transcript): "When I was in Europe, I wasn't just dealing with Leighton and for Alfredo. At a certain point I was looking for Carlos with the same intensity that you carried out your investigation. We were always trying to discover what the Red Brigades were preparing, what were the activities of Baader Meinhof, what the IRA was doing in Ireland or what ETA was plotting in Spain. Thanks to all of these groups, along with the revolutionary faction of the left, the MIR, we discovered contraband arms in shipping containers for electric appliances from Siemens Electric as they were leaving from Hamburg. There were Scorpion M-66 from Czechoslovakia, and also engines, many, many engines." See also Propper and Branch, 324, in which Townley links the two unnamed targets in Paris to Carlos.

221 *Condor presence in Europe:* "Operation Condor Goes Forward," INR Afternoon Summary, September 24, 1976; "Condor Activities Continue," INR Afternoon Summary, November 23, 1967 (Chile Project).

221 *Condor ruined:* Interview with Robert Scherrer. See Dinges and Landau, 237–240.

221 *Knowledge of Paris operation:* Briefing Memorandum, Shlaudeman to Habib, September 25, 1976 (Chile Project and FOIA release to journalist Lucy Komisar, which adds the key line about knowledge of the Paris operation).

222   *Paris mission:* Townley handwritten affidavit to Chilean court, March 1978, document in author's possession.

222   *Wilson Ferreira threat:* Correspondence with his son, Juan Raúl Ferreira. The elder Ferreira died in the 1980s.

222   *Final Condor meeting:* CIA Directorate of Operations cable, April 18, 1977 (Chile Project). Argentina was indeed responsible for leaking information about Condor to FBI legat Robert Scherrer, as reported in his September 28 cable on Operation Condor. But there were other leaks. The CIA knew about the Paris-Lisbon plans before Scherrer learned of it from his Argentine source, and the September 25 briefing memo from Shlaudeman to Habib indicates the Condor countries were aware of the United States' knowledge about the Paris plans.

223   *Bolivian prisoners:* They included Graciela Rutila Artés, Efraín Villa, and Luis Stamponi, who had been captured in Bolivia around the time of the killing of Juan José Torres. Rutila Artes's baby, Carla, was also taken to Argentina, where she was adopted by one of the Orletti taskforce members, Alfredo Ruffo.

224   *Condor party:* Testimony by Captain Eduardo Rodolfo Cabanillas, November 17, 1977, to court martial. The military court was investigating kidnappings allegedly carried out by the Orletti Taskforce 18 team under the leadership of a fellow officer and civilian taskforce chief Anibal Gordon. The case is important in that it demonstrates that some entities of the Argentine army were trying to get some aspects of the dirty war under control, at least insofar as it was investigating kidnappings whose purpose was not to eliminate subversives but rather to extort money for personal gain by the officers involved. Gordon and his group had been involved in such nonpolitical extortion schemes, and the military let it be known that Gordon's illegal activities were the reason for the firing of his boss, General Paladino. The other reason for Paladino's dismissal, the compromised Condor operation, has remained secret until now.

224   *Ecuador joins Condor:* CIA DO, February 14, 1978 (Chile Project), reports that Ecuador joined Condor in January 1978, installed Condortel communications equipment, and received scholarships to send four officers for training at the Chilean intelligence school. Participation of Peru: Chilean Central Nacional de Informaciones No. 201755, April 14, 1978, Secret, to Vice Minister of Foreign Relations (among documents leaked to *La Nación* newspaper in Chile and obtained by author). The memo reports that the Peruvian director of intelligence called the director of CNI to inform him that Peru agreed to the presence of a Chilean Condor representative in Peru. Last document on Condor: Report on exile group *Mopoco* by Pastor Coronel to Francisco Brítez, April 13, 1981, no microfilm numbers (Paraguay Archive). The report say *Mopoco*, a dissident faction of Stroessner's Colorado Party, was trying to organize a large convention of activists but was fearful "about the possibilidad that they will be detected and arrested by the Argentine Armed Forces within Operation 'Condor.' "

225 *Paraguay arrests of Argentines and Uruguayans:* Paraguay Archive documents, all
with letterhead "Police of the Capital, Department of Investigations," March 29,
1977, April 9, 1977, May 16, 1977; May 23, 1977 and undated "Interrogation Report from Nelson Rodolfo Santana Scotto. See also intelligence report on PVP
and OPR-33 groups, DPA 402, 5/23/81, 21:1776 (Paraguay Archive). The group
of suspects included Argentines José Luis Nell, Dora Marta Landi, and José Antonio Loboluso and Uruguayans Gustavo Inzaurralde and Nelson Rodolfo Santana
Scotto. Officers arriving in Asunción to participate in the interrogation were
Lieutenant José Montenegro and Alejandro Stada of Argentina's SIDE, and Major
Carlos Calgagno of Uruguay's SID. A document lists the names of the Argentine
and Paraguayan officers involved in the transfer, the pilot of the plane, and the airplane's license plate number.

225 *Goiburú disappearance:* There are dozens of documents about surveillance, investigation, and arrest of Goiburú in the Paraguay Archive. Most can be found in folder
1051 "Caso Goiburú." The U.S. embassy was following the case closely. See Asunción 4376, October 25, 1977, and State 127171, May 18, 1978 (Dinges FOIA Release). See also Gladys Meilinger de Sannemann, *Paraguay y la operación Condor en
los archivos del terror* (Asunción, 1993), 99; and Alfredo Boccia Paz, Miguel H.
Lopez, Antonio V. Pecci, and Gloria Gimenez Guanes, *En los sotanos de los generales: los documentos ocultos del operativo Condor* (Asunción 2002), 17–31, for an investigative account of Goiburú's capture.

226 *Jaccard case:* Records of the Chilean Comisión Nacional de Verdad y Reconcil-
iación; Buenos Aires 8399, November 9, 1977 (Dinges FOIA Release); and memo
"Update on Stoulman [*sic*] Disappearances," Buenos Aires, July 11, 1979 (Argentina Project). The Chilean commission, in confidential files, concluded that
DINA agents were probably present in Buenos Aires for the operation, and that
Jaccard was taken clandestinely to Chile, where he was executed. The other
Chileans were: Ricardo Ramírez Herrera, in charge of Chilean Communist Party
finances in Buenos Aires; Héctor Velásquez Mardones, CP member based in Argentina; Ruiter Enrique Correa Arce, CP member and newspaper vendor in Santiago; Hernán Soto Gálvez, identified by the CNVR as the "financial liaison"
between Argentina and Chile. Five of the Argentines were members of CP Solidarity committee sheltering the Chileans: Marcos Leder, Mauricio Leder, his son;
Mario Clark, Sergio Clark, his son; Rodolfo Sanchez Cabot, Mardones's em-
ployer. The other four were kidnapped at CP headquarters in Buenos Aires: Luis
Cervera Novo, Ricardo Isidro Gomez, Carmen Candelaria Roman, and Juan Ce-
sareo Arano. A journalistic investigation of this case was carried out in July 2000 by
reporter Lila Pastoriza of *Pagina 12* newspaper.

227 *Campiglia capture:* U.S. Embassy, Buenos Aires, memorandum, Regional Security
Officer James Blystone, April 7, 1980; U.S. Embassy, Buenos Aires, memoran-
dum, Political officer Townsend Friedman, August 21, 1980 (Argentina Project).
The other leader captured with Campiglia in Rio was Mónica Susana Pinus de

Binstock. Lorenzo Ismael Viñas was captured in Uruguayana, near the southern border. TEI members captured elsewhere and disappeared in connection with the same operation were: Julio César Genoud, Verónica María Cabilla, Jorge Óscar Benítez, Angel Servando Benítez, Lía Mariana Ercilia Guangiroli, Angel Carbajal, Matilde Adela Rodríguez de Carbajal, Raúl Milberg, Ernesto Emilio Ferre Cardozo, Miriam Antonio Fuerichs, Marta Elina Libenson, Angel Horacio García Pérez, and Ricardo Marcos Zucker.

228 *Peru operation:* There are more than a dozen U.S. documents on the Peru incident in the Argentina Project collection. The documents indicate that this was one of the rare instances in which U.S. officials tried to use their diplomatic clout, although late in the game and to no avail, to save the victims of an ongoing human rights crime. Other documents used in my reconstruction of the incident include: Memorandum, Townsend Friedman, August 18, 1980; Memorandum, Townsend Friedman, August 19, 1980, "The Case of the Missing Montoneros;" Memorandum, Townsend Friedman, August 21, 1980, no subject (reports on missions abroad to kill Firmenich); Memorandum, James Blystone, "Meeting with Argentine Intelligence Service," June 19; Lima 6226, July 11, 1980, "The Case of the Missing Montoneros"; INR Report, June 25, 1980, "Attempted Repatriation of Montoneros Apparently Foiled"; Geneva 10812, August 8, 1980, "Body of Argentine Exile Discovered in Madrid"; Buenos Aires 5962, July 24, 1980, "Argentine citizens Missing in Peru" (Castro's meeting with Galtieri); Lima 5932, July 3, 1980, "Amnesty International Reportedly Claims 3 Killed in Peru"; Lima 5570, June 20, 1980, "GOP Explains Montonero Deportations, Criticism Continues" (Argentina Project). Further details can be found in CONADEP file 1048, Noemí Esther Gianotti de Molfino. For a gripping account of the Peru operation, based on Peruvian military sources, see Ricardo Uceda, *Muerte en el pentagonito: los cementerios secretos del Ejército Peruano* (Planeta 2004), pp. 346–370.

229 *Goulart investigation:* See Enrique Foch Diaz, *Joao Goulart: El Crimen Perfecto* (Arca, 2001). A Brazilian congressional investigation of Goulart's death was launched in 2000 as a result of new information about Operation Condor.

229 *Frei death:* His daughter, Carmen Frei, now a prominent political figure, said, "We want to have an official investigation opened here in Chile because we have very well founded doubts that there may have been the hands of third persons involved in the death of my father." *El Mostrador,* March 28, 2001.

235 *Arancibia case:* The case is identified, according to court documents, as *"Causa numero 949, Arancibia Clavel y otros por infracción arts 223 y 224 bis del Codigo Penal, que tramitara ante el Juzgado Nacional en lo Criminal y Correccional Federal numero 5, Secretaria Numero 9."* González said she did not remember the judge's name, but other documents list the judge as Dr. Ramon Montoya and his secretary as Dr. Juan A. Piaggio.

236 *Operation Colombo:* The author, with correspondent Rudolf Rauch, published one of the first investigative reports on the scheme, in *Time,* August 18, 1975. The ar-

ticle summed up the arrangement: "A working relationship would well serve the mutual interests of DINA and the AAA. DINA has a long list of names for which it needs bodies and the AAA has bodies for which it needs names." I expanded on the story in a two-part series in *National Catholic Reporter,* October 3 and 10, 1975. See also Mónica González, *La Nación,* July 5, 1990, "Descubiertos los archivos de la DINA en Buenos Aires."

236 *Chilean plebiscite:* U.S. intelligence had firsthand reports of the coup plans and the dramatic actions by Air Force Commander Fernando Mattei to force him to back down. DIA, Top Secret, Chile: Government Contingency Plan, October 4, 1988; and DIA, Chilean Junta Meeting the Night of the Plebiscite, January 1, 1989 (Chile Project). See Peter Kornbluh, *The Pinochet File: A Declassified Dossier on Atrocity and Accountability* (New York: The New Press, 2003), 426–32, for a more detailed account of these events based on U.S. documents.

237 *Plot against Stroessner:* Interviews with survivors of the group Dimas Piris da Motta and Luis Alberto Wagner. Piris da Motta and Wagner's group was called *Ejército Popular Revolucionario* (also identified in some intelligence documents as Ejercito Paraguayo Revolucionario). Goiburú was the leader of a left-leaning faction of Stroessner's party called MOPOCO—Movimiento Popular Colorado. Goiburú and Piris Da Mota are mentioned in an intelligence report on the plot presented in a joint Brazil-Paraguay meeting of security forces, held May 3–6, 1976. See *"IV Conferencia bilateral de inteligencia entre los ejercitos de Paraguay y Brasil,"* undated 78:1674–86 (Paraguay Archive). Asuncion 4932, November 29, 1974, and CIA, Dec. 4, 1974 (Dinges FOIA) indicate it was ERP, on behalf of the JCR, that provided explosives for the bomb. Da Motta's recollection is that Montoneros provided the explosives.

238 *Almada arrest:* Interview with Martín Almada, September 7, 2001.

238 *Almada's quest:* In Panama, Almada wrote a book about his prison experience, which he updated in 1993 with an account of the discovery of the archive: Martín Almada, *Paraguay: la carcel olvidada, el pais exiliado* (Panama 1978, Asunción 1993).

239 *Scene at Lambaré:* Interviews with Martín Almada, Francisco de Vargas, and José Augustín Fernández.

241 *Paraguay Archive:* The discovery of the archive went virtually unreported in the mainstream U.S. press until after General Pinochet was arrested in London in 1998. Three books using the documents merit mention: Alfredo Boccia Paz, Myrian Angélica González, and Rosa Palau Aguilar, *Es mi informe: Los archivos secretos de la policia de Stroessner* (Asunción-CDE, 1994); Stella Calloni, *Los Años del Lobo: Operación Condor* (Buenos Aires, 1999); and Alfredo Boccia Paz, Miguel H. López, Antonio V. Pecci, and Gloria Giménez Guanes, *En los sotanos de los generales: Los documentos ocultos del operativo Condor* (Asunción, 2002).

241 *Italians in Chile:* See John Dinges, "Chile's Global Hit Men," *The Nation,* June 2, 1979; and John Dinges, "Anatomia di un'Anonima omicidi," *La Repúbblica,* May 25, 1979. Patricia Mayorga, *El cóndor negro: El atentado a Bernardo Leighton* (Aguilar

2003), credits the author's revelation of the Italians' presence in Chile as the break-through that led to the initiation of Salvi's judicial investigation.

242 *Salvi at SIDE headquarters:* Interview with Salvi, January 2001. He said the papers had been returned to SIDE by the federal court. Later they were placed again under the custody of the Argentine federal court.

243 *Paris case victims:* George Klein, Chile, September 11, 1973; Alfonso Chanfreau, July 3, 1974, Chile; Etienne Pesle, September 19, 1973, Temuco, Chile; Jean Yves Claudet Fernández, November 1, 1975, Buenos Aires; Marcel Rene Amiel, February 9, 1977, Mendoza, Argentina.

244 *Rome case victims:* The victims listed in the Rome case, with date and place of capture:

Daniel Alvaro Banfi Baranzano, September 13, 1974, Buenos Aires; Gerardo Francisco Gatti Antuña, June 9, 1976, Buenos Aires; Maria Emilia Islas Gatti de Zaffaroni, September 27, 1976, Buenos Aires; Armando Bernardo Arnone Hernández, October 1, 1976, Buenos Aires; Juan Pablo Recagno Ibarburu, October 23, 1976, Buenos Aires; Dora Marta Landi Gil, March 29, 1977, Alejandro José Logoluso, March 29, 1977, Asunción; Andrés Humberto Domingo Bellizzi Bellizzi, April 19, 1977, Buenos Aires; Héctor Giordano Cortazzo, June 7–9, 1978, Buenos Aires; Horacio Domingo Campiglia Pedamonti, March 12, 1980, Rio de Janeiro; and Lorenzo Ismael Viñas Gigli, July 26, 1980, Uruguayana, Brazil. Landi, Logoluso, Campiglia, and Viñas are Argentine citizens; the rest are Uruguayan. Banfi and Bellizzi were arrested in separate operations in Argentina.

244 *Prats indictments:* Also included in the indictment were Jorge Iturriaga Neumann, Raul's civilian brother, and José Zara Holger, also of the Exterior Department.

244 *Chile is profoundly different:* Statement July 2003, FASIC (Fundacion de Ayuda Social de Iglesias Cristianas), text dated July 26, 2003, obtained from Web site, www.fasic.org.

245 *Condor case defendants (titles before retirement):* **Argentines:** Jorge Rafael Videla, lieutenant general, former president and member of the military junta; Carlos Guillermo Suárez Mason, general, former commander of the First Corp of the military; Eduardo Albano Harguindeguy, general, former interior minister. **Chileans:** Augusto Pinochet Ugarte, general, member of the military junta, president; Manuel Contreras, general, chief of Dina; Pedro Espinoza, coronel, DINA. **Paraguayans:** Alfredo Stroessner, division general, president of the Republic of Paraguay; Francisco Brítez, general, chief of police; Pastor Coronel Milcíades, head of the Department of Investigations of the Capital Police; Benito Guanes, colonel, chief of the Military Intelligence Service. **Uruguayans:** Julio Vadora, Armed Forces commander in chief; Guillermo Ramírez, colonel; José Nino Gavazzo, major; Manuel Cordero, major; Enrique Martínez, major; Jorge Silveira, capitán; Hugo Campos Hermida, police commissioner. **Bolivian:** Hugo Banzer, president.

245 *Judge Canicoba Condor case victims:* Seventy-two Condor case victims: Agustín Goiburú Jiménez, Fausto Augusto Carrillo, Juan José Penayo, Federico Jorge Tatter, Dora Marta Landi Gill, Esther Ballestrino de Careaga, Antonio Maidana, Emilio Roa Espinosa, Alejandro José Logoluso, Gustavo Edison Insaurralde, Raúl Edgardo Borelli Cattáneo, Nelson Rodolfo Santana Scotto, José Luis Nell, Juan Alberto Filártiga Martínez, Ary Cabrera Prates, Elba Lucia Gándara Castroman, León Duarte Luján, Juan Pablo Recagno Ibarburú, Ruben Prieto González, Cecilia Susana Trías Hernández, Washington Cram González, Daniel Pedro Alfaro Vásquez, Adalberto Soba, Armando Bernardo Arnone Hernández, Rafael González Lezama, María Emilia Islas Gatti de Zaffaroni, Carlos Federico Cabezudo Pérez, Miguel Angel Moreno Malugani, Washington Domingo Queiro Uzal, Raúl Tejera, Carlos Alfredo Rodriguez Mercader, Eduardo Efraín Chizzola Cano, Jorge Zaffaroni Castilla, Ileana García Ramos de Dossetti, Edmundo Sabino Dossetti Techeira, Casimira María del Rosario Carretero Cardenas, Claudio Epelbaum, Lila Epelbaum, Mónica Sofia Grinspon de Logares, Claudio Ernesto Logares, José Hugo Méndez Donadío, Francisco Edgardo Candia Correa, Juan Pablo Errandonea Salvia, Simón Antonio Riquelo, Miguel Angel Río Casas, María Asunción Artigas Nilo de Moyano, Alfredo Moyano, Alberto Cecilio Mechoso Méndez, Horacio Domingo Campiglia, Susana Pinus de Binstock, Norberto Armando Habegger, Erasmo Suárez Balladores, Juan Carlos Jordán Vercellone, Graciela Rutila Artes, Luis Stamponi Corinaldeci, Oscar Hugo González de la Vega, Efraín Fernando Villa Isola, Edgardo Enríquez Espinosa, Miguel Ivan Orellana Castro, José Luis de la Masa Asquet, Manuel Jesús Tamayo Martínez, Carmen Angélica Delard Cabezas, José Luis Appel de la Cruz, Gloria Ximena Delard Cabezas, Cristina Magdalena Carreño Araya, Jara Angel Athanasiú, Frida Elena Laschan Mellado, Pablo Germán Athanasiú Laschan, Luis Enrique Elgueta Díaz, Carlos Patricio Rojas Campos, Alexis Vladimir Jaccard Siegler, María Claudia Iruretagoyena.

245 *Condor narrative:* Court filing dated April 11, 2001, referring to John Dinges, "Los Archivos de Condor," *La Nación* (Argentina), August 8, 1999.

245 *Kissinger questioning:* Judge Le Loire was the first to seek to question Kissinger. His request was voluntary, and Kissinger rejected it out of hand. Canicoba's request had the authority of the MLAT agreement and produced the only official response. Judges in Brazil and Chile have also sought to question Kissinger, to no avail. Kissinger called off a planned trip to Brazil to avoid the possibility of being served with an embarrassing subpoena while in that country.

245 *Uruguayans sought:* The officers are José Nino Gavazzo, Manuel Cordero, Jorge Silveira, and police officer Hugo Campos Hermida. Campos Hermida died of cancer in 2001, just weeks after he told the author he wished to testify about the Argentine missions, which he said he knew about but denied partipating in.

246 *Military travelers:* Le Loire, as only one example, issued international warrants for 150 officers he wanted for questioning. Another Argentine officer, Jorge Olivera,

was arrested in August 2000 and held briefly pending extradition to face charges in Le Loire's court in Paris.

252 *Plans were known:* Rogers and Shlaudeman, who coordinated their responses to author's questions, also asserted that the phrase "no further action" in the September 20, 1776, cable does not exclude the possibility that the Kissinger démarche was delivered prior to September 20. If that were the case, it would certainly be documented in cables in which the ambassadors reported back to Kissinger on the meetings he ordered them to seek. Both Rogers and Shlaudeman have the security clearances necessary to see cables still kept secret from the public, and would be able to back up their argument with evidence if it existed.

INDEX

and Kissinger address to OAS, 162
Letelier assassination plot and, 177,
190–91
and MIR refugees in Argentina, 144,
207–8
Cuban Nationalist Movement (CNM),
190

de Vargas, Francisco, 239
Defense Intelligence Agency (DIA),
212–13, 219
Delle Chiaie, Stefano ("Alfa"), 128,
130–32, 133, 163, 241–42
Diaz, Victor, 163
Dickens, Charles Bertram, 197
DICP (Paraguay's Department of
Investigations of the Police of the
Capital), 90, 94, 95, 96, 240
Dignity Colony, 129
DINA (Dirección de Inteligencia
Nacional), 64–71
Argentina operations, 110–12, 115–16,
141–43
Battalion 601/DINA operations in
Argentina, 141–43
CIA and, 68–71, 101–5
CIA operational jobs within, 70
CIA training of, 68–70, 107
and Condor's Phase Three
assassination plans in Europe,
129–30, 219–21
Contreras and DINA Exterior
Department abroad, 126–34, 163,
177
Contreras on concept and effectiveness
of, 66–68, 101
Contreras's early plans for Condor and
DINA's expansion, 105–10, 119
Contreras's meetings with CIA, 68,
101–4
coordination with other intelligence
agencies, 66, 70, 79–80
creation of, 12, 49, 64
dissolution of, 228

early joint operations of Operation
Condor, 110–13, 115–16, 141
Fuentes interrogation and, 108–9
Koch assassination plans and, 16
Leighton assassination plot and,
130–32, 133
Letelier assassination and, 7, 69, 177,
190–92
Malloco raid against MIR, 112–13,
114–15, 119
MIR and, 84, 100, 112–13, 114–15,
119
killing of MIR's Miguel Enríquez, 84,
100–101
Operation Colombo, 235–36
Osvaldo Rawson/DINA operation
against JCR, 110–13, 115–16, 141
Pinochet and, 64, 65, 228
political intelligence and, 66–68
power of, 64–66
Prats assassination and, 20, 68, 73–81,
126, 130
torture methods, 65, 99, 100
Townley and, 75–76, 78–79, 126–34,
219–22
U.S. military intelligence on, 64–65
Villa Grimaldi operational center, 100,
108–9, 113–14
indictment and conviction of leaders
of, 28, 228
See also Contreras Sepúlveda, Manuel;
DINA Exterior Department and
operations abroad
DINA Exterior Department and
operations abroad
Contreras and, 105–10, 119, 126–34,
163, 177
Contreras's early plans for Condor
and, 105–10, 119
Cuban exiles, 128, 132–33, 163, 177,
190–91
Europe, 129–30, 177
Germany, 129
investigation of, 241–42